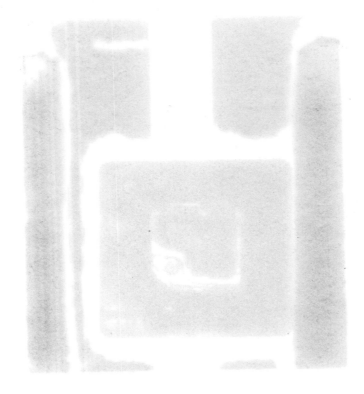

ELECTRIC
GUITARS

*" guitarmen, wake up
and pluck wire for sound,
let 'em hear you play "*

CHARLIE CHRISTIAN 1939

ELECTRIC
GUITARS

THE ILLUSTRATED ENCYCLOPEDIA

**CHARTWELL
BOOKS**

18 June 13
B+T
24.99 (13.62)

Brimming with creative inspiration, how-to projects, and useful information to enrich your everyday life, Quarto Knows is a favorite destination for those pursuing their interests and passions. Visit our site and dig deeper with our books into your area of interest: Quarto Creates, Quarto Cooks, Quarto Homes, Quarto Lives, Quarto Drives, Quarto Explores, Quarto Gifts, or Quarto Kids.

Copyright © Outline Press Ltd. 2017

This edition published in 2018 by Chartwell Books
an imprint of The Quarto Group
142 West 36th Street, 4th Floor
New York, NY 10018
T (212) 779-4972 F (212) 779-6058
www.QuartoKnows.com

Chartwell titles are also available at discount for retail, wholesale, promotional, and bulk purchase. For details, contact the Special Sales Manager by email at specialsales@quarto.com or by mail at The Quarto Group, Attn: Special Sales Manager, 401 Second Avenue North, Suite 310, Minneapolis, MN 55401, USA.

10 9 8 7 6 5 4 3 2 1

ISBN-13: 978-0-7858-3572-1

Printed in China

MIX
Paper from
responsible sources
FSC® C008047
www.fsc.org

contents

An extreme example of the decorated soundhole "rose" (right), this one from Italy in the 17th century. Decoration eventually gave way to practicality when the soundhole was cleared and pure sound poured forth. This music book (far right) dates from 1632, an Italian work by Giovanni Foscarini accentuating single-note playing over chordal strumming.

Almost from the beginning, guitarists have wanted their guitars to be louder. To discover why, we'll have to travel back to the start of the 16th century. Once there, we might find an instrument more or less recognizable today as a guitar.

Take a look at the rare example of the early guitar pictured directly below. You can see that it has a hollow body with a subtle but definite figure-of-eight shape. There's a round soundhole, as well as a long neck that leads to a headstock with tuners, and a bridge glued to the top of the body. All these things tell us that it is a guitar. But there are clear differences to a modern acoustic guitar. The frets are tied on to the neck; there are ten strings in five paired "courses;" and there is a decorated "rose" situated in the body's soundhole. These were all common features at the time.

Already players and instrument makers were striving to increase the volume and the "cutting power" of the guitar during the 16th century. This is most evident in the way that the courses (one, two or three gut strings together) had increased since the guitar's first appearance. Around 1500 the guitar generally had four courses, usually with two strings at the lowest-pitched course for extra power. However, by about 1560 the trend was to a larger guitar with five courses, offering more volume. The four-course guitar continued, but by the end of the 16th

century the louder five-course variety was dominant. It's from this time that the oldest surviving guitars date, the very oldest being an instrument made around 1580.

Into the 17th century, and in Italy the fashion was to achieve still more volume by fitting metal strings – often on a guitar with fixed metal frets, too. This instrument was known as the chitarra batente. The metal frets were adopted in other countries, but it would be some time before metal strings would find their true place. Gut strings continued to be played – quietly – on most guitars.

There were some important developments in the 18th century, not least the standardization of tuning of the five-course guitar to A-D-G-B-E, in other words exactly as today but without the lowest sixth string. By around 1770 the sixth course began to appear, at first usually doubled. But by about 1810 the move to six single strings – tuned E-A-D-G-B-E – was completed, and the guitar looked even more like today's instrument. While basic finger-picking similar to contemporary lute technique was used for the guitar's more delicate repertoire, strumming was a popular technique, especially for the dance music and songs where the guitar was finding an important voice. Strumming was less common on other stringed instruments of the time; guitarists had simply developed this way of playing to give more projection to their sound.

While these principal developments in the guitar's design in the early 19th century were taking place in Spain, Italy, and France, it was the Spaniard Antonio de Torres

Lyre guitars were made around 1800 when a classical revival made fashionable such combinations as guitar and lyre or guitar and harp. This Wornum lyre guitar (above left) was made in London around 1810, with the six single strings then becoming predominant. A similar example is seen in the contemporary print (far left). This "English guitar" (above) made by Preston in about 1775 is in fact a cittern, with six metal-string courses.

This book of music (opposite) is a collection of Italian songs from about 1620, hand-written with tablature and rhythmic symbols for a strummed guitar accompaniment. The three hands (below) are from a Fernando Sor guitar method of 1832, the two on the right "to be avoided."

Four early guitars are pictured on these pages. On the opposite page, above the music, is a five-course guitar made around 1590, probably in Portugal. Unseen is its flat back, but quite visible are the tied-on frets and fine decoration, all typical of the period. Very few guitars of the 16th century have survived, and this restored example conjures up a glorious period of guitar-making. On this page, the top (horizontal) guitar was made by Jean-Baptiste Dehaye Salomon in Paris around 1760. It was later modified to incorporate an additional sixth course to keep up with fashion. Below the Salomon, on this page, is an instrument built around 1804 in Cadiz by Josef

Pagés. He was one of the most influential makers working in Spain in the early 19th century, and is best known for the introduction of fan-strutting under the guitar's top, to provide strength and improve tone. A similar system was later used by the great classical guitar-maker, Torres. The main guitar here, spread over both pages, was made by Louis Panormo in London in 1836. Panormo's father was a violin-maker working in Paris and London. Louis's work often includes elements from some of the best guitars made at the time (compare its shape with that of the Pagés, for example). Panormo regularly fitted superior machine heads at this time rather than pegs.

7

Antonio de Torres Jurado – better known as Torres – redefined the guitar in the 19th century to form the "classical" guitar. This Torres guitar (below) was made in 1876. At the center of the picture below is Andrés Segovia watching Miguel Llobet play, among other admirers. Llobet was a leading player, and often used a Torres guitar.

Another important address in classical guitar history – that of Antonio de Torres, in Seville – is seen on this guitar label (above).

The guitar pictured (right) was made by José Ramirez I in Madrid in 1897, and is strongly influenced by his teacher Francisco González, whom he had joined as an apprentice at the age of 12. Ramirez set up on his own around 1882, a business that developed into a dynasty of Spanish guitar-makers, still in evidence today. Ramirez in turn took on apprentices – including famous names of the immediate future such as his brother Manuel Ramirez, Enrique Garcia,

Francisco Simplicio, and his son, Jose Ramirez II. The label from the guitar (above) includes an illustration of two guitars and a Spanish metal-string bandurria. It also shows one of the most famous addresses in classical guitar history: Concepción Jerónima No.2, in Madrid, which the Ramirez family occupied for close to one hundred years.

The beautiful decoration at the soundhole of this Ramirez I guitar was made using mother-of-pearl in colored mastic and wood.

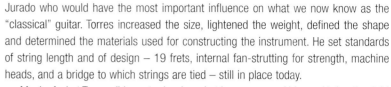

The Paraguayan guitarist and composer Agustin Barrios is seen (below) on a signed photograph dated 1921. The talented musician may have been the first to make recordings of the classical guitar. Far and away the most famous and influential classical guitarist was Andrés Segovia, pictured here as a young man (right).

Jurado who would have the most important influence on what we now know as the "classical" guitar. Torres increased the size, lightened the weight, defined the shape and determined the materials used for constructing the instrument. He set standards of string length and of design – 19 frets, internal fan-strutting for strength, machine heads, and a bridge to which strings are tied – still in place today.

Much of what Torres did was to develop what he saw around him and bring the right ingredients together. However, one of his innovations was the "tornavoz," a metal cylinder that connected the soundhole to the guitar's back, increasing its volume. The device did not last, but it shows that even makers such as Torres were being asked by customers for a louder instrument.

Other "classical" makers built on the Torres tradition. Some, like José Ramirez, developed Torres's ideas; others, including Bouchet and Fleta, changed the instrument beyond Torres's templates, again aiming for a more distinctive and powerful sound. But few makers of classical guitars today have gone further in this direction than the Australian, Greg Smallman, who uses an ultra-thin top with unusual "lattice" strutting and heavy back and sides, all designed for peak volume and projection.

While Torres and his contemporaries were working on the gut-string "classical" instrument in Spain and elsewhere in the 19th century, the guitar was developing in a different direction in the United States. German immigrant Christian Frederick Martin

Santos Hernández built this fine concert guitar (below) in Madrid in 1933. Hernández was a pupil of Manuel Ramirez, and made instruments for both flamenco and concert guitarists.

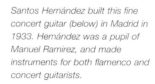

Flamenco guitars use thin woods for a piercing tone. This one was made by Domingo Esteso in 1934. Great flamencos (right) include Sabicas and Ramón Montoya (pictured twice).

Christian Frederick Martin (left) emigrated to the US in the 1830s. The Martins moved to Cherry Hill, just outside Nazareth, PA, in 1839. In the new setting, Martin began to experiment and develop the designs of his guitars, creating a more personal identity and gradually moving away from the styles he had brought with him to America from Stauffer (1820s Stauffer guitar, below) and Vienna. During the 1850s Martin introduced specific body "Sizes" (from the largest Size 1 to the smallest Size 3) and body "Styles" (where a higher number indicated more decoration and refinement).

started his instrument business in New York in the 1830s, at first making guitars in the style of his mentor Johann Georg Stauffer. The banjo was still the most popular stringed instrument in America at this time, and Martin's belief in the validity of the guitar had to wait a number of years before popular demand caught up with his ideas. While still using gut strings, Martin developed during the 1850s an x-shaped bracing pattern inside the guitar, in due course recognized as the best type for steel-string flat-tops.

Some American guitar makers began to use steel strings in the early years of the 20th century. Orville Gibson was one. He had moved from New York State to Kalamazoo, Michigan, probably around 1880, and started making archtop mandolins and guitars there in the mid 1890s. The famous Gibson company was formed in 1902 when Orville teamed up with some businessmen, but he soon left the operation. A type of instrument that the new Gibson company continued to make was the "harp guitar," offering a six-string neck with accompanying sympathetic strings alongside, over the body, to create sustained accompaniment that increased the instrument's power.

Carl Larson and his brother August, based in Chicago, also recognized that guitarists had to be heard alongside loud banjos and mandolins, and so used steel strings on their guitars from an early date. Martin made the move during the 1920s to steel strings from the traditional gut it had used in the meantime, offering steel on all

This Martin Stauffer-style guitar (right) was made in the 1830s, soon after Christian Martin arrived in the United States. (The case pictured above it is typical of the "coffin" cases Martin supplied with his instruments at the time.) In the 1820s Martin had been a foreman at the Vienna workshop of instrument-maker Johann Stauffer, but some years before Martin made his trip across the Atlantic he had moved back home to Germany and tried to set up as a guitar- and violin-maker there. He was not successful, which is fortunate for American guitar history. Martin's company would become the most important modern maker of flat-top acoustic guitars, and is still much in evidence today.

Two harp guitars are pictured here. This Gibson Style U (above) was made around 1906, and shows the magnificent "arm" construction and the extra resonant strings attached to it. The Gibson 1920s catalog reflects the company's main business at the time: mandolins. The other harp guitar (right) is from about 1920 and attributed to the Larson Brothers, among the first US makers to use metal strings and to strengthen their guitars accordingly.

Orville Gibson invented the idea of the hand-carved archtop guitar. This instrument (left, made around 1898) is a wonderful example of his ground-breaking craftsmanship. The carved construction meant that Orville did not need (or want) internal bracing, and unusually he cut the sides of his mandolins and guitars from solid wood. The headstock decoration is a typical touch of the maker. The guitar was made around four years before Orville formed the Gibson company with a number of businessmen. He left the operation soon afterwards.

By 1928 Lyon & Healy sold the Washburn name to Tonk, who used it on the products of several makers, notably Regal, until World War II. For the more recent history of the brandname, see the Washburn entry further into this book.

Washburn was another important early American guitar brand, having first appeared around 1880 for the Lyon & Healy company of Chicago. The unusual shape of Washburn's "Bell" guitar (right, Style 5271, made around 1929) was intended to provide a new, louder tonal characteristic, although the fact that other makers did not leap on the new design tells its own story.

Martin's new "dreadnought" guitars made an impact, especially in the world of country music. This picture (left) of the otherwise little-known Oklahoma Sweethearts, taken around 1941, depicts a typical line-up seen in the country string-bands of the time, with musicians playing guitars, banjo, fiddle and bass. By this time the guitar had all but replaced the banjo, with the sheer volume and presence of the new dreadnoughts an important factor in the guitar's continuing dominance. The Sweetheart to the right holds a Martin D-28 (the "D" is for dreadnought), first introduced as the briefly-named D-2 in 1931. It was the middle guitar in a famous trio of Martins: the D-18, D-28 and D-45.

Martin's D-45 was the top-of-the-line of the company's new dreadnought series of the 1930s. Singing cowboy Gene Autry had ordered the first D-45. Since 1934 dreadnoughts had a neck joining the body at the 14th fret, following the success of this on Martin's OM models. The larger body of the D series guitars offered a much rounder sound and a louder bass presence, suiting string-instrument ensembles or bass-heavy accompaniment to singing. This D-45 (right) was made in 1941. Such was their opulence and expense that only 91 D-45s were made between 1933 and 1942. These have since become among the most collectable acoustic guitars of any period and maker. Martin reintroduced the model in 1968.

This rare Martin-made Paramount Style L (below) from around 1930 has an unusual "double" body. The intention was to provide more volume, but few were made. The brand is better known on banjos.

Gibson's L-5 guitar was launched in 1922 (1929 example here) and defined the new f-hole archtop. Early models were signed by designer Lloyd Loar; some were fitted with an disc inside for sound "improvement," the Virzi Tone Producer.

Martin models by the end of the decade. The combination of the company's strong X-bracing and loud steel strings – plus the inherent quality of the instruments – put Martin into a dominant position for flat-top guitars for many years. At the same time, Martin began to modify the size of the guitar, and in the 1910s hit on the important "dreadnought" guitar design. The thick waist and wide, squared shoulders of the large dreadnought body increased still further the flat-top's volume, power and tonal versatility. Other makers offered their variations, such as Gibson's Jumbo.

Meanwhile at Gibson the other modern type of acoustic guitar, the archtop, was in development. Lloyd Loar's Master Series L-5 guitar of 1922 defined the genre, apparently having more in common with a violin than a guitar. It had a carved arched top, two f-holes instead of a single round soundhole, a floating height-adjustable bridge with strings fastened to a separate metal tailpiece, and a neck-strengthening truss-rod. Most of this was again designed to create fine tone and to improve sound projection. Other archtop makers would follow, including D'Angelico and Stromberg.

Resonator guitars were introduced by National in Los Angeles in 1927. This attempt to provide a louder guitar was more unconventional: inside a metal body, three metal resonator discs were mounted underneath the bridge, acting like mechanical loudspeakers to thrust the brash sound of the guitar forward. The result was relatively crude, but effective, and created a different sound. However, it was becoming clear that

This Selmer Maccaferri Jazz was made in France in 1932. Designed by Mario Maccaferri, some included an extra internal soundbox intended to increase sound projection.

Elmer Stromberg built guitars in Boston. His grandest creation was the Master 400 Cutaway, designed to be the biggest, loudest archtop. This one was made around 1952.

Willi Wilkanowski produced some of the most unusual archtop acoustics in the US. This example dates from about 1940, with the maker's customary violin-like design.

Martin was among the leaders in subtle but impressive decoration of guitars, and this D-45 (left) is a perfect example of the company's tasteful style. Note the extensive use of abalone inlay around the perimeter of the body, in the soundhole rings, and along the fingerboard edges, as well as for that special "C.F. Martin" headstock logo.

National's remarkable resonator principle is demonstrated with this guitar (above), a Style 4 "Tricone" that was made around 1931. The shot of another Tricone with the cover removed (near left) shows the three metal discs that provide the instrument with its unique "acoustic amplified" tone. The Dobro company later developed a similar system using a single resonator (example with cover off, far left).

Gibson's answer to Martin's dreadnought guitars was the jumbo. This SJ-200 (below) dates from 1954 and was the famous leading model among the company's "narrow waist" jumbos. The model has been known variously during its long and distinguished career as the Super Jumbo, the SJ-200, and the J-200. Whatever the name, it offers a huge handful of sound.

Charlie Christian (right) virtually invented the idea of jazz on an electric guitar. His recording career lasted less than two years, yet he managed to define the role of the guitar as a single-note solo vehicle in a new and fresh manner. After Christian, the electric guitar could never be the same again.

the limits of what could be achieved with a purely acoustic instrument had been reached. Dance-band guitarists generally opted for archtop guitars, and while the size and overall dimensions of these instruments had grown in order to increase volume, there was only so much that could be comfortably accommodated – and the band meanwhile was growing louder. Players of flat-top acoustic guitars had also seen their instruments growing larger and more unwieldy.

The answer was clear to some: electric amplification. A number of players and guitar-makers began to experiment during the 1920s and 1930s with the idea of a pickup attached to the guitar's body, near the strings, which would feed an amplifier and loudspeaker. The theory was that the resulting sound could be increased in volume with almost no regard to the physical limitations of the guitar's acoustic properties. The guitar player would at last be heard properly alongside his fellow musicians.

This book documents some of those early electric experiments as well as most of the changes and developments that have appeared subsequently. Much of the pioneering work on electric guitars was done in the United States, and as with most inventions there were several people independently working along similar lines. But a handful of significant explorers did more than most to devise what we now know as the electric guitar. Chief among these were George Beauchamp and Paul Barth, who put together a basic magnetic pickup for guitar. Their research culminated in 1931 with an

Adolph Rickenbacker (pictured below left) ran a California company that pioneered the electric guitar with the "Frying Pan" prototype of 1931 (three views, above left) and production guitars such as this Spanish of 1947.

14

Rickenbacker's Electro Spanish model (below) was a semi-solid Bakelite creation, this one made about 1936. The picture of The Sweethearts Of The Air (left) shows the Electro Spanish (right) and the "Hawaiian" lap-steel version (center). Django Reinhardt (right) is known for using a Maccaferri, but he briefly played an electric guitar too.

experimental one-off instrument, the wooden Rickenbacker "Frying Pan" guitar, so-called because of its small round body and long neck. It was the first guitar to feature an electro-magnetic pickup, and thus the basis for virtually all modern electric guitars. Several of the earliest electric guitars were in "Hawaiian" style, played on the lap.

A number of other US makers began to add magnetic pickups to existing acoustic guitars, but also started to develop models that were built entirely as electric instruments. At first these were primarily in the archtop style and were produced by companies such as National, Rickenbacker, Epiphone and Gibson. The pickups and associated amplifiers were crude. Before World War II, little interest was generated among musicians for these new electric guitars.

It was after the war that the electric guitar began to make its mark, and soon every manufacturer of note was producing electric models as the instrument found its place in the new styles of popular music that were beginning to emerge. The most significant development was the solidbody electric guitar, with Fender leading the way.

The rest of this book is devoted to the enormous range of ideas and designs that followed the early electric experimenters. Guitarists today no longer need their guitars to be louder – the problem of volume was solved long ago. As this book shows, if there is a problem now, then it's one of bewildering choice. So choose carefully: somewhere in these pages your ultimate guitar might well be lurking.

Les Paul exercised his curiosity for electric instruments and his flair for technical experimentation by adapting and modifying an Epiphone guitar he owned. The result is pictured (left), the famous "log." Paul says he would visit the empty Epiphone factory at weekends, probably around 1940, to fiddle with this guitar. The nickname was derived from a 4-by-4 solid "log" of pine which Paul inserted between the cut halves of the dismembered body. Using some metal brackets, he re-joined the neck to the pine block, on to which he mounted a couple of his crude home-made pickups. A little later he modified a second and third Epiphone, which he called his "clunkers," this time chopping up the bodies to add metal strengthening braces, again topped with Paul's own pickups. Despite their makeshift origins, the semi-solid log and the modified clunkers often accompanied Les Paul on stage and in recording studios throughout the 1940s and into the early 1950s. During the 1940s, Paul decided he would take his log idea to a major company, to see if he could generate interest in its commercial potential. He went to Gibson, but was turned away as "the guy with the broomstick." Some years later, Gibson noted the upstart Fender's new solidbody guitar, and decided to design its own version. Paul, by now a famous musician with pop hits, was called up to endorse the new-for-1952 guitar, the Gibson Les Paul.

Gibson's ES-150 (main guitar here, this one made around 1939) was the company's first archtop electric guitar, and the instrument used by Charlie Christian to such devastating effect (see top of page). The type of "blade" pickup fitted to ES-150s of this vintage has since become known as the "Charlie Christian" in honor of the great jazzman's achievements. While Gibson drew on their long-established manufacturing and business contacts to promote

the new guitar, Fender started business in the 1940s as a new and rather green outfit. As first, Leo Fender worked with Doc Kauffman as K&F (amplifier from around 1945, right, with an enlargement of the impressive logo, left). They soon parted, and in 1946 Leo started his new Fender Manufacturing, renamed the Fender Electric Instrument Co at the end of 1947. A few years later, Leo and his partners commercialized the solidbody electric guitar.

In its own way the electric guitar was vital in helping what I've achieved, or what the Stones have achieved. Where would I be without it? Playing awfully quietly, for a start **KEITH RICHARDS**

ELECTRIC GUITAR

A DIRECTORY

ACOUSTIC

Known primarily for amplifiers, the Acoustic Control Corporation of Los Angeles introduced Black Widow solidbody guitars with a protective red "spider" back pad in 1972, endorsed by jazzman Larry Coryell. Most were built in Japan, but around 200 were made by Semie Moseley in California before their demise in 1975.

AIRLINE

This 1950s/1960s brandname was used by the Montgomery Ward mail-order company on instruments supplied by a number of manufacturers. Some were produced by Kay, or Valco, the company that made National and Supro guitars. Most of the Valco-made Airlines were similar to Supros, though some had unconventional body shapes. In recent years, Eastwood has produced a number of reissues.

ALAMO

Remembered for colorful, exotic shapes, Alamo guitars were made under the direction of Charles Eilenberg for Southern Music in San Antonio, Texas, beginning with lap-steels and amps around 1950. Student-grade solidbodies appeared around 1960, with a change to hollow-core bodies from 1963 to 1970; amps continued into the 1980s.

ALEMBIC

While the California maker is best known for bass guitars, its use of exotic woods, multi-laminate through-neck construction and pioneering active electronics generally influenced many guitar-makers during the 1970s and after. Alembic started in southern California in 1969 as an electronics workshop among the community that gradually grew up around the Grateful Dead. Alembic worked in the warehouse where the Dead rehearsed in Novato, California, about 30 miles north of San Francisco. At first the idea was for Alembic to make improved recordings of Dead concerts. This developed into a general interest in the improvement of studio and live sound quality, and Alembic branched out into three main areas: a recording studio; a developer of PA systems; and a workshop for guitar repair and modification.

The combination of the woodworking talents of Rick Turner, a one-time Massachusetts folk guitarist and guitar repairer, and the electronics knowledge of Ron Wickersham, who had worked at the Ampex recording-equipment company, soon turned the workshop into a full-fledged guitar-making operation. In 1970 Alembic moved to San Francisco, and became a corporation with three equal shareholders: Rick Turner, Ron Wickersham and recording engineer Bob Matthews.

At first they customized instruments, what they called "Alembicizing." The first official Alembic instrument made to the new company's own design was a bass built for Jack Casady around 1971. A few years later L D Heater of Portland, Oregon, began US distribution of Alembic instruments, and production increased. By 1974 Alembic's guitar workshop was at Cotati, about 40 miles north of San Francisco, handling

An Acoustic Black Widow from about 1971 (near right, with a 1974 ad featuring Black Widow endorser Larry Coryell); an Airline fiberglass-body model (center) made by Valco around 1964; and an Alamo Titan produced in Texas in 1962 (far right). Ron and Susan Wickersham (Kaman strings ad, opposite page) were two of the original founders of Alembic. The main Alembic guitar shown (opposite page) is a Series I dating from 1978.

Professionals.
Larry Coryell
and Acoustic's
Black Widow Guitar.

Alvarez made this Dana AE650 "Scoop" model (left), with one of the deepest cutaways ever attempted, in 1992. Ampeg teamed with guitar-maker Hagstrom for the Patch 2000 guitar synthesizer, seen in an ad (above) from 1978.

"I can't stand a man who won't try something new!"
—Lita Ford

Lita Ford is seen (above) in an Alvarez ad promoting the Scoop models in 1993.

woodwork, metalwork and pickups, while at the Alembic office in nearby Sebastopol Wickersham dealt with electronics production. All guitar production moved to Cotati in 1977 and to Santa Rosa two years later.

Alembic had gradually standardized a regular line of short-scale, medium-scale and long-scale basses, with equivalents in guitars, primarily the Series I and Series II. Alembic has always produced many more basses than guitars. The instruments featured a high quality multi-laminate through-neck construction using attractive, exotic woods (such as walnut, myrtle, zebrawood, padauk, vermilion and cocobolo), heavy tone-enhancing brass hardware and active-electronics systems with external power supplies. All this came at a price, and Alembic virtually established the idea of the specialist, high quality, high price guitar.

Alembic continues today in Santa Rosa, California, primarily as a prestigious high-end bass specialist, but offering some guitars. Current six-string models include the Orion and the Skylark.

ALVAREZ

Alvarez was a brand for acoustic guitars until 1991 when US distributor St. Louis Music used it to replace Westone on its electrics. The change brought a significantly reworked Korean-made line, and only Trevor Rabin's signature model remained much the same, with styling derived from the earlier Westone Pantera. Many of the all-new Alvarez

the revolutionary dan armstrong guitar from ampeg

This 1970 Ampeg ad has Keith Richards discovering the joys of six strings and a transparent body.

electrics were devised by guitar-maker/designer Dana Sutcliffe. They included the Scoop, a radical solidbody sporting long, slim and sharp horns and the right cutaway sweeping around the end of the neck. It was claimed this enhanced sustain and resonance... but Sutcliffe later admitted it was actually due to a carving accident.

Other Alvarez models included the equally rock-orientated Paramount and Successor, while the later LA Scoop and Nashville Scoop were more Fender-flavored. Alvarez then made safer designs; by 2000 only the Classics offered anything individual in a much-reduced line.

AMPEG

In the late 1940s New York bassist Everett Hull had tackled the problem of amplifying double-basses by producing an amplification system that consisted of a microphone which fitted inside the bass's pointed "peg," the spike that supports the instrument at its base. This "amplified peg" gave Hull's new company its name – Ampeg – and their adaptation of existing double-basses to amplified sound proved a moderate success for the fledgling operation.

Through the following decades Ampeg grew and became principally known for its excellent line of instrument amplifiers. The company first tried to get into the electric guitar market in 1963, importing four Burns guitar models from Britain – Jazz Split Sound, Nu-Sonic, Split Sonic and TR-2 – identical to the UK originals apart from an

Ampeg logo on the pickguard. Few were sold, making these Ampeg-Burns rare catches today. The Ampeg-Burns deal ended in 1964.

By 1968 Ampeg were still keen to grab some of the burgeoning electric guitar business, and local New York City guitar repairman Dan Armstrong was hired to design a new line of guitars. Armstrong decided to carve the bodies from blocks of clear Lucite (perspex), intending to provide a distinctive looking instrument as well as to exploit the sonic potential of the material.

Ampeg offered the See-Through guitar with six slide-in/slide-out pickups designed by Bill Lawrence: Rock, Country and Jazz, each in treble and bass versions. Two of these units were supplied as standard with every new guitar; the others were available to keen See-Through players as accessories that could be purchased through their friendly local Ampeg dealer.

Despite all this invention, Ampeg's imaginative See-Through models lasted little more than a year in production, hindered by conservative players and an expensive manufacturing process. Pro users of the See Through have been few, although an honorable exception was Keith Richards.

In 1999, Ampeg's Japanese-made ADAG1 clear-plastic-body reworking of the original See-Through was launched, later renamed the ADA6, and more recently a wood-body version appeared, the AMG100.

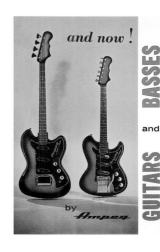

Ampeg made a small number of its Dan Armstrong models in black plastic, including this 1969 example (near left). Most were in clear Lucite (perspex), most famously played by Keith Richards (left). Ampeg had earlier imported to the US a selection of Burns models from England. They included the Burns Split Sonic rebadged as the Ampeg De Luxe Wild Dog model, as seen in this ad (above) from 1963.

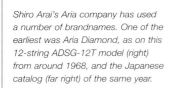

Shiro Arai's Aria company has used a number of brandnames. One of the earliest was Aria Diamond, as on this 12-string ADSG-12T model (right) from around 1968, and the Japanese catalog (far right) of the same year.

Another Aria brandname was Aria Pro II, as used from the mid 1970s. This Aria Pro II PE-160 (below, right) made in 1977 came with an unusual carved dragon motif on the body.

This ad for the Aria Pro II Knight Warrior model (far left) dates from 1984, with the heavy-duty vibrato of the period. The sultry 1983 ad next to it promotes revamped RS models.

ARIA

Aria has been one of the seminal companies in the globalization of guitar-making, with a history that includes major involvement in the 1970s "copy era." Along the way, Aria produced an extraordinary number of guitar models in a variety of different styles and guises. The sheer magnitude of Aria's guitar lines and the worldwide markets in which they have been sold is daunting.

The company was founded in Japan as an importing operation by classical guitarist Shiro Arai during the early 1950s. Arai began manufacturing classical guitars around 1956 and entered the market for electric guitars in 1960. The company developed a mix of solidbody and hollowbody models (including one style with a "violin"-shape body) and these bore the Arai, Aria, Aria Diamond and Diamond brandnames. The factory also manufactured instruments for other companies.

The turning point came at the NAMM instrument trade show in the US in 1968 where Gibson was exhibiting its newly reissued Les Pauls. This inspired Arai in 1969 to build the first Japanese-made bolt-on-neck copy of the Gibson classic, formally kicking off the "copy era" of the 1970s. Copies of the Ampeg Dan Armstrong clear Lucite (perspex) guitar and Fender's Telecaster quickly followed, and this soon mushroomed into the copying of virtually all popular and significant American guitar models. In the mid 1970s Aria added another electric-guitar brand, Aria Pro II, including

models with fancy inlay. The Aria brandname continued to be used in a number of different markets. Many of the better models were built at the Japanese Matsumoku factory, until that closed its doors to guitar-building in 1987. Copies continued until 1978, the year Aria picked up its first big-name endorser in Herb Ellis, whose PE-175 was a Gibson-inspired archtop electric. Full-body and thinline electrics would be mainstay Aria offerings from this time.

However, 1977 saw the introduction of Aria's first truly original design, the Matsumoku-made PE Prototype series. These were either set-neck or bolt-on-neck single-cutaway guitars with carved tops and a sweeping curve that came down from the body's upper shoulder into the cutaway opposite. The Japanese PE Prototypes, many with luxurious appointments, some with vibratos and P.J. Marx pickups, were succeeded by Korean-made versions that began to appear in 1988.

More original Aria designs debuted in 1979, including offset-double-cutaway guitars with pointy horns, and a signature hollowbody for British jazzer Ike Isaacs. The first RS Rev Sound series were through-neck guitars made in an Alembic style, with active electronics, and a few double-necks. They lasted until 1982. The TS Thor Sound (also called Tri-Sound) guitars were passive or active, in set-neck, bolt-on-neck and through-neck configurations, and lasted until 1983. Lines offered in Europe included the shortlived YS and NK (Noise Killer) series. In 1981 Aria added to its catalog the CS

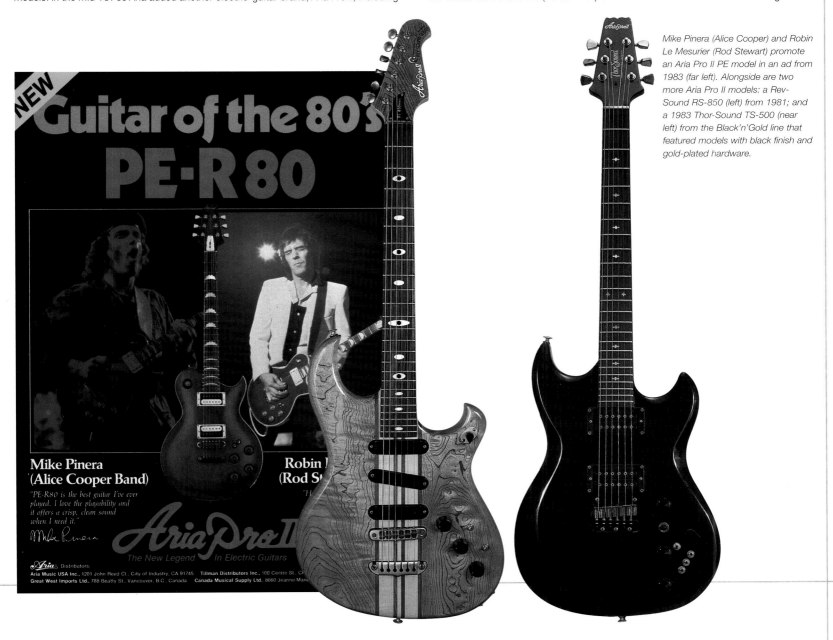

Mike Pinera (Alice Cooper) and Robin Le Mesurier (Rod Stewart) promote an Aria Pro II PE model in an ad from 1983 (far left). Alongside are two more Aria Pro II models: a Rev-Sound RS-850 (left) from 1981; and a 1983 Thor-Sound TS-500 (near left) from the Black'n'Gold line that featured models with black finish and gold-plated hardware.

Jazz guitarist Herb Ellis was honored with the "signature" Aria Pro II PE-175 archtop electric of 1978.

Cardinal Sound series with passive electronics (lots of switches on some models) and either bolt-on- or set-necks. Most of these were available for a few years.

In 1982 Aria helped start a wave of popularity for exotic guitar shapes. The company introduced its B.C.-Rich-inspired Urchin series (which lasted to 1984), the mini-Flying-V-like XX series and the mini-Explorer-style ZZ series, the latter two with fancy paint jobs and available in one form or another through 1987. From 1982 until 1986 various models from different series were rolled into a Black'n'Gold line with appropriate black finishes and gold hardware.

In 1983 Aria introduced a revamped RS Rev Sound line with Stratocaster-like styling and bolt-on necks. In a number of variations, these models would dominate Aria's offerings into the 1990s. The earliest of these second-generation Rev Sounds had elegant thin horns and came either with active or passive electronics, although after 1985 most were passive. Models such as the Bobcat, Wildcat and Straycat suggested the directions that Aria would soon be taking.

By the mid 1980s the RS profile would thicken up to take on even more of a Fender style. Other popular mid-1980s models in this long-running series included the Knight Warrior and Road Warrior. In 1985 the definition of RS was changed to Rock Solid, then the Cat series in 1986. Original Aria locking vibratos were joined by Kahlers in 1986. These guitars lasted through 1987 and the end of Matsumoku's Japanese factory. A

number of other Japanese-made offset-double-cutaway lines were also offered during this period, and these models included such delights as the MM Mega Metal, IC Interceptor, IG Integra, GT and XR series. Many of these were in fact variations on the superstrat, but none was as popular as the Cats.

In 1987 Aria briefly offered a US Custom series of American-made guitars. That same year Aria shifted its general production of electric guitars to Korea, where it continued the superstrat theme, beginning with the SL series and followed by a mind-dizzying list of essentially similar models over the next few years. Mainly these were differentiated by timbers, figured tops, level of appointments and sometimes subtle differences in body contouring.

A few of the better models continued to be made in Japan, but the need to remain at a lower price-point meant that the majority of production was now based in Korea. In 1988, lasting for just a year, came the CT, LB Libra, VA Vanguard, and WR Warrior series. These were supplanted in 1989 by yet more superstrats including the Polaris, VS, and AW series.

Those superstrats were in turn replaced by the FS, JS, XL Excel, VP Viper and MA Magna series in 1990, many of which remained in the catalog for a few years. In 1991 the high-end AQ Aquanotes appeared, which would later evolve into the CR Cobra line. These were followed by the current and decidedly low-end STGs in 1993. Most of

Aria Pro II's first "pointy"-shape guitars were marketed as the Urchin series in 1982, with clear influence from the US brand B.C. Rich. The catalog from 1982 (above) includes the Urchin Deluxe (right). The Titan Artist series began in 1981; this TA-60 (far right) dates from 1989.

these were gone by the mid 1990s. Aria has during its history never had a great many "signature" models in its lines, reflecting the company's relatively low-key presence among leading pro players. It has always seemed as if Aria guitars have been more popular with amateur and semi-pro guitarists, even though the quality of some of the instruments would seem high enough to attract pros. However, during 1991 Aria made a line of Ventures signature models, revived in 1999. The Ventures have always been more successful in Japan than anywhere else, so it was not too surprising that an oriental manufacturer would court the group and its many fans.

In 1994 Aria's US distributor NHF Industries unveiled a single-cutaway model originally called the Nashville 93. This model was styled by British designer Trev Wilkinson, and was at first produced in the United States. However, Gretsch soon objected to Aria's use of the "Nashville" name, which the US company had used for some time on one of its models. So it was that the Aria guitar was renamed as the 615 Custom – at least reflecting Nashville's telephone area code. Lower-grade 615s were manufactured in Korea until 1998.

Also launched in 1994 was the Strat-like Fullerton series, with further Wilkinson input. The top models were made in the US, most others in Korea. At the end of the decade the Aria Pro II line was anchored by PEs (renamed Pro Electrics), Fullerton and STG solidbodies, plus the long-running TA thinlines and FA "jazz" guitars.

Aria Pro II continued with angular shapes for the ZZ series, which included this 1985 ZZ Deluxe (main guitar, left) and the ZZ Bladerunner (featured in 1985 ad, above left). By the time this sparkle-finish M-650T appeared (left) in 1999, Aria had like many guitar-makers embraced "retro" fashion. More mainstream tastes were indulged with the Fullerton series (1998 ad, below).

25

Baldwin in the US bought the Burns
company of England in 1965. This
ad (above) from that year shows
three models from the line, including
the green sunburst Double Six 12-
string (main guitar, right). Baldwin's
catalog (above right) is from 1967 –
could it be any other time? – and has
a groovy lady posing with a Marvin
model. The smaller guitar picture on
this page (right) is from Bartolini, a
wonderful example of the accordion-
influenced plastic-covered guitars
made in Italy during the 1960s.

When it first appeared in 1976 the Bich from B. C. Rich was a ten-string guitar. This 1982 ad features the six-string version, still boasting the bizarre cut-out and pointy body.

BALDWIN

In the 1960s this Ohio-based specialist maker of pianos and organs briefly dabbled with electric guitars. In 1965 they bid unsuccessfully for Fender but bought the Burns company of England for $250,000. Burns already had some American experience through distributor Lipsky and by badging some models with the Ampeg brand.

After Baldwin took control there were "transition" examples; a few guitars even carried both Burns and Baldwin brands. In 1966 the existing Nu-Sonic, GB65 and GB66 models were dropped and various changes made. Most significant was a new "flattened-scroll" headstock, replacing the original Burns type on most models. The Baby Bison and Vibraslim were redesigned with a new, short Rezo-tube vibrato.

In 1967 Baldwin introduced the Gibson 335-like 700 series, with Italian-made bodies. By 1968 bar-magnet pickups were being fitted to the Marvin and Bison models. In 1970 Baldwin discontinued Burns production, concentrating their particular management skills on Gretsch, which they had acquired in 1967.

BARTOLINI

The early-1960s guitar boom overtook many Italian accordion makers, who survived by catering for the new craze. Bartolini was one of numerous brands appearing on the flamboyant results. Styling varied but multiple pushbutton selectors and an abundance of sparkle or pearloid plastic were shared by most, echoing the accordion ancestry.

B.C. RICH

B.C. Rich founder Bernardo Chavez Rico was a pioneer in through-neck, pointy-shaped solidbody guitars with onboard "active" pre-amps and a host of knobs and switches. Rico's instruments became favored by heavy guitarists such as Tony Iommi, Rick Derringer, Nikki Sixx, Blackie Lawless and Lita Ford. It's ironic to note, therefore, that Rico began as a flamenco and classical guitarist making acoustic guitars in his father's Los Angeles shop in the mid 1950s.

The first guitars branded B.C. Rich were acoustics, beginning around 1966, while the first electrics were fancy Gibson copies in 1969. Rico's first original through-neck, heel-less design appeared as the single-cutaway Seagull model, around 1971 – and it had an extra little point on the upper bout which indicated B.C. Rich's future direction that would include points just about everywhere. Early pickups were Gibsons and Guilds, followed by DiMarzio humbuckers from 1974 to 1986. The Seagulls were endorsed by Dominic Troiano and Dick Wagner.

Then came the studies in graceful angularity for which B.C. Rich is known, including the Mockingbird and novel ten-string Bich (1976), the Warlock (1981), and Ironbird, Wave and Stealth models (1983). Fancy woods and bright paint jobs were typical, and Craig Chaquico was an endorser in 1980. A few bolt-neck B.C. Riches were built in the late 1970s, including the Nighthawk (Eagle-style) and Phoenix (Mockingbird). Strat-

Three examples of the B.C. Rich approach to guitar style on this page: a typically "pointy" Bich NJ model from 1999 (left); a rather more subdued Eagle of 1981 (center); and a classic Mockingbird Standard made in 1979. This 1978 ad (below) highlights the horned Beast model.

style guitars (ST, Gunslinger, Outlaw) debuted in 1987. B.C. Rich began making guitars outside the US in 1976 with a small number of B.C. Rico-brand Eagles produced in Japan. Oriental production resumed in 1984-86 with the Japanese-made NJ Series (for Nagoya, Japan). These instruments were versions of popular designs as well as some Standard thinlines that came in a Gibson 335-style. There was also the US Production Series, which consisted of US-assembled Korean kits. The Korean-made Rave and Platinum Series followed in 1986, and in the same year the NJ Series shifted production to the Cort factory in Korea.

Marketing of the B.C. Rich guitars not made in the United States was taken over in America in 1987 by a company called Class Axe, based in New Jersey. Class Axe introduced its own design, the Virgin, that year. In 1989 Bernie Rico began a three-year break, licensing to Class Axe the rights to B.C. Rich. During his vacation, Rico built a number of handmade guitars with the Mason Bernard brand.

During 1994 Rico resumed building B.C. Rich guitars, in Hesperia, California. These included fancy versions of classics (figured woods, abalone trim), variations of other popular guitars (Junior V, Tele-style Blaster), signature models (Jeff Cook, Kerry King), and new designs (super-pointy Ignitor; contoured-top, Tele-style Robert Conti six- and eight-strings). Rico died in 1999, and Hanser bought the company in 2001. In 2016, Hanser licensed production of B.C. Rich guitars to Praxis.

Some B.C. Rich guitars were made in Korea during the late 1990s, including this conservative EMI model of 1997 (near right). The multi-point 1995 US-made Ignitor (main guitar, right) is much more in the classic Rich style. Two ads (right) highlight Body Art limited editons, with a Beast (top, 2003) and a Mockingbird (2004).

Paul Bigsby's most famous guitar is this early semi-solidbody electric (left) which he custom-made for country guitarist Merle Travis in 1948.

Paul Bigsby's lasting contribution to guitar-playing is his vibrato bridge, an example of which is fitted to this remarkable double-neck (below), the first electric of its kind, made by Bigsby in 1952 for another country musician, sessionman Grady Martin. He is pictured with the instrument on the sleeve of a 1954 solo release.

BIGSBY

Paul Bigsby of Downey, California, was a major influence on country music in the late 1940s and early 1950s. He is often credited with building the first solidbody electric guitar. In fact, the ground-breaking instrument he built for Merle Travis in 1948 had a solid through-neck section with hollow body "wings." Nonetheless, the instrument is of enormous historical importance, being closer to what we now think of as a solidbody electric guitar than anything that had existed before. Bigsby is, however, most famous for his bolt-on hand vibrato unit for guitar, also developed for Travis.

Bigsby also offered replacement necks that sported his distinctive six-in-line headstock, and helped musicians create an identifiable "country sound" with his innovative pedal-steel guitars, first used by Speedy West and quickly adopted by others. All Bigsby's custom creations are now rare. In addition to the thin Les-Paul-shape Travis-style guitar, Bigsby offered the Electric Standard (similar except for a scrolled upper shoulder) and Billy Byrd double-cutaway guitars.

Bigsby made at least one thick-bodied guitar (for Jack Parsons) and built electric mandolins, the first in 1951 for Tiny Moore. He also made double-necks, including one for Nashville great Grady Martin; most were guitar/mandolins, but at least one was a guitar/bass. In 1956 Bigsby designed two guitars and a steel for amplifier maker Magnatone. He continued to offer guitars until 1965, and died three years later.

B O N D

Bond's shortlived mid-1980s Electraglide guitar had a novel "stepped" fingerboard. Bond was set up in Scotland by guitar-maker Andrew Bond, Ian Flooks of the Wasted Talent artist agency, and two others. The company had a new factory built at Muir Of Ord, near Inverness, and the first Electraglides began to appear in 1984.

Where a normal guitar fingerboard has a row of frets, the Bond's "pitchboard" was a one-piece construction, with a step and gentle incline between each "fret" position. Some players found there was not enough room to bend strings. It was also impossible to "dress" frets conventionally for personal playability. It quickly became apparent that the success of a conventional frets-and-fingerboard construction is partly due to its potential for modification to suit different string types and different players.

There were other unusual aspects of the twin-cutaway Bond. Composite plastic was used for most of the instrument, as popularized a few years earlier by Steinberger, and the Electraglide was without normal control knobs. Instead it used touch-switches with color-coded LEDs for volume, active tone, pickup switching and phase, and employed a small digital read-out facing up to the player to reveal setting levels. Again, these novelties served mainly to underline the strengths of a conventional control system. The instrument certainly looked futuristic, and was clearly different in many approaches – but it did not necessarily address players' concerns, and might have worked better as

The Bond Electraglide (near right), with novel stepped fingerboard and digital read-outs, was made in Scotland in 1984; the Brian Moore M/C1, with custom fingerboard inlay by Ray Memmels, was made in New York in 1999. A Brian Moore ad from 2004 (center) features the i1000 and i2000 synth-access hybrid guitars.

a custom instrument made in small numbers. Amid production problems, Bond collapsed during 1985 having made around 1,400 guitars. In its brief life the company found that many players couldn't be bothered to adapt to the new guitar's oddities, though it did attract Mick Jones, who loved the way it played, as well as John Turnbull and Dave Stewart.

BRIAN MOORE

One of a new breed of makers that emerged in the 1990s, Brian Moore aimed to achieve a fine balance between conventional wood and newer composite materials. Patrick Cummings, ex-Gibson general manager, teamed up with Brian Moore, ex-Steinberger plastics expert, to produce high-end, exclusive guitars, starting in 1994 and based in Brewster, New York. The first model was the M/C1 (Moore/Cummings). Its composite semi-hollow body had a center-block inside to acoustically "tune" the instrument, and an arched figured-wood top. Recent instruments have been virtually all wooden. The Korean-made iGuitar, a synth-access hybrid, and the more conventional iSeries debuted in 2000.

BURNS

These legendary British guitars of the 1960s include a handful of classics, and have a style all their own. Jim Burns was born in north-east England in 1925. His first production guitar, the Ike Isaacs Short Scale model, appeared on the market in 1958

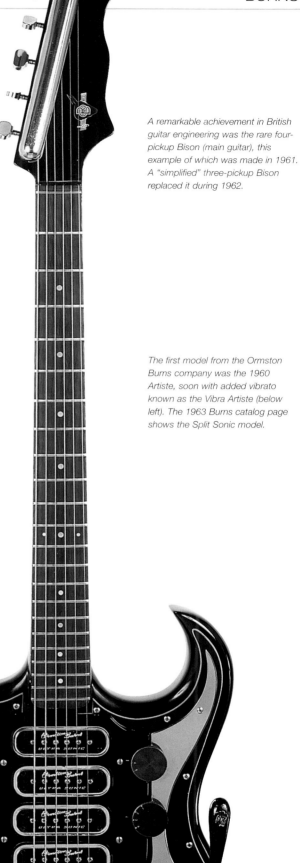

A remarkable achievement in British guitar engineering was the rare four-pickup Bison (main guitar), this example of which was made in 1961. A "simplified" three-pickup Bison replaced it during 1962.

The first model from the Ormston Burns company was the 1960 Artiste, soon with added vibrato known as the Vibra Artiste (below left). The 1963 Burns catalog page shows the Split Sonic model.

ORMSTON
BURNS

THE FINEST IN MUSICAL ENGINEERING *Burns* LONDON

The most desirable Burns guitar among collectors is the 1964 Marvin (main guitar). Co-designer Hank Marvin is seen holding one with the rest of The Shadows in a 1964 portrait (top of page), above a 1960s catalog. This 1977 Burns UK Flyte (right) was apparently modeled on the supersonic Concorde airliner.

with the Supersound brandname. Only about 20 were made. In 1959 Jim joined forces with Henry Weill. Burns-Weill guitars were somewhat crudely constructed and among the earliest British-made production solidbodies. The line included the small-bodied Fenton and the RP (named for British session player Roy Plummer). The angular body shape and Art Deco headstock of the RP soon earned it the nickname "Martian cricket bat." Few Burns-Weill guitars were made; by late 1959 the partnership was over.

In 1960 Jim Burns formed Ormston Burns Ltd (though many guitars were branded "Burns London"). The first guitar was the Artiste, with advanced features for its time including a heel-less set neck and 24 frets. With a Burns vibrato tailpiece it soon became the Vibra Artiste. The Sonic was a popular twin-pickup small-bodied solid aimed at beginners.

The first high-end Burns was the Bison, launched in 1961. The body's long, sweeping horns curved upwards, inwards and forwards to create a unique sculpture in wood. Originally the Bison appeared as a set-neck, four-pickup guitar liberally adorned with gold-plating, plus ebony fingerboard, a new bridge/vibrato unit boasting maximum sustain and smooth operation, a patented "gear box" truss-rod system (later adopted by Gretsch), and low-impedance Ultra Sonic pickups linked to new circuitry that included a novel Split Sound effect. Only 50 were built before a revised version was introduced in 1962 with bolt-on neck, rosewood fingerboard, three pickups, simplified vibrato and chrome-plated hardware. While not as eye-catching as its predecessor it was a more playable, practical instrument, and arguably the epitome of Burns design, character, quality and innovation.

More new models appeared in 1962 including the Jazz Split Sound and Split Sonic guitars, with Bison-style circuitry linked to three Split Sound pickups. Cheaper partners were the two-pickup Jazz and three-pickup Vista Sonic. In 1963 Burns ventured into semi-acoustics with the twin-pickup TR2. Its on-board "active" transistorized pre-amp, for wider tone colors, was an idea ahead of its time. The TR2 was superseded in 1964 by the similarly-styled but passive Vibraslim line.

The next Burns classic was the Marvin, introduced in 1964, designed in conjunction with Hank Marvin. The Marvin copied the construction, scale-length and circuitry of Hank's famous Fender Strat. But the headstock had a distinctive "scroll" top, and a two-bar handrest and three-piece pickguard completed the visual distinctions. The Marvin's new Rez-o-Matik pickups were modeled on Fender, although unlike the Strat all three were angled. The main innovation was a new Rezo-tube vibrato unit which had a knife-edge bearing and six tubes to anchor the strings rather than Fender's single metal block. The vibrato was largely responsible for the Marvin's tone, somewhat sweeter and deeper than the Fender. Only about 400 original Marvins were produced. The Bison was restyled to match the new Marvin, losing much of its distinctive

character in the process. Also launched at this time was the Double Six 12-string. Players have included Mike Pender, Chris Britton and Hank Marvin plus, later, Mark Knopfler and Gaz Coombes. Further down the line, the Sonics were replaced by the Nu-Sonics; Vista Sonics and Split Sonics were gone by 1965. Additions included the GB65, GB66 and Virginian semis, the latter with the round soundhole of a flat-top acoustic.

In September 1965, the Baldwin Piano & Organ Company bought Burns for $250,000 (see Baldwin). The last Burns to appear prior to the Baldwin takeover was the Baby Bison, coincidentally produced for export only. Baldwin acquired sole rights to the Burns brand, so Jim Burns used his middle name, Ormston, as a brand for his late-1960s instruments, including a semi-solid six-string that prompted the line of Hayman guitars he helped develop in 1969 (see Hayman).

In 1973 the Burns UK company was formed. First and best-known model was the Flyte, endorsed by Dave Hill and Marc Bolan. The body design was apparently based on the Concorde aircraft, and two poor Mach One Humbuster pickups were fitted alongside the Dynamic Tension bridge/tailpiece. The Mirage and Artist followed in 1976, later joined by the final Burns UK model, the LJ24. This better guitar came too late to revive the company, which collapsed later that year.

The new Jim Burns company was launched in 1979. Despite commercial pressure to revive the best of the past, the company decided to produce new models. First was

Three more Burns: a peculiar Jim Burns Scorpion (this page, far left) from 1979; a Nu-Sonic from 1996 (center); and a Club series Marquee model from 1999, also featured in this 2004 ad (below).

Those who know that The Shadows were first called The Drifters will understand the reference in the model name of this Burns London Drifter (left) of 1999. The ad from 2004 (above) features remakes of Burns's classic Steer and Double Six models.

Burns fan Gaz Coombes (left) of Supergrass plays a recent Nu-Sonic.

the odd Scorpion. The body had two carved Scorpion-like lower horns and a headstock that might have represented the sting in its tail. Next came the Steer, reminiscent of the Virginian, and the budget Magpie.

In 1981 the company finally acknowledged demand for vintage styles and issued revised versions of the Marvin and Bison. But economies were made and the revivals lacked much of the character and quality of the original 1960s instruments. In 1983 the Bandit model appeared, a small-bodied solid that came with unusual multi-angled styling. This last effort was the best made by the operation, but by 1984 the erratic and misguided Jim Burns company had ceased trading.

Jim himself returned to inactivity and obscurity, while many of his early creations continued to attract more interest on the "vintage" market. In 1991 a British company, Burns London, began producing authentic reproductions and updates of 1960s classics. These included 30/50 Anniversary editions of the Bison and others in 1994. The following year saw the Nu-Sonic, an old name on a Telecaster-style instrument. In 1999 a new Club series was launched, including the Marquee and Cobra models.

In its heyday of the 1960s, Burns represented the best of British guitar design and construction. While not always equal to some of the competition in sound, Burns quality and playability was rarely in question. Jim Burns died in 1998, but his original designs stand as testimony to the man regarded by many as the British Leo Fender.

CARVIN

Uniquely relying and thriving almost exclusively on mail-order marketing, Carvin guitars had their roots in the Kiesel-brand Bakelite lap-steels and amps made in Los Angeles by Lowell C. Kiesel, beginning in 1947.

A distribution problem led in 1949 to a change of brandname – Carvin was named for Lowell's sons Carson and Gavin – and relocation to Covina, California, plus a switch to mail-order. Since mail-order Carvins are basically custom-made, a variety of options has been available since the beginning.

Carvin began to re-market Harmony and Kay Spanish guitars outfitted with Carvin pickups in 1954, offering its original, Kiesel-designed SGB solidbody with a distinctive body point from 1955 to 1961. Early endorsers of the Carvin instruments included country stars such as Joe Maphis and Larry Collins. From 1962-68 a more Fender-style body with a steep lower cutaway was used; Bigsby vibratos became standard-issue in 1963. This model was later played by John Cippolina. German Hofner-made necks were used from 1964-76.

In 1968 Carvin relocated to Escondido, California, changing its model designations to SS, briefly using Japanese Strat-style bodies, then switching to German-made bodies the following year. Gibson-style double-cutaway AS55B and AS51 "Thin Acoustical Guitars" began about this time. During 1976 the operation moved to a larger

Craig Chaquico of Jefferson Starship (above) prepares to blast out on Carvin's pointy V220 in a 1986 ad. This Carvin SGB-3 (left) was made in California around 1959; the pointy V220T (right) dates from 1985.

Jason Becker (above) of the David Lee Roth band demonstrates his left-hand technique on a Carvin DC200C in this ad from 1990.

The Carvin 2-MS double-neck (main guitar) was built around 1965, while this Allan Holdsworth signature Carvin (below, centre) was made in 1997. Casio's PG-380 guitar synthesizer (below right) dates from 1988. Jason Becker teamed up with Carvin again in 2010 (ad, right) for the JB200C tribute model.

factory, where it began producing its first hex-pole pickups. The newly-located Carvin company also produced new electrics, the CM96 or DC150 Stereo Gibson-style solidbodies, now with Carvin-made necks.

Carvin guitar construction switched to set-necks in 1978. During 1980 the company's distinctive sharp-horned offset-double-cutaway body shape appeared on the DC200 model, which was designed by Mark Kiesel. The following year this was offered as the DC200K in koa, marking the beginning of Carvin's use of more exotic timbers, available as standard on high-end models but also offered as options on a number of other models in the line.

Carvin's DC production models continued to proliferate with different pickup configurations. From around 1985-88 a DC160 version of the DC150 appeared in quilted maple. By 1989 the typical Carvin three-tuners-a-side headstock was replaced with a pointy-droopy six-in-line version, and several double-neck options were available. That year the flamed-maple DC400 version of the DC200 also debuted.

In 1985 Carvin made its first venture into exotic shapes with the four-point V220, similar to a Dean ML and endorsed by Craig Chaquico. This was followed in 1987 by the Ultra V, inspired by the Jackson Randy Rhoads. In 1988 Carvin changed construction again to through-neck style, and this became Carvin's favored form of manufacturing. The original Explorer-style headstocks on these changed to pointy-

Stanley Jordan's touch/tapping style
of playing found an unusual home on
Casio's PG-380 guitar synthesizer, as
publicized in this 1989 ad.

droopy six-tuners-in-line in 1989. A more pointy X220 replaced the V220 in 1990. Pointy guitars were gone from the Carvin line by 1993.

From 1987 to 1990 Carvin offered another thinline electric, the SH225, a double-humbucker guitar with very rounded equal cutaways. In 1989 only a rounded-horn version of the offset-cutaway model was offered, the DC145. By the late 1980s Carvin products were used by a host of pros including Elvin Bishop, Jeff Cook, Larry Coryell, Marshall Crenshaw, Lita Ford, Ray Gomez, Alex Lifeson, Steve Lynch and Rick Nielsen, among many others. Later endorsers of Carvin's various models would also include Jason Becker and Al DiMeola.

In 1991 Carvin augmented its catalog (and factory showroom) by setting up and opening two new retail outlets. These were based in Hollywood and Santa Ana, California, and would be followed later by several European stores. That year a 12-string version of the DC200, the DC120, appeared.

In 1993, with "vintage" guitar designs prevalent throughout the rest of the guitar industry, Carvin added the classic Telecaster-style shape to its repertoire with the TL60 model. This was joined the following year by the f-holed AE185. The trend was "solidified" with the solidbody Tele-like SC90 in 1996, the same year that Carvin introduced its flagship Allan Holdsworth signature guitar. In 2015, the Carvin guitar company was renamed Kiesel Guitars.

CASIO

Best-known for digital watches and keyboards, this Japanese company took a tentative step into guitar synthesis in 1987 with the MG-500 and MG-510 MIDI six-strings.

Roland had paved the way, but in 1988 came Casio's superior PG-380 offering a more player-friendly, full-fledged alternative. This Fender-influenced, Floyd Rose-equipped solidbody had all the technical bits arranged in a very accessible manner. Famous names such as Stanley Jordan and Curtis Mayfield obviously agreed. The less expensive PG-300 debuted in 1990, with Strat-style pickup layout and vibrato. Casio's final guitar synth came three years later with the simplified and shortlived G-393.

CHANDLER

Originally a supplier of guitar components, and based in California, Chandler expanded operations during 1991 to include complete instruments. These included custom-built examples and a selection of standard production models initially offered in kit form.

Additions to Chandler's fully-assembled line in the following year included the Rickenbacker-like 555 as well as the ultra-offset Austin Special. This single-cutaway solidbody equipped with lipstick pickups was based on a guitar originally made for Keith Richards by US luthier Ted Newman-Jones.

Later models included the Fender-derived Telepathic and Metro, offered in various guises, along with the equally California-flavored Futurama and Spitfire.

Sonny Sandoval of P.O.D. models a
Carvin custom shop CS6M in this 2014
ad (far left), while the earlier Chandler
Austin Special (left) dates from 1992.
The ad (bottom) from the same year
highlights the Texan charm of that
guitar, while the other ad (top) alludes
to the Rickenbacker-like qualities of
Chandler's 555 model.

C H A R V E L

Charvel grew from a small supplier of guitar parts in the late 1970s to a major producer of rock guitars in the 1980s. In 1974 Wayne Charvel set up a guitar repair business in Azusa, northern Los Angeles, California (and soon moved to nearby San Dimas). Charvel began supplying much-needed hardware replacement parts, and from this humble beginning the line would expand to include bodies, necks, pickups and, ultimately, complete guitar kits.

Financial problems struck in 1977, and late the following year Wayne Charvel signed over his name and the entire operation to employee Grover Jackson. (Charvel himself went on to run several shortlived companies in the 1980s, and launched the Wayne brand in 1999.)

Grover Jackson continued to offer a customizing service at Charvel for instruments brought in by customers, while continuing to develop and hone his own ideas on guitar design. The results eventually appeared in limited form in 1979 with the first Charvel-brand guitars. One of the early efforts was seen under the fast-moving fingers of a rising guitar star, Edward Van Halen.

At the start of the 1980s Jackson added a new line under his own name (see Jackson). The Charvel brand was reserved for bolt-on-neck guitars with essentially Fender-style bodies and necks – as well as Gibson- or Vox-inspired alternatives and an original four-point "star" shape. Options in 1981 also included various DiMarzio pickups as well as distinctive flashy custom paint jobs.

Business grew as Grover Jackson's efforts led to high-profile associations with key emerging guitar heroes. In 1986 a joint venture with distributor IMC of Fort Worth, Texas, resulted in a less-expensive made-in-Japan Charvel line sporting Jackson's by now established drooped "pointy" headstock. Jackson/Charvel relocated a few miles east to Ontario, California, around this time.

The new Charvel line remained Fender-styled: Models One, Two, Three and Four each employed a bolt-on neck and Strat-like body shape. Models Five and Six featured 24-fret through-neck construction allied to a slimmer-horned body. This and the pointy headstock would become characteristics of the new "superstrat" styling, as would Model Six's sharkfin-shape fingerboard markers. Pickup layouts included a single bridge humbucker, as well as the two-single-coils-plus-bridge-humbucker strongly identified with the new rock-oriented superstrats. Vibratos too were considered to be mandatory equipment back then.

By 1988 the line had expanded, but the following year saw a major revamp signified by a new Charvel logo in a "script" style as on Jacksons. Models were split into named series including Contemporary, Classic, Fusion and Professional. The market for superstrats was now clearly defined, and the new Charvels – fine examples of high-

Charvel's first Japanese line featured models still largely Strat-based, such as this 1986 Model Four (near right), as well as in the new superstrat style, like this 1986 Model Five (center). Superstrats prevailed: this Fusion Custom (far right) was made in 1988.

*A couple of Charvel/Jackson ads
from 1992: for the Charvel Surfcaster
(right) and the Jackson Randy
Rhoads Limited Edition (far right).*

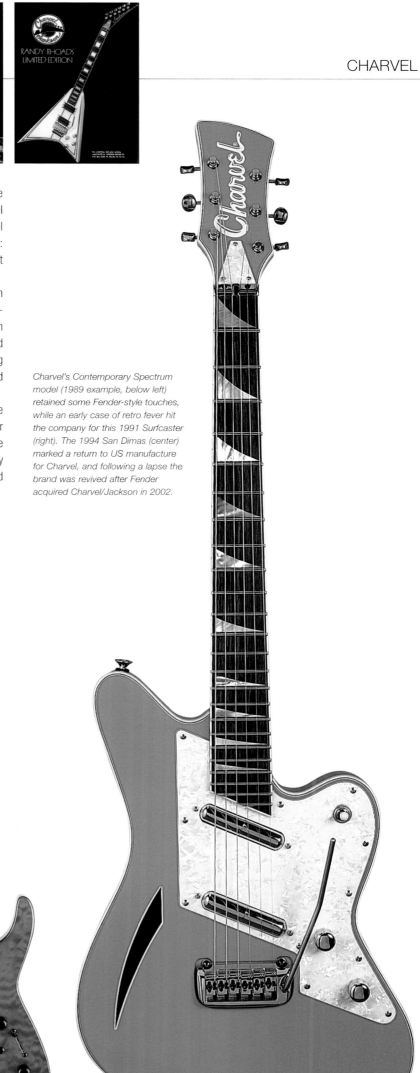

end Japanese mass-manufacture – were intended to fill every niche. A Korean-made line, new for 1989, was branded Charvette By Charvel and clearly aimed at entry-level players. However, by 1991 all instruments regardless of origin were branded Charvel once more. Some new 1990 models catered for traditional as well as extreme tastes: the Strat-style STs and Tele-like TE contrasted the Avenger's offset-V shape that echoed Jackson's Randy Rhoads.

One of the first determined moves into original yet retro-flavored design came in 1991 with the Surfcaster semi-solidbody, something of a mutated Jazzmaster-meets-Rickenbacker-meets-Danelectro. The Surfcaster had started life as a custom Jackson model, but the Charvel versions initially came in six-string (vibrato or fixed-bridge) and 12-string models. Then the CX series took over from the Charvettes, maintaining Charvel's low-end presence. A new overtly Fender-style headstock was soon amended to a design intended to calm trademark lawyers.

In 1994 Charvel's San Dimas series was introduced, named for the location of the old Charvel facility. This marked a return to US manufacture (though three years earlier there had been a limited-edition remake of the original late-1970s model), while the budget CHS series was launched in 1995. Charvel/Jackson was acquired in 1997 by Akai, which dropped the Charvel brand, and then in 2002 by Fender, which licensed Charvel (and Jackson) production to JCMI.

*Charvel's Contemporary Spectrum
model (1989 example, below left)
retained some Fender-style touches,
while an early case of retro fever hit
the company for this 1991 Surfcaster
(right). The 1994 San Dimas (center)
marked a return to US manufacture
for Charvel, and following a lapse the
brand was revived after Fender
acquired Charvel/Jackson in 2002.*

CORAL

In 1966 the entertainment conglomerate MCA bought Danelectro. MCA maintained the company's base in its existing premises in Neptune, New Jersey, along with founder Nat Daniel, but one of the changes that the new owner made was the addition of a new Danelectro-made brand in 1967, which they called Coral. The name came from one of MCA's record labels. (See the Danelectro entry for models that continued at this time with the Danelectro brand.)

The first Coral-brand instruments shared the Jaguar-like shape and short Strat-style head of contemporary Danelectros, but were solidbodies with a Coral logo and the unusual "crackle" finishes of the Dane D series. Models included the two- or three-pickup Hornet and 12-string Scorpion.

Joining these Corals in 1967 was the vaguely US-map shaped Coral Sitar, endorsed by Al Nichol and Tom Dawes. Like the earlier Danelectro Bellzouki 12-string, it was co-designed by session-man Vinnie Bell who had spotted a demand in New York studios in the mid 1960s for trendy sitar sounds, popular since George Harrison used a real sitar on The Beatles' 1965 track 'Norwegian Wood.'

Bell prompted Danelectro to devise an electric guitar that would make a sitar-like sound. The secret was the flat plastic "bridge" that gave a buzzy sound – and made intonation almost impossible. There was also a bank of 13 extra "drone" strings tuned in half-steps. A similarly-shaped Coral Bellzouki 12-string was also introduced. New, too, were the f-hole thinline hollowbody Firefly, flat-top Vincent Bell Combo, and Long Horn Series (f-hole hollow versions of the older Danelectro Long Horns). Coral died along with Danelectro in 1969.

CORT

The Korean guitar-making powerhouse of Cort was established in 1973 by Jack Westheimer of Chicago, Illinois. Westheimer, formerly the US importer of Teisco, used the factory to produce Cortez-brand acoustic guitars, made in Japan since 1960. Cort also produced some Cortez-brand copies of American electric guitars during the 1970s, and supplied guitars for other companies too. Around 1978 Cort developed an efficient way to produce through-neck versions of popular guitar designs; some were sold with the Arbor brand.

In 1983 Cort built a new, modern factory in Korea and began to use timbers and electronics imported from North America. By 1985 Cort was producing lines for Kramer and B.C. Rich. Soon after the new factory opened the Cort brandname itself appeared on various beginner-grade copies of American guitars.

Then Cort bought a license to Ned Steinberger's headless guitar design and has offered a version for some years. By 1986 Cort was offering exotic guitars such as the Effector, with built-in effects, the Sound, with built-in amp and speaker, a star-shaped

Steve Howe on stage with Yes in 1973 (above) about to play a Coral Sitar on his guitar "tree" that enabled a fast changeover between different guitars. Howe first used the Coral Sitar on 'Siberian Khatru,' a track on the band's 1972 album Close To The Edge (below).

A Coral Sitar from 1967 (left), which had a "buzzy" bridge and drone strings, and a thinline Coral Firefly (right) from the same year.

Vinnie Bell worked with Danelectro on the design of the Coral Sitar and appeared in this shameless ad (left) in 1967. New York sessionman Bell played the Sitar on many 1960s pop hits, including 'Green Tambourine' by The Lemon Pipers (1967 album, opposite page).

model, plus Strat-style and Explorer-style models with elaborate pearl dragon inlays. Original designs followed two years later including the pointy-horned Strat-style Solo series and the exaggerated extended-horn double-cutaway Starfires.

By 1989 there was the curly-maple-topped, scalloped and contoured deep-double-cutaway Viva Deluxe guitar, plus a Heavy Metal model that came with a built-in octave-splitting effect. In addition to various copies, the Viva and Starfire (offered as the S-Series) would anchor the line through the 1990s.

During 1992 Cort's line was reorganized into the Performer Series, now including Stratocaster-style guitars that were called the Stature, Mega, Statos, Retro and STAT. These models were offered with various options in materials and the pickup layouts. Also debuting at this time were the thinline Source (in a Gibson ES-335-style) and the full-bodied Yorktown Deluxe archtop (this in Super-400-style). From 1994 for around three years Cort offered the Artist Series, which included a high-end Viva CM with Bartolini pickups, as well as a swamp ash superstrat, the A2000.

Around 1997 Cort began to work with well-known guitar-makers to develop new designs. Luthier Jerry Auerswald came up with the EF (Environmentally Friendly) Series made from the synthetic "luthite." A year later the Solo Series superstrats were introduced, as well as the Signature Series. This included the TRG, an archtop with cats-eye soundholes designed by Nashville luthier Jim Triggs; the LCS-1, a Gibson-style archtop endorsed by Larry Coryell; and the MGM-1, a carved PRS-like solid endorsed by Matt "Guitar" Murphy.

By 1999 the Cort line had moved further to higher-end instruments, with several archtops endorsed by Joe Beck, some very fancy Solo models including the birdseye-maple HBS Hiram Bullock Signature, plus a sleek deep-cut Viva Gold II and the dramatic Music Man Silhouette-style S Series. By 2017 Cort continued to concentrate on solidbody models, including the Classic Rock, G, KX, M, MS, X, and Zenox series, alongside a few hollowbody guitars.

CUSTOM KRAFT

This was a brand applied to entry-level guitars and amplifiers made for Bernard Kornbloom's St. Louis Music, based in Missouri. The line got underway during the mid 1950s with some archtops made by Kay. From 1961 until the middle of the decade many Custom Krafts were variants of Kay hollowbodies (including versions of Kay's Thinline series). At first these were joined by Japanese-made solidbodies.

In 1963 the Valco-made Ambassador solidbodies debuted. Somewhat inspired by Burns, these were variants of Valco's existing National and Supro models. Valco purchased Kay in 1967; in '68 the Mod line of hollowbodies appeared. Despite the demise of Valco/Kay that year, Custom Krafts continued to 1970, increasingly using non-US parts. More recently, Eastwood offered a tribute Custom Kraft model.

This angelic ad by Cort from 2009 (above) was designed to make guitarists aware of the company's Z6-EVL model, which had pentagram and cross-shape fingerboard inlays.

On this page: a Cort Larry Coryell signature model from 1999 (far left), and a Custom Kraft Ambassador Vibramatic (left). a model that was made by Valco in the US in 1966. The company's ad from the following year (above) attempted to link Custom Kraft with the popular sound of the moment from the UK.

Jimmy Page on-stage with Led Zeppelin (opposite), and on a 1970s magazine cover (left), playing the Danelectro Standard he favored for slide work. This Standard 3021 (opposite), made around 1965, is similar to the one used by Page.

DANELECTRO

Probably no other instruments so humble have garnered as much reverence as Danelectro guitars of the 1950s and 1960s, thrust into immortality primarily through association with the mail-order catalog of Sears, Roebuck.

Before competition from Japanese and other importers, Danelectros – or "Danos" as they're often called – were the beginner guitars of the post-war Baby Boom generation. A Danelectro is reported to have set Jerry Garcia on the road to eventual stardom, but the guitars also found their way into recording studios because of an individual sound that attracted pro players. Danelectros can be heard on records that range from 'Sugar, Sugar' by The Archies to 'I'm A Believer' by The Monkees and 'The Sound Of Silence' by Simon & Garfunkel. The instruments have been played by artists as diverse as Jimi Hendrix, Jimmy Page and Los Lobos.

Danelectro's founder was Nathan I. (Nat) Daniel. He began his career in 1933 building amplifiers for a department store in New York City. Some time during the following year Daniel was recruited by Epiphone man Herb Sunshine to build the earliest Epiphone Electar amps. Until 1942 Daniel would continue to supply Epiphone with a number of products.

The Danelectro company was founded in 1946 and began supplying amps for mail-order company Montgomery Ward in 1947, and for Sears in 1948. In 1954 Danelectro expanded into solidbody electric guitars, introducing its own Danelectro-brand models. That same year, in the Fall Sears catalog, Danelectro-made guitars branded Silvertone replaced the solidbodies that had previously been made for the mail-order company by Harmony. These Dano-origin Silvertones were small, Les-Paul-shaped guitars that came with either one or two single-coil pickups concealed underneath a melamine pickguard. The Danelectro-brand versions were covered in white tweed vinyl and were distinguished by wide "bell"-shape headstocks, while the similar Silvertone models came in maroon vinyl but were topped by equally distinctive wide "Coke bottle"-shape headstocks. Most Danelectro guitars of the time sported simple metal bridge/tailpiece assemblies with a moveable rosewood saddle.

In 1955 the small ginger-colored Model C "peanut" appeared with a Coke-bottle headstock. The pickguard had shrunk in size and the pickups were now exposed, first wrapped in brown vinyl tape, followed by unplated and then chrome-plated "lipstick" pickups – the covers actually purchased from a lipstick-tube manufacturer.

The similar U-1 and U-2 models replaced the Cs in 1956, the main difference being their availability in a line of new colors (black, copper, royal blue, coral red, surf green and so on). A Danelectro innovation was the six-string bass, introduced as the short-scale UB-2 model around 1956. This was effectively a guitar that was tuned an octave lower than usual. Dano six-string basses of various designs also began to appear on

Danelectro's popular electrics included the early U-1 and U-2 models, seen in the company's two-sided flyer from 1956 (above). The company sold a number of instruments to the Sears mail-order catalog with the Silvertone brand. This 1958 Silvertone G01301L (right) was the Sears version of Dano's masonite-and-pine U-2.

records, including such gems of Dano twanginess as Duane Eddy's 'Because They're Young.' A three-pickup U-3 regular guitar was added in 1957, and that same year saw the U series Danos also available with the Silvertone brand. However, by the close of the 1950s the Silvertone line had reduced to just a few Danelectro models, replaced largely by Harmony- and Kay-made guitars. Single-pickup Silvertone U models got a new, skinny "dolphin"-shape headstock that had six tuners in-line. This style would last on Danelectro instruments through 1961.

In 1958 Danelectro relocated the guitar and amplifier factory to new premises in Neptune, New Jersey. It was at this time that the company introduced its legendary semi-hollowbody guitars, the Standard (with one or two pickups and Coke-bottle headstock), the Deluxe (two or three pickups) and the oddly-named Hand Vibrato (with "duck foot"-shape headstock, and vibrato).

These are now known as Danelectro's "short-horn" models because of their widely flared double-cutaway horns which are shorter than those of the later "long-horn" style. The various models came with laminated masonite (hardboard) tops and backs over wooden frames of either poplar or pine; sides were covered in vinyl. These instruments would typify the Danelectro line through 1966, but three other classic Danos had been introduced in 1959. These comprised a short-horn guitar/bass double-neck in white-to-brown sunburst, the wood-grained, hollowbody Convertible

that came with or without pickup, and the white-to-bronze sunburst Long Horn Bass with its distinctive "lyre"-shape long-horn body.

In 1958 studio guitarist Vinnie Bell became associated with Danelectro and it was in 1961 that the Bellzouki model he helped to design was introduced. It was an electric 12-string guitar – at this time one of the few such production models available. Its body looked something like a Greek bouzouki, hence the name. The one-pickup version had a teardrop shape, while the two-pickup model added four extra points. Both had a "mustache" pickguard under the strings and a duck-foot head.

Meanwhile, by 1962 the only Danelectro guitar offered by Sears was the new amp-in-case guitar, a single-pickup short-horn in black metalflake. The brilliantly simple idea was that built into the guitar's case was a three-watt amp and 6″ speaker, providing the guitarist with a portable electric guitar outfit. This was joined in 1963 by a two-pickup version in red sunburst that came with a deafening five-watt amp, 8″ speaker and tremolo. The six-tuners-in-line headstocks now looked like meat cleavers. In 1967 the amp-in-case guitars changed to a new Fender Jaguar-style shape.

During 1963 Danelectro rolled out the little Pro 1 solidbody guitar which, with its asymmetrical, square-ish shape, looked something like a poor guitarist's Guild Thunderbird. It did however introduce Nat Daniel's neck-tilt adjustment. It was followed on to the market by the exotic Guitarlin model which sported the long-horn lyre-shaped

Danelectro's short-horn double-neck (left) combined guitar and four-string bass, this one from 1960. Stevie Ray Vaughan clutches one with guitar and six-string bass on a 1990s cover (above). Dan'o was a pioneer of six-string bass: this 1958 Long Horn Model 4623 (center) belongs to Duane Eddy.

Danelectro's Bellzouki (right), first sold in 1961, was one of the first 12-string electric guitars. This two-pickup version dates from around 1965. The publicity material (above) from Danelectro's 1967 catalog pictures sessionman Vinnie Bell, who helped design the Bellzouki.

body and a fingerboard that sported no less than 31 frets. In 1966 the entertainment conglomerate MCA bought Danelectro and, while they kept Daniel in charge, made big changes. Alongside the Danelectro-brand guitars, the new owner would also introduce a new Coral brand, named for one of the MCA's record labels, but still manufactured in the Danelectro factory (see Coral).

The 1967 Danelectro Slimline guitars were semi-hollowbody models with a Jaguar-style shape, distinctive vinyl side-trim, stubby Strat-like head and two or three pickups, with or without vibrato. A 12-string version was also offered. The Hawk line was similar, with one or two pickups but without the vinyl side trim.

Also similar to the Slimlines, the 1967 Dane Series had four basic sub-groups: A (one or two pickups); B (two or three pickups); C (crackled two-tone "gator" finish); and D ("gator" finish plus deluxe pickguard in a swirled plastic and brushed-chrome control panel). Finally during 1967 a new Danelectro-brand Electric Sitar debuted (see Coral for the better-known model). The Danelectro sitar was a one-pickup instrument with rounded, sitar-like body shape and matching headstock style.

By 1968 demand for guitars had declined and in 1969 MCA closed the Danelectro factory. Guitar-maker Dan Armstrong obtained some leftover parts and in 1969 sold them with his own pickups as Dan Armstrong Modified Danelectros. Later, some Danelectro models would became collectable cult items, especially after players of the

Two more Danelectro guitars on this page: an Electric Sitar (center) made in 1967, and a UB-2 six-string bass from 1958 (right). This 1999 ad from Japan (above) features some of the reissues produced by the revived Danelectro brand.

The Sitar sound is something else . . .
(so is the price)

New DANELECTRO **electric sitar . . . $139 list**

This 31-fret Guitarlin from 1966 (left) was in Danelectro's distinctive long-horn style. Dano's advertising was something else, exemplified by this 1967 ad (above) for the Electric Sitar.

stature of Jimmy Page were seen using the instruments. Page would often opt for a Standard short-horn on stage for slide work, exploiting the bright, cutting sound of the guitar's pickups that was enhanced by the cheap but effective construction.

Nat Daniel died in 1994. In 1995 the Evets Corporation obtained rights to the Danelectro name, introducing a line of effects pedals in 1997 followed by guitars in 1998. The new Danelectros were similar in look and construction to the vintage models, with reproduction "lipstick" pickups and similar hardware, although by 1999 the line had begun to expand into retro sparkle finishes and new electronic switching. There were also a number of new designs such as the Hodad (1999) as well as more recently the '59, '63, '64, '66, '67, and Convertible models.

D'ANGELICO

New York City guitar-maker John D'Angelico is best known for his superb acoustic archtop instruments built from the early 1930s to the early 1960s. Some owners of these fine instruments would inevitably fit the guitars with "floating" pickups to allow amplified playing. Other customers would sometimes take more drastic action, such as Chet Atkins who unleashed his toolkit to permanently fix a Gibson pickup into the top of his D'Angelico instrument. This is enough to make guitar collectors weep today, because D'Angelicos are among the most valuable "vintage" guitars. However, due to continuing demand from a number of guitarists who would visit his busy Manhattan

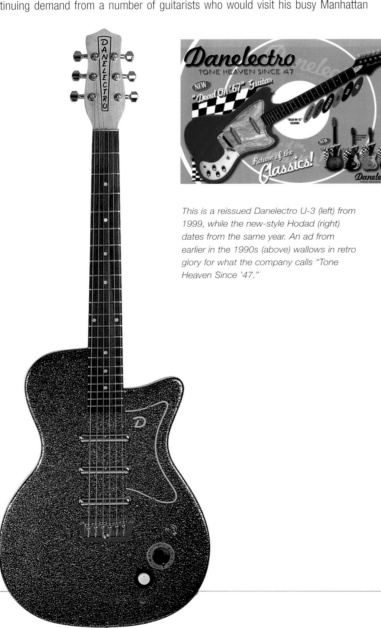

This is a reissued Danelectro U-3 (left) from 1999, while the new-style Hodad (right) dates from the same year. An ad from earlier in the 1990s (above) wallows in retro glory for what the company calls "Tone Heaven Since '47."

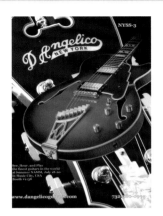

The D'Angelico brand died with John D'Angelico himself in 1964, but it was revived in 2011 for a line of modern guitars, a couple of which are featured in these ads from 2003 (right top) and 2013 (right below).

shop, John D'Angelico decided to offer during the 1950s and early 1960s a line of budget archtops with permanently built-in pickups and controls, sometimes referred to as G-7 models. Most had plywood bodies that D'Angelico would buy in from local suppliers such as United Guitars or Codé of New Jersey, but the necks at least were made by D'Angelico himself. More recently, the brand was revived in 2011 and has appeared on a line of imported and US models, including modern electric archtops.

D'AQUISTO

Jimmy D'Aquisto worked with the New York archtop guitar-maker John D'Angelico from 1959. Following D'Angelico's death five years later, D'Aquisto began making guitars in his own right.

Gradually D'Aquisto developed his own style, and while primarily working in the acoustic archtop field he did make a number of flat-top guitars as well as some fully electric instruments. The electric models culminated in the luthier's Les Paul-shaped semi-hollowbody Centura Electric model. This stylish guitar debuted in the early 1990s. It included typical D'Aquisto touches such as a wooden tailpiece and pickguard, as well as the maker's customary employment of the finest neck and body timbers. D'Aquisto also designed electrics for Hagstrom (the Jimmy model) and for Fender (the D'Aquisto Deluxe, Elite and Standard models). D'Aquisto died in 1995 at the age of just 59. He once described his guitars as "a way that I can make the world a bit better."

The D'Angelico electric archtop shown here (far left) was made around 1960; this D'Aquisto Centura Electric (center) dates from 1991; and the D'Aquisto Jazz Master (right) was produced around 1987.

By the time of this 1997 Dean ad with Pat Travers (left) and a Cadillac Ultima, a new owner was in place.

D E A N

Dean rode to fame in the late 1970s making fancy versions of Gibson-style designs, originally with flamboyant "wishbone" headstocks. Dean was founded in 1976 by Dean Zelinsky of Evanston, Illinois. Production of the Z (Explorer-like), V (Flying V-style) and a hybrid of the two, the much-emulated ML, began in 1977. Dean guitars had figured tops and loud DiMarzio pickups.

The Les-Paul-inspired E'Lite and Cadillac appeared in 1979-80, followed by a downsized Baby series in 1982, as favored by Rik Emmett and Sammy Hagar. The 1983 Bel Aire's bolt-on neck came from ESP in Japan and was one of the first guitars (along with the Kramer Pacer) sporting the humbucker/single-coil/single-coil pickup layout that practically defined the coming "superstrat" genre.

Debuting in 1985 were the Hollywood models from ESP in Japan, the Signature series from Korea, and the "heavy metal" Mach V (Japan) and VII (US). Manufacture of Dean's conventional Fender-style guitars shifted to Korea in 1986, including 1987's Eighty-Eight, Jammer and Playmate series.

In 1990 Zelinsky licensed the Dean name to Tropical Music of Miami, Florida, and a year later Korean Strat-style solidbodies debuted. A Reissue Series of early Dean designs was produced in 1993-94 in California, supervised by Zelinsky, becoming American Customs made in Cleveland, Ohio, in 1994. In 1995 a new Dean factory

An example of Dean's blatantly sexist ads (top), this one from 1982, plus a more thoughtfully clothed Dave Mustaine and V-shape Dean pictured in an ad from 2007.

Dean absorbed Gibson influences into its original trio of models – the Explorer-like Z (1978 example, near right), the Flying-V-style V, and a combination of the two, the ML – all detailed in this 1977 ad (below). Dean's Explorer-meets-V ML model

would itself spawn a good number of imitators in the pointy-guitar world. Dean's Golden E'lite (far right) added a traditional rounded base to the design; this one dates from 1983.

opened in Plant City, Florida, managed by Armadillo Enterprises, offering US-made American Customs and the US Series with Korean bodies, all variations on classic Dean designs. Models made in the US and Korea (American Spirit) were offered in 1997, including a Korina series and new Icon models inspired by PRS's designs.

Zelinsky left in 2008 and set up his own new brand, DBZ. The Dean brand continued, offering models such as the classic MLs, Vs, and Zs, the Dimebag-inspired Razorbacks, Rebels, and Stealths, and a number of other signature guitars.

DE ARMOND

De Armond has been famous as a brandname for pickups and effects-pedals, starting back in the 1940s. In 1997 it was acquired by Fender, who subsequently decided to apply it to a line of Korean-built electrics to represent a less expensive alter ego of Guild, which had been in Fender ownership since 1995.

The De Armond guitar line debuted in Europe in 1998, the American launch following a year later. Including solidbodies, semi-solids and archtop electrics, the line consists of models based on well-known Guild designs, some re-created more closely than others, and employing similar or identical names to the originals.

The Starfire Special closely resembles its early-1960s single-cutaway inspiration, complete with reproduction De Armond single-coil pickups and Bigsby-style vibrato tailpiece, while the standard Starfire replicates the later equal-double-cutaway version.

The humbucker-equipped M75 solid recalls Guild's own Les Paul-style equivalent, and is also offered as the M75T with sparkle-finished front, single-coils and vibrato.

The Jet-Star approximates the style of the odd 1960s Guild Thunderbird, but with simplified fixtures and fittings – no built-in stand or Hagstrom vibrato here. The single-cutaway X155 archtop electric embodies classic Guild features, including a stepped pickguard, harp tailpiece and two humbuckers.

Cheaper Indonesian-made versions of the various solidbodies were later added to the De Armond line, generally identified by bolt-on-neck construction and more basic appointments. Additions during 2000 included the T400 thinline hollowbody, and two seven-string solidbodies, the S67 and Seven Star. The lines were switched to the Squier brand in 2002, but three years later these, too, had disappeared.

DUESENBERG

Dieter Gölsdorf started Duesenberg in Hannover in northern Germany in 1995 with a firm interest in the combination of retro design (especially the art deco style) and modern technology. Models include the semi-solid Starplayers, the solidbody 49er, 59er, and Bonneville, and signature models for Dave Stewart and Mike Campbell.

DWIGHT

Epiphone, like some other makers, occasionally made special versions of existing models for particular retailers. Dwight was a US outlet whose sole claim to guitar fame

This Duesenberg Starplayer TV (far left) was made in 2004, while the two Duesenberg ads date from 2006 (Double Cat model, left) and 2008 (Mike Campbell signature model, top of page). The two other guitars here are a solidbody Domino Baron (center), made in 1967, and a Dwight-brand guitar (right), a specially badged version of an Epiphone Coronet, made in 1962.

An object lesson in how to excite gadget-freaks with a pushbutton-laden multi-pickup guitar, as taught by Eko in a catalog from 1964.

was a special custom-branded edition of the New York company's solidbody Coronet that it commissioned during the early 1960s. It had a Dwight headstock logo and "D"-badged pickguard, but was otherwise identical to the Epi Coronet.

EGGLE

Here was a serious attempt to establish a quality UK guitar brand. Patrick Eggle began his professional guitar-making career in 1990 with the shortlived Climaxe instruments, but a year later Patrick Eggle-brand guitars burst on to the scene from a factory that was based in Coventry, England.

The Patrick Eggle Guitar Company was formed by Eggle and businessman Andrew Selby. The guitars themselves – the small-body fixed-bridge PRS-like Berlin and the similar Berlin Pro, one of the first guitars to be fitted with a Wilkinson VS-100 vibrato – were well conceived and good value.

But problems arose when the company tried to maintain production levels, discovering the marked differences between building one guitar a month and 20 a week. So there followed a liaison with Swiss-based maker Gary Levinson, with the Coventry factory making Eggles as well as Levinson's own Blade-brand guitars. In the midst of the problems, Eggle himself left early in 1994. At first he produced Redwing guitars, but soon retreated to custom-making.

The Eggle/Levinson operation itself folded early in 1995, but a new Eggle company

was back in business within a month. Despite having noted hardware designer Trev Wilkinson on board, this too failed, and Eggle was sold to Birmingham-based distributor Musical Exchanges at the end of 1996, from where Patrick Eggle Guitars operates today. Wilkinson remains as creative director, and has his own Fret-King brand. Current Eggles include the set-neck double- or single-cutaway Macon and the bolt-on 96, available in droptop style, meaning a bent contoured top.

EGMOND

This Dutch maker provided affordable, low-end electrics for many aspiring axe heroes in Europe. Some Egmonds exported to the UK were branded with distributor Rosetti's name. A 1950s example was the Solid 7, actually a thin hollowbody with a floating assembly incorporating two pickups and controls. At just £19 ($32) it was the first electric for many players, including Paul McCartney. Models in the 1960s included the Fender-influenced solidbody Airstream 2 and 3, the semi-solid Sheer-Line 7, the Jazzmaster-like Rosetti 3 and the relatively luxurious three-pickup Princess 3. By the early 1970s the Egmond operation had closed.

An Eggle Berlin Pro from Britain is shown here (near right), made in 1991, the first year of production. The ad (below) was published during the company's direct-sale period in 1995. This Dutch-made Egmond (center) is a model 3 from 1965, while the fabulous Italian Eko is a 700/4V of 1964 – an early showing for multi-cutaway design.

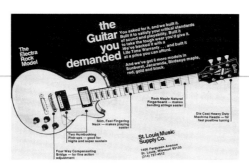

An object lesson in how to attract trademark lawyers with a very close visual copy of a Les Paul, as taught by Electra in a 1975 ad.

EKO

Among Italy's best-known guitar-makers, and one of the country's biggest exporters, Eko was established in the late 1950s by Oliviero Pigini & Co of Porto Recanati. Pigini at first made accordions, with Eko electric guitars following around 1960.

In 1961 Eko teamed up with American distributor LoDuca of Milwaukee, Wisconsin, and the new duo was marketing electrics by 1962. The models included sparkle- and marble-plastic-covered solidbodies and "violin"-shape guitars. During the 1970s Eko sold Gibson-like guitars primarily in Europe. The brand appeared on a line of Korean copies in the late 1980s. During the late 1990s a series of retro electrics revived Eko's 1960s designs. and in recent years there were a number of more conventional models.

ELECTAR

Electar was a brandname on Epiphone's early electric guitars and amplifiers from around 1935 to 1939. New York-based Epiphone had roots in banjo-making but began making guitars in the late 1920s. Its Electar models gave it an early start in the new electric guitar business. Some Electar guitars have large Rickenbacker-like horseshoe pickups, but the company's Master pickup, in use by 1939 and designed by Herb Sunshine, was among the first with individually adjustable polepieces, enabling the relative volume of each string to be set. Around 1939 Epiphone logically began to use its own brandname for electric guitars.

ELECTRA

A top 1970s "copy" brand in the US, Electra succeeded Custom Kraft and Apollo for importer St. Louis Music, beginning in 1971 with an Ampeg Dan Armstrong copy. Primarily made in Japan by Matsumoku, these early copies of designs made famous by Gibson and Fender quickly improved. By 1974 they had gained in quality enough to be endorsed by Nashville ace Paul Yandell. Innovations included US pickups and, in 1976, the MPC line with onboard modular effects, as endorsed by Peter Frampton. Original designs followed a 1977 industry lawsuit over copying, and included the Phoenix line, plus "pointy" shapes by 1983. St. Louis Music replaced the brand with Westone guitars around 1983.

ELECTRO

A brandname originally used by Rickenbacker for its earliest electric guitars. These included the cast aluminum "Frying Pan" lap-steel model of 1932, the world's first electric guitar with magnetic pickup to be put into production. From about 1934 the company added Rickenbacker (or "Rickenbacher") to its logo plates, the same year its manufacturing operation was named the Electro String Instrument Corporation. Rickenbacker alone took over as the company's sole brandname in the 1950s, but the Electro name was briefly revived in 1964 for two solidbody models, the ES-16 (based on the Rickenbacker Model 1000) and ES-17 (based on Rickenbacker's 425).

Three similar brandnames, three very different guitars on this page: Electar was Epiphone's early brand for electric guitars, and this Century model (far left) dates from around 1937; Electra was a brand used on guitars imported to the US by St. Louis Music, including this pointy Lady XV1RD (center) from 1983; and Electro was an early Rickenbacker-related brand revived in the mid 1960s for two models, including this ES-17 of 1964 (near left).

Epiphone's archtop guitars have been popular not just as full-fledged electrics, but as acoustics with "floating" pickups, as demonstrated by Duke Robillard in this 1998 ad.

This Epiphone Zephyr (near right) was made around 1941 and was one of three archtop electrics made by Epiphone at the time, alongside the Century and Coronet models. The ad in the background dates from 1950 and shows sessionman Al Caiola with a Zephyr Deluxe Regent.

An Epiphone Zephyr Emperor Regent made in 1954 is shown (below, far right), at the time a startling mix of old and new, with traditional archtop body topped by an up-to-the-minute bank of six tone-modifying switches.

E P I P H O N E

Many younger readers may only know Epiphone as a brand primarily of bargain-price entry-level versions of Gibson- and Fender-style models. But back when archtops ruled the earth, in the years before and after World War II, Epiphone was one of the most respected guitar companies, making midrange to high-end instruments often used in big-band jazz orchestras.

The Epiphone company dates back to the 1870s in Smyrna, Turkey, where Greek-born founder Anastasios Stathopoulo crafted his own-label fiddles, lutes and Greek lioutos. Stathopoulo moved to the United States in 1903 and continued to make instruments, including mandolins, in Long Island City, Queens, New York.

Anastasios died in 1915 and his son Epaminondas took over. He was generally and helpfully known as "Epi." Two years later the company became known as the House Of Stathopoulo and, following World War I, began making banjos. In 1924 the company's Recording line of banjos was introduced and four years later the official name was changed to the Epiphone Banjo Company.

Epiphone began producing guitars around 1928, introducing its first round-soundhole Recording archtop models, and in the early 1930s the company's famous Masterbilt line of f-hole archtops debuted. By the end of the decade Epiphone was a major competitor to Gibson, which by now was generally acknowledged as the leading

By the mid 1990s the Emperor was redesigned with two pickups, and it had the benefit of an endorsement by jazzman Joe Pass (ad, left).

manufacturer of archtops. The Epiphone operation was renamed Epiphone Inc in 1935 and introduced a line of electric archtops and amplifiers, initially called Electraphone but quickly changed to Electar.

Many of the early Electar amps were made by Nat Daniel who would later found Danelectro. Early Electar guitars were non-cutaway archtops (and lap-steels) that had pickups with large handrests over the strings. By 1939 Epiphone-brand electric archtops included the Century, Coronet and Zephyr (fitted with a large distinctively shaped oval pickup). In 1939 Epiphone's Herb Sunshine was one of the first to conceive of adjustable polepieces on pickups to achieve a better balance of sound, and these soon began to appear on Epiphones.

Epi Stathopoulo died in 1943 and control of Epiphone went to his brothers Orphie and Frixo. Pre-war electric archtops continued following World War II, joined by the Kent model in 1949. Epiphone introduced in 1948 its first single-cutaway archtop acoustics, versions of the earlier Emperor and DeLuxe, and added Tone Spectrum pickups to them in 1949. Among the pros who played Epiphones during these early years were George Van Eps, Tony Mottola, Al Caiola and Oscar Moore.

However, Epiphone's challenge to Gibson was about to fall apart. In 1951 a strike shut down Epiphone's New York factory for four months, and Epiphone relocated its factory to Philadelphia, Pennsylvania. During the Philadelphia tenure the company

Epiphone was bought by Gibson in the late 1950s. Production was shifted to Kalamazoo, Michigan, starting in 1958. The "new" electric Emperor had a more conventional control layout, seen on this 1959 example (left). By the time this 1964 Emperor (right) was made, mini-humbucking pickups were standard.

experimented with some interesting prototypes of solidbody electric guitars, but none ever got so far as to be put into production. During 1955, Epiphone introduced an archtop instrument equipped with a DeArmond pickup and endorsed by Harry Volpe. However, in 1957 Frixo Stathopoulo died – and this sad occasion would in effect mark the end of Epiphone's independence.

Gibson purchased Epiphone and relocated it to Kalamazoo, Michigan, turning the brand into its second-tier line. In 1958 Gibson started to manufacture and market its new Epiphone lines. These included the first Epiphone solidbody electric guitars, similar in style to Les Paul Specials and Juniors: the equal-double-cutaway, slab-bodied, two-pickup Crestwood; and the low-end one-pickup Coronet. Both models were fitted with small pickups now known as "New York" types because they were devised and originally used when the company occupied its east-coast premises. The pickups had arrived with various other leftover parts from Epiphone with the purchase. All Gibson-made Epiphones had set-necks in the new owner's customary style.

Also in 1958, Gibson reworked the old Century electric archtop into a thinline electric fitted with one P-90 pickup. This was followed by the twin-humbucker, double-cutaway Sheraton thinline in 1959. This model would later appeal to Noel Gallagher in Oasis, while a John Lee Hooker signature Sheraton would be introduced to the Epiphone line just over 40 years later, in 2000. Back in 1959, the Epi solidbody line

The Sheraton was the second most expensive f-hole electric in Gibson's new Epiphone line. This natural-finish E212TN version was made in 1962. In the fishy 1966 ad (above) the company wondered why celebrities didn't endorse Epi guitars. Maybe because they were too busy helping to promote Gibsons instead.

This jolly gathering (above) is for the cover of Epiphone's 1964 catalog, where the night will be long, the guitars loud... and ties preferred.

was expanding. The Crestwood was renamed the Crestwood Custom, restyled with a trimmer, more rounded body that sported New York pickups until a change was made to mini-humbuckers in 1963.

The Coronet remained, but now came with a P-90 single-coil pickup. New in 1959 was the Wilshire, effectively a Coronet fitted with two P-90s. Both models adopted the new "rounded" Crestwood body style in 1960, the same year seeing the introduction of the single-cutaway Olympic (single pickup), Olympic Double (two pickups) and double-cutaway Olympic Special. Some Epiphones of the period came with a simple flat-spring vibrato, although after 1961 the rosewood-clad Maestro vibrato was also offered, mainly on Crestwood Customs.

Epiphone thinlines continued to expand with the single-pointed-cutaway Sorrento (two mini-humbuckers) in 1960, double-cutaway Professional (mini-humbucker) and Casino (two P-90s) in 1961, the non-cutaway Granada (one Melody Maker pickup) and double-cutaway Riviera (two mini-humbuckers) in 1962, and the double-cutaway Al Caiola Custom (two mini-humbuckers) in 1963. The Caiola Standard with two P-90s followed in 1966. In 1964 Epiphone introduced the Howard Roberts Standard with one sharp cutaway, oval soundhole and a mini-humbucker.

Popularity of the thinlines increased in the 1960s when first Paul McCartney acquired a Casino for Beatle studio work, followed by John Lennon and George Harrison who each used new Casinos on-stage in the final fab-four concerts of 1966. The group's new Epis were also all over the band's latest *Revolver* LP, and the Beatle connection has ensured that the Epiphone thinlines in general and the Casino model in particular enjoy a continuing popularity among pop groups who find themselves keen on reactivating a Merseyside-style mix.

In 1963 the Epi solidbodies were redesigned to feature a longer upper horn as well as a scalloped "batwing" six-tuners-in-line headstock. A three-pickup Crestwood Deluxe joined the line, and in 1966 a Wilshire 12-string was offered.

Gibson was purchased from Chicago Musical Instruments (CMI) in 1969 by Norlin, an international conglomerate. Kalamazoo-made Epiphone solidbodies continued to be available through 1970, although by that time plans were already underway to transfer production to Japan. The first Japanese-made Epiphones came on to the market around 1970. These bolt-on-neck electrics included the 1802 Stratocaster-style solidbody and the 5102T ES-335-style thinline, each fitted with a pair of black-and-white "Art Deco" single-coil pickups. Ironically, Gibson-owned Epiphone thus offered copies similar to those of Aria… the Japanese company that had started the "copy era" by replicating Gibson's Les Paul Custom.

In 1972 Gibson renamed the 1802 as the ET-270 and the 5102T as the EA-250. The company also added two bolt-on-neck "copies" of its venerable Crestwoods, the

Three more Epiphones on this page: a first-type Crestwood solidbody from 1959 (far left); a Crestwood Custom from 1964 (center); and a Sorrento hollowbody from 1968.

ET-278 (bound fingerboard) and ET-275, both with two humbuckers, vibrato and Gibson-style headstock. This Epiphone line-up remained unchanged into the early 1970s. By 1975 the Stratocaster-style guitar was gone, and the ET-278 (which was now fitted with a stoptail bridge) and the ET-275 acquired new finishes and fresh appointments. The EA-250 thinline remained in the line. These were joined by another Crestwood, the ET-290N in natural maple with a maple fingerboard, and a high-end, walnut-topped EA-255 thinline, these last two both with gold hardware.

In 1976 Epiphone added the distinctive new Scroll models to its catalog. These were distinguished by a carved "scroll" on the upper cutaway horn, and were joined by the set-neck SC550 (block-shape fingerboard inlays) and SC450 (dots), and the bolt-on-neck SC350. All of these came fitted with two humbuckers and pre-Gibson-style Epiphone headstock, differing in finishes and trim. They were available through 1979.

From around 1977-79 Gibson marketed the Epiphone "Rock'n'Roll Star Solid Body Line Up" in Japan, guitars similar to the Scrolls but with equal cutaways and no scrolls, bearing the old Epi names Olympic Custom, Olympic and Wilshire. From 1979-81 Gibson offered the Epiphone Genesis series, again made in Japan. Featuring set-neck, mahogany body with carved maple cap, twin humbuckers and the old Epiphone-style headstock, the Genesis models had various appointments and levels of trim and included the Custom (block inlays, gold hardware), Deluxe (crown inlays, chrome

A Crestwood Deluxe from 1966 (near right) alongside Paul McCartney's very own Epiphone Casino, made in 1962 and used on many Beatle records such as 'Paperback Writer.' Epiphone's 1961 ad (below) sets out the advantages of the company's new Tremotone vibrato bridge.

56

Paul McCartney was attracted to Epiphone's Casino in the 1960s because it came with the Bigsby vibrato that he'd heard used so well by Duane Eddy. But years after the break-up of The Beatles he still counted it among his favorites, often playing it in concert (below) as well as in the studio.

Epiphone's Professional model (1963 example, left) had five Tonexpressor controls, and its special amplifier could be adjusted from extra controls on the guitar. This did not prove very popular.

Epiphone designed the Caiola Custom (1964 example, below right) in collaboration with studio guitarist Al Caiola (he played the Bonanza theme among many others) as a slightly more conventional version of the earlier Professional. The Caiola ad dates from 1967.

hardware) and Standard (dot inlays). An even more basic model called simply The Genesis was added to the Epiphone line in 1981, but the entire series was gone by the end of that year. Following the demise of the Genesis series, in 1982 Gibson briefly offered some Japanese-made Epiphone hollowbody electrics: the Emperor, the Sheraton, the Casino and the Riviera.

Competition had taken its toll on Gibson during the 1970s, particularly the success of Japanese manufacturers. Beginning at this time Gibson began slowly transferring production to a new factory in Nashville, Tennessee, where labor costs were lower than in Kalamazoo. With idle production capability in Kalamazoo, Gibson decided to make Epiphones in America again.

Calling back laid-off workers, in 1982 Gibson unveiled the Kalamazoo-made Epiphone Spirit version of the same-name Gibson model. This was a set-neck, equal-double-cutaway guitar that was clearly inspired by Gibson's own Les Paul Special shape. The Gibson Spirit featured an Explorer-style headstock, whereas the Epi had a typical Gibson-style "open-book" head. The Epiphone Spirit came with either one or two humbuckers. The Spirit was joined in the new catalog by the Epiphone Special, which was in effect an SG available with one or two humbuckers. Very few of these Specials were made, and the American-made Epiphones were gone from the line by the end of the year. As Gibson's Kalamazoo factory wound down to a close, one final Epiphone

The inimitable Stacie Jones gets herself back to the garden for a Korean Epi Coronet in 1996.

solidbody was made, a US-map-shaped guitar. This featured a Gibson-style neck glued into a body cut out in the shape of the continental United States. It was intended to be a promotional item but was well received, so Gibson decided to re-brand the "map" guitars with the Gibson logo.

This was the (temporary) end of Epiphone guitar production, and for the time being at least marked the cessation of an operation that stretched back to the late 1920s, deep into early American guitar history.

In 1984 Gibson closed down its guitar-making at Kalamazoo, selling part of the facility to former employees who formed the Heritage guitar company. During this period Gibson offered a few Japanese-made Epiphone electric thinlines, including the round-cutaway Emperor II and double-cutaway Sheraton, both fitted with two humbuckers. A year earlier a few Epiphone solidbody models had been sourced from the Samick factory in Korea.

By the early 1980s Gibson's parent company Norlin seemed to have lost interest in guitar-making altogether. However, in 1984 Gibson was turned over to a broker and at the beginning of 1986 the company was purchased by Henry Juszkiewicz, Dave Berryman and Gary Zebrowski. They promptly revived the Epiphone brand, primarily as a vehicle for Korean-made low-end instruments, although a select few Epi models would be made at Gibson's Nashville plant in subsequent years. The new 1986

Epiphone By Gibson line included versions of both Gibson and Fender stalwarts: copies of the Flying V (V-2) and the Explorer, plus five S-series Stratocaster-style guitars. By the end of the year these early Korean-made Epiphones were being replaced by a considerably expanded line. Included were three new bolt-on-neck Les Pauls, all now equipped with Steinberger KB locking vibratos. The Les Paul 3 had the popular humbucker/single-coil/single-coil pickup layout. The Les Paul 2 was similar but with two humbuckers, while the Les Paul 1 had a single lead humbucker. Also offered were two Epiphone Firebirds, through-neck guitars with Steinberger KB vibrato and optional layouts of EMG Select pickups.

Six Strat-style guitars were offered in late 1986, including four superstrats with Kramer-style "hockey stick" (or "banana") six-tuners-in-line headstocks plus locking Steinberger KB vibratos. The top-of-the-line X-1000 had through-neck construction, EMG Select pickups in a humbucker/single-coil/single-coil layout, and chevron-shape fingerboard inlays. The X-900 was similar except the body was more like a wide Ibanez Roadstar, with triangular sharktooth inlays. The S-800 was basically a bolt-on-neck version of the X-900.

The S-600 was another similar bolt-on-neck guitar shaped more like contemporary Kramers. The S-400 (maple fingerboard, humbucker/single-coil/single-coil pickup layout, and locking vibrato) and S-310 (three single-coil pickups and traditional fulcrum

Three more Epiphones on this page: a Coronet made in 1965 (far left); a Riviera 12-string (center) from 1968; and an ET-270 from 1973 (near left). The 270 was first called the 1802T, as in this 1971 catalog (below).

vibrato) also had the Kramer body styling. Most of this line-up continued to be available into 1989. Epiphone tapped a host of celebrities to endorse its new lines, including Les Paul, Chet Atkins (for a new Country Gentleman II thinline) and Howard Roberts (new HR Fusion II and HR Fusion III thinline models), as well as Billy Burnette, Julio Fernandez, Zakk Wylde, Vinnie Zummo and Ed Ott.

Gibson planned a new series of Japanese-made guitars in 1987 to be called the Nouveau By Gibson line, with several new designs including a superstrat similar to the X-1000, an archtop and a model patterned in the style of a PRS solidbody. Whether these ever got beyond the prototype stage is unknown, but in 1988 the PRS-like solidbody did provide the basis for the Epiphone Spotlight series, sporting through-neck construction, fancy carved maple cap, EMG Select pickups and "chevron"-shape fingerboard inlays. A traditional-style vibrato was offered, although some versions featured the locking Steinberger KB unit. The Spotlight models lasted only a year in the line before high costs made them impractical.

While earlier Epiphones had flirted with the idea of copying popular designs, in 1988 Gibson hit on the formula that would bring success to the Epiphone brand in the 1990s and beyond. Two new proper set-neck Les Paul copies were introduced, the Custom and the Standard (plus a bolt-on-neck Les Paul 2, now with stoptail). In 1989 Epiphone revamped the whole line. The Les Paul Custom and Standard, plus the old

Strat-style S-310, were joined by the G Series of Gibson SG copies, the G-400 being a set-neck copy of Gibson's SG 62, and the G-310 being a bolt-on-neck version of a 1967-style SG. Also new was the Epiphone Flying V, a copy of Gibson's 1967-style V, and the T-310. This was a Telecaster-like copy, but underlining its Gibson association was a "hockey stick" Explorer-like head.

Though fast becoming passé, three superstrats with Floyd Rose locking vibratos continued to be offered: the bolt-neck 435i and 635i (humbucker/single-coil/single-coil pickup layout) and the neck-through-body 935i (humbucker and one single-coil pickup), all with Explorer-style headstock.

During the 1989 makeover Gibson returned to making a few special Epiphones in Nashville. This time it was the USA Pro, a superstrat-style replacement for the previous X-1000, though with a bolt-on neck, plus locking Floyd Rose vibrato system and a Gibson lead humbucker and neck single-coil pickup.

Another American-made Epiphone was introduced in 1990, the USA Coronet. This presented a clever combination of old and new, reviving the defunct 1960s Epiphone shape and set-neck design, and adding a new reverse-Explorer headstock plus a five-way pickup selector switch, as well as a circuit board that provided humbucker, single-coil, out-of-phase and series/parallel sounds. The USA Coronets came with gold hardware and stoptails or black hardware and Floyd Rose locking vibrato systems. In

An Epiphone Scroll 250 from 1977 (far left); a gold-finished USA Coronet made at Gibson's Nashville plant in 1990 (center); and an ES Les Paul with f-holes from 1999 (right). The two promo cards (left) from 1983 highlight two of Epi's reissues, here featuring the Emperor (top) and the Sheraton.

The Mark
of Great Guitarists.

Epiphone
The Epiphone Company
1818 Elm Hill Pike · Nashville, TN 37210
Call 1-800-444-2766 for a FREE Catalog!!!

Some guitars on this page from Epiphone's lines of the 1990s include two "copies" of established Gibson faves: a Les Paul from 1998 (center) and a Flying V from 1999 (far right). This Epiphone Supernova (left), a Noel Gallagher signature model, was made in 1997. More Epi fans are included in the 1994 ad (above), namely John Lennon, John Lee Hooker, Lenny Kravitz, and Stevie Ray Vaughan.

1991 two more new Epiphone "copies" debuted, the EM-2 and EM-1, being Korean-made, bolt-on-neck versions of Gibson's new M-III, slightly offset-cutaway solidbodies with a dramatically extended horn and reverse-Explorer headstock.

The Epiphones were plainer than the original Gibson models. However, they used the same electronic switching system, a combination of a two-way toggle and five-way switch to control the humbucker/single-coil/humbucker pickup layout. This offered either humbucking or single-coil tonalities depending on the position of the two-way switch. The EM-2 featured a locking Floyd Rose vibrato, whereas the EM-1 had a traditional "fulcrum" vibrato.

In 1991 Epiphone briefly added to the bottom of its line an inexpensive bolt-on-neck Les Paul, the LP-300, and the Stratocaster-style S-300, which would last only a year. Epiphone also continued to add pro endorsers, including Mick Cribbs, Tracii Guns, Dan Toler, Frank Hannon, Pete Pagan, John Ricco and Tom Keifer.

A management change occurred in 1992 when Jim Rosenberg was hired from electronic instrument manufacturer E-Mu Systems to take charge of Epiphone. It was at this time that Epiphone revived the trend of marketing musical instruments through mail-order catalogs. By 1993 a new low-end bolt-on-neck LP-100 model Les Paul had joined the line, while the i Series superstrats were gone. Epiphone added another EM-3 Rebel Custom in 1994 to the line derived from the Gibson M-IIIs (the EMs now also called Rebels). This was still a bolt-on-neck guitar, but appointments such as the pick-shape fingerboard inlays were more like the Gibson original. It also had a new Steinberger Jam-Trem vibrato system. New too in 1994 was the Epiphone Explorer, a copy of the famous Gibson model. By 1995 the EM Rebel models had been dropped and American Epiphone production had ended.

More Gibson "copies" were introduced, while reissues of earlier Epis proliferated too, including the Casino, Riviera, Emperor Regent, Sheraton and Sorrento. A signature Supernova model appeared in 1997 for Noel Gallagher, though it lacked the Oasis guitarist's subtle British flag graphic that brightened up the body of his own Sheraton.

The most striking aspect of recent Epiphones has been the veritable explosion of Les Paul variants. Appointments range from exotic, transparent and sparkle finishes to good looking flamed-maple and birdseye-maple caps. There are seven-string versions, one with f-holes, and there's even a Metal Edition, as well as a signature model for Slash of Guns N'Roses that comes with a suitable snake graphic.

In the company's thinline series, a swathe of old names still manages to conjure up the heritage of 1950s and 1960s designs. These make available a vintage-style alternative to parent company Gibson's thinlines, always more fashionable in this area. Nonetheless, new signature Epiphone thinlines launched in 2000 underlined their continuing appeal to some players. There was the already mentioned John Lee Hooker

1964 Sheraton, available with two bridge/tailpiece options, and the Jorma Kaukonen Riviera Deluxe, a wonderful cherry and gold concoction.

Epiphone opened its own new factory in Qingdao, China in 2002, and by that year the Epi lines included signature guitars for John Lennon (Casino) and Ace Frehley (Les Paul Custom), along with many Gibson-influenced models. There were a number of more original designs, too, including the Kat single-cutaway semi-solids.

Epi marked what would have been John Lennon's 70th birthday in 2010 with a new limited-edition tribute instrument, the John Lennon 70th Anniversary Casino. It was produced in a limited run of just 70 guitars, and they were sold only on the Japanese market. Each one came with a certificate and had Lennon's birthdate, October 9 1940, set into an inlay at the guitar's 12th fret. A portion of the proceeds of the sale of these instruments was donated to the BMI Foundation for the John Lennon Scholarship, which helps support music education.

More signature models appeared from Epiphone for the likes of Robb Flynn of Machine Head, with the Love/Hate Baritone-V of 2011, and Zakk Wylde, probably better known for his Gibsons but a perfect fit for Epiphone and the Graveyard Disciple model, with a black body and case shaped like a coffin. There also several Epiphone versions of Wylde's bullseye Gibsons. In 2016, Epiphone offered a new signature model for Brendon Small of Dethklok, a virtual metal band featured in the animated show

Noel Gallagher from Oasis (above) playing one of his Epiphone Sheratons with Union Jack graphic.

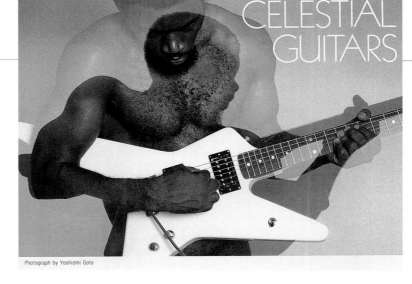

This striking ESP ad published in 1982 (right) features a metal-inclined model from the Navigator line.

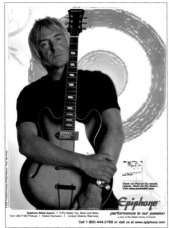

A good trawl of Epiphones pictured here: an Emily The Strange G-310 from 2009 (opposite, far left), a Robb Flynn Love/Hate Baritone Flying V made in 2011 (opposite, left); and a 1958 Explorer from 2008 (right). The ads feature Marcus Henderson with his Apparition (2008, opposite); Zakk Wylde with Epi versions of his Gibson bullseye and buzzsaw models (2011, top); and Paul Weller with an Elitist Casino (2010, above).

Metalocalypse. Small's Snow Falcon V came in an all-white finish, and it was yet another Gibson-influenced model in the Epi lines. Today, it seems as if there are almost enough Epiphones to compete with Gibson... just like it was in the old days.

E S P

This high-end Japanese maker began in 1975 by offering handmade guitars with the Navigator brandname. A move to guitar parts came in 1978; ESP-brand instruments soon followed. Many maintained Fender styling, and were joined in the 1980s by graphic-finished superstrats and models for metal players. ESPs were made in the US and Germany as well as Japan; quality (and prices) stayed high. The less expensive Edwards line appeared in the late 1980s, then the even more affordable Korean-made Grass Roots series (more recent budget Koreans had an LTD logo). Influential endorsers have included Kirk Hammett and Max Cavalera, both with popular signature models.

This ESP Ltd M-250 model (left) was made during 1998 and is from the company's more affordable Korean-made series. Ron Wood has been a long-standing and important endorser of ESP instruments, and he is portrayed in this 1993 ad (below) with one of the more traditional products of the Japanese-based company.

Fender's Broadcaster is historically the most important electric guitar ever made. It was the first instrument to commercialize the concept of the solidbody electric guitar – and put Fender on the map. This example (main guitar) was made, like all Broadcasters, in 1950.

This ad (below) was the first to feature and name the Esquire, the earliest version of Fender's new solidbody electric in its pre-production form. It's clear from this 1950 ad that Fender's main business was still in amps and steel guitars, but it effectively marks the birth of marketing for the solidbody electric.

FENDER

No other company has contributed more to the look and sound of the solidbody electric guitar than Fender. Clarence Leo Fender's original firm changed the course of popular music by revolutionizing the design and manufacture of electric guitars.

So successful did Fender become that in 1965 the business was sold to the giant CBS conglomerate for $13 million, an unprecedentedly large figure. Yet the whole affair had started around 20 years earlier when Leo made some electric steel guitars with a few thousand dollars that he'd earned from a record-player design. From these humble beginnings grew one of the largest, most influential and splendidly original musical instrument manufacturers in the world.

Despite spectacular later successes, during its early years the southern California company came perilously close to failing. It was Leo Fender's sheer determination, combined with his luck in surrounding himself with clever, dedicated people, that helped pull the Fender company through difficult times.

Leo was born in 1909, in a barn near the Anaheim/Fullerton border in the Los Angeles area. His parents ran a "truck farm," growing vegetables and fruit for the market, and had put up the barn first before they could afford to build a house. A friend once recalled that when Leo was small his father had told him that the only thing worthwhile in the world was what you accomplished at work – and that if you weren't

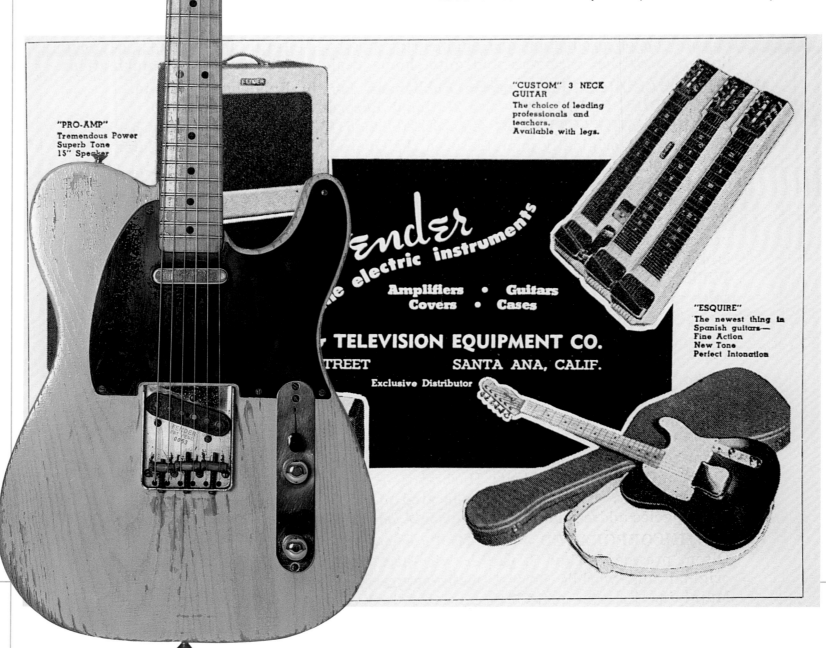

"PRO-AMP"
Tremendous Power
Superb Tone
15" Speaker

"CUSTOM" 3 NECK GUITAR
The choice of leading professionals and teachers.
Available with legs.

Amplifiers • Guitars
Covers • Cases

TELEVISION EQUIPMENT CO.
TREET   SANTA ANA, CALIF.
Exclusive Distributor

"ESQUIRE"
The newest thing in Spanish guitars—
Fine Action
New Tone
Perfect Intonation

working you were lazy, which was a sin. It seems that Leo would judge himself and everyone else around him by that measure... and himself hardest of all.

Although he went on to study accountancy and began his working life in the accounts sections of the state highway department and a tire distribution company, Leo's hobby was always electronics, and in his 20s he built amplifiers and PA systems for use at public events such as sports and religious gatherings as well as dances. In about 1939 Leo opened The Fender Radio Service, a radio and record store at Fullerton in the Los Angeles area. Leo had lost his accounting job earlier in that decade of depression. His new shop brought instant introductions to many local musicians including professional violinist and lap-steel guitarist "Doc" Kauffman. Doc had worked on electric guitar designs for another local company, Rickenbacker.

Lap-steel guitar playing, or Hawaiian guitar playing, had been fashionable in the United States since the 1920s and was still tremendously popular at the time Leo opened his new store. A lap-steel guitar is one that sits horizontally on the player's lap, and its strings are stopped not by the frets, but with a sliding steel bar held in the player's non-picking hand. As the most prevalent type of guitar in America at the time, lap-steels were thus the first guitars to "go electric" in the 1930s. Several innovative companies, with Rickenbacker in the lead, had started to experiment with electro-magnetic pickups, attaching them to guitars and connecting them to small amplifiers.

During the 1930s and later the term "Spanish" was used to identify the other (less popular) hold-against-the-body type of guitar.

Leo had by this time already begun to look into the potential for electric guitars and to play around with pickup designs. Leo and Doc built a solidbody guitar in 1943 to test these early pickups, as well as a design for a record-changer good enough to net them $5,000. Some of this money went into starting their shortlived company, K&F (Kauffman & Fender), and the two men began proper production of electric lap-steel guitars and small amplifiers in November 1945.

Another significant person with whom Leo started working at this early stage was Don Randall, general manager of Radio & Television Equipment Co ("Radio-Tel") which was based in Santa Ana, some 15 miles south of Fullerton. Radio-Tel, owned by Francis Hall, became the exclusive distributor of K&F products in 1946 – around the time that Leo and Doc Kauffman decided to split. In 1946 Leo called his new operation Fender Manufacturing (renamed the Fender Electric Instrument Co in December 1947). Leo continued to make lap-steels and amps as he had with K&F, but gradually developed new products. He also expanded into larger premises in Fullerton, separate from the radio store and described by one observer as two plain, unattractive steel buildings.

Yet another important member of the growing Fender team, Dale Hyatt, had joined the company in January 1946. Hyatt later became a crucial member of the Fender

The Esquire model name had been used for Fender's earliest solidbody prototype, but was soon revived for the single-pickup production version. This Esquire (far left) was made in 1953. The two-pickup Broadcaster's name was changed to Telecaster after Gretsch complained about prior use. At first Fender removed "Broadcaster" from its decals, making "Nocaster" models (see headstock picture, right), but during 1951 had the new Telecaster name in place. The Telecaster shown here (near left) was made in 1953. Gene Vincent's guitarist Russell Wilaford, replacing a just-departed Cliff Gallup, plays a Telecaster (above) on the set of The Girl Can't Help It movie in 1956.

sales team, but one of his early tasks, in late 1947 or early 1948, was to take over the radio store business because Leo was trying to get things started at the new buildings in Pomona Avenue. Next to join Fender's company was George Fullerton, who was to become what one colleague describes as Leo's faithful workhorse. Fullerton started working at Pomona Avenue in February 1948.

Karl Olmsted and his partner Lymon Race had left the services in 1947 and decided to start a much-needed tool-and-die company in Fullerton, making specialist tools, as well as dies that customers could use to stamp out metal parts on punch presses. They were looking for work, and Leo had reached the point where he needed dies to be made for production work. He'd been making parts by hand, cutting out raw metal. But of course Leo now needed to make several identical copies of each component. Race & Olmsted continued to make Fender's tooling and most metal parts for the next 30 years and more, progressing to more complicated, sophisticated and high-production tooling as time went on.

Fender's electric lap-steels enjoyed some local success, and Leo began to think about producing a solidbody electric guitar of normal shape and playing style: an "electric Spanish" guitar. Normal Spanish archtop hollowbody "f-hole" acoustic guitars with built-in electric pickups and associated controls had been produced by makers such as Rickenbacker, National, Gibson and Epiphone at various times since the

The first famous user of the Fender Stratocaster in the 1950s was Buddy Holly, and he's seen (above) with his Strat on the first Crickets LP, released in late 1957.

Two early Stratocasters are shown on this page. This first-year 1954 example (below left) in non-standard color has serial number 0001; behind is the cover of Fender's catalog of the same year. The fine 1957 Strat (main guitar) is the standard sunburst model of the time.

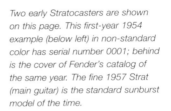

Fender's 1958/59 catalog (left) was the first to show a custom color guitar, the Fiesta Red Stratocaster above the man's head.

1930s, but without much effect on player's habits. And while demand was rising from danceband guitarists who found themselves increasingly unable to compete with the volume of the rest of the band, most of the early electric hollowbody guitars were effectively experimental. They were only partially successful from a technical standpoint, and electric guitars were still some way from becoming a great commercial sensation. Leo's plans would change all that.

A number of guitar makers, musicians and engineers in America were wondering about the possibility of a solidbody instrument. Such a design would curtail the annoying feedback often produced by amplified hollowbody guitars, at the same time reducing the guitar body's interference with its overall tone and thus more accurately reproducing and sustaining the sound of the strings.

Rickenbacker had launched a relatively solid Bakelite-body electric guitar in the mid 1930s – the type that Leo's friend Doc Kauffman had played – while around 1940 guitarist Les Paul built a personal test-bed electric guitar in New York which used parts

from a variety of instruments mounted on a solid central block of pine. In Downey, California, about 15 miles to the west of Fender's operation in Fullerton, Paul Bigsby had a small workshop where he spent a good deal of time fixing motorcycles and, later, making some fine pedal-steel guitars and vibrato units. He also ventured into the solidbody electric guitar and mandolin field, hand-building a limited number of distinctive instruments. He'd started this in 1948 with the historic Merle Travis guitar, an instrument with through-neck construction and hollow body "wings."

It's difficult to judge whether the design of Fender's first solidbody electric guitar was influenced very much by those earlier instruments of Bigsby's. George Fullerton says that he and Leo knew Paul Bigsby and had seen Merle Travis playing his Bigsby guitar. On the other hand, it's possible that Fender and Bigsby just made something similar at the same time.

Leo started work in the summer of 1949 on the instrument which we now know as the Fender Telecaster, effectively the world's first commercially marketed solidbody electric guitar, and still very much alive today. The guitar, originally named the Fender Esquire and then the Fender Broadcaster, first went into production in 1950. Early prototypes borrowed their headstock design from Fender's lap-steels, with three tuners each side, but the production version had a smart new headstock with all six tuners along one side, allowing strings to meet tuners in a straight line and obviating the

An enviable 1950s Strat collection: a "Mary Kaye" Strat from 1958 (far left) with blond body and gold-plated hardware; an early example of the Fiesta Red finish on a 1959 Strat (center); and a gold-finish model (near left) dating from 1958.

67

traditional "angled back" headstock. Fender's new solidbody electric guitar was unadorned, straightforward, potent, and – perhaps most significantly – ahead of its time. As such it did not prove immediately easy for the salesmen at Fender to sell, as Don Randall of Radio-Tel found when he took some prototypes to a musical instrument trade show in Chicago during the summer of 1950. In fact, Randall was aghast to find that competitors generally laughed at the new instrument, calling the prototypes canoe paddles, snow shovels and worse.

A very few pre-production one-pickup Esquire models without truss-rods were made in April 1950, with another tiny production run of two-pickup Esquires two months later. General production of the better-known single-pickup Esquire with truss-rod did not begin until January 1951.

But in November 1950, a truss-rod was added to the two-pickup model, its name was changed to Broadcaster, and the retail price was fixed at $170. The Broadcaster name was shortlived, halted in early 1951 after Gretsch, a large New York-based instrument manufacturer, indicated its prior use of "Broadkaster" on various drum products. At first, Fender simply used up its "Fender Broadcaster" decals on the guitar's headstock by cutting off the "Broadcaster" and leaving just the "Fender" logo; these no-name guitars are known among collectors today as Nocasters. The new name decided upon for the Fender solid electric was Telecaster, coined by Don Randall. The

This Fender Musicmaster was made in 1957, and it has an anodized aluminum pickguard. Fender also made a two-pickup version, called the Duo-Sonic, and a Duo-Sonic with vibrato, known as the Mustang.

Fender's cheaper models have been popular with more recent musicians looking for an affordable instrument. Liz Phair, whose folk-grunge Exile To Guyville album appeared in 1993, is seen (below) playing a Duo-Sonic.

Fender began an enjoyable and often inventive series of ads in the late 1950s where a guitar was placed in an unlikely setting, with the tag-line: "You won't part with yours either..." This one (left), with a nautical Jazzmaster, was published in 1960.

Telecaster name was on headstocks by April 1951, and at last Fender's new $189.50 solidbody electric had a permanent name.

At Fender, practicality and function ruled. There was no hand-carving of selected timbers as one would find in the workshops of established archtop guitar makers. With the Telecaster, Fender made the electric guitar into a factory product, stripped down to its essential elements, built up from easily assembled parts, and produced at a relatively affordable price. Fender's methods made for easier, more consistent production – and a different sound. Not for Fender the fat, Gibson-style jazz tone, but a clearer, spikier sound, something like a cross between a clean acoustic guitar and a cutting electric lap-steel.

One of the earliest players to appreciate this new sound was Jimmy Bryant, best known for his staggering guitar instrumental duets with pedal-steel virtuoso Speedy West. Bryant soon took to playing the new Fender solidbody. He was respected by professionals in the music business for his session work, including recordings made with Tennessee Ernie Ford and Ella Mae Morse among others. Bryant also made television appearances on country showcases, and would highlight Fender's exciting new solidbody for the growing TV audience.

It was western swing, a lively dance music that grew up in Texas dancehalls during the 1930s and 1940s, that popularized the electric guitar in the US, at first with steel guitars. Many of its steel players used Fender electrics, notably Noel Boggs and Leon McAuliffe, but there were also some electric-Spanish guitarists in the bands, like Tele-wielding Bill Carson.

Business began to pick up for the Fender company as news of the Telecaster spread, and as Radio-Tel's five salesmen began to persuade instrument store owners to stock the instrument. Early in 1953 Fender's existing sales set-up with Radio-Tel was re-organized into a new Fender Sales distribution company, which was operational by June. Based like Radio-Tel in Santa Ana, Fender Sales had four business partners: Leo, Don Randall, Radio-Tel owner Francis Hall and salesman Charlie Hayes. Hayes was killed in a road accident and in late 1953 Hall bought the Rickenbacker company, so in 1955 Fender Sales became a partnership owned by Leo and Don Randall. It was Randall who actually ran this pivotal part of the Fender business.

The sales side of Fender was, therefore, in capable hands. Another important addition to the Fender team occurred in 1953 when steel guitarist Freddie Tavares, best known for his swooping steel intro over the titles of the *Looney Tunes* cartoons, joined the California guitar maker, principally to help Leo design new products. Also in 1953 three new buildings at South Raymond Avenue and Valencia Drive were added to the company's manufacturing premises. As well as just two electric guitars, the Telecaster and Esquire, Fender had at this time a line of seven amplifiers (Bandmaster,

Three Jazzmasters on this page. This early example in standard sunburst finish (far left) was made in 1959, while the 1963 model (center) is in lurid Foam Green. This 1966 instrument (near left) was originally finished in Blue Ice Metallic, but a gradual "yellowing" of its outer skin has transformed it to more of a green. It also displays the change to bound fingerboard and block-shape fingerboard inlays made to the Jazzmaster during 1965 and 1966. The Jazzmaster hang-tag (below) would be fastened to the guitar's tuner button in music stores.

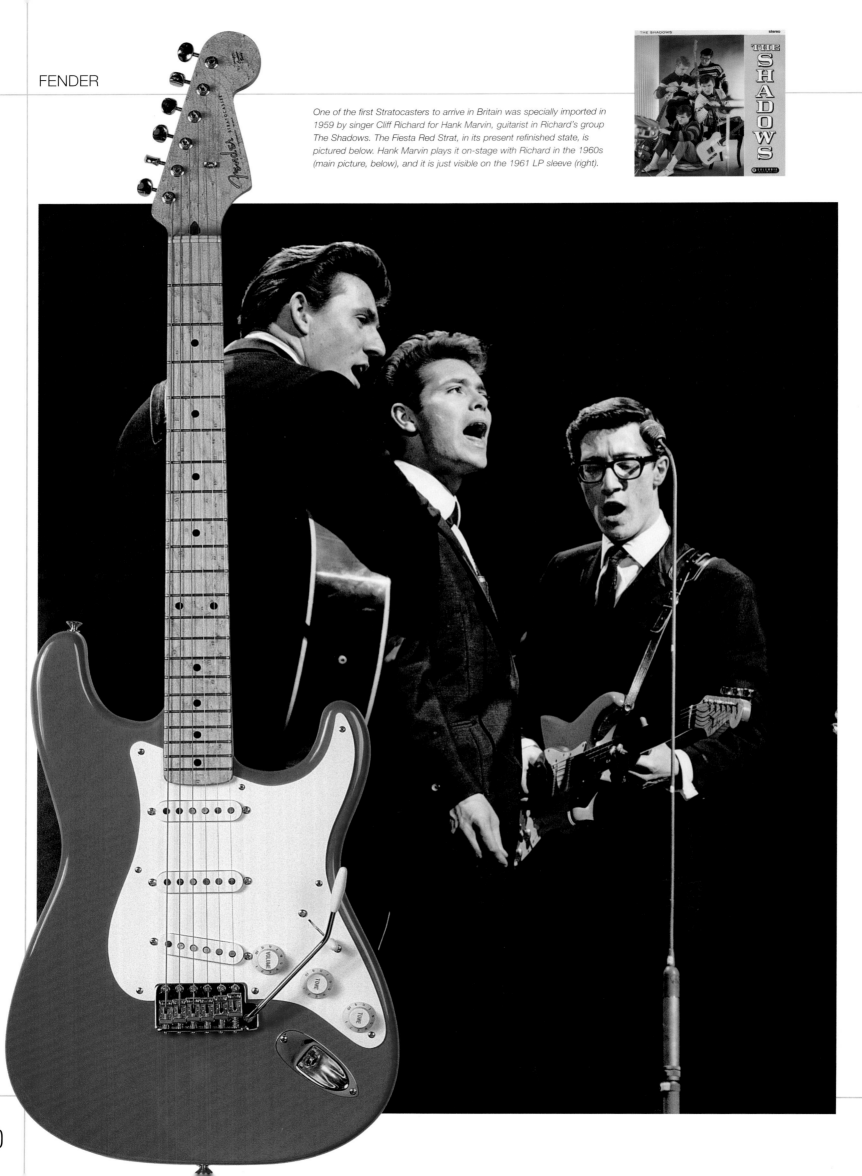

One of the first Stratocasters to arrive in Britain was specially imported in 1959 by singer Cliff Richard for Hank Marvin, guitarist in Richard's group *The Shadows*. The Fiesta Red Strat, in its present refinished state, is pictured below. Hank Marvin plays it on-stage with Richard in the 1960s (main picture, below), and it is just visible on the 1961 LP sleeve (right).

Two further late-1950s ads in the "You won't part with yours" series feature a Jazzmaster on a Porsche in the California hills (far right) and somewhere above (near right).

Bassman, Champ, Deluxe, Princeton, Super, Twin Amp), five electric steel guitars (Custom, Deluxe, Dual, Stringmaster, Student) and its revolutionary electric bass guitar, the Precision, that had been introduced two years earlier.

Another newcomer was Forrest White. He had joined the company after Leo asked if he'd be interested in helping sort out some "management problems" at Fender. White was shocked by the disorganized mess he found at the Fender workshops, and agreed to come in and work for Leo, beginning in May 1954. White soon began to put the manufacturing operations into order.

Now Leo had able men – Forrest White and Don Randall – poised at the head of the production and sales halves of the Fender company. He had a new factory, and a small but growing reputation. All he needed now, it seemed, was more new products. And along came the stylish Fender Stratocaster, the epitome of tailfin-flash American design of the 1950s.

Leo was listening hard to players' comments about the "plain vanilla" Tele and Esquire, and during the early 1950s he and Freddie Tavares began to formulate the guitar that would become the Stratocaster. Some musicians were complaining that the sharp edge on the Telecaster was uncomfortable, so the team began to fool around with smoothed contouring on the body. The Stratocaster was eventually launched during 1954 – samples around May and June were followed by the first proper

production run in October. It was priced at $249.50 (or $229.50 without vibrato) plus $39.50 for a case. The new Fender was the first solidbody electric with three pickups, and also featured a new-design built-in vibrato unit (or "tremolo" as Fender called it) to provide pitch-bending and shimmering chordal effects for the player. It was the first self-contained vibrato unit: an adjustable bridge, tailpiece and vibrato system all in one. Not a simple mechanism for the time, but a reasonably effective one. It followed the Fender principle of taking an existing product (in this case the Bigsby vibrato) and improving on it. Fender's new Strat vibrato also had six saddles, one for each string, adjustable for height and length. The complete unit was typical of Fender's constant consideration of musicians' requirements and the consequent application of a mass-producer's solution.

The Strat came with a radically sleek, solid body, based on the shape of the earlier Fender Precision Bass, contoured for the player's comfort and finished in a yellow-to-black sunburst finish. Even the jack socket mounting was new, recessed in a stylish plate on the body face. The Strat looked like no other guitar around – and in some ways

Three Strats, all featuring the new rosewood fingerboard introduced during 1959: a 1964 example (far left) in Sonic Blue; another made in 1961 (center) in Burgundy Mist Metallic; and a sunburst model dating from 1964 (near left).

FENDER

Esquires and Telecasters also gained a rosewood fingerboard during 1959, as featured in this page (right) from Fender's 1963/64 catalog .

Three custom color Telecasters are shown on this page. This one in Fiesta Red (near right) dates from 1960, while the Shoreline Gold model (center) was made in 1963. The pale green Tele from around 1964 (far right) was originally finished in Sonic Blue but has since "faded" to a green color. It has been fitted with a Parsons-White B-Bender that can raise the pitch of the B-string to provide string-bends that emulate pedal-steel type sounds.

Temptation... Jaguars and Jazzmasters on a 1960s hang-tag (far left) and a luscious Jaguar with gold-plated hardware on the cover of Fender's 1963/64 catalog (near left).

seemed to owe more to contemporary automobile design than traditional guitar forms, especially in the flowing, sensual curves of that beautifully proportioned, timeless body.

The Stratocaster's new-style pickguard complemented the body lines perfectly. Indeed, the overall impression was of a guitar where all the components ideally suited one another. It's not surprising, therefore, that the Strat is still made today, over 45 years since its birth in the Fender company's functional buildings in Fullerton, California. The exemplary Fender Stratocaster has become the most popular, the most copied, the most desired, and very probably the most played solid electric guitar ever.

On its 40th anniversary in 1994 an official Fender estimate put Stratocaster sales so far at between a million and a million-and-a-half guitars – and that's without the plethora of unsubtle copies or more subtly "influenced" guitars that subsequently appeared from hundreds of other guitar-makers. The Stratocaster has appeared in the hands of virtually every great guitarist over the years. Back in the 1950s it was a more specialized market, but nonetheless the Strat fired the music then of players such as Buddy Holly, Carl Perkins and Buddy Guy.

Fender's next model introductions came in 1956 with a pair of new "student" electrics. These had a shorter string-length than was usual for Fender. The "three-quarter size" one-pickup Musicmaster and two-pickup Duo-Sonic were described in the company's literature as "ideal for students and adults with small hands." They were

clearly designed for players on a tight budget, for those who were starting out on electric guitar and were flocking to the music-retailer "schools" that were springing up everywhere in the US at the time.

Fender then created a decidedly high-end instrument. The Jazzmaster first appeared on Fender's pricelists in 1958, and at $329 was some $50 more expensive than the Strat. At that sort of price Fender couldn't resist tagging its new Jazzmaster as "America's finest electric guitar... unequaled in performance and design features." Immediately striking to the guitarist of 1958 was the Jazzmaster's unusual offset-waist body shape and, for the first time on a Fender, a separate rosewood fingerboard glued to the customary maple neck. The vibrato system was new, too, with an ill-conceived "lock-off" facility aimed at preventing tuning problems if a string should break.

The sound of the Jazzmaster was richer and warmer than players were used to from Fender. The name Jazzmaster was not chosen at random, for Fender aimed the different tone at jazz players. But jazz guitarists found little appeal in this new, rather difficult solidbody guitar, and mainstream Fender players largely stayed with their Strats and Teles.

All in all, the Jazzmaster was a distinct change for Fender, and constituted a real effort to extend the scope and appeal of its guitar line. Ironically, and despite significant early success, this has been partly responsible for the guitar's lack of long-term

Fender's Custom Telecaster, new in 1959, had a bound body. This example (far left) was made in 1963. Two Fender Jaguars are shown next to it: a sunburst model from 1963 (center) and one finished in Candy Apple Red from the following year.

popularity relative to the Strat and Tele, mainly as a result of players' dissatisfaction with the guitar's looks and sounds. Nonetheless, the Jazzmaster remained near the top of the Fender pricelist until withdrawn around 1980.

Most Fender guitars of the 1950s came officially only in sunburst or varieties of the original "blond" (some rare early Esquires were black). But a few guitars, specially made at the factory effectively as one-offs, were finished in solid colors. The rare surviving examples indicate that this practice was underway by 1954, but few players then seemed interested in slinging on a colored guitar, and Fender's main production remained in sunburst and blond instruments.

The company's early production of special-color guitars was certainly casual, often no doubt the understandable reaction of a small company to lucrative if unusual orders from a handful of customers. But this informal arrangement was given a rather more commercial footing in the company's sales literature of 1956 when "player's choice" colored guitars were noted as an option, at five per cent extra cost. In the following year these Du Pont paint finishes were described in Fender's catalog as "Custom Colors" (a name that has stuck ever since) and in the pricelist as "custom Du Pont Duco finishes," still at five per cent on top of normal prices.

Fender also announced, early in 1957, a Stratocaster in see-through blond finish and with gold-plated hardware. Don Randall says the gold plate was influenced by

The Mustang was a relatively low-end Fender that first appeared in 1964; the example pictured (below left) dates from around 1971. Another Fender popular with grunge acts in the 1990s, a Mustang is pivtured here with Steve Turner of Mudhoney (above).

Thurston Moore of Sonic Youth was also a 1980s fan of "other" Fenders, such as the much modified Mustang (below left) that he used alongside Jaguars and Jazzmasters.

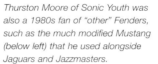

Joining the Fender line in 1965 as a high-end model was the Electric XII 12-string. The two shown here both date from 1966, the one on this page finished in Candy Apple Red, the other (opposite) in the more subtle shade of Olympic White.

Shown (below, right) is a second prototype for Fender's ill-fated Marauder project, which never saw production. This 1966 Marauder has multiple switches and angled frets. The original prototype was even odder, with pickups concealed below the pickguard (as pictured in Fender's 1965/66 catalog, below).

seeing the new White Falcon model by Gretsch. In fact Fender had trouble getting the gold-plate to stay on the its components. But the gold-hardware blond Strat was in effect Fender's first official Custom Color guitar – although the term has always been more popularly applied since to solid-color varieties. The blond/gold Strat was later known as the "Mary Kaye" model thanks to musician Kaye regularly appearing with such a model in Fender catalogs.

Fender eventually came up with a defined list of its choice of available Custom Colors. In the early 1960s, when many more Custom Color Fenders were being made, the company issued color charts to publicize the various shades. There were three original charts: the first, in about 1960, featured Black, Burgundy Mist Metallic, Dakota Red, Daphne Blue, Fiesta Red, Foam Green, Inca Silver Metallic, Lake Placid Blue Metallic, Olympic White, Shell Pink, Sherwood Green Metallic, Shoreline Gold Metallic, Sonic Blue and Surf Green; the second, around 1963, had lost Shell Pink and gained Candy Apple Red Metallic; and the third, in 1965, lost Burgundy Mist Metallic, Daphne Blue, Inca Silver Metallic, Sherwood Green Metallic, Shoreline Gold Metallic and Surf Green, and gained – all Metallics – Blue Ice, Charcoal Frost, Firemist Gold, Firemist Silver, Ocean Turquoise and Teal Green.

The automobile industry was clearly having a profound effect upon US guitar manufacturers in the 1950s, not least in this ability to enhance the look of an already

Fender's 1965/66 catalog included this page with three harmless Jaguars (right) and two Marauders (left) with pickups hidden underneath the pickguard. The Marauder never actually went into production.

During 1967 George Harrison painted his Strat (opposite) in a suitably psychedelic/rockabilly style. He played it in the Magical Mystery Tour movie and regularly after The Beatles split. Preferring a Tele at the end of the 1960s was country picker Clarence White on The Byrds' Sweetheart Of The Rodeo (left).

stylish object with a rich, sparkling paint job. Fender used paints from Du Pont's Duco nitro-cellulose lines, such as Dakota Red or Foam Green, as well as the more color-retentive Lucite acrylics like Lake Placid Blue Metallic or Burgundy Mist Metallic. Decades later the guitars bearing these original Fiesta Reds, Sonic Blues, Shoreline Golds and the like have proved very desirable among collectors, many of whom rate a Custom Color Fender, especially an early one, as a prime catch. This is despite the prevalence of recent "refinishes" which have become so accurate that even alleged experts can be fooled into declaring some fake finishes as original. Some players find it difficult to understand why collectors can pay a very high premium simply for the promise that a particular layer of paint is "original."

At Fender in the late 1950s a few cosmetic and production adjustments were being made to the company's electric guitars. The Jazzmaster had been the first Fender with a rosewood fingerboard, and this material was adopted for other models around 1959. The company also altered the look of its sunburst finish at the time, adding red to give a three-tone yellow-to-red-to-black effect. By 1959 Fender employed 100 workers in nine buildings occupying some 54,000 square feet.

The last "new" Fender electrics of the 1950s were the bound-body Custom versions of the Esquire and Telecaster, new for 1959. Forrest White got advice on the process of binding from Fred Martin, head of the leading American flat-top acoustic

guitar manufacturer Martin. The Customs each listed at just $30 more than the regular unbound versions, but far fewer of these were sold.

As Fender entered the 1960s, the company boasted an extended list of products in addition to its electric guitars. The company's July 1961 pricelist, for example, noted 13 amplifiers (Bandmaster, Bassman, Champ, Concert, Deluxe, Harvard, Princeton, Pro Amp, Super, Tremolux, Twin Amp, Vibrasonic, Vibrolux), five steel guitars (Champ, Deluxe, Dual, Stringmaster, Studio Deluxe), two pedal-steel guitars (400, 1000) and two bass guitars (Jazz, Precision).

The next new electric six-string design to leave Fender's production line was the Jaguar, which first showed up in sales material during 1962. It used a similar offset-waist body shape to the Jazzmaster, and also shared that guitar's separate bridge and vibrato unit, though the Jaguar had the addition of a spring-loaded string mute at the bridge. Fender rather optimistically believed that players of the time were so obsessed with gadgets that they would prefer a mechanical string mute to the natural edge-of-the-hand method. They were wrong. There are many elements of playing technique that simply cannot be replaced by hardware.

Despite the surface similarities, there were some notable differences between the new Jaguar and the now four-year-old Jazzmaster. Visually, the Jaguar had three distinctive chrome-plated control panels, and was the first Fender with 22 frets on the

Three Stratocasters are shown on this page with the new larger headstock that began to appear during 1965. Two date from 1966: one finished in Lake Placid Blue Metallic (far left); the other in Black (center). The black guitar is said to have been given by Jimi Hendrix to sessionman Al Kooper in the late 1960s. The 1968 example in Olympic White (near left; since yellowed) has the optional maple fingerboard offered at the time.

Fender developed unusual colors for some of its new Coronado models. Antigua was a white-to-brown shaded finish, as featured in this Fender leaflet (left) of 1968. Stranger still was the Wildwood effect (1968 flyer, right) achieved by injecting dyes into beech trees for spectacular streaked and striped colors.

We planted
a whole forest...
to give you
Fender
Wildwood

Wildwood Guitar, Bass and 12-String

Truly a happening in sight and sound. *You only have to look and listen to know it can only be FENDER.* These are the NEW WILDWOODS...the new distinctive look in guitars. Exciting rainbow hues of greens, blues and golds are exclusively FENDER...grown in a private forest to bring you the wildest, richest grains of natural color in acoustically perfect and musically oriented beechwood. Vivid colors matched only by the colorful sounds of the guitar itself. Vivid sound created only the way FENDER master craftsmen can build a musical instrument. Moreover, each instrument is exclusively individual in appearance...each has its own wild colorful pattern . . . *no two alike!* Only FENDER gives you this distinction.

Designed for tomorrow's "turned-on" world ...FENDER'S WILDWOOD Series is a kaleidoscope of sound:

FENDER WILDWOOD GUITAR ■ Custom Grover Rotomatic Pearl Button Keys ■ Slimline 1-11/16" semi-acoustic body ■ Modern "F" hole and entire body custom bound ■ Removable and adjustable neck mounted without a heel for playing ease and extremely fast, low playing action ■ Two all-new high efficiency custom built pickups—better sensitivity and higher output with maximum shielding for hum cancellation ■ Ultra-wide response range for dynamic sound—harmonic content full-bodied and distortion-free ■ Custom pickups designed for full adjustments: Pole pieces are individually adjustable to achieve balanced string response and tonal effects to suit individual requirements ■ Fully adjustable bridge allows custom string length and height settings, bridge saddle may be raised at either end for personal playing requirements ■ Distinctive tail piece is functional allowing easy string replacement ■ Neck has adjustable reinforced truss rod . . . is custom bound and inlaid with bold position markers ■ Slimline precision Tremolo provides smooth operation and accurate return to pitch without variance

■ Three position switch selects either or both of the new high efficiency pickups—variations range from rich, mellow to sharp biting rock.

FENDER WILDWOOD 12 STRING ■ Custom Grover Rotomatic Pearl Button Keys ■ Fast, low action neck is truss rod reinforced, fully bound and has bold inlaid position markers ■ Neck mounted without heel for added reach ■ Ultra-thin body with bound "F" hole and multiple binding on both front and back edges ■ Individual barrel type bridges—each varies in size to conform to the fingerboard contour and each is independently adjustable for

length—master bridge is adjustable for height at either end ■ Two all-new high efficiency pickups—better sensitivity and higher output with maximum shielding for hum cancellation ■ Three position tone switch to permit use of each pickup separately or together ■ Maximum flexibility in tonal shadings with individual tone and volume controls ■ Individual bridges are adjustable for length and custom playing height ■ Fully bound body and neck ■ Fast action truss-reinforced neck in removable and mounted without a heel for playing ease enabling the player to easily reach the highest fret ■ Full-bodied and precisely muted bass response — traditionally FENDER—dynamic and distortion-free.

FENDER WILDWOOD BASS ■ Slimline 1-11/16" thin body ■ Two custom built high efficiency bass pickups—better sensitivity and higher output with maximum shielding for hum cancellation ■ Three position tone switch

CBS Musical Instruments
Columbia Broadcasting System, Inc.

fingerboard. The Jaguar also had a slightly shorter string-length than usual for Fenders, closer to Gibson's standard, making for a different playing feel.

The Jaguar had better pickups than the Jazzmaster. They looked much like Strat units but had metal shielding added at the base and sides, partly as a response to criticisms of the Jazzmaster's tendency to noisiness. The Jag's electrics were even more complex than the Jazzmaster's, using the same rhythm circuit but adding a trio of lead-circuit switches. Like the Jazzmaster, the Jaguar enjoyed a burst of popularity when introduced. But this top-of-the-line guitar, "one of the finest solidbody electric guitars that has ever been offered to the public" in Fender's original sales hyperbole, has never enjoyed sustained success.

As the 1960s got underway it was clear that Fender had become a remarkably successful company. In a relatively short period Fender's brilliantly inventive trio of Telecaster, Precision Bass and Stratocaster had established in the minds of musicians and guitar-makers the idea of the solidbody electric guitar as a viable modern instrument. The company found itself in the midst of the rock'n'roll music revolution of the late 1950s and early 1960s... and were happy to ensure that players had a good supply of affordable guitars available in large numbers.

Fender had captured a huge segment of the new market. Many buildings had been added to cope with increased manufacturing demands, and by 1964 the operation

Two Coronado models: first, a Wildwood II six-string (near right) from 1968, with Fender's special injected-wood finish; second, a Coronado XII (center) in Teal Green, dating from around 1968. A new low-end model was the Bronco, with a standard red finish. This example (far right) was made in about 1972.

At the start of his success, Jimi Hendrix (first two albums, both 1967, above) was using a battered sunburst Fender Stratocaster. Soon he began to acquire more Strats, usually opting for a black- or white-finished model on stage (he's seen with a white rosewood-fingerboard Strat, opposite). From around the middle of 1968, Jimi's preference moved to maple-fingerboard models.

This Olympic White Stratocaster (main guitar) dating from around 1968 was sold at Sotheby's saleroom in London in April 1990 as the instrument that Hendrix used at the Woodstock festival in 1969, among other performances. It was sold by Jimi's drummer, Mitch Mitchell, and fetched a record price of £180,000 (about $270,000).

whereas Fender's old guard – the team that had done much to put Fender where it was at the time – were long-serving craft workers without formal qualifications.

Leo's services were retained, CBS grandly naming him a "special consultant in research and development." In fact, he was set up away from the Fender buildings and allowed to tinker as much as he liked – with very little effect on the Fender product lines. A couple of years after the sale to CBS, Leo changed doctors and was given a huge dose of antibiotics which cured his sinus complaint. He completed a few projects for CBS but left when his five-year contract expired in 1970. He went on to design and make instruments for Music Man and G&L.

But Leo was not the first of the old team to leave CBS. White departed in 1967; he died in November 1994. Randall resigned from CBS in April 1969, and formed Randall Electric Instruments, which he sold in 1987. Fullerton left CBS in 1970, worked at Ernie Ball for a while, and with Leo formed the G&L company in 1979, although Fullerton sold his interest in 1986. Hyatt, who resigned from CBS in 1972, was also part of the G&L set-up, which was sold to BBE Sound Inc after Leo Fender's death in March 1991.

Back at Fender Musical Instruments, the Electric XII – a guitar that had been on the drawing board when the CBS sale took place – finally hit the music stores in the summer of 1965. Electric 12-strings had recently been popularized by The Beatles and The Byrds, who both used Rickenbackers, so Fender joined in the battle with its own

This 1973 natural-finish Strat (near left) features the new neck truss-rod system introduced along with a three-bolt neck fixing by Fender to some models during 1971. The new "bullet" truss-rod adjuster is visible on the headstock by the nut.

After using a variety of guitars in his early career, Eric Clapton settled down to long-term Stratocaster use, beginning around 1970. Since that time he played Strats regularly on-stage (far right) as well as on some great records such as his Derek & the Dominos studio album, Layla, and with Delaney & Bonnie.

rather belated version. An innovation was the Electric XII's 12-saddle bridge which allowed for precise adjustments of individual string heights and intonation, a luxury hitherto unknown on any 12-string guitar. But the 12-string craze of the 1960s was almost over and the Electric XII proved shortlived, lasting in the line only until 1968.

One of Fender's first CBS-era pricelists, dated April 1965, reveals a burgeoning line of products in addition to the company's 11 electric guitar models (namely the Duo-Sonic, Electric XII, Esquire, Esquire Custom, Jaguar, Jazzmaster, Musicmaster, Mustang, Stratocaster, Telecaster and Telecaster Custom).

The other lines included three bass guitars (the Jazz, Precision, and VI), six flat-top acoustic guitars (the Classic, Concert, King, Malibu, Palomino and Newporter) and 15 amplifiers (Bandmaster, Bassman, Champ, Deluxe, Deluxe Reverb, Dual Showman, Princeton, Princeton Reverb, Pro Reverb, Showman, Super Reverb, Tremolux, Twin Reverb, Vibro Champ, Vibrolux Reverb). These were accompanied by various Fender-Rhodes keyboards, a number of steel and pedal steel guitars, and a solidbody electric mandolin, as well as reverb and echo units.

Uniquely for Fender, a guitar appeared in its 1965/66 literature that never actually made it into production. Naturally a company makes many designs and prototypes which do not translate to commercial release, but for an instrument to get as far as printed sales material, and then be withdrawn, implies a serious error of judgement

somewhere along the line. It was the first sign that CBS might be losing its grip. The guitar was the Marauder, and its obvious distinction was summed up by Fender as follows in the hapless catalog entry: "It appears as though there are no pickups. There are, in reality, however, four newly created pickups mounted underneath the pickguard." The design had been offered to Fender by one Quilla H. Freeman, who had a patent for his idea of hiding powerful pickups under a guitar's pickguard.

Forrest White later remembered that there were problems with weak signals from the pickups, and George Fullerton said he thought there was also a dispute between Freeman and CBS concerning the patent. Whatever the circumstances, we know that Freeman later took the hidden-pickups idea to another California company, Rickenbacker, who also got no further than prototypes.

A second proposed version of the Marauder was worked on at Fender during 1966. Eight prototypes were built of the new version, this time with three conventional, visible pickups, plus some complex associated control switching. Four of these trial guitars also had slanted frets. It was in this state that the Marauder project finally died.

During 1966 CBS completed the construction of a new Fender factory, which had been planned before its purchase of the company. It cost the new owner $1.3million, and was situated next to Fender's buildings on the South Raymond site in Fullerton. Meanwhile, some cosmetic changes were being made to various Fender models. In

The Telecaster Thinline gained humbucking pickups in 1971, as on this example from around 1977 (near right). Two other "new" Teles from the period were the Telecaster Custom with neck humbuckers (1977 example, center) and the twin-humbucker Telecaster Deluxe (1976 example, far right).

According to Fender the illustration in this 1977 ad (left) was of a hard-charging, sharp-toothed Starcaster. Now extinct.

This unusual Rhinestone Strat, made in 1975, has a bonded metal and fiberglass body by British sculptor Jon Douglas, specially ordered by Fender's UK distributor. Some, like this one, have rhinestones set into the heavy relief design. Only a very small quantity was produced. A later unauthorized version made in the 1990s has an identifying plaque on the back of the body.

Fender's second attempt at a semi-solid instrument was the Starcaster (below right), this one dating from around 1978. Despite the quality, it was not popular. A Starcasting minstrel is pictured on the cover of Fender's 1976 catalog.

1965 the Stratocaster gained a broader headstock, effectively matching that of the Jazzmaster and Jaguar. Also during 1965 the fingerboards of the Electric XII, Jaguar and Jazzmaster were bound, while the following year the same trio was given block-shaped fingerboard inlays rather than the previous dot markers. Generally, CBS seemed to be fiddling for fiddling's sake.

A firm innovation – at least for Fender – came in the shape of a new line of hollowbody electrics. These were the first such electrics from Fender who until this point were clearly identified in the player's mind as a solidbody producer. Evidently the strong success of Gibson's ES line of semi-solidbodies and to a lesser extent models by Gretsch and others must have tempted CBS and its search for wider markets.

German maker Roger Rossmeisl had been brought into the company by Leo Fender in 1962 to design acoustic guitars, and Rossmeisl also became responsible for the new electric hollowbodies. Launched in 1966, the Coronado thinline guitars were the first to appear of Rossmeisl's electric designs for Fender and, despite their conventional, equal-double-cutaway, bound bodies with large, stylized f-holes, they employed the standard Fender bolt-on neck and headstock design. Options included a new vibrato tailpiece, and there was also a 12-string version that borrowed the Electric XII's "hockey-stick" headstock. Rossmeisl was also among the team which came up with a lightweight version of the Tele in 1968. The Thinline Telecaster had three hollowed-out

THE COLLECTED WORKS OF FENDER

cavities inside the body and a modified pickguard shaped to accommodate the single, token f-hole. It was also around this time – and quite apart from Fender – that Byrds guitarist Clarence White and drummer Gene Parsons came up with their "shoulder strap control" B-string-pull device that fitted into a Telecaster. It was designed to offer string-bends within chords to emulate pedal steel-type sounds.

It was at this time that Rossmeisl was let loose with a couple of guitar designs that were even less like the normal run of Fenders than the Coronado models had been. Rossmeisl's specialty was the so-called "German carve" taught to him by his guitar-making father, Wenzel Rossmeisl. This applies a distinctive "dished" dip around the top edge of the body, following its outline. Rossmeisl adopted this feature for the new hollowbody archtop electric Montego and LTD models, all eminently traditional but still obstinately using Fender's customary bolt-on neck. From all reports there were very few of these made, and the models are rarely seen today.

Toward the end of the 1960s came firm evidence that CBS was trying to wring every last drop of potential income from unused Fender factory stock that would otherwise have been written off. Two shortlived guitars, the Custom and the Swinger, were assembled from these leftovers.

As the close of the 1960s loomed, Fender took a boost when an inspired guitarist by the name of Jimi Hendrix applied the Stratocaster's sensuous curves and glorious tone to his live cavorting and studio experiments. Salesman Dale Hyatt once said, only half-jokingly one suspects, that Jimi Hendrix caused more Stratocasters to be sold than all the Fender salesmen put together.

One of the few top bands apparently absent from Fender patronage during the 1960s was The Beatles, who at least on-stage contented themselves with a mix of primarily Gretsch, Rickenbacker, Gibson, Epiphone and Hofner guitars. In fact, George Harrison and John Lennon had each acquired a Stratocaster in 1965 for studio use, and Paul McCartney bought an Esquire a year or two later. But the public face of the band remained distinctly Fender-less, which led Don Randall to try to persuade manager Brian Epstein to get his boys into Fender. Probably during 1969, Randall managed to secure a meeting with Lennon and McCartney at the band's Apple headquarters in London. The results were the band's Fender-Rhodes pianos, a Jazz Bass and a VI six-string bass, as well as George Harrison's Rosewood Telecaster – all visible at various times during the *Let It Be* movie.

The 1970s are believed by many players and collectors to be the poorest years of Fender's production history, and there can be little doubt that quality control slipped and more low-standard Fenders were made during this decade than any other. But some fine Fender guitars were made in the 1970s as well. It's just that there were more average guitars made than good ones – and it often seems as if the good

Three more Stratocasters on this page: a 25th Anniversary model in fetching silver finish from 1979 (far left); a 1980 example of the Strat (center), a shortlived official use of the common abbreviation; and a regular Stratocaster model from 1980 finished in Capri Orange, one of several lurid "International Colors" offered briefly at this time.

instruments that do turn up were produced in spite rather than because of the company's policies and activities during that decade.

The 1970s would be a time when CBS management cut back on the existing Fender product lines and offered hardly any new models. The last Esquire of the period was made in 1970, the year in which the Duo-Sonic also died. The Jaguar disappeared around 1975, and by 1980 the Bronco, Jazzmaster, Musicmaster and Thinline Tele had all been taken out of production.

Elsewhere in Fender's guitar lines, the original acoustic flat-tops had all gone from the catalog by 1971. Ten years later the steels and pedal-steels had all disappeared, with only amplifiers (some 14 models) offering anything like the previous market coverage. Most of the original Custom Colors had been discontinued during the late 1960s and early 1970s.

So it was that by the start of the 1980s the guitarist who wanted to buy a new Fender electric had little choice beyond the company's ever-reliable Strats and Teles. And apart from a few shortlived exceptions, these came mostly in sunburst, blond, black or natural. It was hard to resist the feeling that the newly-important calculations of the balance sheet had become firmly established at Fender, and had taken precedence over the company's former creativity. A few new electric Fender models did get introduced in the 1970s, but mostly these were variations on familiar themes. Part

Fender launched its first Vintage reissue series of guitars in 1982, a masterstroke that allowed it to capitalize on its own valuable history. This example of the Vintage 57 Stratocaster (main guitar) was made in 1987. There was also a Vintage 62 Stratocaster that had a rosewood fingerboard among other features associated with early-1960s Strats.

The shortlived Standard Stratocaster (1982 example, below left) returned to a more traditional look and feel for the Strat, abandoning features such as the "large" headstock, three-bolt neck fixing and headstock-located bullet truss-rod adjuster. The ad from 1983 shows a close-up of that year's Elite Stratocaster (details opposite).

Fender's catalog of 1982 (below) featured famous Fender players on the cover (left to right): Buddy Holly, James Burton, The Ventures, Steve Cropper, Jimi Hendrix, Eric Clapton. The page from inside shows Fender's new low-end Lead III model pictured in a punky dressing room, somewhat in contrast to the cover stars.

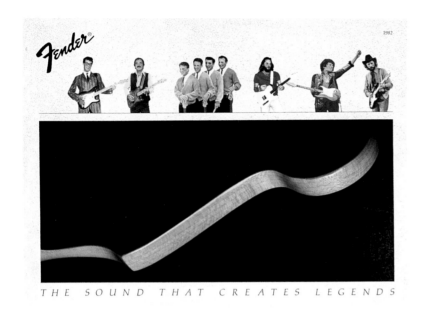

Three more new-in-the-1980s Fenders on this page: a '52 Telecaster vintage reissue, this one (far left) made in 1984; a Stratocaster Elite (center) dating from 1983, with pushbutton pickup selectors and finished in Blue Stratoburst; plus a Elite Telecaster from 1983 with two new-design humbucking pickups.

of Fender's distinction had come from using bright-sounding single-coil pickups; the warmer, fatter-sounding humbucking types were always considered then as a Gibson mainstay. Nonetheless, in keeping with changing market trends, the Telecaster was given a humbucking pickup at the neck position to create the Telecaster Custom in 1972, and similar dabbling led to a sort of Tele-meets-Strat-meets-Gibson: the two-humbucker, Strat-necked Telecaster Deluxe of 1973.

The company made another attempt at thinline hollowbody electrics with the ill-fated Starcaster in 1976, again aimed at competing with Gibson's ever-popular ES line. The Starcaster had left the Fender list by 1980.

By 1976 Fender had a five-acre facility under one roof in Fullerton and employed over 750 workers. Some new "student" models appeared at this time to replace the Musicmaster, Bronco, Duo-Sonic and Mustang. The Lead I and Lead II guitars of 1979 were simple double-cutaway solids, though not especially cheap at $399. They were followed by the single-cutaway Bullet series which began production in 1981. Fender did briefly attempt to have these models produced in Korea, to eliminate tooling costs, but after a number of problems manufacturing resumed in the US.

In the early 1980s the CBS management appears to have decided that Fender needed some new blood to help reverse the decline in the company's fortunes. During 1981 key personnel were recruited from the American musical instrument operation of

A radically different design was the shortlived Performer (main guitar), this one made in 1986.

This D'Aquisto Deluxe (below left) was made at Fender's Custom Shop in 1997. The 1986 ad shows sessionman Tommy Tedesco with the earlier and similar Japanese-made D'Aquisto Elite model.

One of the Stratocaster's leading advocates during the 1980s was Edge of U2 (left), who did much to keep the instrument in public view.

the giant Japanese company Yamaha, including John McLaren, Bill Schultz and Dan Smith. It appeared that they were brought in to turn around the reputation of Fender, to get the operation on its feet and making a profit once again.

One of the new team's recommendations was to start alternative production of Fenders in Japan. The reason was relatively straightforward: Fender's sales were being hammered by the onslaught of orientally-produced copies. These Japanese copyists made their biggest profits in their own domestic market, so the best place to hit back at them was in Japan – by making and selling guitars there. So, with the blessing of CBS, negotiations began with two Japanese distributors to establish the Fender Japan company. A joint venture was officially established in March 1982.

In the States the new management team was working on a strategy to return Fender to its former glory. The plan was for Fender in effect to copy itself, by recreating the guitars that many players and collectors were spending large sums of money to acquire: the Fenders made back in the company's glory years in the 1950s and 1960s. The result was the Vintage reissue series, begun in 1982. The guitars consisted of a maple-neck "57" and rosewood-fingerboard "62" Strat, as well as a "52" Telecaster. These Vintage reproductions were not exact enough for some die-hard Fender collectors, but generally the guitars were praised and welcomed. Production of the Vintage reissues was planned to start in 1982 at Fender US (Fullerton) and at Fender

Fender joined in the mid-1980s trend for weird body shapes with the shortlived Katana model (far left), this one made in 1985. A longer stay in the Fender line was enjoyed by the 12-string Strat XII (1990 example, center). Fender Japan launched a Paisley Stratocaster and a Blue Flower Stratocaster in 1988, two finishes first used in the 1960s – on Telecasters. This Blue Flower Strat (near left) dates from 1989.

FENDER

Fender's Custom Shop began to operate officially in 1987, and the company was soon publishing ads like this one (near right) to underline the traditional role of a custom shop making one-off "fantasy" guitars. Fender acquired the rights to products bearing Floyd Rose's name in 1991 (ad from that year, far right).

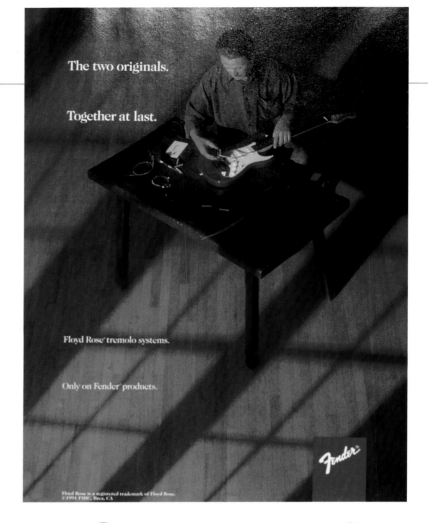

Japan (Fujigen). But changes being instituted at the American factory meant that the US versions did not come on-stream until early 1983. Fender Japan's guitars at this stage were being made only for the internal Japanese market, but Fender's European agents were putting pressure on the Fullerton management for a low-end Fender to compete with the multitude of exported models being sold in Europe and elsewhere by other Japanese manufacturers.

So Fender Japan made some less costly versions of the Vintage reissues for European distribution in 1982, with the Squier brand (see Squier). At the end of 1983, with the US Fender factory still not up to the scale of production the team wanted, Fender Japan also built a Squier Stratocaster for the US market. This instrument, together with the earlier Squier Stratocasters and Telecasters, saw the start of the sale of Fender Japan products around the world, and a move by Fender to become an international manufacturer of guitars.

A shortlived pair from the US factory at this time was the Elite Stratocaster and Elite Telecaster, intended as radical new high-end versions of the old faithfuls. Unfortunately the vibrato-equipped Elite Strat came saddled with a terrible bridge, which is what most players recall when the Elites are mentioned. In-fighting at Fender had led to last-minute modifications of the vibrato design and the result was an unwieldy, unworkable piece of hardware. The Elite Strat also featured three pushbuttons for pickup selection,

Fender's American Standard series re-established the good name of the Stratocaster and Telecaster with efficacious updates. The Stratocaster American Standard (1991 example, near right) first appeared in 1985; the Telecaster American Standard (1991 example, far right) in 1988. Both remain popular and important models in Fender's line. The company's first signature model was the Eric Clapton Stratocaster; this example (center) dates from 1990.

92

The 40th Anniversary Telecaster was the Fender Custom Shop's first limited-edition guitar. This exquisite 1989 example (main guitar) is number 221 of 300.

Fender's Yngwie Malmsteen signature Strat has a scalloped fingerboard – "scooped" rather than flat between each fret, to enable faster playing.

which were not to the taste of players brought up on the classic Fender pickup switch. There were good points – the new pickups, the effective active circuitry, and an improved truss-rod design – but they tended to be overlooked. The Elites were also dropped by the end of 1984.

Three new-design Fender lines were introduced in 1984, made by Fender Japan and intended to compete with some of Gibson's popular lines. The overall name for the new instruments was the Master Series, encompassing electric archtop D'Aquisto models, with design input from American luthier Jimmy D'Aquisto, and semi-solid Esprit and Flame guitars. Significantly, they were the first Fender Japan products with the Fender rather than Squier headstock logo to be sold officially outside Japan, and the first Fenders with set-necks. Their overtly Gibson image was to be their undoing. Most players wanted recognizable Fenders from Fender. This recurring theme has jarred with all Fender's attempts to introduce new-design guitars.

For a variety of reasons, CBS decided during 1984 that it had finally had enough of this part of the music business, and that it wished to sell Fender Musical Instruments. CBS invited offers and at the end of January 1985, almost exactly 20 years since acquiring it, CBS confirmed that it would sell Fender to an investor group led by Bill Schultz, then president of Fender Musical Instruments. The contract was formalized in February and the sale completed in March 1985 for $12.5million. It's interesting to

Swedish heavy metal guitarist Yngwie Malmsteen is pictured in this 1990 ad (above) with one of his Fender signature Stratocasters.

compare this with the $13million that CBS originally paid for the company back in 1965 (which translates to around $90million at 1985 prices).

The problems facing the new owners were legion, but probably the most immediate was the fact that the Fullerton factories were not included in the deal. So US production of Fenders stopped in February 1985. However, the new team had been stockpiling bodies and necks, and did acquire some existing inventory of completed guitars as well as production machinery. The company went from employing over 800 people in early 1984 down to just over 100 in early 1985.

Fender had been working on a couple of radical guitar designs before CBS sold the company, and these instruments became victims of the crossfire. One was the Performer, which started life intended for US production. But with nowhere to build it in the States, Fender had it manufactured at the Fujigen factory in Japan.

The Performer had a distinctive body shape, twin slanted pickups, 24 frets, and an arrow-shape headstock quite different from the usual Fender Strat derivative, a reaction to the newly popular "superstrat" design popularized by American guitar makers such as Jackson and including a drooped "pointy" headstock. All in all, Fender's Performer was a thoroughly modern instrument with few nods to the company's illustrious past, but this brave move was killed by the CBS sale. The Japanese operation became Fender's lifeline at this time, providing much-needed product to the company which still had no US factory. All the guitars in Fender's 1985 catalog were made in Japan, including the new Contemporary Stratocasters and Telecasters which were the first Fenders with the increasingly fashionable heavy-duty vibrato units and string-clamps.

One estimate put as much as 80 per cent of the guitars that Fender US sold from around the end of 1984 to the middle of 1986 as Japanese-made.

Fender finally established its new factory at Corona, about 20 miles east of the now defunct Fullerton site. Production started on a very limited scale toward the end of 1985, producing only about five guitars a day for the Vintage reissue series. But Dan Smith and his colleagues wanted to re-establish the US side of Fender's production with some good, basic Strats and Teles that would be seen as a continuation of the best of Fender's American traditions. That plan translated into the American Standard models: the Strat version was launched in 1986; the Tele followed two years later.

The American Standard was an efficacious piece of re-interpretation. It drew from the best of the original Stratocaster but was updated with a flatter-camber 22-fret neck and a revised vibrato unit based on twin stud pivot points. Once the Corona plant's production lines reached full speed, the American Standard Stratocaster proved extremely successful for the revitalized Fender operation. By the early 1990s, the instrument was a best-seller, and was notching up some 25,000 sales annually. In

Three Fenders made in the 1990s are shown on this page: a Strat Plus of 1990 (near right), the first with Fenders low-noise Lace Sensor pickups; the Prodigy II (1991 example, center) acknowledged the superstrat trend, and was one of the first Fender's worked on at the company's new Mexican factory; and this Strat Ultra (far right), with doubled-up single-coil pickup at the bridge, was made in 1991.

Japanese-made Jaguar and Jazzmaster models appeared in this 1995 ad (left). By 2000 Fender Japan was primarily supplying its domestic market, exporting just a handful of small-run basses, as Fender's Mexican plant and new US factory – plus offshore suppliers – took care of demand elsewhere.

Meanwhile there were truly new guitars. Well... almost new guitars. Larry Brooks in the Custom Shop had built a hybrid guitar for grunge supremo Kurt Cobain in 1993 after the guitarist had come up with some ideas for a merged Jaguar and Mustang: the Jag-Stang. A number of also-ran Fender models beyond Stratocasters and Telecasters were proving popular at this time with grunge guitarists: Cobain himself played Jaguars and Mustangs; Steve Turner played a Mustang; J Mascis had a Jazzmaster. And the reason was straightforward. These guitars had the comforting Fender logo on the head, but could be bought more cheaply secondhand than Strats or Teles. The ethics of such deals suited grunge guitarists perfectly.

Cobain, meanwhile, decided to take cut-up photographs of his Jag and Mustang and stick them together this way and that, trying out different combinations to see what they would look like combined. The Custom Shop then took his paste-ups as a basis, assembled the design, and contoured it here and there to improve balance and feel.

After Cobain's untimely death in 1994, the guitarist's family collaborated with the Fender company to release a Japan-made production version of the instrument, which was named the Fender Jag-Stang. Cobain's guitar hit the market in 1996.

Fender opened a brand new guitar- and amp-making factory in November 1998, still in Corona, California. The company described the impressive state-of-the-art factory as arguably the most expensive and automated facility of its type in the world. Since starting production at the original Corona factory back in 1985, Fender had grown to occupy a total of 115,000 square feet of space in ten buildings across the city. Such a rambling spread proved increasingly inefficient, and Fender had begun to plan a new factory during the early 1990s. With this new facility Fender are now clearly geared up for even more expansion, and the new $20million 177,000-square-feet plant affords the continuingly successful Fender a potentially growing production capacity for the future. The new factory, with a staff of 600, also means that Fender's long-standing fight with California's stringent environmental laws are at an end, as the new purpose-built paint section works without toxic emissions.

The new factory may be only 20 miles or so from Fullerton and the site of Leo Fender's original workshops, but it is a universe away from those humble steel shacks that provided the first home for Fender guitar production. However, with his love of gadgetry Leo would undoubtedly have been enthralled by the new plant, not least its

Here's a trio of artist models: a 2002 Custom Shop "Go Cat Go" Tele (left) for rockabilly king Carl Perkins; a Jim Adkins JA-90 Telecaster Thinline (center) from 2009 with semi-solid body and Seymour Duncan pickups; and a Lee Ranaldo Jazzmaster (far right), also from 2009. Keith Richards (on-stage in the 1990s, right) was the alleged inspiration for Fender's Relic series of aged guitars when he complained that some Custom Shop guitars "looked too new."

automated conveyor system that enables the storage and supply on demand to the production line of a vast inventory of guitar components.

In the late 1990s, fashion began to turn to the old humbucker'd Telecaster models: the Thinline (1971–79), which had two humbuckers, regular Tele controls, and an f-hole in the body; the Deluxe (1972–81), with two humbuckers, Strat-like head, and four knobs; and the Custom (1972–81), with neck humbucker, regular bridge pickup, and four knobs. Thom Yorke of Radiohead may have started the trend soon bolstered by members of Snow Patrol, Gomez, Maroon 5 and many others. Fender reacted and reissued the 1970s humbucker'd Teles as part of the Mexican-made Classic series: the '72 Telecaster Thinline (two humbuckers) and the '72 Telecaster Custom (neck humbucker), both starting in 1999, and the '72 Telecaster Deluxe (two humbuckers) in 2004. US-made versions appeared in 2011 in the shape of the American Vintage '72 Telecaster Thinline and '72 Telecaster Custom, and more recently variations such as the Modern Player Thinline Deluxe.

Upstairs in the boardroom at Fender headquarters, Bill Schultz stepped down as Fender Chief Executive Officer in 2005, staying on as chairman of the board of directors, and Bill Mendello became CEO. Mendello retired from Fender in 2010, Larry Thomas took over as CEO, and Thomas was in turn succeeded by Andy Mooney in 2015. Dan Smith waved goodbye to Fender in 2006 after 25 remarkable years with

Fender's American Special series was launched in 2010 as US-made guitars for working players on a budget, and here we've shown a 2011 Strat (below, far left) from the line. At the other end of the scale was the Damien Hirst Spot Telecaster (center), a one-off decorated by Hirst and which sold for nearly $50,000. The Fender Sergio Vallin (right) of 2015 was a distinctive creation for the Maná guitarist, with an offset-Strat shape, HSS pickup layout with rotary switching, and push-pull volume knob. This 1999 ad (right) got close to an American Classic Strat.

the company, his era including the crucial management buy-out from CBS in 1985 and the creative struggle through the years immediately following. Sadly, Schultz died in 2006, Smith in 2016.

The US-made Vintage Hot Rod guitars, new for 2007, were based on vintage reissues but with thin-skin lacquer finishes, flatter fingerboards, bigger frets, modern pickups, and custom wiring. The series kicked off with a '52 Tele and '57 and '62 Strats. Road Worn was the Mexico factory's name for its take on the Custom Shop's aged Relic finish, with the line settling down to distressed-finish 50s and 60s Strats, a 50s Tele, and a 60s Jazzmaster.

By 2017, Fender was offering its electric models in ten series: American Elites, launched in 2016, were high-performance guitars boasting the newest of the new; American Professionals replaced American Standards in 2017 as the prime Fender series; American Specials were described as for the workingman on a budget; American Vintages offered a variety of period-style models; Artist models were star-specific signature guitars, including old faithfuls such as the Jeff Beck Stratocaster and James Burton Telecaster alongside newer offerings like the Troy Van Leeuwen Jazzmaster, Chris Shiflett Telecaster, and Johnny Marr Jaguar; Classics were the Mexico versions of vintage-style guitars; Deluxes were upgraded American Standards; Limited Editions were short runs and oddities; Offsets included the Duo-Sonic and

Mustang; and the Standards were the Mexico models first seen in 1991 that offered standard unchanged designs.

Into the 21st century, and the Fender Musical Instruments Corporation is as aware as ever of the value of its (mostly) illustrious heritage. But many musicians, collectors and guitar dealers are inclined to measure the worth of Fender purely in terms of those past achievements – which must be a continuing frustration for a modern company whose new ideas are often resisted for being "un-Fender."

Fender has reached the enviable point today where it dominates the world's electric guitar market. It has achieved its current successes in a variety of ways, not least by trying to provide a model or models that will appeal to every conceivable type of guitar player at every level of skill and affluence.

In 1999, Fender boss Bill Schultz described his firm's outlook in simple business-like terms that still apply today: "Our goal couldn't be more straightforward. Simply put, we're going to be the world's best guitar and guitar-amp company."

The history of Fender and of Fender electric guitars – which continues as you read these words – has been a remarkable mixture of inspiration and invention, of luck and mishap. But the company's best guitars ensure that the Fender name lives on today, and Fender guitars will no doubt help further generations of players turn strings and frets and pickups into remarkable music.

This Limited Edition American Stratocaster (2015, left) was finished in oiled ash, recalling a 1970s vibe. The Standard Telecaster HH (2015, center) gives the traditional Tele layout the extra punch of a pair of humbuckers, while the Kurt Cobain Jaguar (2016, far right) was a new take on the Nirvana guitarist's battered and modded '65 Jag, here in appropriately left-handed form. Fender's Vintage Hot Rod series (2008 ad for the '52 Tele, right) was a Custom Shop line that took classic models and gave them a twist, seen here in the shape of a Seymour Duncan humbucker at the neck. As such, it exemplifies Fender's continuing search for a satisfying mix of the old and the new.

Fernandes adopted the Sustainer system on a number of instruments, promoted in this 1992 ad (left). Among the more esoteric archtop models from Framus was its Attila Zoller model (1963 ad, right).

attila zoller guitar's....

LUFTHANSA

An instrument of unparalleled quality and beauty!

Emerges from an instrument-crafting tradition extending 350 years!

Combines the experience and skill of generations of master instrument makers!

Designed as a result of collaboration between world's greatest guitarists!

Carries the Framus guarantee of perfection and satisfaction!

FENTON-WEILL

Henry Weill's British company made amplifiers, but Jim Burns formed a partnership with Weill in 1959 to make guitars. After Burns's quick departure, Weill continued, adopting the Fenton-Weill brand for Twinmaster, Fibratone, Twister and other models, also making for Dallas, Vox, Hohner and Rose-Morris. The guitars stopped in 1965.

FERNANDES

At home in Japan, Fernandes has long been one of the biggest brands. Guitar megastar Hotei is a Japanese devotee. Fernandes originated in the early 1970s on copies, but a decade later the catalog had expanded to include flattering imitations not just of Gibsons and Fenders but also Alembic, B.C. Rich and others.

Through the 1980s more players noticed Fernandes, praising accuracy, construction and quality. Name endorsers included Frank Dunnery, Brad Gillis, John Mayall, Steve Stevens and Mick Taylor. Despite Fender's legal successes and its own Japanese-made "copies," Fernandes remained busy in the US and Europe, battling with the likes of Tokai for the role of top copyist.

The 1990s brought a retro flavor to Fernandes, and a new feature: the Sustainer. This was a development of an American electro-magnetic sustain device that had appeared in 1987, refined and incorporated into guitars by Hamer and others. Fernandes developed the system. By the late 1990s it offered regular guitar

A Fenton-Weill Triplemaster from 1962 (near right); a Fernandes FR5S (center) with Sustainer, made in 1993 as a special for a trade show; and a Framus Hollywood 5/132 (far right) produced in Germany around 1959.

Framus is among the few makers to offer a nine-string guitar. This Melodie (left) from 1965 has three pairs of two strings, doubled as on a 12-string, alongside three standard singles for the higher-pitched strings.

This Framus Strato Deluxe from 1965 (below right) has the maker's unusual "Organtone" effect, operated by the small bent handle below the bridge. The 1975 ad is for the Framus Jan Akkerman model.

performance plus controllable, never-ending sustain at any volume. The feature was fitted to numerous Fernandes models from the start of the 1990s, with Billy Gibbons a reported convert. The Fernandes line continues to boast a variety of standard, retro-style and superstrat electrics.

F R A M U S

Even though guitars have been made in Germany for centuries, Framus would become one of the most successful German companies during the fabled guitar boom of the 1960s. During that decade, Framus guitars were especially noted for features such as multi-laminated necks and complex electronics.

Frankische Musikindustrie (Framus) had been founded in the Erlangen area of Germany by Fred Wilfer in 1946, at first making only acoustic instruments. However, in 1954 the Framus operation relocated to Bubenreuth, and began adding pickups. Framus soon began making slimline semi-acoustic electric guitars around 1958, the best known being the single-cutaway Billy Lorento hollowbody (for the jazz guitarist later known as Bill Lawrence).

The late 1950s also brought the flat-topped, Les Paul-shaped Hollywood series of semi-solids, which later had single- or double-cutaway styling. They were succeeded in the early 1960s by Strato solidbodies. A great many solids carried this model name, regardless of shape or configuration, and Stratos came with numerous variations of

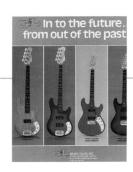

pickups and hardware. By the mid 1960s the shape had changed to a more Fender Jazzmaster-like style, both for solidbody Strato and hollowbody Television models. By 1965, high-end Framus models had an Organtone effect, a spring-loaded volume control with a hook (or "spigot") operated by the little finger. For the exceptionally coordinated player it could simulate an organ swell effect. Better models often had mutes, plus many switches for questionable circuitry tricks.

Double-cutaway thinline hollowbodies offered in the mid 1960s included the Fret Jet and New Sound, both with multiple switches on the upper horn. Exotic examples from this era included the nine-string Melody, and the Electronica with "18 different string outputs" and onboard pre-amp.

Around 1969, Framus collaborated with Bill Lawrence – who was by now a pickup designer – on the BL series of offset-double-cutaway solidbodies with thick waist and chunky upper horn. In the early 1970s Framus also built Fender and Gibson copies, returning to original thinking around 1974 with the Jan Akkerman semi-hollowbody and the broad, solidbody Nashville series.

In 1977 Framus introduced the Memphis, a sort of anthropomorphic wedge-shape solidbody, and several other distinctive models. Framus limped on into the early 1980s before becoming Warwick, a brand more successful with bass guitars. Warwick revived the Framus brandname in 1995 for a line of high-end German-made six-strings.

The G&L ad from 1981 pictured (above, left) shows the first guitar and bass models introduced by the company that Leo Fender started after he'd left Music Man.

This G&L Comanche (main guitar), made in 1989, features Leo Fender's distinctive split-pickup design, echoing the style of the pickups that he devised for the Precision Bass at his original company.

George Harrison (above, behind bassist Stuart Sutcliffe) plays a Neoton Grazioso. The occasion is one of The Beatles' early shows in Hamburg, Germany, probably around 1960. British importer Selmer soon changed the name of the Czech-made Neoton to the easier-sounding Futurama, as seen on this example (right) that dates from about 1960.

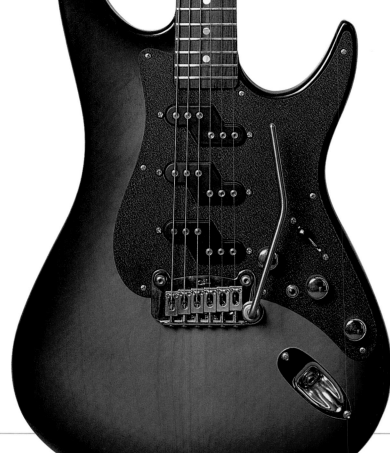

Leo Fender introduced his G&L Broadcaster in 1985 (ad from that year, right) but the Fender company suggested otherwise, and the model was renamed as the ASAT (said by some to stand for "Another Strat, Another Tele," though G&L deny this).

FUTURAMA

These cheap imported guitars for early British would-be rockers were first made by Neoton, which was based in Prague, Czech Republic (then Czechoslovakia). The Fender-style Neoton Grazioso arrived in Britain in 1957, marketed by Selmer. At around £55 ($90) it proved popular with many soon-to-be-famous players such as George Harrison, Albert Lee and Gerry Marsden.

Selmer soon changed the uncommercial Grazioso name to the more evocative Futurama brand. During 1963 Selmer switched sources, using the new brand on guitars made by Hagstrom of Sweden. The Futurama Coronado model represented the best in Futurama quality, but Selmer had dropped the brandname by 1965.

G & L

G&L provided the final vehicle for Leo Fender's ideas on guitar design, continuing the tradition established by one of the industry's most famous names. Leo sold Fender to CBS in 1965. After leaving his Music Man operation, he started G&L in Fullerton, California, in 1979.

The name for the company, G&L, was in fact an abbreviation of "George and Leo," partner George Fullerton having worked with Leo at Fender. George Fullerton sold his interest in the G&L company in 1986. The first guitar model from the new company was the F-100, and this went on to the market during 1980. The two-humbucker

F-100 model displayed several design touches that were unmistakably the work of Leo Fender. G&L then addressed the less expensive end of the market with its first SC series, debuting in 1982 with a body reminiscent of Fender's Mustang. High-end models continued to appear, many being variations on a now-established G&L template. Most striking of the high-end G&Ls was the limited-edition Interceptor which had an unusual X-shaped body.

In 1985 Leo refined his original Telecaster for the G&L Broadcaster. Body shape and control plate were familiar; other aspects remained staunchly G&L. Fender objected, so in 1986 G&L's Broadcaster became the ASAT, which went on to be a popular model.

During the late 1980s all-new rock machines included the Invader, Rampage and Superhawk. The Interceptor was modified with extended body horns and a Kahler vibrato, but in 1988 became a more conventional superstrat. In the same year the Comanche appeared, one of Leo's last designs. Signature versions of some models bore Leo's autograph logo on the body. The limited-edition Commemorative marked Leo's death in March 1991.

In late 1991 G&L was sold to BBE Sound of Huntington Beach, California. A Japan-only Tribute series of Japanese-made G&Ls appeared in 1998, including an ASAT. In the US the Comanche model was revived the same year, reintroducing for this as well as other models Leo's distinctive split-coil pickups, now called Z-coils.

Two more G&L guitars: the classic ASAT (far left, this one made in 1989), and a Cavalier (near left) from 1984. Seattle grunge-man Jerry Cantrell of Alice In Chains is seen playing his decorated G&L Rampage on stage around 1993.

Charlie Christian, the original electric guitarist of jazz, is seen playing a Gibson ES-150 (main picture, in New York 1939, and album sleeve, top of page). This example of the ES-150 (left) dates from 1937. Introduced during the previous year, it was Gibson's first electric guitar (other than an earlier lap-steel model).

Gibson's 1937 catalog features its new
ES-150 electric guitar and associated
amplifier, along with pictures of players
of the 150 and of Gibson's related lap-
steel electrics of the period.

GIBSON

Gibson is one of the greatest and most significant fretted instrument manufacturers, and has been in existence for more than 100 years. Orville H. Gibson was born in 1856 in upstate New York, near the Canadian border. He began making stringed musical instruments in Kalamazoo, Michigan, probably by the 1880s, and set himself up as a manufacturer of musical instruments there around 1894.

Orville Gibson had a refreshingly unconventional mixture of ideas about how to construct his mandolin-family instruments and oval-soundhole guitars. He would hand-carve the tops and backs, but would cut sides from solid wood rather than using the usual heating-and-bending method. Also unusual was the lack of internal bracing, which he thought degraded volume and tone. Gibson would often have his instrument's bodies decorated with beautiful inlaid pickguards and a distinctive crescent-and-star logo on the headstock. The only patent that Orville ever received – which was granted in 1898 – was for his mandolin design that featured the distinctive one-piece carved sides, as well as a similarly one-piece neck.

In 1902 a group of businessmen joined Orville Gibson to form the Gibson Mandolin-Guitar Manufacturing company. The instruments that the new operation produced illustrated the diverse range of fretted stringed instruments available in the United States during the early decades of the 20th century. The mandolin was clearly the most popular, and Gibson would soon find itself among the most celebrated of mandolin makers, thanks in no small part to the enormously influential F-5 model that would appear in 1922. Gibson also instigated a successful teacher-agent system to sell its mandolins. This was in contrast to the normal distribution operated by most instrument companies that would be based on a network of retailers.

Orville had left the Gibson company in 1903, receiving a regular royalty from the company for the following five years and then a monthly income until his death in 1918. A year earlier the company had moved to new premises on Parsons Street, Kalamazoo (which it occupied until 1984).

Once Orville left Gibson, changes began to be made to his original construction methods, apparently for reasons of efficiency, for ease of production and, indeed, for improvement. Orville's sawed solid-wood sides were replaced with conventional heated-and-bent parts, and his inlaid, integral pickguard was replaced around 1908 with a unit elevated from the instrument's surface: the "floating pickguard." It was devised by Gibson man Lewis Williams, and the general design is still in use today by many producers of archtop guitars.

The guitar began to grow in importance during the late 1920s and into the 1930s, largely replacing the previously prominent tenor banjo. It became essential that any company demanding attention among guitarists should be seen as inventive and

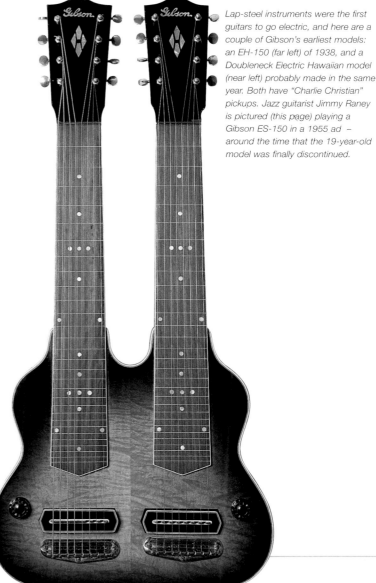

Lap-steel instruments were the first
guitars to go electric, and here are a
couple of Gibson's earliest models:
an EH-150 (far left) of 1938, and a
Doubleneck Electric Hawaiian model
(near left) probably made in the same
year. Both have "Charlie Christian"
pickups. Jazz guitarist Jimmy Raney
is pictured (this page) playing a
Gibson ES-150 in a 1955 ad –
around the time that the 19-year-old
model was finally discontinued.

forward-thinking in this vital new area. Gibson obliged with many six-string innovations, including Ted McHugh's adjustable truss-rod that did an excellent job of strengthening the instrument's neck. Truss-rods are virtually obligatory on today's guitars.

Thanks to the creativity of gifted employees such as Lloyd Loar, Gibson also established individual landmarks like the L-5 guitar of the early 1920s. With its novel f-holes and "floating" pickguard, this model virtually defined the look and sound of the early archtop acoustic guitar. It soon established itself and was played in a variety of musical styles, none more appealing than the "parlor jazz" music epitomized by the incomparable guitarist Eddie Lang.

Lloyd Loar was an experienced musician who had started to work at Gibson in 1919 as a designer, and his best-known achievements were the Master Models series that included that ground-breaking L-5 guitar. Loar left Gibson in 1924 and around 1933 formed a company with ex-Gibson man Lewis Williams, primarily to manufacture electric instruments, which they called Vivi Tone or Acousti-Lectric.

The still barely understood potential of electric instruments fascinated Loar, who had devised an early experimental electric pickup while at Gibson in the 1920s. But Loar and Williams's offerings appear to have been too radical and ahead of their time to make any commercial impact, and within a few years of its inception their company had closed. Loar died in the early 1940s at the age of 57.

The ES-300 (1941 example, near right) was Gibson's most expensive pre-war electric guitar. This ES-350 (far right) was made in 1952, still with an old-style control layout. The ad (above) for the new ES-5 model was published in 1950.

Two more Gibson-wielding jazzmen, both of whom usually favored ES-175 models: Kenny Burrell, in a 1956 ad (near left), and Herb Ellis, seen in an ad from 1957 (far left).

As players demanded more volume from their guitars, Gibson dutifully increased the size of its acoustic instruments, introducing the superb, huge archtop Super 400 model in 1934. Later in the decade came Gibson's "jumbo" J-series flat-tops. It was around this time that Gibson introduced its first electric guitars, the Electric Hawaiian E-150 cast aluminum steel guitar in 1935, and the following year the EH-150 steel plus an f-hole hollowbody, the ES-150, Gibson's first archtop electric.

The non-cutaway ES-150 electric guitar was a very significant addition to the catalog for Gibson. It effectively marked the start of the company's long-running ES series – the initial letters standing for "Electric Spanish." It's worth noting that, in this context, the term "Spanish" of course had nothing at all to do with nylon-string round-soundhole guitars. Instead, it was being used to distinguish this type of guitar from its Hawaiian-style cousin, the one generally played on the lap.

The ES-150 was famously taken up by Charlie Christian, the genius who showed jazz players what an electric guitar was for. Playing clear, single-note runs as if he were a horn player, Christian virtually invented the idea of the electric guitar solo. The "bar" pickup of the earliest ES-150 models, which was designed by Walt Fuller at Gibson, has subsequently become known as the "Charlie Christian" pickup as the guitarist was by far its best-known user, even though Christian's career was cut tragically short by his early death in 1942 at the age of just 25. Gibson tentatively built on these low-key

electric experiments, adding the budget ES-100 archtop in 1938, and following this with its most expensive pre-war electric model, the ES-300, in 1940. When America entered the war two years later Gibson effectively put a halt to its guitar production. As instrument manufacturing gradually recommenced afterwards, Gibson rightly concluded that the electric guitar was set to become an important part of its reactivated business.

Around this time Gibson also manufactured instruments with a number of brandnames in addition to the most famous one. A good deal of the instruments bearing these names were acoustics, but electrics did appear with the following brands: Capital (made for Jenkins mail-order); Cromwell (for a variety of mail-order houses); Kalamazoo (a low-end in-house brand); Old Kraftsman (made for Spiegel mail-order); and Recording King (for Montgomery-Ward mail-order).

A controlling interest in Gibson was purchased in 1944 by the Chicago Musical Instrument Company (CMI), founded some 25 years earlier in Chicago, Illinois, by Maurice Berlin. Gibson's manufacturing base remained at its original factory, purpose-built in 1917 at Kalamazoo, which was roughly equidistant between Detroit and Chicago. The latter city was the location for Gibson's new sales and administration headquarters at CMI. It was at this time that Gibson began to pioneer electric guitars with cutaways. A cutaway offered easier access to the now audible and musically

Gibson's ES-175 that debuted in 1949 (this example, far left, was made in 1953) has proved popular with jazzmen, including Jim Hall (pictured). Another new model for 1949 was the three-pickup ES-5: this attractive natural-finish model (near left) was made in 1952.

GIBSON

Steve Howe, long-standing guitarist in Yes (1971 album, right), has a large guitar collection, but among his firm favorites is this ES-175D (below) that dates from 1964. Like many active players, Howe regularly modifies his instruments to enhance playability and to suit personal taste.

Wes Montgomery, among the greatest of jazz guitarists, is seen on this 1973 magazine cover with a Gibson L-5CES. Montgomery sometimes played custom-made single-pickup versions of this model.

useful area of the upper fingerboard, previously of little use to quiet acoustic players who tended to limit their fret-based ramblings primarily to the headstock end of the neck. Talented and imaginative guitarists openly welcomed the artistic potential of the cutaway... and began to investigate the dusty end of the fingerboard.

Significant new archtop electric guitars debuted in the late 1940s. The ES-350 of 1947 and two years later the ES-5 and sharp-cutaway ES-175 were all aimed at players who were prepared to commit themselves to fully integrated electric instruments designed and built as such by Gibson.

Gibson's ES-350 of 1947 was the first of the company's new-style cutaway electrics (and at first it bore the "Premier" tag of the pre-war cutaway acoustics). The 350 was followed in 1949 by the new single-pickup ES-175, Gibson's first electric with a "pointed" cutaway style and a pressed, laminated top. This construction contributed a distinctively bright, cutting tone color to the 175. A two-pickup version, the ES-175D, was added in 1953.

The ES-175 became a popular instrument and was Gibson's first really successful electric guitar. It has made a particular impact among electric jazz musicians, including such luminaries as Joe Pass, while also attracting eclectic modern players like Steve Howe and Pat Metheny.

The ES-5 also debuted in 1949 and was the first electric guitar with three pickups – it was effectively a three-pickup ES-350. However, before long, players found that it was less controllable than they wanted. As with all Gibson's immediate post-war electric guitars, the ES-5 had no pickup switching. Instead, each pickup had a separate volume control, which meant that the only way to achieve a balance between the pickups was to set the three volume knobs at relative positions.

So it was that in 1956 Gibson issued the ES-5 model with redesigned electronics, this time with a new name: the ES-5 Switchmaster. Three individual tone knobs were added alongside the three volume controls, and near the cutaway a four-way pickup selector switch was added, hence the new model name. The switch, explained a Gibson catalog of the time, "activates each of the three pickups separately, a combination of any two, or all three simultaneously."

At a time when Fender had just launched its stylish three-pickup Stratocaster, and Epiphone was offering models with a six-button "color tone" switching system, Gibson probably felt the ES-5 Switchmaster was a potential market leader. But it never caught on. And anyway, by now Gibson had produced proper electric versions of its great archtop acoustics, the L-5 and the Super 400.

In 1951 Gibson became serious about the electric guitar, launching the Super 400CES and the L-5CES (the initials stand for Cutaway, Electric, Spanish). For the 400CES, Gibson built on its existing Super 400C acoustic model, and for the L-5CES

Gibson's two new high-end electric archtops, first issued in 1951: the Super 400CES (1953 example, far left) and the L-5CES (1951 example, near left). The letters stand for Cutaway Electric Spanish. Elvis Presley's guitarist Scotty Moore was an early fan of the Super 400CES. Moore is seen with the Gibson in this 1956 photograph (far left) that he sent to amplifier-maker Ray Butts to illustrate his handiwork in action.

Gibson's first solidbody electric guitar was the Les Paul Model of 1952, endorsed by the popular guitarist in this launch-year ad (center). The striking pair of gold-top instruments on this page – a regular right-hand model and a special-order left-hand version – also date from the Les Paul's debut year of 1952.

Gibson
Les Paul model

It's a Sensation!

Designed by Les Paul—produced by Gibson—and enthusiastically approved by top guitarists everywhere. The Les Paul Model is a unique and exciting innovation in the fretted instrument field; you have to see and hear it to appreciate the wonderful features and unusual tone of this newest Gibson guitar. Write Dept. 101 for more information about it.

Gibson, Inc., Kalamazoo, Mich.

Gibson boss Ted McCarty holds a custom-made gold-finished hollowbody guitar (above, right) that provided the inspiration for the company's gold-top Les Paul model and all-gold ES-295.

An ES-295 (main guitar) made in 1952, the model's first year of production. This was in effect a gold-finished version of the ES-175D.

combined elements of its acoustic L-5C and electric ES-5 guitars. The new electric models had modified and stronger internal "bracing" to make them less prone to feedback when amplified.

The generally large proportions of the 18″-wide acoustic bodies of the earlier models were retained for these impressive new electrics in the Gibson line. For the 400CES model, the acoustic 400's high-end appointments remained – such as split-block-shape fingerboard inlays, a "marbleized" tortoiseshell pickguard, and a fancy "split-diamond" headstock inlay.

At first the electric 400 and L-5 came with a pair of Gibson's standard single-coil P-90 pickups, but in 1954 changed to more powerful "Alnico" types with distinctive rectangular polepieces. The Alnico nickname comes from the magnet type used in these pickups. A "rounded"-cutaway body style lasted from the launch of the two electrics in 1951 until 1960, when a new "pointed" cutaway was introduced. Gibson reverted to the original rounded design in 1969.

An immense variety of players has at different times been drawn to the power and versatility of Gibson's two leading archtop electrics. The Super 400CES has attracted bluesman Robben Ford, country players like Hank Thompson and Merle Travis (whose custom 400 was described in 1952 as Gibson's "most expensive guitar ever"), rock'n'roller Scotty Moore, and a number of fine jazz guitarists including George

Following on from the original gold-top Les Paul model came the high-end black-finish Les Paul Custom. This example (left) dates from the first year it was made, 1954. Bill Haley & His Comets did much to popularize rock'n'roll in its early years, and Haley's guitarist Frank Beecher is seen in this 1957 Gibson ad (below) with his favored Les Paul Custom. Haley himself is playing an acoustic Gibson Super 400C.

ANOTHER POPULAR GUITARIST IN THE...

Gibson GALLERY OF STARS

JUST AS UP AND COMING GUITARISTS THROUGHOUT THE COUNTRY CHOOSE GIBSON FOR THEIR GUITAR SO DOES POPULAR BILL HALEY WHO RECOMMENDS THAT YOU SEE THE MAGNIFICENT GIBSON LINE AT YOUR LOCAL DEALER.

BILL HALEY
and his Comets

Gibson , INC., KALAMAZOO, MICH.

113

Benson and Kenny Burrell. The L-5CES has also had its fans and adherents over the subsequent years, including jazzmen such as Wes Montgomery and John Collins, as well as the fine country-jazzer Hank Garland.

Ted McCarty had joined Gibson back in March 1948, having worked at the Wurlitzer organ company for the previous 12 years. In 1950 he was made president of Gibson. Gibson was finding it hard in the post-war years to get back into full-scale guitar production, and McCarty's first managerial tasks were to increase the effectiveness of supervision, to bolster efficiency, and to improve internal communication.

Gibson began to work on a solidbody design soon after Fender's original Telecaster-style model had appeared in 1950. McCarty had a good team working on the project, including production head John Huis, as well as employees Julius Bellson and Wilbur Marker, while the sales people were regularly consulted through manager Clarence Havenga. It took them all about a year to come up with satisfactory prototypes for a new Gibson solidbody – at which point McCarty began to think about guitarist Les Paul, who was just about the most famous guitar player in America.

In the 1940s Les Paul had been a member of the supergroup Jazz At The Philharmonic, and had played prominent guitar on Bing Crosby's hit 'It's Been A Long Long Time.' Crosby encouraged Paul to build a studio into the garage of the guitarist's home in Hollywood, California, and it was here that he hit upon his effective "multiple"

recording techniques. These early overdubbing routines allowed Paul to create huge, magical orchestras of massed guitars, arranged by the guitarist to play catchy instrumental tunes. Les Paul and his New Sound was signed to Capitol Records, with the first release 'Lover' a hit in 1948.

Paul found even greater popularity when he added vocalist Mary Ford to the act. They had married in 1949, and the following year the duo released their first joint record. Guitars and now voices too were given the multiple recording treatment, and big hits followed for Les Paul & Mary Ford including 'The Tennessee Waltz' (1950) and 'How High The Moon' (1951). The duo performed hundreds of personal appearances and concerts, and were heard on NBC Radio's *Les Paul Show* every week for six months during 1949 and 1950. Their networked TV series *The Les Paul & Mary Ford Show* began in 1953, beamed from their extravagant new home in Mahwah, New Jersey. As the 1950s got underway, Les Paul & Mary Ford – "America's Musical Sweethearts" – were huge stars.

Les Paul's obsessive tinkering with gadgetry was not restricted to the recording studio. The teenage Lester, drawn to the guitar, had soon become interested in the idea of amplification. In the late 1930s his new jazz-based trio was broadcasting out of New York on the Fred Waring radio show, with Paul at first playing a Gibson L-5 archtop acoustic, and later a similar Epiphone. The guitarist exercised his curiosity for electric

Gibson added more Les Paul models to its line, including relatively low-end models such as the single-pickup Junior (near right, 1956 example) and two-pickup Special (center, 1955 example), both with uncarved "slab" body and simple appointments. The Byrdland (1957 example, far right) was among Gibson's first "thinline" electric archtops, with a more comfortable, less deep body.

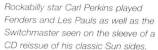

Rockabilly star Carl Perkins played Fenders and Les Pauls as well as the Switchmaster seen on the sleeve of a CD reissue of his classic Sun sides.

Another of Gibson's new thinline models was the ES-350T (main guitar). This fine natural-finish example was produced during 1957.

Rock'n'roller Chuck Berry favored Gibson's ES-350T, and is seen (below) taking the instrument on one of his classic on-stage "duck walks."

instruments and his flair for technical experimentation by adapting and modifying the Epiphone guitar.

Around 1940, Les Paul used to go at weekends into the empty Epiphone factory in New York in order to fiddle with what he would call his "log" guitar. The nickname was derived from the 4″ by 4″ solid block of pine which the guitarist had inserted between the sawed halves of the body that he'd just dismembered. He then carefully re-joined the neck to the pine log, using some metal brackets, and mounted on the top a couple of crude pickups he'd made for himself.

Later he modified a second and third Epiphone, which he called his "clunkers," this time chopping up the bodies to add metal strengthening braces, and again topped off with Paul's own pickups. Despite their makeshift origins, the semi-solid "log" and the modified "clunker" Epiphones often accompanied Les Paul and Mary Ford on stage and in recording studios throughout the 1940s and into the early 1950s.

Paul was not alone in his investigations. Several unconnected explorations into the possibility of a solidbody electric guitar were being undertaken elsewhere in America at this time, not least at the California workshops of Rickenbacker, National, Bigsby and Fender. A solidbody electric was appealing because it would dispose of the involved construction of an acoustic guitar, and instead use a body or section of the body made of solid wood (or some other rigid material) to support the strings and pickups. Also, it

The ES-5 was redesigned in 1955 with a new pickup selector switch for easier operation, and renamed the ES-5 Switchmaster. This example with its exquisitely flamed maple top was made in 1957.

would curtail the annoying feedback produced by amplified acoustic guitars, and reduce the body's interference with the guitar's overall tone, thus more accurately reproducing and sustaining the sound of the strings.

During the 1940s, Paul had decided that he would take his "log" idea to a major guitar manufacturing company in order to try to generate some real interest in its commercial potential. He decided – accurately, as it turned out – that Epiphone would not continue in its present form as a strong force in the guitar world. So around 1946 Paul took his crude log guitar to Gibson's parent company, CMI in Chicago, with the intention of convincing them to market such a semi-solid guitar. No doubt with all the courtesy that a pressurized city businessman could muster, the boss of CMI showed Les Paul the door. A startled Paul recalls that they laughed at his guitar, dismissing him as "the guy with the broomstick."

But some years later, as we've seen, Gibson was developing ideas for a solidbody electric guitar in the wake of Fender's new instrument, and Gibson president Ted McCarty decided to contact the now hugely popular Les Paul. A meeting took place, probably in 1951. McCarty's intention was to interest Paul in publicly playing Gibson's newly designed guitar in return for a royalty on sales – an arrangement generally referred to now as an "endorsement" deal. It was certainly not a new arrangement for Gibson: the company's Nick Lucas flat-top acoustic model of 1928 had exploited the

During 1957 Gibson began to fit its new humbucking pickups to the instruments in its electric lines. This ES-5 Switchmaster (1961 example, near right) has three humbuckers, and also features the new "sharp" cutaway that Gibson began applying to its archtop electrics from 1960. The Les Paul Custom turned into a three-pickup instrument when it was switched to the new humbuckers, as this example made in 1957 (main guitar, far right) illustrates.

Robert Fripp (pictured below) regularly played an original three-humbucker Les Paul Custom from his early days in the first King Crimson (1969 album sleeve, left).

popularity of Lucas, known as "the crooning troubadour," to produce the contemporary guitar industry's first "signature" instrument.

Gibson's meeting with Les Paul around 1951 was the first opportunity the guitarist had to see the prototype of what would soon become the Gibson Les Paul solidbody electric. A deal was struck: Paul's royalty on Les Paul models would be five per cent, and the term of the contract was set at five years. Paul's respected playing and commercial success added to Gibson's weighty experience in manufacturing and marketing guitars made for a strong and impressive combination.

The new Les Paul guitar was launched by Gibson in 1952, probably in the spring of that year, and was priced at $210 (this being around $20 more than Fender's Telecaster). Today, this first style of Les Paul model is nearly always called the "gold-top" because of its distinctive gold-finished body face. The gold-top's solid body cleverly combined a carved maple top bonded to a mahogany "back," uniting the darker tonality of mahogany with the brighter sound of maple.

Gibson had made a one-off all-gold hollowbody guitar in 1951 for Paul to present to a terminally ill patient whom he had met when making a special hospital appearance. This presentation guitar presumably prompted the all-gold archtop electric ES-295 model of 1952 (effectively a gold-finished ES-175) and was probably the inspiration for the color of the first Les Paul model. Almost all the other design elements

Gibson's new humbucking pickups were developed at the company's headquarters in Kalamazoo, Michigan, as illustrated in this 1950s catalog (above). The Les Paul gold-top received humbuckers in place of its original P-90 pickups during 1957, the year in which this example (below left) was made. The left-handed gold-top (main guitar) was also made in 1957, and is owned today by Paul McCartney. Gold-tops continue to be popular, as seen in this hectic Neil Young/Pearl Jam gathering (below).

Scotty Moore used mainly Gibson guitars – including a Super 400CES and an ES-295 – to drive the sound of Elvis Presley's great Sun records.

of the first Gibson Les Paul have precedents in earlier Gibson models. For example, the instrument's layout of two P-90 single-coil pickups and four controls (which comprised a volume and tone pair for each pickup) was already a feature of Gibson's CES electric archtops that had been launched the previous year.

The general body outline and glued-in mahogany neck also followed established Gibson traditions, and the "crown"-shape inlays on the rosewood fingerboard had first appeared on the 1950 incarnation of the ES-150 model. Several Gibson acoustics had already appeared with the same scale-length as the new Les Paul.

The model came with a new height-adjustable combined bridge/tailpiece which was bar-shaped, joined to long metal rods that anchored it to the bottom edge of the guitar. This was designed by Les Paul, intended for use on archtop guitars (and Gibson also sold it as a separate replacement accessory). It proved unsuitable for the new solidbody, and was quickly replaced by a new purpose-built "stud" bar-shaped bridge/tailpiece, phased in around 1953. This was mounted to the top of the body with twin height-adjustable studs, hence the nickname.

The original gold-top sold well at first in relation to Gibson's other models. Electric guitars were clearly catching on. In 1954 Gibson's historian Julius Bellson charted the progress of the company's electric instruments. Consulting records, Bellson estimated that back in 1938 electric guitars had made up no more than ten per cent of Gibson

guitar sales, but that the proportion of electrics to the rest had risen to 15 per cent by 1940, to 50 per cent by 1951, and that by 1953 electric guitars constituted no less than 65 per cent of the company's total guitar sales.

In a move designed to widen the market still further for solidbody electrics, Gibson issued two more Les Paul models in 1954, the Junior and the Custom. The cheaper Junior was designed for and aimed at beginners, although over time it has proved itself well enough suited to straightforward pro use.

Although the outline of the Junior's body was clearly Les Paul-like, the most obvious difference to its partners was the flat-top "slab" mahogany body, finished in traditional Gibson sunburst. It did not pretend to be anything other than a cheaper guitar: it had a single P-90 pickup, simple volume and tone controls, and the unbound rosewood fingerboard bore plain dot-shape position markers. It featured the stud bridge/tailpiece as used on the second incarnation of the gold-top.

By contrast, the high-end two-pickup Custom looked luxurious. It came with an all-black finish, multiple binding, block-shape position markers in an ebony fingerboard, and gold-plated hardware. It was, naturally, more expensive than the gold-top.

The Custom had an all-mahogany body, as favored by Les Paul himself, rather than the maple/mahogany mix of the gold-top model, and this gave the new guitar a rather more mellow tone. The Custom was promoted in Gibson catalogs as "The Fretless

Existing Gibson electrics began to be fitted with humbucking pickups from 1957, including the Byrdland (1959 example, far left) and Super 400CES (1962 example, near left). The 400 also shows the "sharp" cutaway introduced in 1960, a contrast to the earlier "rounded" cutaway as seen on Scotty Moore's 400 (above).

Jimmy Page of Led Zeppelin (albums from 1969, far left, and 1971) plays one of his Les Paul Standards on-stage (below) in the 1970s.

Wonder" thanks to its use of very low, flat fretwire, different than the wire used on other Les Pauls at the time. It was the first Les Paul model to feature Gibson's new Tune-o-matic bridge, used with a separate bar-shaped tailpiece and offering for the first time on Gibsons the opportunity to adjust individually the length of each string, thus improving intonation (tuning accuracy). These new units were gradually added to other models in the Gibson line.

In 1955 Gibson launched the Les Paul TV model, essentially a Junior in what Gibson referred to as "natural" finish – actually more of a murky beige. Also that year the original line-up of Les Paul models was completed with the addition of the Special, effectively a two-pickup version of the Junior finished in the TV's beige color (but not called a TV model).

A number of well-known players from a variety of musical styles were drawn to Gibson Les Paul models during the 1950s. These musicians included rock'n'roller Frannie Beecher, bluesmen such as Guitar Slim, Freddy King and John Lee Hooker, as well as rockabilly rebel Carl Perkins.

Gibson launched three hollowbody electrics during 1955 in a new "thinline" thinner-body style, aiming to provide instruments more comfortable than their existing deep-bodied archtop cutaway electrics which were generally around 3.5″ deep. The ES-225T, the ES-350T and the Byrdland had shallower bodies, around 2″ deep, and the

During his time with Led Zeppelin, Jimmy Page mainly used these two Les Paul Standards. His "number one" (main guitar) is probably a 1958 model, while "number two" (far left), a gift from Joe Walsh, is from 1959. Both have replaced tuners. Gibson issued a Page signature model Les Paul in 1995 (ad, above). Original 1950s Les Pauls tend to have a strip of binding in the cutaway that follows the contour of the body (below, top picture) while some Les Pauls made after that period have a deeper strip of binding (below, lower picture) that continues down to the line where the guitar's maple cap meets its mahogany "back."

latter two also boasted a shorter scale-length and a shorter, narrower neck, all designed for an easier, more playable feel. Top of the new line was the Byrdland, a kind of thinline L-5CES. It was inspired by country guitarist Billy Byrd and sessionman Hank Garland, hence the combined model name.

An important player who grasped the possibilities of these new friendlier electrics from Gibson was Chuck Berry, the most influential rock'n'roll guitarist of the 1950s. Berry chose a brand new natural-finish ES-350T to fuel his startlingly fresh hybrid of boogie, country and blues. In hindsight, it's remarkable that this great player did not appear in any Gibson advertising at the time – but then nor did any other black guitarists of the period.

Jazz players still kept Gibson's name prominent in the archtop electric field. Of the guitarists in the poll for the prestigious US jazz magazine *Down Beat* in 1956, Gibson could count six of the top ten as being loyal to the company: Barney Kessel (most often seen with an ES-350); Tal Farlow (also principally a 350 man); Les Paul (no prizes for guessing his six-string choice); Herb Ellis; Jimmy Raney; and Jim Hall (the last three all favoring Gibson ES-175s).

New humbucking pickups were developed by Seth Lover in the Gibson workshops. The idea was to cut down the hum and electrical interference that plagued standard single-coil pickups, Gibson's ubiquitous P-90 unit included. Lover contemplated the

Eric Clapton teamed his 1950s Les Paul Standard with a 50-watt Marshall combo for some startling work on John Mayall's 1966 album, Blues Breakers (sleeve, above), often referred to now as the peak of recorded white blues.

Keith Richards had been one of the first British guitarists to bag a Standard, having returned to Britain with one after The Rolling Stones' summer 1964 US tour. He's pictured (below left) searching for a pick with which to attack his Les Paul.

This trio of rare and desirable Les Paul Standards illustrates the variety of visual effects brought about by the original wood used by Gibson in their production, and the way in which the paints used in the finish can change over time. This 1958 Standard (opposite) has a virtually plain, unfigured maple top, but with most of the original sunbursting color intact. This spectacular 1959 example (near right) is the kind that collectors dream about. The maple is highly figured, and the sunburst colors are rich and clear. The 1960 Standard shown (far right) is of a type called an "unburst" by some collectors. It has some attractive figuring in the timber used for the top, but the sunburst colors have all but faded away, leaving behind a uniform honey color. However, beyond all considerations of aesthetics and appearance, many of them sound superb.

The close-up of this Standard with pickguard removed (below) reveals how the fading of sunburst colors is due to exposure to light. Where the finish has been protected under the pickguard, traces of the red paint remain. One imagines that Eric Clapton (pictured left) had little concern for the color of his Les Paul, though the supplier of the jacket might have argued otherwise.

GIBSON

Peter Green was in the original line-up of Fleetwood Mac (albums from 1968 and 1969, right) and did much to define the potential of the Gibson Les Paul Standard in the hands of a great guitar player.

Pictured on-stage with Fleetwood Mac in the late 1960s is Peter Green (above). The 1959 Les Paul Standard that he played with the group (main guitar) was later owned by guitarist Gary Moore. The neck pickup was famously reversed by Green and is said to aid the instrument's particular tone. Moore has, wisely, never had this modification "corrected."

During his brief but notable career, Paul Kossoff used a number of Les Paul guitars. One of his favorites was this battered Standard (main guitar, made around 1959), used by the guitarist while a member of Free.

Paul Kossoff plays the pictured Les Paul Standard on-stage (below right) with Free, around 1970. One of the band's finest singles was 'Wishing Well' (reissue sleeve, top of page).

humbucking "choke coil" found in some Gibson amplifiers, installed to eliminate the hum dispensed by their power transformers.

From those beginnings, Lover extrapolated a pickup design that employed two coils wired together electrically "out of phase" and with opposite magnetic polarities. The result was less prone to picking up extraneous noise, in the process giving a fatter, thicker tone than single-coil types. Ray Butts came up with a similar principle around the same time while working for Gretsch.

During 1957 Gibson started to fit its electric guitars with the new humbuckers. The Les Paul Custom was promoted to a three-pickup guitar in its new humbucker-equipped guise. Today many guitarists and collectors make a point of seeking out the earliest type of Gibson humbucking pickup, which is now known as a "PAF" because of the small "patent applied for" label that is attached to the underside. The PAF labels appear on pickups on Gibson guitars dated up to 1962 (even though the patent had been granted in 1959). Some who prefer the sound of PAF-label humbuckers say that later humbuckers sound different because of small changes made to coil-winding, magnet grades and wire-sheathing.

Gibson purchased the old Epiphone brand of New York in 1957, relocating the operation to its base at Kalamazoo, Michigan. The following year Gibson released the first of its new Epiphones, effectively creating for itself a second-tier line. Some of

these "new" guitars continued existing Epiphone models, but others were new Epiphone equivalents of Gibson models – for example the Casino, very similar to a Gibson ES330 (but with an Epiphone logo, of course).

In fact, 1958 proved to be one of the most significant years in Gibson's entire history. During that heady 12 months the company issued the radical new Explorer and Flying V solidbodies, changed the finish of its Les Paul model to a gorgeous sunburst, introduced the brand new semi-solid ES-335 and ES-355 guitars, changed the body outlines of the Les Paul Junior and Les Paul Special to a useful double-cutaway shape, and brought out its first double-neck electric guitars. All these various designs would to a greater or lesser extent become classics over the coming years, and today some of them qualify as the most revered electric guitars ever made.

The Gibson Modernistic series of guitars was first seen in public during 1958. Fender's flamboyant designs such as the Stratocaster and the new-that-year Jazzmaster had been leaving Gibson's rather staid electric models behind as rock'n'roll burst forth. Guitar makers became increasingly aware that, beyond the usual considerations of quality and playability, there was an immense and largely untapped value in sheer visual appeal.

So the designers at Gibson temporarily set aside their customary preoccupation with curvaceously elegant forms to come up with the boldly adventurous Flying V and

Another collector's-dream Les Paul Standard (main guitar), this one made during 1960.

A few Standards were fitted with Bigsby vibratos, like this 1959 example (below left), pictured alongside some Gibson hang-tags of the period.

Another remarkable instrument from Paul McCartney's working collection, this left-handed Les Paul Standard was made in 1960.

Paul McCartney is seen in the photo (below) holding the pictured guitar during the late 1980s.

Explorer. Here was a pair of stark, linear creations. The body of the Flying V had an angular, pointed, arrow-head shape, while that of the Explorer was an uncompromising study in offset rectangles.

Most Explorers have a long, drooping headstock with the tuners in a line on one side – a design that would later inspire the superstrat's "pointy" headstock of the 1980s. But a small number of early Explorers (sometimes referred to as Futura models) had an unusual V-shaped head.

Both Flying V and Explorer were made from Korina, which was a timber tradename for an African relative of mahogany, sometimes known as limba. Gibson used a different control layout on the V and Explorer than the one they generally employed on two-humbucker electrics: on the Modernistics, the player was offered a volume knob per pickup but just one overall tone control.

"An asset to the combo musician with a flair for showmanship," insisted Gibson's 1950s publicity for the new Modernistic pair. The company urged its dealers: "Try one of these 'new look' instruments – either is a sure-fire hit with guitarists of today!" But customers ignored the designs as too futuristic, too un-Gibson and too un-guitar. One story has a number of the new oddball Gibsons reduced to hanging as signs outside guitar shops: if you can't sell them, flaunt them.

The small numbers produced would turn the Modernistics into future collectables

of the rarest kind. In fact, only 98 of the original Flying V were made, with a further 20 or so assembled in the early 1960s from existing parts.

Gibson's factory records for the original Explorer are not so clear, but the best estimates among collectors and other experts put production at just 22 instruments, with a further 16 assembled later. A good number of reissues and redesigns of both the Flying V and Explorer has followed, especially during their bouts of popularity with metal guitarists and others in subsequent decades.

Among players drawn to the Flying V in its various guises were Albert King in the 1950s, Jimi Hendrix in the 1960s, Marc Bolan and Andy Powell in the 1970s, Mick Mars and Michael Schenker in the 1980s, and Jim Martin and Tim Wheeler in the 1990s. Perhaps more importantly (or disgracefully, depending on your viewpoint) this late-flowering popularity of Gibson's Modernistic duo of Flying V and Explorer has been the trigger for any number of outlandishly shaped solidbody guitars, especially during the late 1970s and 1980s.

A third guitar in the original 1958 Modernistic series, the Moderne, was planned but never actually reached general production or distribution, even though a patent for the design was filed in summer 1957 along with similar documents claiming the Flying V and Explorer designs. No prototype or other incarnation of the original Moderne has ever turned up, despite much searching by desperate collectors. Some keen Gibson

The Modernistic series launched by Gibson in 1958 included guitars with radical body shapes. This prototype Flying V (far left) was produced – probably in 1957 – so that Gibson's case manufacturer could design a special fitted case for the unusual guitar. Even models from the Flying V's first production run are rare, such as this 1959 example (main guitar). Despite the lack of popularity at the time, Flying Vs have attracted a number of players since, including Tim Wheeler of Ash, pictured (above) with a recently reissued model.

fans have even described this virtually fictional guitar as the company's "holy grail." If a Moderne should ever surface, it would surely be the ultimate collectable Gibson instrument. It might even prove to be the first million-dollar guitar.

Also in 1958, Gibson made a radical design-change to three of the Les Paul models, as well as a cosmetic alteration to another that would later take on enormous importance. The single-pickup Les Paul Junior and TV models were revamped with a completely new double-cutaway body shape, apparently as a reaction to players' requests for more access to the top frets than the previous single-cutaway design allowed. The new cutaways did the trick. The Junior's fresh look was enhanced with a new cherry red finish. The TV adopted the new double-cutaway design as well, along with a rather more yellow-tinged finish.

When the double-cutaway design was applied to the two-pickup Les Paul Special during the following year, the construction was not an immediate success. Gibson had overlooked the fact that the cavity for the neck pickup in the Special's new body severely weakened the neck-to-body joint. In fact, the neck could potentially snap off at this point. The error was soon corrected when Gibson's designers moved the neck pickup further down the body, resulting in a stronger joint. The new double-cutaway Special was offered in cherry or the new TV yellow (although the yellow Special was never actually called a TV model).

Sales of Gibson's Les Paul gold-top had gradually declined during the late 1950s, and so in a bid to improve sales in 1958 Gibson changed the look by applying its more traditional cherry sunburst finish. This sunburst Les Paul is generally known as the Les Paul Standard, although Gibson did not refer to it as such in their literature until 1960, and the guitar itself never bore the name.

Gibson must have deduced that the unusual gold finish of the original Les Paul model was considered too unconventional. To some extent they were proved right. Sales of the gold-top had declined from a high of 920 in 1956 to just 434 in 1958, the year of the new Standard. After the sunburst model appeared, sales then climbed to 643 in 1959. But when they dipped again in 1960, Gibson decided that this change of finish had not been enough, and that the only way to attract new customers was to completely redesign the Les Paul.

So the sunburst Standard was dropped, having existed for a little short of three years. Here again was one of Gibson's sleeping giants: almost ignored at the time, this instrument would become an ultra-collectable object in later years. Players and collectors came to realize that the guitar's inherent musicality, as well as its short production run (some 1,700 examples were made between 1958 and 1960), added up to a modern classic. This re-evaluation was prompted originally in the middle and late 1960s when a number of guitarists discovered that the Gibson Les Paul had

The other Gibson Modernistic guitar launched in 1958 was the Explorer. This first-year example (far left) has the rare early "split" headstock. This was soon changed to a "drooped" style, as seen on the Explorer (near left) made in the early 1960s from leftover parts, and with nickel-plated rather than gold-plated hardware. Eric Clapton is pictured in a 1975 Music Man amps ad playing an original Explorer, as heard briefly on the 1975 album EC Was Here.

ERIC CLAPTON in concert

enormous potential for high-volume blues-based rock. It turned out that the Les Paul's inherent tonality coupled with its humbucking pickups – played through a loud tube amp – made a wonderful noise.

Of course, this newly discovered sonic potential of the Les Paul was something that neither Gibson nor Les Paul could possibly have planned. Leading early members of the Loud Les Appreciation Society were Mike Bloomfield in America and Eric Clapton in England. Demand for the old instruments rocketed. (As we shall see, Gibson would reintroduce original-design Les Pauls in 1968.)

The original sunburst Gibson Les Paul Standard – the "burst" in guitar-speak – has since achieved almost mythological status. The revised model appeared on Gibson's November 1959 pricelist, where it was shown to have a retail cost of $280. That's equivalent to about $3,500 at today's prices, but even this is far short of the five-figure sums that genuine originals now fetch on the active collector's market. Oddly, however, the value of these instruments is not only determined by their sound or playability or rarity – but often by their individual look.

Gold-top Les Pauls mostly had maple tops made from two or more pieces of wood, safely hidden under the gold paint. Now that this maple top was on show through the transparent sunburst finish of the Standard, Gibson's woodworkers were more careful in selecting wood of good appearance, and would usually bookmatch the timber. This

More great Gibsons were first offered during 1958. The semi-solid ES-335 (1959 example, with vibrato, near right) had the thinline body style, detailed in this 1960 catalog page (above). The company's first electric double-necks were the EDS-1275 Double 12 six-string/12-string (1960 example, far right) and EDS-1235 Double Mandolin.

There have been many notable users of Gibson 300-series semi-solids through the years, including blues-boom guitarist Alvin Lee of Ten Years After, and Suede fretman Bernard Butler, who left the group to go solo later in the 1990s.

is where a piece of wood is sliced into two, then matched together like an open book, the pieces opened out down a central join to give symmetrically similar patterns.

The most celebrated "bursts" are those that display through the top's finish the most outrageous wood pattern. This is often called "flame," but more correctly "figure." Figure is caused by a kind of genetic anomaly in the growing tree that makes ripples in the cells of the living wood. The visual effect of figure is also determined by the situation of the original tree, and the way in which the timber is cut from it. Quarter-sawing – cutting so that the grain is generally square to the face of the resulting pieces – usually produces the most attractive results. The illusion can exist of roughly parallel rows of three-dimensional "fingers" or "hills and valleys" going across the face of the timber. In extreme cases this can look spectacular.

Another factor that can make sunburst Standard models look quite different from one another is color-fading. The colored paints used to create the sunburst effect, especially the red element, can fade in varying ways over time, depending primarily on how the guitar has been exposed to daylight during its lifetime. Some apparently sharp-eyed collectors claim to be able to tell exactly how long a particular guitar spent in the shop window. In some cases the original shaded sunburst will have almost totally disappeared, leaving a uniform and rather pleasant honey color on such guitars, now affectionately known as "unburst" examples.

A further innovation of 1958, and one that proved to be more successful at the time, was Gibson's new ES-335 guitar. This was a development of the company's thin-body "thinline" design that had begun with the Byrdland and the ES-350T three years earlier. When it came to the new 335, however, Gibson deployed a radical double-cutaway design, as well as the use of a novel solid block within the otherwise hollow body to create a new "semi-solid" structure.

Gibson's idea was effectively to combine a hollowbody guitar with a solidbody, not only in terms of construction but also in sonic effect. A problem for hollowbody electric guitar designers had been the screeching "feedback" that often occurred when the guitar was played with its amplifier set at high volume. The 335's solid maple block inside what Gibson described as its "wonder-thin" body tamed the feedback and combined pure solidbody sustain with the woody warmth of a hollowbody. This quality would endear the 335-style Gibson to a wide range of players, especially bluesmen such as B.B. King, but also to a number of other guitarists from jazz stylist Larry Carlton to Britpop pioneer Bernard Butler.

The "dot neck" 335 – one with dot-shape fingerboard markers and made between 1958 and 1962 – has become a prime collectable guitar. In 1962 Gibson replaced the dots with block-shape markers. Not that this makes the guitar sound less good, but collectors feel the dot-neck feature marks a "better" period of quality and

Here are three 1959-made examples of the instruments in Gibson's new double-cutaway semi-solid series: the ES-335 (far left); the stereo ES-345 (center); and the deluxe ES-355 (near left).

Punks often sought cheaper, straightforward guitars, so it's hardly surprising that Mick Jones of The Clash regularly used a double-cutaway Les Paul Junior.

manufacturing standards, and therefore denotes a more desirable instrument. Players tend to be less selective and will generally tend to choose a 335 from any period, that plays well and feels good, and that is financially within reach.

The earliest 335 models were officially named ES-335T, the "T" at the end standing for "thinline" to emphasize and underline one of its most important features. Soon, however, a "D" was added by Gibson, meaning double pickups, as well as an extra "N" for natural-finish examples, resulting in the rather overwhelming model description of ES-335TDN. The sunburst 335 was originally made in greater numbers than the natural version, which was dropped in 1960. From that year the 335 was also available in a cherry red finish, known as the ES-335TDC.

A more high-end version of the 335 model also appeared in 1958, a cherry-finish guitar that was named the ES-355. This guitar was distinguished by multiple binding on the neck, body and headstock, the latter also bearing Gibson's luxurious split-diamond inlay. The 355 generally gleamed with gold-plated hardware, as well as boasting an ebony fingerboard and a Bigsby vibrato as standard.

The idea of a stereo guitar had originally been investigated by Jimmie Webster at Gretsch in New York. He had filed a patent for a stereo pickup system in 1956, leading to Gretsch's as-ever wonderfully titled Project-O-Sonic guitars of 1958. Gibson's first take on the stereo idea, the ES-345, appeared in the following year, along with optional

stereo wiring for the ES-355. "Stereophonic" and its more common diminutive "stereo" had become buzzwords in the late 1950s, as first stereo pre-recorded tapes and then stereo records hit the market.

Gretsch's pioneering system had worked by effectively splitting each pickup on a two-pickup guitar into two, so that one pickup could feed the output from the instrument's lower three strings to one amplifier, while the other pickup sent the higher three strings out to another amp.

Gibson would certainly have known about and examined the Gretsch system, and when it came to their own stereo guitars adopted a rather more straightforward system in 1959. Gibson's two-pickup circuitry simply directed the output of each complete pickup to a separate amplifier. In contemporary advertising, Gibson assured the guitarist of the day that it would soon be customary to plug in to a pair of amps and produce "a symphony of warm, full stereophonic sound."

Another new Gibson feature in the search for fresh electric tonalities was the Varitone control, offered on the ES-345 and some ES-355s. This switch selected one of six preset tone options, in combination with the pickup selector expanding to 18 possible tonal shades.

However, Gibson's Varitone and stereo capabilities were never especially popular among guitarists. Often, players would simply disconnect the confusing Varitone and,

Gibson changed the Les Paul Junior and Special from the old single-cutaway style (as detailed in this 1957 catalog, below) to a new double-cutaway body shape, introduced during the late 1950s. This Junior (near right) dates from 1958, while the Special (center) was made in 1959. This L-5CES (far right) was made in 1964 and bears the "sharp" cutaway of that period.

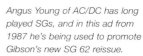

despite the stereo option, would just get on with playing what was undoubtedly a very good guitar in conventional "mono" mode.

Gibson's doubtless exhausted development team added one more innovation to the line during 1958: the company's first double-neck guitars. Always something of a compromise between convenience and comfort, the double-neck electric guitar was a relatively new idea, the first one having been custom-made by Paul Bigsby in California in 1952. The concept would have been obvious to Bigsby because he also made pedal-steel guitars, on which multiple necks are common.

A double-neck instrument is designed so that it can offer the player two different guitars in one instrument. An instant changeover from one neck to another saves the guitarist having to swap between separate instruments. Clearly, this is especially useful for the stage musician. The most obvious drawback to the double-neck electric is the increased weight of the resulting instrument, as well as the general awkwardness involved in reaching beyond a neck in an ideal playing position to the other that is invariably too high or too low for comfort.

Gibson launched two double-necks in 1958. The EDS-1275 Double 12 had what became the most common combination for electric double-necks, mixing a six-string and a 12-string neck. It looked something like an extended ES-175 with its twin pointed cutaways. The more unusual EMS-1235 Double Mandolin had one standard

More new designs from Gibson were the SG solidbodies, at first still called Les Paul models. These transition examples have since become known as SG/Les Pauls: this white SG/Les Paul Custom (main guitar) dates from 1962, and the cherry-finish SG/Les Paul Junior (far right) was made in 1961. A notable player of SG-style Gibsons was John Cipollina of Quicksilver Messenger Service, pictured above with his decorated SG around 1972.

six-string neck, plus a short-scale neck with six strings tuned an octave higher than a guitar, supposedly to mimic the sound of a mandolin.

These first Gibson double-necks were produced only to special order, their hollow bodies made with carved spruce tops and maple backs and sides. The instruments are rare today. Around 1962 Gibson changed the double-necks to a solidbody style, which made them look more like extended SG models. They remained custom-order-only instruments. The most famous player to opt for a Gibson double-neck was Jimmy Page who regularly used one on stage.

Gibson's first low-end solidbody – aside from earlier Les Paul Juniors – was the Melody Maker, launched in 1959. At first it had a simple "slab" single-cutaway body, though this was modified to a double-cutaway body two years later. An option was a short scale-length, another feature aimed at the smaller fingers of beginners. The last change to the Melody Maker came in 1965 when it adopted the style of Gibson's SG solidbody. This type of body design would last until the Melody Maker was dropped from the Gibson line during the early 1970s.

Considering all the Les Paul models as a whole, sales declined in 1960 after a peak in 1959. As we've seen, by 1961 Gibson had decided on a complete re-design of the line in an effort to try to reactivate this faltering model. The company had started a $400,000 expansion of the factory in Kalamazoo during 1960 which more than

This SG Standard (main guitar), made around 1965, was acquired by Eric Clapton early in 1967, probably to replace his stolen Les Paul Standard. Soon Clapton had a Dutch group of artists called The Fool paint the guitar. Clapton used the guitar widely with Cream, both on-stage (pictured far right) and on recordings such as the Disraeli Gears and Wheels Of Fire albums. Some of the original hardware has been replaced, and areas of the paintwork have been restored. From 1974 the instrument was owned for some time by Todd Rundgren.

Two more SGs are shown here (below left): an SG Special from 1966 finished in Pelham Blue that has aged to green; and an SG/Les Paul Standard from 1961 in regular cherry finish.

Eric Clapton on-stage with his painted SG (below) tests the sustain of humbuckers-and-Marshall during a Cream performance in 1967. Clapton recorded the band's Disraeli Gears album (far left) in New York in May 1967 using the SG. Dutch art group The Fool, who decorated the SG, made their own LP (near left).

Charlie Whitney used his Gibson double-neck on tour with Family. The band's set often featured songs from the second album, Entertainment, released in 1969, including their anthem 'The Weaver's Answer.'

doubled the size of the plant by the time it was completed in 1961. It was the third addition to the original 1917 factory, other buildings having been added in 1945 and 1950. But this new single-story brick-and-steel building was more than twice the size of the previous additions combined, resulting in a plant of more than 120,000 square feet that extended for two city blocks at Parsons Street in Kalamazoo. Clearly, Gibson was expecting its business to expand rapidly in the coming years.

One of the first series of new models to benefit from the company's newly expanded production facilities was the completely revised line of Les Paul models. Gibson redesigned the Junior, Standard and Custom models, adopting a new, distinctly modern, sculpted double-cutaway design. The "Les Paul" name was still used at first, but during 1963 Gibson began to call these new models the SG Junior, the SG Standard and the SG Custom. (Confusingly, the SG name had been used earlier on old-style Les Pauls: the old-design TV and Special had been renamed as the SG TV and the SG Special in 1959.) The transition models – those produced between 1961 and 1963 – had the new SG design but the old Les Paul names, and these are now known to collectors and players as SG/Les Paul models.

Les Paul's name was dropped for a number of reasons. Partly it was because the connection with the guitarist was less of a commercial bonus for Gibson than it had been. His popularity as a recording artist had declined: he'd had no more hits after

1955. Crucially, Les Paul and Mary Ford had separated in May 1963 and were officially divorced by the end of 1964, and Paul did not want to sign any fresh contract with Gibson that would bring in new money while the divorce proceedings were underway. So his contract with Gibson was terminated in 1962, and the following year Les Paul models became SG models ("Solid Guitar").

From 1964 until 1967 inclusive there were no guitars in the Gibson line that bore the name of Les Paul, either on the actual guitars themselves or in the company's catalogs, pricelists and other advertising material.

Production did increase at the Gibson factory of the new SG-style designs, with the output of Gibson Les Pauls from the Kalamazoo plant settling at just under 6,000 units every year for 1961, 1962 and 1963. SG-style solidbodies have attracted a number of players over the years, including John Cipollina, Eric Clapton, Tony Iommi, Robby Krieger, Tony McPhee, Pete Townshend, Angus Young and Frank Zappa.

Gibson produced a number of new electric archtop signature models in the 1960s named for jazz guitarists such as Barney Kessel and Tal Farlow, both best known for their fine playing which had come to the fore in the previous decade. The body of the Gibson Barney Kessel (1961) featured an unusual double "sharp" cutaway. More successful as an instrument was the Tal Farlow model (1962), visually distinguished by an ornate swirl of extra binding at the cutaway. Back in the solidbody department,

Double-neck instruments provide the on-stage guitarist with a (relatively) portable opportunity to swap between six-string and 12-string (or bass) necks on one guitar. Family's guitar player Charlie Whitney used this Gibson solidbody EDS-1275 (right, made in 1966) throughout the band's career, and the road-weary guitar has been modified and restored over the years. Whitney is pictured with his Gibson in front of Family vocalist Roger Chapman around 1971. On the opposite page is a white EDS-1275 made in 1964, used by Steve Howe on many Yes tours. The main picture shows Rush guitarist Alex Lifeson with his similar double-neck, on-stage in 1979.

Gibson was determined to take on its chief rival, Fender, and came up with the Firebird guitars (and matching Thunderbird bass). Launched in 1963, the Firebirds clearly recognized the solidbody style of the West Coast firm while retaining the style and workmanship for which Gibson was known. Gibson called upon car designer Ray Dietrich to out-Fender Fender.

Dietrich devised the new Firebird line with sleek, asymmetrical bodies that looked a little as if Gibson's old Explorer design had been modernized with some additional curves. The new elongated body shape featured a "horn-less" upper portion that had the effect of making the lower cutaway appear to protrude further. This unbalanced "lop-sided" effect has since gained the original Firebirds the nickname "reverse body" among collectors and players.

There were four models in the 1963 Firebird line. The Firebird I had a single pickup and was the only model without a vibrato unit. The Firebird III had two pickups and a "stud"-style bridge, while the Firebird V had two pickups and a Tune-o-matic bridge. The glorious top-of-the-line Firebird VII had three pickups.

They were the first Gibson electrics to employ through-neck construction. They were also unusual in that they featured a "flipped Fender" headstock which was fitted with banjo-style tuners. This meant that players had to adjust tuning in an unfamiliar way, reaching around to the back of the headstock. But at least the design of the

Two albums from the jazz guitarists whose Gibson signature guitars are pictured here: Tal Farlow's 'Tal' from 1956 (above left) and an eponymous Barney Kessel record of the 1950s.

Another signature Gibson made in collaboration with a jazz great was the Tal Farlow model (main guitar, made in 1964). The instrument was similar to an L-5CES, but with a decorated scroll near the cutaway recalling early Gibson instruments, and a slightly shallower body.

This Barney Kessel Custom (near right) was made by Gibson during 1961, and unusually features double-cutaways on a deep body. This Custom version has gold-plated hardware, while the Regular model had nickel plating.

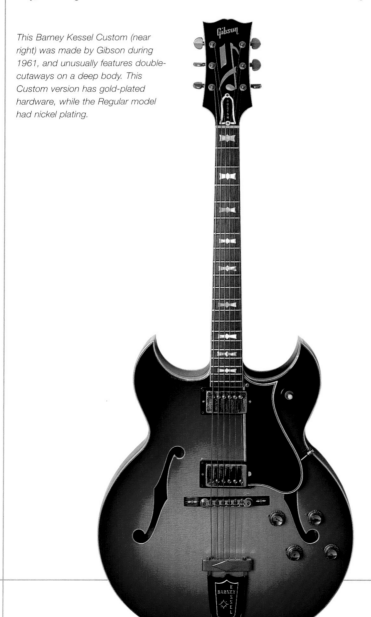

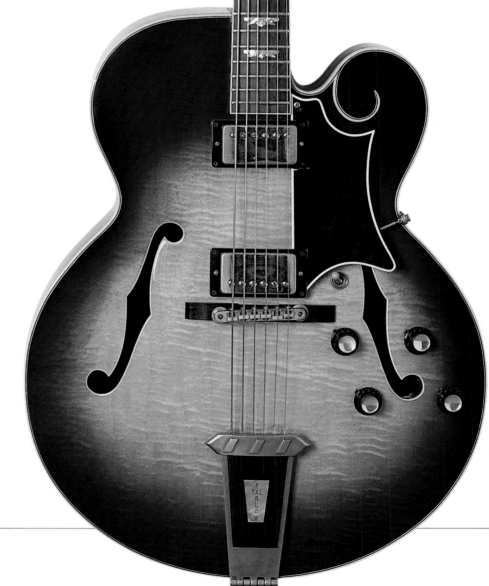

Eric Clapton plays his Gibson ES-335TDC (pictured right, made in 1964) at London's Royal Albert Hall in November 1968 during the final dates of Cream's last tour.

Johnny Winter (1969 album, right) has regularly used a "reverse body" Firebird, as seen on a magazine cover from 1974 (far right).

headstock showed a clean outline to the audience. The Firebirds were all fitted with special smaller-than-normal humbucking pickups which were without adjustable polepieces. Standard finish for the Firebirds was sunburst. However, Gibson went further than adopting just a Fender vibe for the new line.

The company also borrowed Fender's custom color idea, applying to the new line of guitars a range of paints more often employed to brighten up the look of the latest automobiles. One of Gibson's ten new Firebird colors was in fact identical to a Fender color. However, Gibson used the Oldsmobile name for it – Golden Mist – while Fender had opted for the Pontiac term, Shoreline Gold.

Despite the striking appearance of the Firebirds, and their prominent use in the 1960s and later by players such as Brian Jones and Johnny Winter, the ploy didn't work. Gibson's sales of electric guitars during the 1960s had to rely on classic 1950s designs such as the great semi-solid ES-335. Fender understandably complained about similarities to its patented "offset waist" design feature, pointing primarily to the Jazzmaster and Jaguar in its line, and so Gibson tried to fix things by reworking the Firebirds in 1965.

Gibson came up with a new Firebird shape that flipped the old one into a slightly more conventional if still quite Fender-like outline, known now as the "non-reverse" body. Gibson also dropped the through-neck construction in favor of its customary set-

Gibson's color chart for the Firebird models illustrates the ten optional finishes beyond sunburst, as well as instruments from the Firebird guitar and matching Thunderbird bass lines. Two of these "reverse body" Firebirds are pictured on this page: a sunburst Firebird I (far left) made in 1964, and a Firebird V (main guitar) manufactured during the following year and finished in Cardinal Red.

*Phil Manzanera used this Firebird VII
(pictured left, made around 1964)
with Roxy Music both on-stage
(above) and in the studio (first album,
released in 1972, top of page).*

Jimi Hendrix was best known for playing a Strat, but during the last half of 1967 this Flying V was his favorite guitar. Jimi painted the guitar himself. It's a pity he didn't paint the cover of Electric Ladyland (1968, left), a remarkably kitsch document that Jimi apparently hated.

neck. The new Firebird I had two single-coil pickups, the Firebird III three single-coil pickups, the Firebird V two mini-humbuckers, and the Firebird VII three mini-humbuckers. Still unsuccessful, the Firebirds were grounded by 1969. Since then, the non-reverse Firebirds have been used even less by well-known players than the marginally more favored reverse versions. However, Oasis's new rhythm guitarist Gem Archer was to be seen on the band's 2000 dates occasionally strapping on a non-reverse Firebird, which must have pleased a number of vintage guitar dealers.

Back in the 1960s, Gibson enjoyed good sales in Britain amid the mushrooming of pop music talent there. Distribution of Gibson in Britain had been patchy until Selmer, a wholesale company that was based in London, started officially to import Gibson guitars to the UK during 1960. In fact, British musicians had virtually been starved of any American-made guitars between 1951 and 1959, thanks to a government ban on importation during that period.

Selmer was in the right place when the ban was lifted. The company's famed retail store in London's Charing Cross Road was at the heart of an area alive with music publishers, small studios and instrument retailers, a mecca for both the budding and successful musician. Jeff Beck bought his first Les Paul Standard from the Selmer store; Steve Howe purchased his favorite ES-175D there; and Robert Fripp acquired his prized Les Paul Custom at the store in 1968.

As noted earlier, Gibson had since the 1930s used the Kalamazoo brand – named for the location of its factory in Michigan – for cheaper products unworthy of the full Gibson marque. In 1965 the Kalamazoo brand was revived as Gibson decided to feed a strong demand for bargain electric guitars. At first the entry-level Kalamazoo electrics had Fender-style offset cutaways, although later in the 1960s a shape more like Gibson's own SG was adopted. A handful of different models appeared in this KG series, but they were all dropped by the turn of the decade.

There was a newly revised version of the Flying V launched by Gibson during the second half of the 1960s. The reworked model had more conventional hardware than the original late-1950s V, without the through-body stringing. Gibson also redesigned the control layout for these models first issued during 1967, with the three knobs now forming a triangular group rather than the three-in-a-line style of the original. These new-style Vs would stay in the Gibson catalog until the late 1970s.

Guitar sales in general in the United States – including acoustic as well as electric instruments – had climbed throughout the early 1960s, hitting a peak of some 1,500,000 units in 1965, after which sales declined and fell to just over a million in 1967. CMI's sales of Gibson guitars and amplifiers hit a fiscal peak of $19million in 1966, but then began to fall in line with the general industry trend, and were down to $15million-worth by 1968. As well as the general decline in demand for guitars,

Gibson revised the Firebird body design in 1965 to the "non-reverse" shape seen on these two examples: a Firebird I from 1965 (far left) and a Firebird III made in 1966. The catalog from the same period illustrates the other two models in the line, the Firebird VII and Firebird V.

Gibson's production had been hit by a number of strikes in the 1960s, including a 16-day stoppage in 1966. Gibson president Ted McCarty and his number two, John Huis, left that year after purchasing the Bigsby musical accessories company of California, which they re-established in Kalamazoo.

In February 1968, after a number of short-stay occupants in the president's chair, Stan Rendell was appointed as the new president of the Gibson operation. Rendell immediately set about his task of improving the company's fortunes.

Meanwhile, as we've seen, the blues-rock boom had made players aware of the potential of old Les Paul guitars. Musicians began to hunt for the instruments, and prices for secondhand examples began gradually to climb. Gibson at last decided to do something about their deteriorating position in the electric guitar market, and specifically about the increasing demand for their old-style Les Paul guitars.

Les Paul's musical activities had been very low-key since the mid 1960s, but in 1967 he began a new association with Gibson that resulted in a reissue program for Les Paul models. By the time Stan Rendell became president of Gibson in early 1968 the decision to re-commence manufacturing Les Paul guitars had been made by the CMI management in Chicago, principally by Maurice Berlin and Marc Carlucci, and a new contract was negotiated with Paul. For some reason, Gibson decided to re-introduce the relatively rare two-humbucker Les Paul Custom, and the gold-top Les

Paul with P-90 pickups and Tune-o-matic bridge. They were launched at a June 1968 trade show in Chicago. Gibson's ads publicizing the revived guitars admitted that the company had virtually been forced to re-introduce the guitars: "The demand for them just won't quit. And the pressure to make more has never let up. Okay, you win. We are pleased to announce that more of the original Les Paul Gibsons are available." The new Les Pauls sold well, and Gibson clearly had a success in the making. The only mystery so far as many guitarists were concerned was why they'd waited so long.

An important change to Gibson's ownership occurred in 1969. The new owner, Norlin Industries, was formed that year with the merger of Gibson's parent company, CMI, with ECL, an Ecuadorian brewery. The Norlin name was arrived at by combining the first syllable of ECL chairman Norton Stevens' name with the last syllable of that of CMI founder Maurice Berlin.

Norlin was in three businesses: musical instruments, brewing, and "technology." The takeover was formalized in 1974 and Maurice Berlin, a man widely respected in the musical instrument industry, was moved sideways in the new structure, away from the general running of the company.

Many people who worked at Gibson during this period feel that there was a move away from managers who understood guitars to managers who understood manufacturing. Some of the instruments made during the period soon after Gibson

Gibson reintroduced original-design Les Paul models in 1968 after a number of years when guitars with the SG design had replaced them. Shown on this page are the two "new" models, both made in 1968: the revived gold-top (near right, this one with some non-standard features on the headstock) and a Custom (center). The Les Paul Deluxe model was introduced in 1969. This example from about 1975 (far right) is in a custom blue sparkle finish.

A 1972 ad for the Les Paul Recording model, highlighting the multiple controls that left most musicians somewhat baffled.

The Les Paul Recording model replaced two earlier models with low-impedance pickups, the Les Paul Personal and Professional, in 1971. This example of the Recording (main guitar) was made around 1972. A British catalog of the period details the Recording and its matching bass guitar, the Les Paul Triumph.

were taken over have a bad reputation today. The new owners are generally felt now to have been insensitive to the needs of musicians. Clearly this was a sign of the times, as economic analysts were busily advising many of the big corporations that they should diversify into a range of different areas, pour in some money... and sit back to wait for the profits.

There was a shift in emphasis at Gibson toward the rationalization of production, and this meant that changes were made to some of the company's instruments built during the 1970s (and, to some extent, to those made into the 1980s). Generally, such alterations were made for one of three reasons. The first and apparently most pressing requirement was to save money. Second, Gibson wished to limit the number of guitars returned for work under warranty. Lastly, there was a distinct desire to speed up production of Gibson guitars at the Kalamazoo factory.

The guitar design department at Gibson gave a change of style and name to the recently re-introduced Les Paul gold-top model in 1969, when the Les Paul Deluxe took its place. The Deluxe was the first "new" Les Paul model for 14 years, and was prompted by calls for a gold-top with humbucking pickups rather than the single-coil P-90s of the existing reissue model.

Gibson ended up using small Epiphone humbuckers for the Les Paul Deluxe model that were surplus to requirements. At first the Deluxe was only available with a gold

The first Les Paul model with an f-hole was the Les Paul Signature (1976 example here), a gold-finished guitar with low-impedance pickups.

145

top, but gradually sunbursts and other colors were introduced, and it lasted in production until the mid 1980s.

Back in the 1950s and 1960s one of guitarist Les Paul's more out-of-step tastes had been for low-impedance pickups. Today, low-impedance elements are more often used as part of a pickup design, thanks to improvements in associated components, but back then Paul was largely on his own. The vast majority of electric guitars and guitar-related equipment was (and still is) high-impedance.

The chief advantage of low-impedance is a wide and all-encompassing tonal characteristic. This might appear at first to be an advantage, but in fact the tonal range offered isn't necessarily to everyone's taste. Another disadvantage is that low-impedance pickups must have their power boosted at some point before the signal reaches the amplifier (unless the player is plugging the guitar straight into a recording studio mixer, as Les Paul did).

When Paul had gone to Gibson in 1967 to discuss the revival of Les Paul guitars, he'd talked with great passion about his beloved low-impedance pickups, and how Gibson should use them on some of their instruments. So in 1969 along came the first wave of Gibson Les Paul guitars with low-impedance pickups: the Les Paul Professional and the Les Paul Personal. The Personal was, as the name implied, in keeping with one of Paul's own modified Les Paul guitars, even copying his odd feature

of a microphone socket on the top edge of the body. The Personal and Professional had a complex array of controls, seemingly aimed at recording engineers rather than guitarists. These included an 11-position Decade control, "to tune high frequencies," a three-position tone selector to create various in- and out-of-circuit mixes, and a pickup phase switch. The Personal also provided a volume control for that handy on-board microphone input. Both guitars required connection with the special cord supplied, which had an integral transformer to boost the output from the low-impedance stacked-coil humbucking pickups to a level suitable for use with normal high-impedance amplifiers.

Predictably, the guitars were not a great success, and did not last long in the Gibson line. Their rather somber brown color, achieved with a natural mahogany finish, could not have helped in an era when most of the competition was busily turning out simple guitars finished in bright colors.

The company did have another go at low-impedance instruments during 1971. First, Gibson decided to scale down the body size of the Professional/Personal style, virtually to that of a normal Les Paul, and to give it a contoured back. Second, the company located the still-necessary transformer into the guitar itself, and provided a switch on the guitar to give either low-impedance output or normal high-impedance output. Third, Gibson re-titled the guitar to the more appropriate Les Paul Recording. It

The Les Paul Artisan (near right, from 1982) had a fancy fingerboard; the S-1 (far right, from 1976) unusually for Gibson had a bolt-on neck. Meanwhile, Al DiMeola promotes the L-6S (above).

would remain in the line until 1980. Another low-impedance-equipped model came along in 1972, the L-5S. The name of this single-cutaway solidbody alluded to Gibson's great old electric hollowbody model, the L-5CES — but beyond that, any obvious kind of connection was unclear.

There seemed to be even less chance of guitarists being attracted to low-impedance pickups on an instrument that didn't even have the cachet of the Les Paul name. So it was that a few years into its life the new L-5S was changed from low-impedance pickups to regular humbuckers — but that still made no difference to its popularity. Even the use of the new L-5S by the fine jazzman Pat Martino had apparently little impact on other musicians. Gibson's final fling with low-impedance pickups was reserved for the company's thinline style, and was launched during 1973 as the two-pickup gold-colored Les Paul Signature.

Some of the new Signature model's controls were similar to those found on previous low-impedance models, but an extra feature on the Signature was the inclusion of two jack sockets. One was on the side of the body, for normal high-impedance output; the other on the face of the body was for connection to low-impedance equipment such as recording mixers. (A similar facility was offered on the final version of the Recording model.) The Signature models never really fired players' imaginations, and by the end of the 1970s they were out of production. By now Gibson

A luxurious high-end guitar, even by Gibson's sometimes lofty standards, was The Les Paul. The instrument was made in very limited numbers from 1976 to 1979 at Gibson's original factory at Kalamazoo, Michigan. Work there on these special new Les Pauls was at first overseen by local luthier Dick Schneider. Very fine rosewood and maple was used for many of the parts of The Les Paul that would not normally be made from wood, and the result was a very beautiful and, at $3,000, a very expensive instrument. Two magnificent examples from the run of under 100 The Les Pauls are shown on this page: number 48 (main guitar, alongside its highly-figured back), completed on March 8th 1978; and number 51 (far left) which was finished two days later.

employed around 600 people at its Kalamazoo factory, and was producing something like 300 guitars every day. Demand for guitars had increased during the early 1970s, and so management decided to build a second Gibson factory at Nashville, Tennessee, some 500 miles south of Kalamazoo. Recent strikes at Gibson had cost Norlin dear, and the new plant of 100,000 square feet was also constructed with a view to decreasing costs through advantageous labor deals.

Work began in 1974 on the new facility, five miles to the east of Nashville, and the factory eventually opened in June 1975. Gibson's original intention was to keep both Kalamazoo and Nashville running. Nashville was designed to produce very large quantities of a handful of models, while Kalamazoo was more flexible and had the potential to specialize in small runs. Nashville was thus the obvious choice to produce the models in Gibson's solidbody line required in the greatest volume at the time – the Les Paul Custom and Deluxe models – along with various other solidbody models.

As if to highlight the contrast between the capabilities of the two plants, Gibson introduced two new Les Paul models in 1976. First was the Les Paul Pro Deluxe, effectively a Deluxe with P-90 pickups and an ebony fingerboard. It was produced in large quantities at Nashville.

The other new model was The Les Paul, a spectacular limited-edition model that was notable for Gibson's employment of various fine woods for virtually the entire instrument. Many parts that on a normal electric guitar would be made from plastic were hand-carved from rosewood. These included the pickguard, backplates, control knobs and truss-rod cover.

Raw bodies and necks of attractive maple and an ornate ebony and rosewood fingerboard for the The Les Paul were produced at Gibson's Kalamazoo factory. Further work on the multiple colored binding, abalone inlays and handmade wooden parts was continued at the workshop of freelance luthier Dick Schneider, who was based about a mile from the factory in Kalamazoo.

Very few of The Les Pauls were made, with probably well under 100 produced from 1976 to 1979, primarily in the first year. During this time Schneider moved away from Kalamazoo, and later examples of The Les Paul were therefore produced entirely at the Gibson factory. As the limited stocks of Schneider's handmade wooden parts ran out, so normal plastic items were substituted, along with less ornate binding.

Each example of The Les Paul had a numbered oval plate on the back of the headstock. Number 25 was presented to Les Paul just prior to the 1977 Grammy Awards ceremony where Paul and Chet Atkins received a Grammy award for their *Chester & Lester* album. The $3,000 price tag on The Les Paul made it four times the cost of the next most expensive Les Paul model on the 1976 pricelist. During the previous year, Gibson had in fact introduced a number of other new models and a

Three guitars with Gibson's new active circuitry are shown on this page: an RD Artist from 1979 (near right); a Les Paul Artist (center) made in 1979; and an ES Artist (far right) that dates from 1980.

reissue. These included a revitalized Explorer, plus two new solidbodys: the all-maple single-cutaway L-6S, as endorsed by Carlos Santana, and the Les Paul-shape bolt-on-neck Marauder with humbucker and angled single-coil pickups. The S-1 was a sort of three-pickup Marauder that also sported that model's V-shape headstock, and it joined the line in 1976. None of these lasted long.

The 25/50 Les Paul was intended to celebrate Les Paul's 25th year with Gibson (presumably it had been planned for 1977) and his 50th year in the music business. The silver and gold themes generally associated with these anniversaries were reflected in the guitar's chrome- and gold-plated hardware, while Chuck Burge in Gibson's R&D (research and development) department designed the special intricate inlay in pearl and abalone on the guitar's headstock.

The guitar bore a three-digit edition number on the back of the headstock as well as a standard serial number. Once again Les Paul himself was presented with a special example: this time he received guitar number one at a party given in his honor by Gibson, who launched the Les Paul 25/50 Anniversary model during 1978. Despite its relatively high price the Kalamazoo-made 25/50 sold well, bringing into sharp focus for Norlin the ready market for more costly Les Paul models

Gibson's new RD models first appeared in 1978, and incorporated a package of complex "active" electronics. This kind of circuit had been popularized by Alembic at

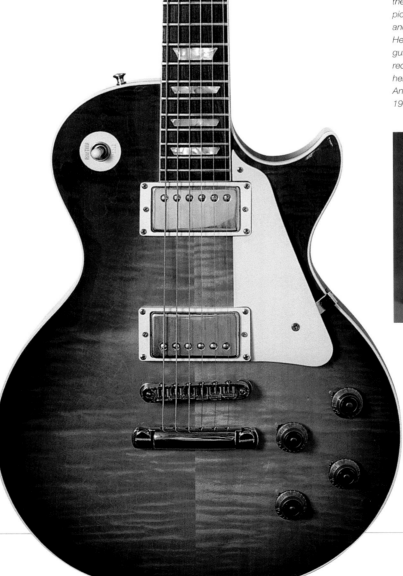

This V-II (far left) from 1981 updated the Flying V with "boomerang" pickups and a sandwiched walnut-and-maple construction. Gibson's Heritage Series Standard 80 (main guitar, 1980) was an early attempt to recapture previous glories. The ads here are for the gold-top's 30th Anniversary model (1982, above) and 1979's The SG (below).

the start of the 1970s and was designed to boost the signal and widen the tonal range of a guitar. The circuit was powered by an on-board battery. The body of the RD series was an even curvier version of the previous decade's Firebird "reverse body" design.

This kind of "hi-fi" guitar was prompted by the apparent competition from synthesizers, which had become big business during the late 1970s. Gibson's parent company Norlin figured that a hook-up with Moog, one of the synthesizer field's most famous names of the time, might re-capture some of the ground that guitars seemed to be losing to the new keyboards.

In fact one of the RD models – the Standard – was a regular electric, without the active circuit, which was reserved for the Custom and Artist models. Gibson's RD line did not, however, prove popular and was soon gone from the catalog. Many guitarists disliked what they considered the "unnatural" sounds of active circuitry, and this was a major factor in the downfall of the RD series. Gibson believed that the radical styling was more to blame for the lack of popularity, and moved to combine the RD technology with some of its traditional body designs.

In 1979 Gibson did this, expanding the RD concept into two of its more mainstream electric series, the ES thinlines and the Les Pauls. Gibson had to re-design the large RD circuit board to fit into these more confined body designs. Each of the new Artist models had three knobs, for volume, bass and treble, and three switches for

brightness, expansion and compression. However, these models also failed to grab many guitarists, and the Artists did not last for very long: the Les Paul Artist hobbled on to 1981, while the ES Artist managed to last until 1985.

A happier project was the Les Paul Heritage Series, one of the first conscious attempts by Gibson to try to make Les Pauls in a way that many players thought was no longer possible. A reasonably healthy market had been building since the late 1960s in so-called "vintage" guitars (which used to be called merely "secondhand," or "used," or just plain "old guitars").

This trend was fueled by the general feeling that Gibson "didn't make them like they used to," combined with the prominent use of older instruments by many of the most popular guitarists of the day. While to some extent this was flattering in general to the Gibson name (and to others such as Fender and Gretsch whose guitars were also associated with the vintage trend), it did not help a manufacturer whose main priority was to continue to sell new guitars and especially its new models.

Some US dealers such as Strings & Things and Music Trader who specialized in older instruments had already begun to order selected new models with vintage-style appointments from Gibson's Kalamazoo plant, which since the onset of the Nashville factory was beginning to lean more heavily toward shorter, specialized runs of guitars. For the Heritage Series Les Pauls, Gibson's team used a 1954 pattern sample for the

Nobody seemed ready for the sheer ugliness of Gibson's Corvus model (1983 example, near right; ad, below, from 1984). Better was the Les Paul Spotlight Special (1983, center) with its central walnut block between some beautiful maple. This prototype Explorer (far right) was made in 1980 as a pattern for the limited-edition Explorer Heritage reissue of 1983.

hollowbodies appeared from 1986, not dissimilar in style to some of the well-known Gretsch Chet Atkins models, but with distinct Gibson touches. Models include the Country Gentleman and the Tennessean.

The superstrat-like US-1 model debuted during 1986 and introduced musicians to a new idea from Gibson in the construction of solidbody guitars. For the new US-1, the company decided to employ a core of "chromite" (balsa wood) at the heart of the guitar, primarily for the material's low weight and its resonant qualities. Chromite had the effect of reducing the weight of the maple-top US-1, and Gibson also applied the new material to the Les Paul Studio Lite model in 1991.

New in 1991 was the solidbody M-III line, a series of radically styled double-cutaway guitars fitted with flexible circuitry. The M-III guitars used the popular humbucker/single-coil/humbucker pickup layout, in the process aiming to provide Stratocaster-like and Les Paul-style tones from a five-way switch.

Unfortunately, Gibson's customers felt the design and the electronics of the new M-III guitars were, again, too "un-Gibson," and they did not rush to buy the instruments. So it was that in a move reminiscent of the marriage of RD and Artist ten years before, Gibson decided to apply the electronics from the strange M-III to the more familiar environment of the Les Paul design. This resulted in two new models, the Classic/M-III and the Studio Lite/M-III. However, even this made little difference to players'

allegiances, and the original M-IIIs as well as these Les Paul versions were gone from the Gibson line by the late 1990s.

Gibson's first official Custom Shop had started in the 1960s at Kalamazoo, building one-offs to customers' requirements, although of course non-standard orders had been undertaken from the company's earliest days. The Custom Shop idea was revived in the 1980s at Nashville, running from 1983 to 1988, and has now been running again since another new start in 1992.

The present Custom Shop at Gibson continues the traditional role of making oddities for wealthy players, but also provides more mainstream inspiration for the current Custom Shop Collection series that includes everything from a Zakk Wylde signature Les Paul to Tony Iommi's SG model.

The most recent new solidbody from Gibson was the single-cutaway humbucker/single-coil/humbucker Nighthawk, launched in 1993 in Standard, Special and Custom guises, but dropped by the end of the decade. Semi-hollow versions, the Blueshawk and B.B. King Little Lucille, followed in 1996 and 1999.

A relatively simple cosmetic alteration provided Gibson with its Gothic series that first appeared in 1999, with matt black finish and matt black hardware. Two of the models chosen for this line of instruments aimed at the solid rocking guitarist were obvious: the Flying V and the Explorer. However, the all-black 335 was a more

This Gibson Flying V Gothic (far left) is a black ultra-rock machine, this one from 1999; the Dickey Betts '57 Redtop (center) was one of a pair of Betts signature models, this one made in 2001; and the Johnny A. Signature (near left) was a hollowbody electric with "gamba" soundholes, the one pictured here dating from 2004.

surprising choice, and did not last in this particular category of Gibson's Designer Collection, which also finds room to contain models such as the Explorer 1976 and EDS1275 double-neck reissues.

Reissue "repros" of more vintage glories were featured in Gibson's 2000 catalog, including Firebirds, Flying Vs, 175s, 295s, 335s, Explorers, CESs and SGs. These are in addition to a long list of Les Paul reissues, some of which were mentioned earlier. One interesting addition to the burgeoning line of Gibson's "new/old" Les Pauls was the Aged 40th Anniversary model, which first appeared in 1999. Essentially, this was yet another move toward a more accurate reproduction of those hallowed 1959-period flame-top Les Paul Standards. The engineers at Gibson responsible for this particular attempt explained that they had virtually started again from scratch (which is what they usually say), finding new sources of materials and components.

But the major difference with the 40th Anniversary recreation was, however, the aged finish. There's no doubt that this was influenced by the success that Fender had found with its Relic series, introduced in the mid 1990s after the company had almost jokingly displayed a couple of aged repros of early models at a trade show – and received an incredibly positive reaction (for which read many orders from dealers visiting the show). So it was that a trained team at Gibson set about giving the 40th Anniversary model a look that suggests it has actually been gigged and used for 40

years. Thus the paint colors were made to appear faded, the nickel parts on the instrument such as the pickup covers were realistically tarnished, the lacquer "skin" was cracked and effectively dulled, and there were all manner of dings and knocks over the guitar. Like Fender and its Relics, Gibson aimed to recreate the almost indefinable allure of a vintage guitar with this model – at a stiff price, of course.

More signature models have appeared from Gibson, including an L-5CES named for Wes Montgomery (1993) that reproduces the great jazzman's custom requirement of a single pickup. There have been many Les Pauls, including models for Jimmy Page (1995, 2004, 2008, 2009), Joe Perry (1996, 2003, 2013), Slash (1997, 2003, 2008, 2010), Ace Frehley (1997), Zakk Wylde (1999, 2004), Peter Frampton (2000, 2006), Gary Moore (2000, 2010, 2013), Dickey Betts (2001, 2002), Gary Rossington (2002), Duane Allman (2003, 2013), Neal Schon (2005), Pete Townshend (2006), Warren Haynes (2007), Keith Richards (2007), Joe Bonamassa (2008), Michael Bloomfield (2009), Billy Gibbons (2009), Jeff Beck (2009), Eric Clapton (2010), Don Felder (2010), Paul Kossoff (2012), Joe Walsh (2013), Tom Scholz (2013), Alex Lifeson (2014), Mark Knopfler (2016), and Mike McCready (2016).

Gibson's first signature SG was the Custom Shop's Tony Iommi model of 1999, followed three years later by a factory version. Further SG artist guitars have appeared for Angus Young (2000, 2009), Pete Townshend (2000, 2011), Robby Krieger (2009),

This Pete Townshend Deluxe #1 (near right) was a Gibson Who-related replica from 2006; the Robot SG Limited (center) from 2008 was fitted with the Robot self-tuning system; and the Zakk Wylde Les Paul BFG Bullseye (far right) from 2009 was another in the line of Wylde signature models. A 2002 ad (right) for the thinline ES-446S with integral top bracing.

Dickey Betts (2011), Derek Trucks (2012), and Frank Zappa (2013). As these latest models come off the Gibson production line, it's interesting to observe that the company's classic designs, many of which are decades old, seem more than ever before to reflect the needs of contemporary musicians.

A new take on the semi-solid 335 came along in 1996, the ES-336. It had a smaller body than a 335 (about two inches less wide) and a modified Les Paul-like construction (a mahogany one-piece back with routed areas that in effect left a central block, plus a routed solid maple cap with f-holes, glued together, and the top carved). Further variants on this comfortable design followed, including the upscale ES-346/Paul Jackson model, the CS-336 (a renamed ES-336), the CS-356 (355-like features), a number of Midtown models, and the ES-339, which was a proper scaled-down 335, plus 349 and 359 versions that had 345 and 355-like features.

Gibson opened a new factory in Memphis in 2000. The Nashville factory was working at full capacity, so it made sense to keep (and expand) solidbody production there and create a new factory primarily for the ES models. Since 1990, Gibson's acoustic guitars had been built at a separate factory, over in Montana, so there was a precedent for moving production. Memphis is just over 200 miles west of Nashville, and one of the reasons it was chosen as the location for the new factory was probably its long association with the blues, and especially B.B. King, who was of course a

celebrated ES player. King opened the first of his chain of blues clubs in Memphis in 1991, on Beale Street, revered as the historical centre of the city's blues scene. Gibson built its new plant just around the corner, on a block bordered by South B.B. King Boulevard. With Memphis a tourist destination, Gibson's building included what it called the Beale Street Showcase, hosting factory tours and with a shop.

Gibson's high-tech ambitions became evident in 2006, when the company began shipping its long-promised digital guitar, the HD.6X-Pro, a Les Paul with an additional hex pickup that allowed the player to feed various combinations of strings to a computer, for use with recording software or similar programs.

The next tech step came in 2007 with Gibson's clever Robot self-tuning system. Various regular models – mainly Les Pauls and SGs – were offered with the Robot's powered tuning pegs, auto-tuning bridge, and data-transmitting tailpiece, which offered standard tuning plus six programmable tunings.

A further development in 2008 was the Dark Fire, a Les Paul that linked an improved Robot system with some of the digital guitar's features and potential. The hi-tech Dark Fires failed to catch on with players, who (to generalize) are inclined to a conservative and somewhat skeptical outlook when it comes to apparently complex new technology. The Dark Fire model was gone within two years. The Robot system itself was further revamped in 2013 as a self-contained unit that could mount to the

Three more Gibsons here: a Trini
Lopez With Stopbar reissue from
2010 (far left), recalling his original
Standard model from the 1960s but
with a stopbar tailpiece; a 2010
ES-335 Block reissue (center),
recalling an original from around
1963; and an example of the
shortlived Dusk Tiger Les Paul (right),
this from 2009, with Robot self-
tuning, ten preset tones, and an
exotic figured top.

Gibson has long made models that reference great guitars used by the best players, and this Randy Rhoads Les Paul Custom (main guitar) from 2012 is a tribute to the '74 Custom played by the talented Ozzy guitarist who was killed at just 25 years old in an aircraft accident. The single-cutaway Les Paul Junior has been in production, with some breaks and lapses, since 1954: here we show how the instrument looked in 2012 (far right). Essentially... much the same. The CS-336 (2003 ad, right) was a small-body take on Gibson's 335 semi-solid style, although it was made with a routed back and cap rather than with the central-block construction of the 335.

rear of any headstock, and Gibson took the opportunity to rename it, at first as the Min-ETune, and then in 2015 the G Force. It's been available since as a feature or an option on a number of models.

Among the greatly increased competition of today's guitar market, Gibson seems well positioned to serve up its own true, traditional flavor – but with all the benefits of the improvements made in modern manufacturing and all of the advances that have taken place among the electric guitar's technical appointments.

By 2017, Gibson's lines included a large number of Les Paul variations. For example, the USA factory output was split into "Traditional" and "High Performance" versions. There was vintage vibe in the Trad camp, such as the Tribute T, with keystone tuners, slim neck profile, plain A grade maple top, classic controls, and nickel-plated hardware, and there was contemporary class in the Performance camp, like the Classic HP, with autotune, zero fret, fast-access heel, maple-cap weight relief, and push-pull controls. Gibson offered plenty more beyond the ubiquitous Les Pauls, drawing upon its other core designs, the ES-335, SG, Flying V, Explorer, and Firebird. The Custom Shop continued to specialize in vintage re-creations, and Historic Les Pauls, especially from the golden era of 1958-60 sunburst Standards, were as ever at the heart of the offerings. With all this history in mind, Gibson electrics still seem set for many new adventures in the hands of present and future generations of musicians.

G I T T L E R

"Less is more" was the philosophy behind the unique minimalist guitars of inventor Allan Gittler. Born in 1928, Gittler made his first electric guitar – basically a wooden neck – while living in New York City in 1974. This quickly evolved into a stainless steel headless "skeleton" built around a central rod or "spine" on to which were mounted machined-tube frets. There was also a small pickup housing and a volume control, plus knurled knobs to tune strings that were tied at the nut. A moveable "arm" served as an armrest or legrest. In 1982, Gittler changed his name to Avraham Bar Rashi and emigrated to Israel, where his guitars were built by the Astron company from 1986-87. As a concession to guitarists who needed more neck, some featured a metal extension behind the frets. The Gittler guitar continues today – Bar Rashi has described it as a 20th century classic and "now a 21st century marvel."

G O D I N

This large Canadian maker has popularized "synth-access" guitars, and is also among those offering "hybrid" instruments that mix electric and acoustic qualities.

The company is located in Canada and the US, headed by Robert Godin. Godin first set up his LaSiDo shop in La Patrie, Quebec, in the early 1980s to build replacement electric-guitar necks and bodies. Soon LaSiDo was building instruments and parts for a number of big-name guitar brands – this continues today – but also developed its

The Canadian-based Godin company produced this G-1000 (main guitar) during 1996. Earlier attempts by Godin at solidbody electrics leaned heavily on Strat-style and Tele-style shapes, but for the Artisan and then this G-1000 a more original design was employed. Two Godin ads below feature Eric McFadden (2012, top) and Mark Potter (2011, bottom). Allan Gittler's peculiar guitar (below, far left) is little more than a skeleton that retains only the essential elements of an instrument. This example was made in Israel by Astron Engineering around 1986. The skeleton itself is made from stainless steel, and this one has "open" frets, although some examples were made with an optional "back" to the neck, which was situated behind the wishbone-shape fret system.

own models, for which Godin is the sole electric brand. LaSiDo is still best known as a maker of acoustics and electro-acoustics (making brands such as Seagull, Norman, Simon & Patrick etc). Godin came to prominence with its innovative Acousticaster model of 1987, a Telecaster-size bolt-on-neck electro-acoustic with unusual harp-shape "sound fork" under the bridge, designed to improve the guitar's response.

Moves by Godin into the market for solidbody electric guitars proved relatively unsuccessful for the company until the launch of its LG-X model in 1994. This was a "synth-access" guitar – in other words an instrument with special built-in pickup and circuitry that enables it to be linked directly with (and control) a remote synthesizer module, thus giving the guitarist access to synth sounds. Guitar synthesizers had foundered in the 1980s due to poor compatibility with the synthesizers available, but this new MIDI-based system offered better performance.

The Les Paul-style LG-X now heads a small series of similar instruments, some also with piezo "acoustic"-sounding bridge pickups. The LG-XT of 1998, for example, incorporated the piezo-loaded L.R. Baggs vibrato X-bridge, and as such offers the adventurous player the potential for a variety of different sounds and applications from one instrument. Godin's first synth-access guitar had in fact been the Multiac, launched in 1993, which was a thinline nylon-strung electric-acoustic, and it's joined in the Godin line today by the Multiac Classical and Multiac Steel, plus the budget-price

Solidac. The LGX-SA was a further Godin aimed at players who prefer a solidbody feel. Despite this innovation and industry, the mass-produced, well-made Godin line lacked "classic" styling. So in the late 1990s attempts were made to introduce some guitars with retro-inspired designs. These included the Radiator, launched in 1999, which illustrated a desire by Godin to go beyond its specialist status and move into the mainstream market. Certainly Godin guitars are unusual in offering hybrid pickups and synth-access, but they are almost an underground force within the guitar industry, and at present lack star-name users to attract younger players to their undoubtedly innovative instruments. Godin now also has assembly plants in Berlin, New Hampshire, and Richmond, Quebec, and the guitars are made at the original location in La Patrie.

GODWIN

During the 1970s Sisme, Italian owner of Godwin organs, aimed also to attract guitarists with the ambitious Super Professional Guitar-Organ. It looked impressive, with a vast array of controls, and was big on weight and body dimensions, essential to accommodate the copious electrics. As with the ill-fated Vox guitar organ, frets were wired to tone generators and string contact completed the circuit, creating the "organ" sound. Results could be convincing but performance was, predictably, erratic. In marked contrast, the company later issued a straightforward, Les Paul-like Godwin six-string, which also went nowhere.

Two more Godin guitars are shown on this page. This LG-XT (near right) from 1998 is a modern "hybrid," mixing normal electro-magnetic electric sounds with "acoustic"-like tones from its piezo bridge pickups. The Radiator (1999 example, center) was Godin's retro model. This Godwin Guitar-Organ (far right) from around 1976 required serious study of its multiple controls in order to coax a convincing organ sound.

GORDON-SMITH

The longest-running British manufacturer, Gordon-Smith has operated since 1975 when Gordon Whittam and John Smith started making guitars. Whittam established the shortlived Gordy brand in 1984, but John Smith remained, producing models such as the Graduate, Gypsy and the start-up GS series. Smith's original symmetrical double-cutaway shape based on the Les Paul Junior became established as a good quality workingman's guitar, low on style but offering a notoriously Gibson-like tone with added upper-frequency sparkle. Smith sold to Auden in 2015, and the guitar-making business continues at a base in Northampton in the English Midlands.

GOYA

Levin in Sweden provided some of the first acoustic guitars imported into the US, branded Goya and sold from 1952 by Hershman of New York and David Wexler of Chicago. By 1959 Hershman's Goyas also included Swedish-made Hagstrom sparkle- and swirled-plastic-covered electric hollowbodies.

Hershman switched to Italian-made solidbody and hollowbody electric guitars and basses, including the Rangemaster models with Burns-style pickups and controls, until about 1970. In 1966 the Goya name had passed to Avnet (Guild). It later went to Kustom and then Martin, who imported Japanese Goya solidbodies around 1980 but mainly used the name on imported acoustics.

Goya was a brandname used for guitars imported to the US from various sources. At the end of the 1950s it appeared on the Swedish company Hagstrom's sparkle-top electrics (1959 ad, above), while this Rangemaster of 1968 (near left) came from Italy, probably originating at Eko. The Gordon-Smith Gypsy "60" SS hollowbody (far left) was produced in 1997.

GRETSCH

Making a distinctive mark with some visually arresting guitars, Gretsch has attracted some key players in its long history, including Chet Atkins, Duane Eddy and George Harrison. The company's founder, Friedrich Gretsch, emigrated to the United States from Germany in 1872 at the age of 16.

After working for a manufacturer of drums and banjos in New York City, Gretsch set up his own Fred Gretsch Manufacturing Company there in 1883 to make drums, banjos, tambourines and toy instruments.

Friedrich's son Fred, the eldest of seven children, took over at age 15 on his father's premature death in 1895. During the next five years Fred Sr, as he became known, added mandolins to the company's drum-making and banjo-making operations. In 1916 construction was completed of a large ten-story building at 60 Broadway, Brooklyn, just by the Williamsburg Bridge. This imposing building continued to house the factory and offices of the Gretsch company for many years.

In the early 1930s the guitar began to replace the banjo in general popularity, and about 1933 the first Gretsch-brand guitars appeared, a line of archtop and flat-top acoustics. They were offered alongside Gretsch's burgeoning wholesale list of other makers' instruments, including guitars from the "big two" Chicago manufacturers, Kay and Harmony. The first Gretsch-brand archtop electric was introduced around 1939,

The old-fashioned look of this Corvette, made in 1955, would soon give way to Gretsch's new cutaway electric models.

One of Gretsch's earliest electric guitars was the Electromatic Spanish hollowbody model, pictured in the 1950 catalog (left) alongside a number of more popular lap-steel electrics. The Electro II (main guitar, 1954 example) helped to set Gretsch's more modern cutaway electric archtop style, and would soon evolve into the Country Club model. The Country Club was one of the instruments that started a notable line of color options that Gretsch began to offer at this time. This 1955 Country Club (opposite page, left) is finished in Cadillac Green, further enhanced by gold-plated hardware. The Duo Jet was Gretsch's first "solidbody" electric (actually semi-solid), this one (opposite, center) made in 1955. Another Gretsch color, Jaguar Tan, is seen on this Streamliner (opposite, right), also made in 1955.

the shortlived Electromatic Spanish model, which was made for Gretsch by Kay. At this time Fred Sr was still nominally president of Gretsch, but in fact had effectively retired from active management in the early 1930s to devote himself to banking. He officially retired from Gretsch in 1942.

Fred Sr was replaced as company president in 1942 by his third son, William Walter Gretsch, generally known as Bill, who headed Gretsch until his premature death at the age of 44 in 1948. Bill's brother Fred Gretsch Jr, already the company's treasurer, then took over as president. It was Fred Jr who would steer the company through its glory years during the 1950s and 1960s.

After World War II was over, Gretsch placed a new emphasis on supplying guitars for professional musicians. The first new Gretsch electric guitar of the post-war era revived the Electromatic Spanish model name, this archtop debuting in 1949 alongside a number of Synchromatic acoustic guitars. The single-coil pickup of the Electromatic Spanish was the first of many made for Gretsch by Rowe Industries of Toledo, Ohio, a company run by Harry DeArmond. A few years later that DeArmond pickup would receive its official Gretsch name, the Dynasonic.

Cutaway-body electrics followed in 1951, the Electromatic and Electro II, in effect proving that Gretsch now took seriously the expanding electric guitar business. Helping to launch the models was a new Gretsch man, Jimmie Webster, a qualified piano-tuner

and inspired guitarist. Webster used an unusual "touch" playing system, similar to that popularized much later by Eddie Van Halen. Webster became an important ambassador for Gretsch, probably doing more than anyone else in the coming years to spread the word about Gretsch guitars, as well as doing much in the process to promote electric guitars and guitar-playing in general.

Gretsch certainly noticed the new solidbody electric guitar that Fender began marketing during 1950, mainly because the upstart California company chose to call it the Broadcaster. This was a model name that Gretsch still used – although spelled "Broadkaster" – for a number of its drum products. (Gretsch had made drums since its earliest days, and was important for its pioneering work in new manufacturing techniques, as well as instigating the significant switch among jazz drummers to smaller-size drums in the kit during the 1940s.)

At Gretsch's request, Fender dropped the Broadcaster name, changing it to Telecaster (which was a more appropriately modern name, anyway). When Fred Jr saw that Fender and Gibson were actually beginning to sell these new-style solidbody guitars, he acted swiftly. In 1953 Gretsch launched its first solidbody, the single-cutaway Duo Jet. In fact, the guitar was a semi-solid with routed channels and pockets inside, but the visual effect was certainly of a solidbody instrument. In its early years the new Duo Jet had, unusually, a body front covered in a black plastic material, as

George Harrison bought this 1957 Gretsch Duo Jet (main guitar) early in 1961, and is pictured that year (above) posing proudly with his first treasured American guitar alongside his fellow Beatles (drummer Pete Best was still in the group at that time). Harrison used the Duo Jet throughout the group's rise to fame, only retiring it when he acquired a double-cutaway Gretsch Country Gentleman in summer 1963.

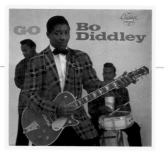

Two keen Gretsch players. Bo Diddley (near right) with a
vibrant jacket and a Jet Firebird, rather more sedate than
the custom-shape guitars Gretsch made for him around
1960. Jeff Beck used a Duo Jet to record his 1993 album
Crazy Legs (far right), a tribute to Gene Vincent – and more
especially to Vincent's Duo Jet-toting guitarist Cliff Gallup.

used on some Gretsch drums. It also had Gretsch's unique two-piece strap buttons (an early take on the idea of locking strap buttons) and the Melita Synchro-Sonic bridge.

The Melita was the first bridge to offer independent intonation adjustment for each string, beating Gibson's Tune-o-matic version by at least a year. Three more solidbodies in the style of the Duo Jet were added to the Gretsch line in 1954 and 1955: the country-flavored Round Up, the Silver Jet, and the red Jet Fire Bird. The Silver Jet came with a silver sparkle finish on the front of its body, and this was another product of Gretsch's helpful drum department.

That same year in the hollowbody lines the non-cutaway Electromatic Spanish became the Corvette, the cutaway Electro II became the Country Club, and the Electromatic became the Streamliner. The Country Club would go on to be the most enduring model name in Gretsch's history.

Another significant addition to the Gretsch line in 1954 was the option of colored finishes for some models, beyond the normal sunburst or natural varieties. We've already noted the company's use of drum coverings on the Silver Jet and the black Duo Jet, but equally flamboyant paint finishes were on the way.

Automobile marketing was having a growing influence on guitar manufacturers in the early 1950s, and the theme was especially evident in Gretsch's colorful campaign of 1954, with a Cadillac Green option for the Country Club and a Jaguar Tan (a sort of

dark gold) for the Streamliner. The paints came from DuPont, a company that also supplied most of the car companies at that time (and later Fender too). Gretsch drew yet again on its experience in finishing and lacquering drum products in different colors, artfully applying know-how that already existed within the operation to help make its guitars stand out in the market.

There had been isolated precedents for colored-finish guitars, such as Gibson's all-gold ES-295 and gold-top Les Paul of 1952, as well as Fender's infrequent and as-yet unofficial custom colors. But for a few years Gretsch made the use of color into a marketing bonus almost entirely its own. Through the middle 1950s Gretsch added a number of pleasant two-tone options – yellows, coppers, ivories – contrasting a darker body back and sides against a lighter-colored body front, for example on archtop electrics such as the Streamliner (launched 1954), Convertible (1955) and Clipper (1956). This two-tone style was yet further evidence of inspiration from long-standing techniques used in the drum department.

The success of Gibson's new Les Paul guitar – well over 2,000 were sold in 1953 alone – alerted other manufacturers, including Gretsch, to the value of a "signature" model endorsed by a famous player. Today the practice is very familiar, but back in the 1950s it was a new, exciting and potentially profitable area of musical instrument marketing. Around 1954 Jimmie Webster succeeded in securing talented Nashville-

Three desirable Gretsch Jet models
are pictured on this page: a Duo Jet
(far left) from 1958; a Jet Fire Bird
(center) made in 1960; and a Silver
Jet (near left) that dates from 1955.

based country guitarist Chet Atkins for this role, a move that in time would completely turn around Gretsch's fortunes.

After various discussions and meetings between the company and the guitarist, the Gretsch Chet Atkins Hollow Body 6120 model appeared in 1955. Atkins wasn't keen on the Western paraphernalia that Gretsch insisted on applying to the guitar – including cactus and cattle inlays, and a branded "G" on the body – but relented because he was so keen to get a signature guitar on to the market.

In fact, the decorations on the Hollow Body model were gradually removed over the following years. Gretsch had also given ground by adding a Bigsby vibrato to the production model, in line with Atkins's request. There was a Chet Atkins Solid Body, too, essentially a Round Up with a Bigsby vibrato – although, despite the name, the Solid Body still had Gretsch's customary semi-solid construction. Atkins had little to do with the Solid Body model, and it was dropped after a few years.

The Hollow Body, however, became Atkins's exclusive instrument for his increasingly popular work. It remained one of the most famous Gretsch models for many years, and Gretsch did good business from the new endorsement deal. Its 1955 catalog trumpeted: "Every Chet Atkins appearance, whether in person or on TV... and every new album he cuts for RCA Victor, wins new admirers to swell the vast army of Chet Atkins fans." The new Chet Atkins model effectively put Gretsch on the map. Not

This Chet Atkins Hollow Body 6120 (main guitar) was made in 1955, the model's launch year, and has all the Western paraphernalia: G-brand on body; engraved fingerboard markers; steer's head on the headstock. Gretsch used Atkins's name extensively, not just on guitars but on accessories such as strings too.

The Solid Body 6121 (far left, 1956 example) was the less popular semi-solid version of the first Chet Atkins models, despite Atkins appearing in ads such as this 1955 promo (below left). The catalog from that same year shows both the Hollow and Solid Chet models with special Gretsch Western straps attached.

pickguard. Very few White Penguins were sold, and the model has since become regarded as one of the most collectable of all Gretsch guitars.

Gretsch benefited from some big success stories among two early rock'n'roll guitarists, both of whom used Chet Atkins Hollow Body guitars to power their sound. Eddie Cochran was an accomplished guitarist who landed a cameo spot in the 1956 movie *The Girl Can't Help It* and then made some blasting rock'n'roll with his Hollow Body at the center of a churning mix of rockabilly, country and blues.

Duane Eddy turned out a string of hit records from the late 1950s, based on his deceptively simple instrumental style that will forever be known by the word that was attached to so many of the guitarist's albums: Twang! That twangy tone came when Eddy concentrated on playing melodies on the bass strings of his Hollow Body. He made full use of the pitch-bending potential of the guitar's Bigsby vibrato, as well as exploiting his amplifier's tremolo effect and the studio's echo facilities.

Ray Butts, a music store owner and electronics wizard from Cairo, Illinois, met Chet Atkins in 1954 and showed the guitarist his new combination amplifier that offered echo from a built-in tape loop, an unusual facility at the time. Atkins and players such as Carl Perkins and Scotty Moore became customers for Butts's amp. Then Atkins, who didn't like Gretsch's DeArmond pickups, asked Butts to come up with an improved type of pickup. Butts devised a humbucking model, around the same time that Seth Lover

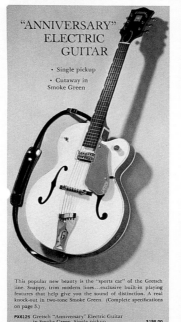
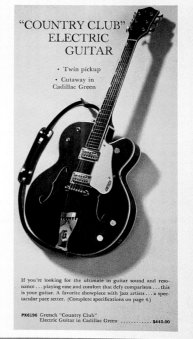

Three more fine Gretsch guitars are shown on this page: a single-cutaway Chet Atkins Country Gentleman (far left) from 1961; a "Single" Anniversary model (center) made in 1959; and a "Double" Anniversary (near left), with two pickups, that dates from 1961. Gretsch's control layouts are often unusual. The one-pickup guitar here has a single volume control near the cutaway and a tone-selector switch opposite. The two-pickup guitars here have a master volume control on the cutaway, a tone-selector switch for each pickup, and a volume control per pickup in the "normal" position, near the bridge. The 1959 catalog (above) also shows these layouts, on a one-pickup Anniversary and a two-pickup Country Club.

over at Gibson in Michigan formulated his humbucker. Gretsch was fitting the new Filter'Tron pickups to most electrics by 1958.

Two new models in the Chet Atkins series were the dark brown Country Gentleman and the red Tennessean. The Country Gent, new in 1957, was the first Gretsch hollowbody to be made with a thinline body – about two inches deep, unlike most of the company's existing hollowbodies which were around three inches deep. The thinline concept had been popularized by Gibson in the preceding years.

The Country Gent was also the first Gretsch Chet Atkins model to be offered with a slightly wider 17″ body, like the company's White Falcon, Country Club and Convertible. The Hollow Body (and indeed the new Tennessean) was closer to 16″ wide. The Gent had what are generally referred to by players and collectors as "fake" f-holes. These have a visual representation of f-holes on the body, to help the general look of the guitar, but are without actual apertures. The Gretsch f-holes would not revert to true holes until the early 1970s.

Atkins had tried to convince Gretsch that in order to cut feedback – and moreover to enhance the guitarist's beloved sustain – it would be useful to make the Country Gent's hollow body more "solid" at certain points by adding wooden reinforcement inside. In fact, what Atkins wanted was a guitar that had a solid wooden section running through the center of the body from neck to tailpiece – exactly as Gibson had done on

its ES-335 model that debuted in 1958. Gibson also needed this solid center to mount the bridge and humbucking pickups that it used at the time, but as Gretsch employed a floating bridge and non-height-adjustable humbuckers they had no need for this facility. Gretsch was content merely to add twin strengthening braces under the top of the Country Gentleman's body.

The new Space Control bridge appeared around this time, another Jimmie Webster design. It was simpler than the Melita, and lacked intonation adjustment. Also new were "Neo-Classic" half-moon-shape markers at the edge of the fingerboard, which appeared around 1957.

In 1958 Gretsch marked the 75th anniversary of the company's founding with a pair of special Anniversary model guitars. These were offered in one- and two-pickup versions that have since been nicknamed as the Single Anniversary and Double Anniversary models. Remarkably, they lasted in the Gretsch catalog until as late as 1977. Meanwhile, the tireless Jimmie Webster collaborated with Ray Butts to come up with the first stereo guitar system, "Project-O-Sonic." At first they achieved a stereo effect by splitting the output of the pickups, sending the sound of the top three strings to one amplifier and the bottom three to another.

This stereo circuitry was first launched as an option on the Country Club and White Falcon models during 1958. Various modifications appeared over subsequent years,

Jimmie Webster devised Gretsch's new stereo guitar system. The two guitars pictured on this page are a White Falcon Stereo (near right) from 1958 and a Country Club Stereo (far right). Webster is seen (above) in about 1962 with a later-style White Falcon Stereo model.

Chet Atkins picks on a double-cutaway Hollow Body while keeping in with the in-crowd.

but stereo seemed too complex to capture many players' imaginations. Another questionable piece of Webster weirdness was "T-Zone Tempered Treble," which translates to the more simple description "slanted frets." Webster claimed that they improved intonation. The White Falcon and the new high-end Viking model bore the skewed frets from 1964, the fingerboard helpfully marked with offset dot markers in the slanted zone to warn innocent players.

The Country Gent, Hollow Body and White Falcon changed to a double-cutaway style during 1961 and 1962. Gibson was as ever the primary inspiration for this decision: since 1958 the Kalamazoo guitar-maker had increasingly employed double cutaways to successful effect. With such a body design, players could more easily reach the higher frets of the fingerboard and make fuller use of this upper register when soloing. George Harrison, who'd previously used a Duo Jet, was a very visible player of the double-cutaway Country Gentleman in the 1960s.

Gretsch's solidbody line moved to a double-cutaway style too, from 1961. Also that year, Gretsch decided that it needed a cheaper solidbody that could compete with Gibson's Les Paul Junior, and so came up with the low-end Corvette (a name borrowed from an early archtop model). This was the company's first true solidbody guitar, and came complete with HiLo'Tron single-coil pickup. The Gretsch Corvette started life with a "slab" body like the Junior, but subsequently gained beveled-edge contours, aping

GEORGE HARRISON
of the BEATLES
and his
GRETSCH CHET ATKINS COUNTRY
GENTLEMEN GUITAR

Gretsch changed many of its models to a double-cutaway style from about 1961. The Country Gent followed the trend: this example (main guitar) was made in 1963. By far the most influential player of the model was George Harrison, seen in a Gretsch publicity shot from 1964 (above). The Chet Atkins Hollow Body 6120 also gained a double-cut body at the time; this one (far left) is from 1962.

Gibson's new SG design. During the early 1960s, Gretsch went on to toy with a number of peculiar solidbody designs – and the Bikini was certainly among the oddest. It consisted of a hinged, folding body-back which could accept slide-in, interchangeable guitar and bass necks. The body-backs were in both single- and double-neck styles. Few Bikinis were made.

The colorful Princess model of 1962 was, according to the boys at Gretsch, "engineered to meet the needs and standards of young women all over the world." Gretsch had, in fact, simply finished the later-style Corvette in special pastel color combinations designed to appeal to the delicate female sensibility.

Another opportunist solidbody based on the Corvette was the Twist of 1962, exploiting the contemporary dance craze. It sported a pickguard with a twisting red and white "peppermint" design. The Astro-Jet of 1963 was a very strange looking guitar, almost as if it had been left out too long on a hot Brooklyn summer day and melted into several disfigured lumps. It also had an apparently randomly styled headstock, with four tuners on one side, two the other.

During the guitar boom of the middle 1960s Gretsch decided to move its drum department out of the Brooklyn factory to another location a few blocks away, while a good deal of the company's wholesaling operations were either ceased or moved to the Chicago office. All this was to allow the whole of the seventh floor in Brooklyn to be turned over to guitar making, not least because of the popularity afforded Gretsch by George Harrison's prominent use of a Country Gentleman.

No Harrison signature model ever appeared, but Gretsch did produce a shortlived Monkees model to cash in on the TV pop group of the 1960s. Through a marketing deal the group featured Gretsch instruments including drums and the company's 12-string thinline electric introduced in 1966. The six-string Monkees model that Gretsch issued that same year had the group's distinctive guitar-shape logo on the pickguard and truss-rod cover.

By the mid 1960s models such as the high-end White Falcon came fitted with a gamut of guitar gadgets created by the ever-fertile mind of Jimmie Webster. They included the weird slanted frets in the upper register that we've already seen. Additionally there was a "standby" on/off switch, which on a stereo-equipped model meant a total of two control knobs and six switches, as well as a couple of levers behind the back pickup to operate padded string-dampers.

Also, the vibrato tailpiece would sport a telescopic adjustable arm, while a Floating Sound frame-like device sat on a "fork" passing through the body and contacting the back. It was positioned in front of the bridge with the strings passing through it and was supposed to enhance tone and increase sustain. Webster's inspiration came from the tuning forks he used regularly as a piano tuner. Thus the top-of-the-line Gretsch

Three Gretsch Corvette-style guitars are pictured on this page: an early-type Corvette (near right) from about 1961; a pastel-colored Princess (center) made in 1962; and a custom-finished "Gold Duke" Corvette (far right) from 1966.

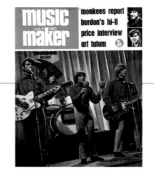

The Monkees received Gretsch gear (1967 magazine cover, right) in return for allowing Gretsch to market an endorsed guitar (pictured below, left).

models of the day were probably the most gadget-laden instruments on the market, assaulting players' imaginations with a plethora of possibilities. But some musicians were simply scared off.

Shockwaves had been sent through the guitar manufacturing industry in 1965 when the Fender companies were sold to the Columbia Broadcasting System corporation for $13million. D.H. Baldwin, an Ohio-based musical instrument company specializing in the manufacture of pianos and organs, was like many actively seeking to purchase a guitar-making operation at this time. In 1965 it had bid unsuccessfully for Fender. So Baldwin bought the Burns guitar company of England (see Baldwin) and then, in 1967, Gretsch.

Baldwin began to diversify away from its original core of music and into financial services, including banking and insurance. The company's Annual Report for 1969 noted a 12 per cent drop in Gretsch sales, conveniently attributing over half the fall to a three-month strike that began in October 1969.

By 1970 plans were underway by Baldwin to move the Gretsch factory out of its 54-year-old home in Brooklyn to a site in Booneville, Arkansas, well over 1,000 miles away. Baldwin already operated a number of factories there, enjoying cheaper and more amenable labor. Of course, the move did not please an already disgruntled workforce at Gretsch, and very few personnel made the move south-west in September

1970. The Brooklyn building continued to house Gretsch sales until that too was moved, first to the Illinois office and then in 1972 to Baldwin's HQ in Cincinnati, Ohio. Thus by the summer of 1972 the very last Gretsch connection had been severed with 60 Broadway, Brooklyn, New York City.

Before production moved in 1970 from Brooklyn to Booneville there was a period when Gretsch made a number of limited-run instruments for various retailers, players, teachers and so on. Not that Gretsch had ever been shy of custom work, most famously exemplified by the handful of odd-shaped solidbodies it made for Bo Diddley around 1960. Some Gretsch personnel have suggested that the company was more likely to do custom work in the summer months – when other business was slower. And collectors have always noted Gretsch as a brand where, as a result of its flexible approach to custom orders, almost anything is possible.

Small-order batches in the 1960s included specially modified models for Gretsch dealers such as Sam Ash (Anniversary-style with cat's-eye shape soundholes), Sam Goody (twin-cutaway archtop with "G"-shape soundholes) and Sherman Clay (gold- and silver-finish Corvettes, later nicknamed the Silver Duke and the Gold Duke).

Special small-run "signature" guitars were also made, including a limited number for New York-based player/teacher/store-owner Ronny Lee, as well as some six- and seven-string models named for guitarist George Van Eps (the seven-string version of

The Monkees gained TV fame and a Gretsch signature guitar (left), this one made in 1967. Other models in the line had gained a double-cutaway shape, including the Silver Jet (1969 example, center). The peculiar Astro-Jet (far right, from 1966, plus side view) and its bizarre body made few friends for Gretsch.

The new Committee model, with the popular laminated through-neck construction style of the time, seen (far left) on the cover of a 1978 catalog. This 1969 catalog page (near left) promotes the new Van Eps seven-string and the double-cutaway version of the Streamliner model.

which remained in the catalog for ten years). Around 1940 the Epiphone company had built Van Eps a custom guitar based on his unusual requirement for a seven-string model, adding a low-A below the existing E-string (over 40 years before Steve Vai came up with a similar idea).

Van Eps once explained that the reason for the additional low A-string was based on his love of deep basslines, and because he approached the guitar as a complete instrument within itself, almost a mini-orchestra.

Gretsch produced the Van Eps single-cutaway archtop models from 1968, in six-string as well as the seven-string versions. This underlined once again the company's compliant approach, enabling the manufacture of small numbers of limited-appeal instruments – even if it did mean tooling-up for the unique 14-pole humbuckers necessary for Van Eps's seven-string.

The first new Gretsch model of the Baldwin era was the undistinguished twin-cutaway thinline Rally, although it did have an unusual built-in active treble-boost circuit. More interesting, though hardly devastating, was a new line of Chet Atkins models. In 1972 the Deluxe Chet and the Super Chet were launched. The big, deep-body, single-cutaway archtop style was the result of a collaboration between Chet Atkins and Gretsch men Dean Porter and Clyde Edwards. The highly-decorated Super Chet sported an unusual row of control "wheels" built into the pickguard's edge, while

the plainer Deluxe Chet had conventional controls. The Deluxe did not last long, but the Super stayed in the line for some seven years.

Two new low-end guitars came along in 1975, the Broadkaster solidbody and semi-hollow electrics. As usual Gretsch was to some extent following Gibson's lead – and on this occasion the path was an unpopular one. Gibson had launched the Marauder, its first solidbody guitar with a Fender-style bolt-on neck, in 1974; likewise, the Broadkaster solidbody was the first Gretsch with a bolt-on neck, while also displaying strong Strat-style influences. Neither of these new Gretsch guitars drew much praise.

More new Chet Atkins signature models appeared in 1977. These were the effects-laden Super Axe, plus the gadget-less Atkins Axe. The distinctive look of these big new solidbody guitars with their sweeping, pointed cutaway was the subject of a patent issued to Gretsch designer Clyde Edwards for "ornamental design." Both were gone from the line by 1980.

There were a couple more solidbody electrics added to the Gretsch line in 1977, the TK 300 and the Committee. The TK 300 was another cheap bolt-on-neck solidbody, this time with a strange, asymmetric body, while the Committee followed a trend of the period for using through-neck construction. But these were uninspiring guitars by any standards, and appeared to be almost totally lacking in the character which had once been at the heart of Gretsch design. The last new Gretsch guitars to appear under

The White Falcon continued into the 1970s, seen here in mono (1975 example, left). The Chet Atkins Super Axe (1977 example, center) was the last new Atkins signature model of the period to appear from Gretsch. One of the last new models from the Gretsch/Baldwin operation was this Country Roc (far right) from 1975.

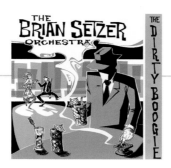

Brian Setzer spearheaded the 1990s rockabilly revival with his Orchestra, Gretsch guitars to the fore as ever, on albums such as this 1998 release, Dirty Boogie (right).

Baldwin ownership were the unappealing Beast solidbodys, launched in 1979. While nobody realized it at the time, they marked the end of an era with a depressingly low note. If Baldwin's performance in handling its fresh acquisition was measured by the aptitude and success of the new Gretsch guitar models that it launched during the 1970s, then the score would be low.

Baldwin fared little better in the business affairs surrounding Gretsch. Although sales picked up a little in the early 1970s, Baldwin was disturbed to find that the business was still not returning a profit, despite various cost-cutting exercises.

In early 1979, Baldwin bought the Kustom amplifier company, and by the end of the year had merged Gretsch with Kustom, moving the sales and administration office for the new combined operation to Chanute, Kansas. Probably during 1980 Baldwin finally decided that they would stop production of Gretsch guitars. Very few instruments were manufactured beyond the start of 1981 (which, somewhat ironically, was two years short of Gretsch's 100th anniversary).

A man called Charlie Roy was running the Gretsch/Kustom operation, which he bought from Baldwin in 1982, moving the offices to Gallatin, Tennessee, just outside Nashville. By now Chet Atkins's endorsement deal had come to a natural end, and he soon transferred allegiance to Gibson. (Gibson began making a number of Chet Atkins signature models from 1986.) Baldwin once again took control of Gretsch in about 1984, when the deal with Roy ceased. Around this time there was a last-ditch plan to revive Gretsch guitar production at a piano-action factory that Baldwin owned in Ciudad Juarez, Mexico. However, only a small trial batch of instruments was assembled, after which the idea was dropped.

Baldwin then sold Gretsch to yet another Fred Gretsch. This one was the grandson of Fred Sr, and we shall call him Fred III. He had originally worked for his grandfather at Gretsch from 1965 until 1971, when he began to run his own business, importing and wholesaling musical instruments. Fred III acquired the Synsonics brandname in 1980 from Mattel, which led to some success with acoustic and electronic percussion as well as electric guitars.

Fred III bought Gretsch from Baldwin at the very beginning of 1985. Gretsch drum production – which had never ceased – continued in Arkansas for a year, then moved to Fred's own premises in South Carolina. It was then that Gretsch guitar manufacturing was started again.

With the help of old Gretsch hand Duke Kramer, Fred III decided to introduce updated versions of the classic Gretsch models of the past, no doubt having noticed the increasing prices that certain Gretsch instruments had been fetching for some time on the "vintage" guitar market. The unique character of Gretsch – in sound, looks and playability – was appealing to yet another new generation of players. Kramer drew up

A new Gretsch company was up and running by 1989. Among the new offerings was a signature model for Brian Setzer (1995 example far left, alongside a Japanese ad from the previous year). Two more modern signature models are pictured here: an Elliot Easton 6128 (center, from 2004); and a Nashville Keith Scott 6120KS (right, from 2005).

Tim Armstrong of Rancid cradles his signature model in this 2006 ad (far left), while a magnificent collection of Eddie Cochran memorabilia graces an ad from 2010 (near left) promoting Gretsch's limited edition Eddie Cochran Tribute Hollow Body 6120EC (example pictured below right).

specifications for the proposed new models, and visited many American makers with a view to US production. But negotiations were unsuccessful, and so Gretsch decided to go "offshore," in guitar-biz-speak — meaning that they contracted a manufacturer based a good distance beyond the shores of the United States. After some searching, Gretsch selected Terada in Japan as its new factory.

However, in 1989 Gretsch offered an unusual forerunner to its forthcoming guitars with a series of Korean-made electrics intended to capitalize on the popularity of the fictional-family supergroup The Traveling Wilburys. The cheap and somewhat primitive guitars were loosely based on the group's old Danelectro instruments, and various models were issued, all boldly finished in what Gretsch called "original graphics" with a travel theme appropriate to the band's name.

Gretsch delivered its first proper models later in 1989. Clearly it could no longer use Chet Atkins's name, now a Gibson property, so while some of the model names were familiar, others were necessarily modified. Nine new Gretsch models were launched. There were five hollowbodies: the Tennessee Rose, recalling a Tennessean; the Nashville; Nashville Western with G-brand and Western appointments; Country Classic, recalling a Country Club; and Country Classic double-cutaway. There were four solidbodies: a Duo Jet; Silver Jet; Jet Fire Bird; and Round Up. This was just the start, and more reissues would come along, including Anniversary models, Country Clubs,

and a White Penguin, and signature models for Bo Diddley, Elliot Easton, Duane Eddy, Keith Scott, Brian Setzer, Stephen Stills, Malcolm Young, and more.

There were new twists, too, such as Falcons finished in black or with silver-colored metalwork, scaled-down versions of various models, a number of colored sparkle-finish Jets, a 12-string or two, a double-neck Jet, and some new Spectra-Sonic models (six-string, baritone, and bass) designed in collaboration with the pickup specialist TV Jones, who created and re-created several pickups and consulted for Gretsch on various matters for a few years from 1998.

The path toward accurate re-creations of old designs started in 1992 with the new firm's attempt at a vintage-style 6120, the Nashville 6120-1960. It was a commendable first try, with thumbnail markers, zero fret, three knobs and two selectors, and a two-and-a-half-inch deep body, but other details like the Bigsby and the bridge seemed adrift.

Further bids for vintage veracity came with oldie-style takes on the Country Classic (Gent), Country Club, Duo Jet, Falcon, Nashville (6120), Silver Jet, and Tennessee Rose (Tennessean), and even the Atkins Axe and Super Chet. But it was a while before the vintage-intended guitars were shuffled much closer to the originals.

Gretsch made an alliance with Fender in 2003, where the Fender Musical Instruments Corporation was granted the exclusive rights to "develop, produce, market,

Three more models from the early 21st century Gretsch lines: a "Billy-Bo" Jupiter Thunderbird 6199 (near right, from 2005), which came about when Billy Gibbons was inspired by Bo Diddley's weird instruments; a model from Gretsch's budget Electromatic sub-brand (center), this a 5120BK from 2009, one of a series of limited editions pinstriped by hot rod graphic artist JimmyC; and a re-creation of Eddie Cochran's 6120 (far right), the Eddie Cochran Tribute Hollow Body 6120EC from 2010, this one in left-handed style.

The headline on this 2003 ad (left) seems to sum up Gretsch's cool vibe, while the other ad here (far left), from a few years later, features the Reverend Horton Heat and his aged signature-model 6120.

and distribute" Gretsch guitars worldwide. Fender made a complete overhaul of the lines, and as a result, Fender-era Gretsches – the regular Japanese-made Professional Series, rejigged in 2003, as well as the high-end US Custom Shop instruments, begun in '04 – seemed more accurate and better made. The Custom Shop has produced notably detailed Tribute re-creations based on famous old Gretsches, including an Eddie Cochran 6120 in 2010 and a George Harrison Duo Jet the following year.

Gretsch regained most of the Chet Atkins model names in 2007. Chet had died in 2001, and Gretsch made a deal with his family. The renamed models, which would be offered in a multitude of different styles and levels, were the Chet Atkins Hollow Body 6120 (previously the Nashville) and the Chet Atkins Country Gentleman 6122 (previously Country Classic). The Chet Atkins name was also restored to the Solid Body 6121. The Chet Atkins Tennessee Rose 6119 was the only model that kept the old name, because Gibson still owned a trademark for the original name, Tennessean.

During recent times Gretsch has added more models, including a line of Center Block models that began in 2013, in the regular Professional series as well as the second-tier Electromatics. They have a solid spruce block running the length of the body (chambered at the lower bout to reduce weight), similar to a Gibson 335.

Gretsch has settled to a pleasing balance between classic models and new ideas, and the old slogan "That Great Gretsch Sound" looks set to be heard for many years.

Gretsch's alliance with Fender in 2003 opened a new path for the company, and in recent years the brand has seemed stronger than ever. This 2014 Brian Setzer Hot Rod 6120SH (left) was a stripped-down Setzer signature, with simpler controls, while the Duo Jet (right) recalled an early-1960s double-cut Jet, although this 2012 example was finished in dark cherry metallic. Gretsch's Center Block models, introduced in 2013, had a chambered 335-like center block through the hollow body. Examples included this Center Block Jr 6112 (far right) from 2016.

GRIMSHAW

On the UK's embryonic electric guitar scene of the late 1950s, Emile Grimshaw's London-based company provided more or less the only practical British-made instruments available for serious players.

Soon-to-be stars such as Joe Brown and Bruce Welch favored the SS De Luxe, a short-scale, slim semi-solidbody. The SS had quite adventurous styling for its type and the era, with a figured sycamore body that featured offset cutaways and unusual "teardrop"-shape soundholes. The guitar conjured a very modern image compared to most of the available competition at the time.

Grimshaw was already well established, having started in business two decades earlier. Although primarily producing numerous acoustic models, the company catered for the 1960s beat boom with an increasing assortment of electrics. Most were hollowbodies, but the Meteor was an early solidbody alternative.

The early 1970s brought more solidbodies to the Grimshaw line in the shape of the GS7 and GS33 models, while the GS30 was one of the first unabashed Les Paul-alikes, and all the more popular among players as a result.

Later models such as the Telecaster-style GTC and the SG-based GSG Custom were more copies, but by the mid 1980s the brand had effectively succumbed to the onslaught of Japanese imports armed with the same intentions.

Underlining Guild's early benefit from an influx of ex-Epiphone workers, this Guild Stratford X-350 (this page, right) made in 1954 was similar in pickup and control layout to Epiphone's Zephyr Emperor Regent model. On the opposite page are three more Guilds: the top electric archtop of its time, a Stuart X-550 from 1958 (left); a Duane Eddy from 1962 (center); and a Bert Weedon Model made in 1966 (right).

Guild first produced its Johnny Smith Award model in 1956, although Smith (seen in 1957 ad, below) apparently did not like it. Guild renamed it the Artist Award during 1961 – the same year that a Gibson Johnny Smith model appeared.

Grimshaw made this striking Electric Deluxe model (near right) in London during the late 1950s.

Jazz guitarist Johnny Smith's allegiance with Guild may have been shortlived, but more regrettable is that his playing career, flecked with masterful, emotive performances, was not much longer itself.

GUILD

For players who've discovered them, Guild guitars have since their inception in the early 1950s always offered a high-quality alternative to the market leaders. Founded in New York City by jazz guitarist Alfred Dronge, Guild was born just as the Epiphone company was embroiled in a labor dispute and was relocating to Philadelphia. Many former Epiphone employees joined the new company and brought their skills to Guild, especially in making carved archtops.

So it's no surprise that Guild's first guitars, introduced around 1953, were non-cutaway and single-cutaway archtops – either electric, or acoustics with an optional pickup. Guild's archtops would always command respect, although the company quickly began to make its reputation with high-quality acoustic flat-tops. The full-bodied, rounded "F"-series and dreadnoughts that debuted in 1954 were played through the years by stars such as Eric Clapton, Ralph Towner and Charlie Byrd (who chose an instrument from the classical Mark series).

Among Guild's 1953 non-cutaway electric archtops were the one-pickup X-100 and two-pickup X-200, replaced the following year by the one-pickup Granada (and renamed the Cordoba X-50 in 1961) which was offered until 1970. Single-cutaway models included the shortlived one-pickup X-300, two-pickup X-400 and three-pickup X-600, plus the luxuriously appointed Stuart X-500 which remained Guild's flagship

archtop until 1994. Other long-running single-cutaway electric archtops introduced the following year were the one-pickup Savoy X-150, two pickup Manhattan X-175, and two-pickup hollowbody Aristocrat M-75, a model that lasted until 1963 and then reappeared a few years later as the semi-hollow BluesBird, transforming into the solidbody M-75 BluesBird in 1970.

In 1956 Guild moved its factory to Hoboken, New Jersey, and picked up its first pro endorsement by jazz great Johnny Smith, beginning a string of artist models. The single-cutaway, single-DeArmond-equipped Johnny Smith Award was introduced that year – renamed the Artist Award in 1961 – and became another high-end mainstay of the Guild line. In 1962 jazz ace George Barnes entered the fold with his single-cutaway, twin-humbucker George Barnes AcoustiLectric model, followed by the "George Barnes Guitar In F" model in 1963, both offered until the early 1970s.

Twangy instrumentalist Duane Eddy also came on board in 1962 with his single-cutaway, twin-DeArmond Duane Eddy Deluxe (lasting to 1987) followed by the Standard in 1963 (until 1974). From 1963-65 the single-cutaway Bert Weedon Model, with two DeArmonds and a Bigsby vibrato, was available, endorsed by the British sessionman and author of the influential teaching book *Play In A Day*.

Guild entered the thinline market in 1960 with its Starfire series, initially single-cutaways (Starfire I with one single-coil pickup, II with two single-coil pickups, III with

The offset-shape Guild Thunderbird (1966 example, left) had a guitar-stand built into the back of the body.

Guild's 1979 ad (below) features a specially built see-through plastic version of the company's "bell-bottom" S series solidbody of the period. Two Guild f-hole electrics are shown on this page: a Starfire III made in 1961 (below, center), and an Artist Award from 1976 (right).

Ax-cessories.

added Bigsby), all but the Starfire I lasting into the mid 1970s. These were joined in 1963 by the double-cutaway Starfire IV (two humbuckers) and V (Bigsby), followed in 1964 by the VI (gold hardware, pearl/abalone block inlays) and the XII 12-string. All but the IV ceased during the 1970s, and all but the I were revived in the 1990s.

In 1963 Guild began making solidbody electrics, producing many excellent instruments – even some classics – yet never really finding great success. Guild's first solidbody was one of the most unusual American guitars of the 1960s, the lumpy "Gumby"-shaped S-200 Thunderbird, available from 1963-68. Not only was the shape unusual, but the guitar featured a very early example of phase-switching (for a different pickup sound) and more importantly was one of only two guitars ever to incorporate a metal stand built into the back.

Despite these oddities, the Thunderbird had enough appeal to win over an eclectic bunch of players, including Muddy Waters, Zal Yanofsky, Jorma Kaukonen and Banana. The Thunderbird was joined by two other similarly shaped solids, the plainer S-100 Polara (also with built-in stand) and the single-pickup S-50 Jet-Star, both gone by the late 1960s. The S-200 and S-100 featured Swedish Hagstrom vibratos.

In 1966 Guild was purchased by Avnet Inc, an electronics firm that also purchased the Hershman company and its Goya guitar brandname that year. Alfred Dronge was retained to manage Guild, and production began to shift over to a new factory in

Westerly, Rhode Island. Guild production continues there today. When Hoboken production ended in 1971 the corporate HQ was moved to Elizabeth, New Jersey.

In 1970 Guild revisited the solidbody market and introduced a new S-100 Polara, more conventionally styled with a slightly offset double cutaway, and twin humbuckers. It's often referred to as "Guild's SG" because of its similarity to the Gibson, though it was closer to Hagstrom's mid-1960s solidbody design. Two low-end companions were also introduced at this time, the S-90 and S-50. An S-100 Deluxe joined the line in 1973 with optional stereo output, followed by the S-100C in 1974, a version with an oak leaf carved into the front. The previously mentioned M-75 solidbody was offered from 1970-80, along with a Deluxe version and, beginning in 1975, the M-85CS.

In 1972 Dronge was killed in an aircraft crash and was succeeded by Leon Tell. Guild briefly participated in the "copy era" in 1973-74 by offering Japanese-made Madeira-brand copies of its own S-100 as well as of Fender and Gibson designs.

The SG-like S series was retired in 1976, supplanted by a new S design with offset double-cutaways and a "bell"-shaped lower bout. With different appointments (some sporting DiMarzio pickups) these included the S-60, S-65, S-70, S-300, and S-400, all offered through 1982.

From 1980-83 the M-80 was available, a double-cutaway version of the M-75. In 1981 Guild introduced its first Strat-style solids, the S-250 and S-25 (both with set-necks) and its first "pointy" guitars, the X-82 Nova and X-79 Skylark. The X-82 Nova was essentially a hybrid Explorer/Flying V similar to Dean's ML model, while the X-79 Skylark was more radically pointed and had a dramatically extended upper horn and sloped lower bout, and a matching headstock shape. Both lasted into the mid 1980s. In 1983 the X-80 Skyhawk joined the line, essentially an X-79 variant. The Madeira brand was revived briefly on a series of original and copy designs in the early 1980s.

During 1983, Guild began offering a number of fairly popular Strat-style models, often with a bewildering variety of model names for the same or similar guitars, and all distinguished by set-necks and Guild's first six-tuners-in-line headstocks. The S series differed primarily in details such as pickup types and layouts and included Flyer, Thunderbolt and Aviator models among others.

In 1984 and '85 Guild offered perhaps its most exotic solidbodies with the X-88 Crue Flying Star (a very pointy variant on the X-82, named for Motley Crue's Mick Mars), the X-100 Bladerunner (almost "X"-shaped, with large holes cut out of the body, designed by luthier David Andrews) and the X-90 Citron Breakaway (shaped something like a Jackson Randy Rhoads V but with detachable wings to make it a travel guitar, designed by luthier Harvey Citron).

In 1985 the single-cutaway solid Bluesbird and semi-hollow Nightbird electrics debuted. It was also during this mid-1980s period that Guild introduced one of its more

Two more Guild guitars are shown on this page. This M-75 BCG BluesBird (far left) was made in 1977, showing the design used for the BluesBird during the 1970s (compare the 1990s example at the top of the page). The S-100 Carved (near left, this one made in 1974) is in Guild's offset-SG-like style used for a number of models in the 1970s. The Carved had an unusual design of acorns and leaves in the top. Soundgarden's Kim Thayil (below, and ad, left) repopularized the S-100 in the 1990s.

collectable models, the Brian May MHM1, promoted as a "copy" of the Queen guitarist's homemade axe, even though it wasn't an exact replica.

A period of turmoil began for Guild. In 1986 Avnet sold Guild to an investment group headed by banker Jere Haskew from Chattanooga, Tennessee. Around this time Guild introduced Telecaster-style guitars in two versions, the fancy T-250 and the T-200 Roy Buchanan, endorsed by the great Tele ace. These were Guild's first bolt-on-neck guitars. In 1987-88 Guild returned to imports with a line of high-quality Japanese-made solidbodies carrying the Burnside brandname, including both Strat- and Tele-style guitars and original "pointy" designs (often with flashy paint jobs). Some had set-necks, others were bolt-ons.

In 1987 Guild experienced financial difficulties, yet managed to introduce some fine electrics including the high-end semi-hollow Nightbird I and II, the solidbody Liberator series and the well-made but otherwise conventional Detonator superstrat. The Liberator Elite was a spectacular set-neck guitar with a carved flamed-maple body cap and fancy rising-sun inlays.

In 1988 Guild went into bankruptcy and ceased solidbody guitar production, although it did continue to manufacture the semi-hollow and hollowbody electrics (which often appear to be solids) for a couple more years. In 1989 the company was sold to the Fass Corporation of New Berlin, Wisconsin (subsequently US Music

Guild collaborated with Brian May for a series of instruments based on his famous home-made guitar, Big Red, beginning with the BHM-1 in 1984, as featured in the 1986 ad (above). Closer to the original was the Brian May Signature (1993 example, opposite), followed by three more May models in 1994.

Guild joined the pointy-body trend with the X-79 model (main guitar), this example dating from 1984.

The "bell-bottom" body shape of the S series (S-70D from 1980, right) took Guild solidbodies into the early 1980s. Later in that decade Guild's particular take on superstrat fashion led to its Flyers (1986 ad, above).

Brian May with his original homemade guitar – Big Red – on stage with Queen (below). May continued to use the instrument regularly for his solo projects following Queen's demise, including the 1998 album Another World (left).

Corporation). While domestic electric production was in hiatus, the Madeira brand was again revived in 1990-91 and was applied to a brief run of Stratocaster-style and Les Paul-style instruments.

After a period when Guild concentrated on its traditional strengths – mainly flat-top acoustics – the company ventured back to solidbodies in 1993-94 by reviving the Brian May guitar with the limited-edition Signature, this time a little closer to the original. This guitar was followed in 1994-95 by three more Brian May models: these were the Pro, the Special, and the Standard, which differed in precise appointments. In 1994 Guild reissued its venerable SG-style solidbody, the S-100 of the 1970s, after its high-profile use by Kim Thayil.

In late 1995, Guild was sold to Fender. The new owner decided to bring Guild designs to a wider market with an additional line of less expensive equivalents marketed with the DeArmond name, after Harry DeArmond whose Rowe company made many of Guild's early pickups (see DeArmond). The Brian May models were dropped from the catalog – later copies of the Queen man's guitar were made by Burns London in the early 2000s, and then May formed Brian May Guitars to produce his own versions – and the accent at Guild was now more on traditional design.

Late-1990s Guilds included revivals of the 1960s-style single-cutaway Starfire semi-hollowbodies, alongside the continuing Bluesbird and S-100 solidbodies. The well

known archtop builder Bob Benedetto was brought into the Guild fold during 2000 in order to redefine Guild's Artist Award and Stuart archtops, and also he was charged with launching a new custom-shop Guild Benedetto line of instruments, which included the small sealed-body Benny model.

In 2001, Guild moved production from its long-standing Westerly, Rhode Island, premises to Fender's factory in Corona, California. Three years later came a further move to Tacoma, Washington, but shortly afterward electric production stopped, and there was yet another move to New Hartford, Connecticut.

Guild opened a Custom Shop in 2013 and launched the Orpheum series, which aimed to reissue a number of Guild's classic electrics of the 1950s and 60s, including Starfire, M-75 Aristocrat, and A-150 Savoy models, with further additions the following year. However, in 2014, Fender sold Guild to the Cordoba Music Group, with Ren Ferguson heading the new venture as vice president of manufacturing and R&D, and production of US-made Guild electrics was reinstated in California.

The reinvigorated operation offered a number of electric models, including a Thunderbird, renamed as the T-Bird, an S-100 and T-bird-shape S-200, the solidbody Bluesbird, and of course a swarm of Starfires, including the III, IV, V, and VI variants. Hollowbody electrics in the 2017 Guild catalog included the M-75 Aristocrat, A-150 Savoy, X-175 Manhattan, C-100D Capri, and T-50 Slim.

GUYATONE

One of the oldest Japanese guitar brands, Guyatone dates from the 1930s when Mitsuo Matsuki set up in Tokyo. The Guyatone brand was based on Matsuki's nickname "Guya," someone who takes care of tools. Guyatone's first solidbody electric debuted in 1955, the "Les Paul Model," styled more like early Nationals and Supros. Exporting began in the late 1950s. Budget Guyatones (some branded Star or Antoria) proved popular in the UK, where little else was available. Hank Marvin was an early customer.

By the mid 1960s the catalog had expanded, with some inspiration from Mosrite, plus originals like the "holed" LG-160T Telstar. The high-end LG-350T Sharp 5 was featured by the Japanese group of that name.

Around 1968 the electric guitar market crashed in Japan. Many companies failed, including Guyatone. It re-emerged as the Guya Co Ltd. When the Japanese "copy era" began during the early 1970s Guyatone was quick to contribute a succession of Fender and Gibson clones. The mid 1970s brought some Guyatone originals and a revival of the Sharp 5. One guitar even came with a basic drum machine on-board.

Matsuki died in 1992. The LGX-II of 1993 employed a novel combination of Gibson and Fender features and was endorsed by the late Rory Gallagher. The Sharp 5 was reissued again in 1996, as was the LG-2100M. Another reissue of a 1960s model was the LG-160T that appeared in 2000 complete with distinctive body hole.

Three Guild instruments are shown on this page: a Blues 90 (near right) made in 2000, with P-90-style pickups; an X-700 Stuart archtop electric (center) from 1995; and a reissue Starfire IV semi-solidbody that dates from 2000.

HAGSTROM

Hagstrom of Älvdalen, Sweden, was a major global operator during the great guitar boom of the 1960s. The company had been founded as an accordion importer in 1921 by Albin Hagstrom. Guitar-making began in 1958 with the sparkle-plastic-covered hollowbody De Luxe and Standard models.

These single-cutaway guitars could in theory at least be played "acoustically," or electrically with modular plug-in assemblies featuring one, two or four single-coil pickups. Their popularity was later boosted when bands such as Roxy Music and ABC displayed them in publicity material. (The guitars were imported into the US from 1959 to 1961 by Hershman, with the Goya brand.)

In 1962 Hagstrom introduced the Kent-brand line of Strat-influenced solidbodies featuring vinyl-covered backs and Lucite (plastic) covered fronts. These were sold in the US by Merson as Hagstroms (the Kent name was already in use by Buegeleisen & Jacobson) and in the UK by Selmer as Futurama guitars. The patented Hagstrom vibrato was licensed to Guild and Harmony and appeared on some of their 1960s solidbodies. The asymmetrically shaped two-pickup Impala and three-pickup Corvette (later Condor) with pushbutton controls appeared from 1963-67.

Kents later lost the Lucite, became distinctly more Strat-like, and gained the Hagstrom brand. By 1965, body-horns had become more pointed, hinting more at

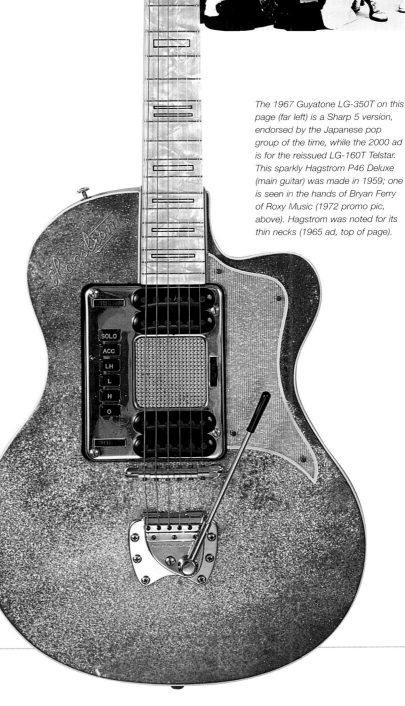

The 1967 Guyatone LG-350T on this page (far left) is a Sharp 5 version, endorsed by the Japanese pop group of the time, while the 2000 ad is for the reissued LG-160T Telstar. This sparkly Hagstrom P46 Deluxe (main guitar) was made in 1959; one is seen in the hands of Bryan Ferry of Roxy Music (1972 promo pic, above). Hagstrom was noted for its thin necks (1965 ad, top of page).

Elvis Presley appeared on his famous December 1968 "comeback" TV special playing a Hagstrom Viking, providing an unexpected PR bonus for Hagstrom's US agent, Merson.

Gibson's SG, and making a classic Hagstrom style. The line included 12-string models (Frank Zappa used one) and Viking thinlines. Hagstrom's most popular model, the Les-Paul-like Swede, was offered from 1973 to 1982. Equipped with a synthesizer pickup it was also offered as the Patch 2000 in the late 1970s (see Ampeg). A fancier Super Swede was made from 1978-83. In 1968 Hagstrom had hired New York luthier James D'Aquisto to design an archtop model, the Jimmy, with f-holes or oval soundhole. A number were produced in 1969, but supply problems delayed main production until the late 1970s. Hagstrom considered sourcing instruments from Japan in the early 1980s, but instead decided to cease production in 1983 to concentrate on music retailing. The brand was revived for electric guitars in 2008, with re-creations of many Hagstrom classics.

HALLMARK

Headed by ex-Mosrite man Joe Hall, this shortlived company was based in Arvin, California. The only Hallmark model was the Swept Wing, its large, thin body having a distinctive offset-arrow outline. A semi-solid version debuted in 1967, followed by a solidbody, and there were six-strings, 12-strings, basses and double-necks.

HAMER

One of the new-generation American makers of the 1970s, Hamer has survived with an enviable reputation. Established around 1975, Hamer grew out of Northern Prairie

Music, a respected repair workshop in Wilmette, Illinois, that included co-founders Paul Hamer and Jol Dantzig. Hamer and chief ideas-man Dantzig preferred Gibson designs and construction. Their early instruments reflected this with liberal use of mahogany, the Gibson scale-length, a 22-fret glued-in neck and twin humbuckers. First up was the Standard, strongly Explorer-based but no clone: high-end features included a bound, bookmatched maple top, and pickups from DiMarzio, the company that Larry DiMarzio had set up earlier in the 70s to make replacement pickups, which at the time was a novel idea.

The Sunburst of 1977 had the outline of Gibson's late-1950s double-cutaway Les Paul Junior. It took the souped-up idea that Dantzig had begun with the Standard, merging several designs into a new and attractive, playable whole. Hamer's dealers had asked for something less expensive than the Standard, and with less of the radical look of that Explorer-shaped model. It became a classic Hamer, sharing the features and deluxe appointments of the Standard and adding Fender-like through-body stringing and a fixed bridge.

The Sunburst was an important model in electric guitar history, because it was a production instrument that took elements of other instruments and combined them to create something new and something attractive to contemporary players, at a time when there were frustrations with what the big makers were producing. It was a time

Three more Hagstrom guitars on this page: a plastic-topped Kent PB24G (near right) made in 1963; a multi-control Impala (center) from 1965; and a Swede model, this 1980 example being part of a Patch 2000 guitar synthesizer outfit. The 2008 Hagstrom ad (right) marked the brand's comeback, cleverly combining a 1967 ad for Frank Zappa and a Hagstrom Viking with a contemporary promo for Frank's son Dweezil Zappa and a Viking TSB model... plus the same wicker chair.

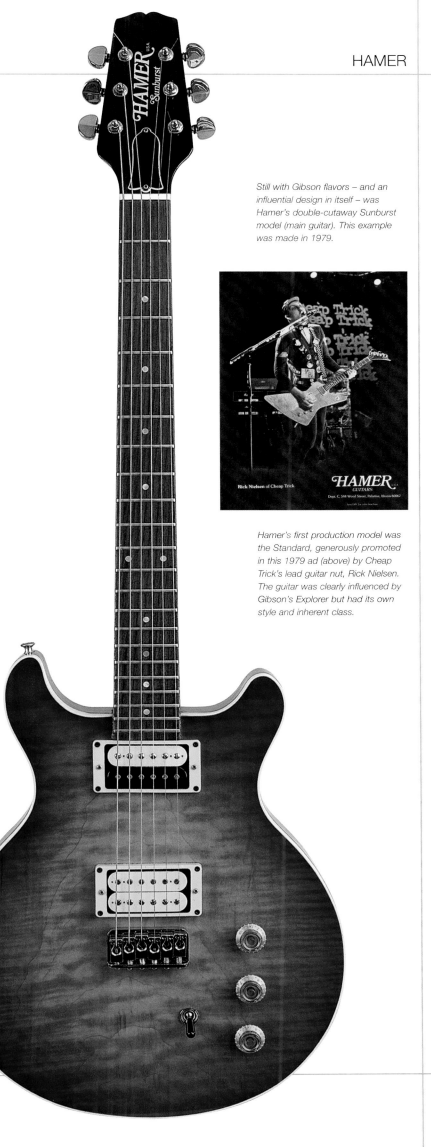

of the growth of the vintage trend – the notion that older guitars were somehow better. At Hamer, meanwhile, the Sunburst was joined by the more basic Special model in 1980, the same year that Hamer relocated to larger premises in Arlington Heights, on the north-west side of Chicago.

The 1981 Prototype was the first with completely original styling, although it was far from a radical guitar. The odd triple-coil pickup did attract Andy Summers of The Police, however. Multi-string basses became a Hamer specialty, including eight- and 12-string versions. Although Cheap Trick's Rick Nielsen was Hamer's highest-profile fan, his unusual taste in guitars precluded a signature production model, so Hamer's first signature guitar was the Steve Stevens model, launched in 1984.

In 1988 Hamer was acquired by Ovation's manufacturer, Kaman. Paul Hamer had left a year earlier, and it was around this time that significant changes were made to the line. Most Gibson-influenced models disappeared, largely replaced by superstrat designs catering for the new breed of fast-gun guitarists. More unusual were the 36-fret Virtuoso and seven-string Maestro, while the Sustainiac infinite-sustain system was a novel option on the Chaparral.

A stylistic balance returned with the reissued Sunburst in 1989, amid a fashionable revival of guitars with two humbuckers and a fixed bridge. Since then this original Hamer has been reborn several times, including high-end Archtops and cheaper

Still with Gibson flavors – and an influential design in itself – was Hamer's double-cutaway Sunburst model (main guitar). This example was made in 1979.

Hamer's first production model was the Standard, generously promoted in this 1979 ad (above) by Cheap Trick's lead guitar nut, Rick Nielsen. The guitar was clearly influenced by Gibson's Explorer but had its own style and inherent class.

Hallmark's only contribution to electric guitar design was this bizarre instrument (left), aptly named the Swept Wing. This solidbody version was made during 1967, and the ad (below) dates from the same year.

Specials. The line became further diversified during the 1990s, following Dantzig's departure early in the decade. Fender derivatives as well as the Korean-made Slammer series, launched in 1993, brought the US designs to more affordable levels.

The Duo Tone was Hamer's hybrid guitar, launched in 1994. In 1998 Hamer revived the 1980s Phantom name but using the shape of the Prototype model. A year later the company issued a suitably deluxe 25th Anniversary model.

In 2008, Fender acquired Kaman, and the deal included the Hamer brand. The future of Hamer seemed unclear, and in 2013 it limped to what seemed like a final halt. Then in 2015, Fender sold Kaman (KMC) to Jam Industries, and two years later KMC announced the reintroduction of Hamer, which KMC described as America's original boutique guitar line. Models included the Sunburst Flame, Vector Flame, Standard Flame, Special Junior, and Monaco Flame.

HARMONY

Before guitars turned global during the 1960s one of the largest mass-manufacturers of bargain and midrange guitars was the Harmony company of Chicago, founded by German immigrant Wilhelm J.F. Schultz in 1892.

By about 1905 the company had become a large supplier of instruments to the Sears, Roebuck mail-order catalog, with a variety of "parlor" guitars. In 1914 Sears introduced Supertone-brand guitars, virtually all Harmony-made, and purchased Harmony in 1916. Schultz died in 1925 and was succeeded by Jay Kraus. In 1928 Harmony introduced a line of acoustics endorsed by Roy Smeck. During the Depression of the 1930s fancier trim was replaced by stenciled designs, typical of cheaper Harmony guitars through the 1950s.

Harmony's first archtop acoustic guitar models appeared during the mid 1930s. However, in 1940 Sears sold Harmony to a group of investors headed by Kraus. Sears changed the in-house brandname used for its guitars to Silvertone, and these were no longer exclusively made by Harmony.

Harmony came relatively late to electric guitars, with an amplified Spanish archtop and Hawaiian lap-steel appearing in 1939. From around 1948 Harmony increasingly applied pickups to full-sized archtops, which continued through the 1960s. Harmony's first solidbody electric debuted in 1953: the small copper-finished, Les-Paul-shaped Stratotone had a neck and body made from one piece of wood.

The Stratotone line expanded in 1955 with the black Doublet and the yellow or green Newport, with aluminum and vinyl strips on the sides. In 1955 electric Roy Smeck guitars appeared, a Spanish archtop and a lap-steel. In 1956 Harmony introduced the one-pickup H65, its first cutaway archtop.

Harmony thinlines began with the single-cutaway Meteor hollowbodies in 1958. By this time the electric models featured single-coil pickups by DeArmond, and bolt-on

Three Hamer guitars here: this Chaparral Elite (near right) of 1990 has a Sustainiac pickup fitted at the neck position, linked to the on-board infinite-sustain system; this Phantom A5 (center) of 1984 boasts a triple-coil pickup, first used by Hamer on its earlier Prototype model; and this Duo Tone of 1994 (far right) was Hamer's hybrid guitar, mixing electric and "acoustic" pickup sounds. "Art Is Where You Find It," Hamer said in this 1996 ad (right) for the Eclipse series, and the 1990 ad (top of page) features Vernon Reid of Living Colour with a custom-finish guitar.

The Stratotone model in its earliest guise was Harmony's first solidbody electric. The yellow Newport H42/1 example (far left) dates from 1957, as does the ad above it where Harmony aims the two-pickup version squarely at country players. This later Stratotone Jupiter H-49 (main guitar) was made in 1960. This exotic 1950s ad (top) had to admit that Harmony's home town was Chicago.

191

A Harmony catalog from 1960 (right) displays the yellow sunburst H75, also available as the cherry sunburst H77 (main guitar, left).

where there's music...
there's Harmony

HARMONY GUITARS
ELECTRIC GUITARS & AMPLIFIERS
MANDOLINS • BANJOS • UKULELES

Copr. 1958 The Harmony Company, Chicago 9, U.S.A.

Arguably Harmony's finest electric creation was its three-pickup 1960s guitar available as the H75 or H77. This cherry sunburst H77 (main guitar, near right) was made in 1964. The Harmony Meteor was a more humble creation; the left-handed version (below, right) dates from 1965. The catalog pictured above was published during 1959. On the opposite page is an impressive Harmony Rocket H59 made around 1964, with its unmistakable curve of six controls: a volume and tone for each of the three pickups.

necks. Harmony's solidbody Stratotones were replaced by a line of slightly larger hollow versions. These consisted of the one-pickup Mercury model, the two-pickup Jupiter, and either one- or two-pickup Mars models, all differing in finish and trim. The Meteors and Stratotones lasted in the Harmony catalog until 1965.

Harmony's famous thin hollowbody single-cutaway Rocket debuted in 1959, offered through 1967. After that the model became a double-cutaway, lasting to 1973. Other thinline electrics introduced in the early 1960s included the high-end three-pickup double-cutaway H75 or H77 (1960), as well as three models with a Telecaster-style curve on the body's upper shoulder: the H74 Neo-Cutaway (launched in 1961); the H66 Vibra Jet with onboard transistorized tremolo (also 1961); and another Roy Smeck-endorsed model, the H73 (debuting in 1963).

Solidbodies returned to the Harmony catalog in 1963 with the Silhouette line. These instruments were shaped roughly like Fender Jaguars and sported headstocks with six tuners in-line, one or two pickups and several vibrato options, including a Hagstrom-made unit. These models lasted until 1973.

In 1966 Harmony put a six-tuners-in-line headstock on its H72 double-cutaway thinline and introduced the H79 thinline electric 12-string. In 1968 most of its previous thinlines were supplanted by the Rebel models that featured pointy double-cutaways, six-tuners-in-line heads and sliding volume and tone controls. Jay Kraus died in 1968

Harmony was a vast company as it entered the 1960s, offering everything from bargain flat-tops with stenciled cowboy scenes to electric archtops (1959 ad, right) and solidbody Stratotones.

and management passed to a trust. Hit hard by imported competition from oriental makers and others, Harmony had dropped its electric lines by 1975, the year in which Harmony purchased Ampeg to handle its distribution.

In 1976 Harmony was auctioned off, the name going to the Global company. During the 1980s some imported low-end double-cutaway solidbodies appeared with the Harmony logo. The brand entered the 1990s on inexpensive beginner guitars, including near-copies of Strats.

HARVEY THOMAS

Based in Kent, Washington State, Harvey Thomas built instruments with gloriously little evidence of design influences from outside the four walls of his workshop.

Thomas's individuality was manifested in distinctive solidbody instruments such as the unusual cross-shaped Maltese model (an example of which would later attract Ian Hunter), the oddball triangular Mandarin, and the deranged mutations of the Mod and the Riot King. Thomas also offered a custom-building service to his customers, resulting in even stranger creations, including ax- and map-shape guitars, as well as a few enormous hollowbody electrics.

Thomas worked near the Spanish Castle outside Seattle, as frequented by a young Jimi Hendrix and immortalized in his song 'Spanish Castle Magic.' Thomas had nothing to do with Thomas Organs, a common misconception.

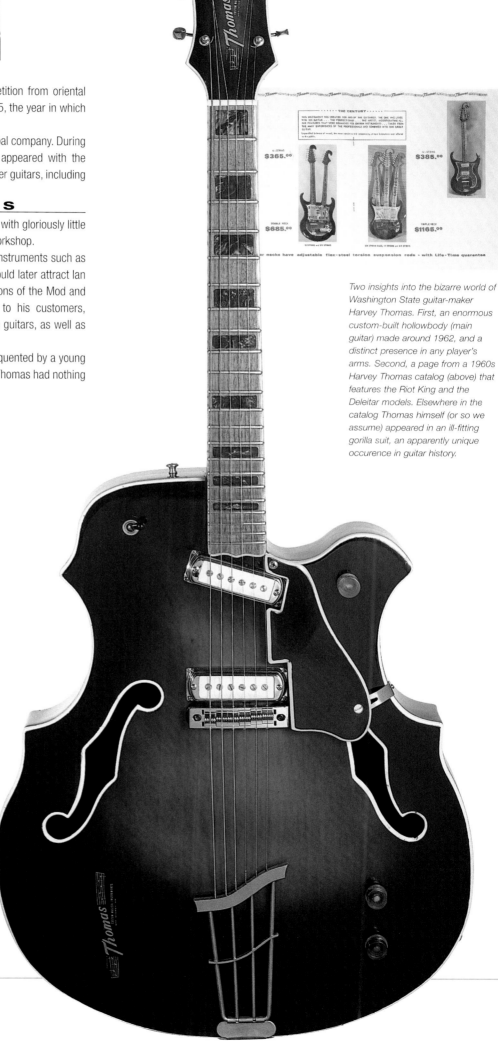

Two insights into the bizarre world of Washington State guitar-maker Harvey Thomas. First, an enormous custom-built hollowbody (main guitar) made around 1962, and a distinct presence in any player's arms. Second, a page from a 1960s Harvey Thomas catalog (above) that features the Riot King and the Deleitar models. Elsewhere in the catalog Thomas himself (or so we assume) appeared in an ill-fitting gorilla suit, an apparently unique occurence in guitar history.

HAYMAN

This dependable British brand provided many amateur 1970s groups with workmanlike tools. Jim Burns, a few years after he sold Burns to Baldwin in 1965, joined forces with ex-Vox man Bob Pearson and distributor Dallas Arbiter to develop a new brand of electric guitars – which became Hayman. Naturally enough, Jim drew on several of his contacts from the Burns-brand days, including Jack Golder's timber firm and Derek Adams's polyester-finishing skills.

Hayman guitars were launched in 1970 with two chunky, distinctive six-strings, the three-pickup 1010 solidbody and two-pickup 2020 semi-solid. The 3030 followed in 1971. Scale-length and 21-fret maple neck followed Fender formats, but the zero-fret and characterful headstock were pure Burns.

Jim left Dallas-Arbiter in summer 1971 and Pearson continued to develop new models. The low-end Hayman Comet appeared in 1974, while the following year's Modular had plug-in modules for changing control circuitry. The White Cloud was the final Hayman, a three-single-coil solidbody produced in small numbers.

At its peak in 1974 Dallas's factory in Shoeburyness, Essex, was producing 200 Haymans a month. But Dallas ran into financial problems in 1975, and Hayman guitars did not survive the sale to CBS/Arbiter that formed Dallas Arbiter. However, Jack Golder continued the spirit of Hayman with his new Shergold brand.

HEARTFIELD

Launched in 1989, Heartfield lasted about four years and represented a joint design effort by Fender Musical Instruments in America and Fender Japan.

Like many of Fender Japan's guitars, the line was manufactured at the Fujigen factory. The Heartfield instruments included the chunky, short-horned RR series, among the first guitars to feature retro styling, which became a growing trend throughout the 1990s. Some versions incorporated novel "touch" selectors governing active circuitry that included stompbox-style distortion.

The EX and Elan lines were more conventionally styled and attired, while the Talon series targeted the rock market with aggressive Ibanez-inspired styling, including a locking vibrato system and other hot-rod hardware.

HERITAGE

Established in 1985, Heritage occupies part of the former Gibson factory in Kalamazoo, Michigan, and numbered among the staff are many ex-employees of that company. Some early Heritage guitars displayed Fender tendencies, but predictably enough the most popular of the company's models echo various facets of Gibson design, often using what seem deliberately similar model designations.

The H-535 and H-555 are equal-double-cutaway thinline semi-solids in ES-335 and ES-355 style, while the H-525 is a Gibson ES-175 style single-cutaway archtop

The three guitars on this page are: a solidbody Hayman 3030 (near right) from 1973; a prototype (center) made at the Fujigen factory in 1989 for Heartfield's Talon series; and a Heritage H-150CM from 1998.

electric. Naturally, Les Paul-like solidbodies abound, including the H-150 and the H-157. Other models such as the Prospect Standard semi and the H-137 solid continue to emphasize the "Gibson alternative."

HOFNER

In the late 1950s and early 1960s German-made Hofner guitars served a growing army of young three-chord hopefuls in the UK. However, a good deal of this intense popularity was the result of the fact that Hofner guitars were, quite simply, available, rather than that they possessed any notable inherent quality.

Hofner saw the potential of the fast-growing market for electric guitars before many of its competitors. The company had been founded in the 1880s by Karl Höfner in Schoenbach, Germany, initially producing violins, cellos and double basses. Guitars were first introduced in 1925, by which time Karl's sons Josef and Walter had joined their father, and the business had developed into one of the largest in the Schoenbach area. After World War II the Höfner family moved to the Erlangen district, an area in what became West Germany and was home to a good number of musical instrument makers. Hofner production began again in 1949, and two years later the company and its factory was relocated to Bubenreuth.

Archtop acoustic guitars were added to the line sold in Germany during the early 1950s, and these were very soon partnered by alternative versions that had floating

This Hofner Club 50 (main guitar) was made around 1958, a two-pickup version of the instrument that started John Lennon's electric-guitar adventures. Hofners had a great effect on British guitarists in the 1950s. Sessionman Bert Weedon played an electrified Committee model (far left) before adopting proper electric models. The German-made Hofner guitars were imported into the UK by Selmer, beginning with acoustics in 1953 and adding electrics two years later. Selmer's 1957 catalog (above) features the Clubs, plus Committee, President and Senator electrics.

pickups attached. Hofner electric guitars with built-in pickups followed on to the German market in 1954, and these thinline, small-bodied, single-cutaway instruments reflected the growing influence among guitarists as well as guitar-makers of Gibson's Les Paul model. Although without f-holes, these Hofners were in fact hollow, and consequently relatively lightweight.

The first Hofner "solids" were launched in Germany in 1956, but these too were more semi-solid than solidbody. Also at this time Hofner's first bass guitar, the 500/1, appeared in the manufacturer's catalog, another small hollowbody instrument. It is better known today by its descriptive nickname, the "violin" bass, and even more as the "Beatle" bass for its most famous player, Paul McCartney, who played one on-stage throughout his mop-top career.

In 1953 Hofner acoustic archtop guitars were first brought into Britain by the busy importer and distributor Selmer. This London-based company began to offer a selection from Hofner's comprehensive lines, and most models were specifically made or modified to Selmer's requirements.

Selmer soon began to realize the value of the instruments coming from its new German supplier. The UK distributor chose to ignore the detailed numbered model designations of the instruments they'd commissioned for the British market, instead giving them distinct model names that were more likely to attract British players. Thus

Selmer would begin to launch such models as the Golden Hofner, the Committee, the President, Senator and Club, the Verithin, and the Colorama and Galaxie.

As already noted, Hofner had introduced its first electric guitars with built-in pickups on to the German market in 1954, and these appeared in the UK in 1955, marketed as the Club 40 and Club 50. They were small, single-cutaway six-string hollowbody models without f-holes, in a loosely Les Paul style, offered with one pickup (the Club 40) or two pickups (the Club 50). They were joined in 1958 by the rather more fancy Club 60, which was distinguished by its bound ebony fingerboard and more decorated position markers. The affordable Club line (£28-£50, about $45-$80) quickly became essential to many aspiring beat-groups, including an embryonic Fab Four wherein John Lennon thrashed a battered Club 40.

Selmer's timing with the introduction of Hofners to Britain was perfect. As the 1950s progressed, Britain was beginning to embrace rock'n'roll – but there was a very limited choice of electric guitars available, mostly due to a ban on US imports that was in effect from 1951 to 1959. British players welcomed the variety, quality and value offered by the Hofner line, and the brand soon became a leading name in the UK, seen in the hands of famous artists such as Bert Weedon and Tommy Steele.

The electric archtop Committee, which appeared in 1957, was designed in conjunction with an advisory group of six leading UK players: Frank Deniz, Ike Isaacs,

Two popular Hofner hollowbody electrics both made in 1959 are shown here: a Committee (near right) and a President (far right). The ad, published in the same year, features an array of bandsmen, sessioneers and would-be rock'n'rollers, including Dickie Bishop and Denny Wright, each of whom played with skiffle king Lonnie Donegan at various times.

Jack Llewellyn, Freddie Phillips, Roy Plummer and Bert Weedon. With an ornate, high-end image, the Committee featured two pickups, a flowery headstock inlay, a harp-style tailpiece, multiple binding all around, and figured maple veneer on the body's sides and back (which also sported a fancy inlaid fleur-de-lis). As with most Hofner hollowbody guitars, finish options were sunburst and natural – or, as Selmer preferred to call them, brunette and blonde.

Slotting into the electric archtop line below the Committee were the more austere two-pickup President and single-pickup Senator, although the general image of the President was improved by triple-dot position markers and the company's six-"finger" Compensator tailpiece.

The Golden Hofner was launched in 1959 and was by far the most luxurious Hofner, going to extremes in size, opulence and price. This top-of-the-line hollowbody electric boasted a hand-carved body, ebony fingerboard, fancy inlay and binding, and gold-plated hardware – including an engraved, shield-shaped tailpiece.

The ornate Golden Hofner also bore the Committee-style inlaid fleur-de-lis on the back of the body, and was described with some justification in Hofner advertising as "a masterpiece of guitar perfection."

By the time the Golden Hofner model was launched in 1959 the Hofner catalog had increased considerably, with a wide variety of large-bodied archtops, thinline versions,

The Golden Hofner was Hofner's high-end hollowbody electric, launched in 1959. The two examples shown here were made in 1961: this Bigsby-equipped model (main guitar) is a thinline Thin model; the other (below, far left) the full-depth version. The Golden Hofner Thin pictured was owned by Bert Weedon, the author of the Play In A Day teaching guide, first published in 1957, that provided the initial inspiration for many later famous guitarists.

smaller semis and an assortment of solidbodies. In Britain at the time Selmer offered eight UK-only electric models in addition to the Golden Hofner: the Committee, President, Senator, Club 40, Club 50, Club 60, and Colorama.

The single-cutaway Colorama solidbodies had first appeared on the British market during 1958, offered in one- or two-pickup models. Later versions of the Colorama modified the body shape to equal-double-cutaways, first seen in 1960, and then to Fender-like offset cutaways, a style that debuted during 1963.

Gibson's successful thinline electrics of the period had prompted Hofner to offer slim versions of its existing archtop electric bestsellers. The Verithin model, first introduced in 1960, offered an even thinner cross-section to the body, as well as some notably Gibson-like touches such as an equal-double-cutaway design and a bright cherry-red finish. This stylish approach and, as ever with Hofner at the time, keen pricing proved very popular in the UK, and the Verithin model became something of a classic among cost-conscious British beat groups.

As 1950s rock'n'roll gave way to the beat group music of the early 1960s, Hofner continued to maintain a healthy share of electric guitar business in Britain. Most Hofner instruments targeted beginners and second-time buyers, and while the guitars could not match Fender or Gibson for quality, Hofners invariably offered a great deal of character, some impressive visuals and fair performance, and as such they attracted

Two classic Hofner guitars are shown on this page: a Galaxie (main guitar) from around 1965; and a Verithin, made about 1961. The groovy Hofner catalog cover (above) dates from 1968.

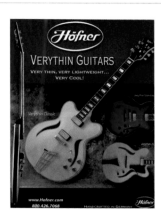

many soon-to-be-famous guitarists during their formative years, including Ritchie Blackmore, Joe Brown, David Gilmour and Roy Wood.

Hofner's second line of solidbody models for the UK appeared during 1963, the Stratocaster-inspired Galaxie series. These instruments were offered bedecked with slider switches and roller controls, and this was in line with the popular trends among electric makers at the time.

Sales of Hofner's guitars peaked in the UK during the 1960s, but the transition into rock music by the end of the decade saw Hofner's British popularity diminishing as competition increased at all price levels. Hofner appeared to be reluctant to modify its product lines and to move with the changing times all around it, and of course the ever-stronger challenge from Japanese manufacturers and the rise of the 1970s "copy era" only increased the pressure.

Ironically, Hofner instruments from the late 1970s to the mid 1980s are very often of markedly better quality than a good deal of the earlier instruments, but they have attracted far less attention.

Hofner battled on through the 1980s and into the 1990s, with sales mainly limited to the company's apparently timeless "Beatle" basses. By the early 1990s business had declined. In 1994 Hofner was sold to Boosey & Hawkes, the British music company, and some years later Boosey closed Hofner's Bubenreuth factory and moved

production west to new premises in Hagenau, just over the border into France. In 2003 Boosey sold its instrument division to a British investment consortium, The Music Group, which quickly sold off the individual companies. The following year, Hofner was sold to Klaus Schöller and Ulrike Schrimpff – Schöller was a former general manager at Hofner and Schrimpff the finance director – and the new company developed Chinese manufacturing in addition to its Hagenau factory for a line of old and new models, some of which reflected changing market trends, while many aimed to recreate former glories.

However, for guitar collectors of a certain age in Britain, it's the UK-only electric archtops that the company produced from the late 1950s into the mid 1960s that remain the most desirable Hofners, mainly for their image and associations with particular artists, but also, of course, for pure and simple nostalgia.

Three more Hofner guitars: a German-market 175 (far left) with special vinyl-covered body, made around 1968; a 459/VTZ "violin" guitar (center, made in about 1965), inspired by the better-known violin-shape "Beatle" bass; and an A2L hollowbody from 1983. The ads here show the Jazzica Custom and the "very cool" Verythin in 2003 (top of page) and the "retro vibe" of the President in 2006 (left).

HONDO

A pioneer of Korean guitar-making, Hondo began in 1969 as a joint venture between Samick of Korea and International Music Corporation (IMC) of Fort Worth, Texas. Primitive solidbody electrics (1972) became low-end Hondo II copies of Fenders and Gibsons (1974). Better models included the Longhorn, an active-electronics take on Danelectro's Guitarlin, made in Japan by Tokai.

In 1982 came the Chiquita Travel model and a Steinberger-like Lazer headless, modeled on Johnny Winter's guitar, plus the weird "pointy" H-2 and Coyote. More Fender/Gibson copies (Fame, Revival) and Fleischman originals appeared in 1984.

IMC purchased an interest in Jackson/Charvel in 1985, and supplanted the Hondo line with Charvels after 1987. In 1991 IMC co-founder Jerry Freed repurchased Hondo, importing beginner instruments. Hondo was owned by MBT International (J.B. Player) from 1995 and ceased trading from 2005.

HOPF

The Hopf name has been associated with German musical instrument making since the 17th century, although the company was officially established in 1906. After World War II, Hopf's manufacturing resumed at a new factory located in Taunusstein, near Wiesbaden, with Dieter Hopf responsible for stringed instruments. The first Hopf electric guitars appeared during the late 1950s, and soon models included the Spezisl

archtop-electric and Harmony H-75-like Galaxie semi-acoustic. The Saturn 63 had a Fender Jazzmaster-style body with metal-rimmed teardrop soundholes, and was featured in publicity material for the fabled Star Club in Hamburg. Later Hopfs included the budget Twisty, while the more high-end Telstar had abundant roller controls, toggles and slide switches. Hopf steadily decreased electric guitar production during the 1970s and ceased manufacturing in the mid 1980s.

HOYER

Hoyer instruments date back to the 19th century, made in the Erlangen area of Germany. Archtop electrics from the 1950s and 1960s were big-bodied and often fancy in typical German fashion, while semi-solids were usually Gibson-like. Early solidbodies were more individual: the mid-1960s model 35, for example, balanced Fender-like features with distinctively German ideas.

Copies prevailed in the 1970s, although solids like the straight-sided HG 651 and UK-designed Foldaxe maintained some original thinking. This mix continued into the 1980s, with Fender- and Gibson-inspired guitars partnering a few oddities.

Some high-end models appeared briefly with the breakaway Walter Hoyer brand around 1984, but both operations had ceased manufacturing by 1990. In 1998 Hoyer returned with various electrics, but by 2005 the brand had a new owner, who used it only for acoustic models.

This Hondo H-2 (near right) was made in Korea in 1983, in a similar style to Ibanez's X series. Two German guitars made around 1965 are here, too: a Hopf Saturn 63 (center) and a Hoyer 35 (far right). The ad (below) for a Hondo Professional dates from 1981.

IBANEZ

No Japanese guitar manufacturer has had more global impact than Hoshino Gakki Ten, a company best known for its primary brandname, Ibanez. Its instruments have been seen in the hands of some of the world's top players, and for half a century Hoshino has contributed classic designs, efficient instruments for working musicians, and countless players' first guitars.

Hoshino was founded in 1909 in Nagoya, Japan, by Matsujiro Hoshino as a supplier of books and stationery, also retailing musical instruments. The company began importing instruments in 1921. Later in the 1920s, Yoshitaro Hoshino succeeded his father and in 1932 the first acoustic instruments appeared carrying the Ibanez brand. However, the company's buildings were destroyed during World War II, and Hoshino did not resume business until 1950.

Yoshitaro's son Junpei became president in 1960 and opened a new factory called Tama Seisakusho (Tama Industries). By 1964 Hoshino was making and exporting guitars with brandnames such as Ibanez, Star, King's Stone, Jamboree and Goldentone. While it's an oversimplification that ignores the many original creations, one can characterize Ibanez guitars historically in terms of stylistic influences, breaking the maker's long history down into three main areas: the 1960s; the 1970s; and the 1980s and later. The 1960s reflected the design influence of Jim Burns of England;

These two early Ibanez electrics illustrate the two body shapes that the brand at first adopted: a Jazzmaster-like outline, as on this Model 882 (far left) from about 1963; and a Burns-inspired shape and multiple-pickguard arrangement, as on this Model 2103 (near left) made around 1964. Four more models are pictured in this catalogue dating from 1962 (left).

the 1970s were heavily dominated by Gibson-style guitars; and the remainder of the century was given over primarily to offset-double-cutaway guitars derived from Fender's Stratocaster design.

In the early 1960s Hoshino first reached the US when it sold acoustic guitars to Harry Rosenblum, founder of Elger Guitars and owner of Medley Music in Ardmore, Pennsylvania. Interested in obtaining an American distribution arm, Hoshino purchased a half interest in Elger around 1962. By that time Hoshino still only made acoustic guitars, but was offering a line of solidbody electrics sourced from other Japanese factories such as Fujigen Gakki, Kasuga, Chu Sin Gakki and others.

These early Ibanez instruments were small-body short-scale low-end guitars aimed at beginners. They came in two basic shapes, one of which was similar to a pointy-horned Burns Bison, the other more like a Fender Jazzmaster, and they were fitted with up to four small single-coil pickups.

Around 1964 Hoshino revised the Burns-style guitar with an interpretation somewhat closer to the original, including three-part pickguards, and replaced the little Jazzmaster-shaped body with one that was slightly more Stratocaster-like. But throughout most of the 1960s Hoshino's principal focus was on acoustic guitars.

Hoshino's serious interest in electric guitars strengthened after Shiro Arai of Aria encountered the newly-reissued Gibson Les Paul Custom — effectively Gibson's own

"copy" of the original — at a US trade show in 1968. Arai took back to Japan the notion of making Les Paul copies, launching what would become the "copy era." By 1969, bolt-neck Ibanez "Les Pauls" had joined those of other Japanese manufacturers, followed around 1971 by an Ibanez version of the Ampeg Dan Armstrong "see-through" Lucite guitar.

Around this time other Japanese manufacturers began to produce full lines of Fender, Gibson and Martin copies, increasingly closer to the originals, as did Hoshino by 1973. It was during the early 1970s that Hoshino began selling Ibanez- and CSL-brand guitars in the UK through distributor Summerfield Brothers, and Jason-brand guitars in Australia. Technical advice from Maurice Summerfield in the UK and Jeff Hasselberger in the US made Ibanez copies even better, with necks lowered into the body and squared-off fingerboard ends.

By 1974, the Ibanez line had exploded with both bolt-on-neck and set-neck variations on Gibson designs, including instruments in the style of the SG (including double-necks), Flying V (called the Rocket Roll), Firebird, Les Paul, Explorer (the Destroyer), Moderne, ES-345 and ES-175, plus a full complement of Fender copies. A number of these were marketed in the UK with the Antoria brand.

No sooner had these full-blown copies arrived than Hoshino began to innovate. In 1974 Ibanez introduced maple fingerboards on Les Paul and thinline copies, plus a

Three guitars from Ibanez's copying period: a 2347 (near right) from about 1974, copying a Gibson SG, including a very Gibson-like headstock shape; a 2364 (center) made in 1975 and copying an Ampeg Dan Armstrong "see-through" guitar; and a 2351 (far right) dating from 1976, copying a Gibson Les Paul, and with Ibanez's later Guild-like headstock shape.

rosewood-capped "Les Paul" with elaborate fingerboard inlays – before Gibson adopted such features. Ibanez had introduced original designs by 1974 (which, combined later, would yield its most popular and respected 1970s model, the Artist).

The 1974 models from Ibanez included four "Artist" electric guitars. Two were double-cutaway thinline types and two were solidbodies. They had fatter horns than the later Artist, but appeared with bolt-on necks with the "castle" headstock shape associated with the later-style Artist. Another solidbody debuted at this time, bearing two small sharply-pointed cutaways, but with an early version of the later Artist's glued-in heel-less neck joint.

Company literature dates the appearance of the carved-top, equal-double-cutaway Ibanez Artist to 1975, although it does not seem to have been advertised until the following year. The new Artist's fast, heel-less, glued-in neck and twin humbuckers competed with Yamaha's similar SG-2000. The Artist models would proliferate through 1982, to include versions with active onboard EQ and various options of switching and appointments. The two players most associated with the Artist were John Scofield and Steve Miller. The Artist solidbody line would be revived during 1997 – but not before the model name had seen more use.

In 1975 a number of Ibanez guitars appeared which are now considered some of the most collectable. They included the Custom Agent (a Les Paul-alike with a Gibson F-5 mandolin-style head and pearl belly inlays), the Artwood Nouveau (Strat-style with a dragon-carved body) and the Artwood Twin (a copy of the double-neck instrument played by John McLaughlin, built for him by luthier Rex Bogue).

These special guitars led to a variety of Les-Paul-style single-cutaway and Artist-style double-cutaway carved ash models, with features including "tree-of-life" inlays. Most of these were produced in limited runs and were referred to as Artist and/or Professional models, although common names had little to do with consistency of features and design. Musicians playing these guitars at the time included Randy Scruggs, Carl Perkins and Bob Weir.

An original-design Ibanez model, the Iceman, debuted In 1976. It was popularized when a custom-made model faced with broken mirror parts was played by Paul Stanley. The Iceman featured a medallion-like body shape with a point on the end and a large, Mosrite-style extended lower-cutaway horn. It was offered in both set-neck and bolt-on-neck versions.

It was at this time that original US distributor Harry Rosenblum sold his interest in Elger to Hoshino, although Hoshino's American subsidiary did not change its name to Hoshino USA until 1981. The strategy of copying US classics was very successful for everyone marketing Japanese guitars in the 1970s, especially Hoshino, and the American companies being copied became increasingly alarmed at the erosion of their

Three more Ibanez guitars are shown on this page, these from the company's transitional period when it was mixing copies and more original styles: a Performer 230 Les Paul-inspired model (far left) with subtle but important body and headstock changes, plus fancy decoration; a limited-edition Artist Professional model (center) from 1977 with tree-of-life fingerboard inlay; and a Firebrand 2348 (near left), a copy of a "reverse" body Gibson Firebird, but with non-reverse headstock. The Firebrand appears in a 1974 ad (left) featuring a fictional band who have three more Ibanez copy guitars: a Rocket Roll (copying a Flying V), a Deluxe 59'er (Les Paul Standard), and an FM Jr. (Les Paul Junior).

The great jazz popularizer George Benson (on-stage, below) was honored with Ibanez signature models in 1977. Benson is seen promoting a GB-10 model in this 1979 ad (far left) and posing with one for the cover of his fine album of 1987 (near left) made with Earl Klugh.

market share. In 1977 Norlin, the parent company of Gibson, filed a federal lawsuit against Elger. It claimed trademark infringement based on the copying of Gibson's headstock design – even though Ibanez had changed to a more Guild-like shape the previous year. It's from this action that copy guitars are sometimes nicknamed "lawsuit" instruments. The suit was settled out of court and, in the US at least, this particular "copy era" ended.

Ibanez's move away from copies was relatively quick and certainly dramatic. First to appear in 1978 was the Performer series, which essentially consisted of set-neck or bolt-on-neck Les-Paul-style instruments with an extra Telecaster-style curve on the upper shoulder, plus that Guild-style headstock. These were followed by the Concert series, which combined more of a Stratocaster-style offset-double-cutaway body with the carved top of a Les Paul.

Ibanez quickly settled on the Studio and Musician series, both of which featured rounded slightly-offset double-cutaways with short, pointed horns that clearly had taken their cue from the designs of Alembic. The Musicians were through-neck guitars with figured ash or walnut "wings" and, on the top models, onboard active pre-amps and equalization, again Alembic-like.

In 1977 Ibanez began what became a long tradition of artist-endorsed models, introducing the Artist Autograph line including versions of the ash-bodied Professional,

now renamed the Bob Weir, a limited-edition Iceman called the Paul Stanley, and two new fancy twin-humbucker single-cutaway archtops named for jazz sensation George Benson, the full-sized GB-20 and the smaller GB-10. The Weir and Iceman models did not make it into the 1980s, but the Benson models, including several variations, would remain Ibanez's flagship archtops.

A sign of Ibanez's shift from Gibson-like designs to Fender styles was the introduction in 1979 of the Roadster. This Stratocaster-style guitar had a bolt-on-neck, non-vibrato bridge and three single-coils. It came with either ash or mahogany bodies, and flamed-maple tops peering through semi-opaque finishes. A year later Ibanez helped start the Dyna factory in Japan to produce Fender-style guitars and introduced the new Stratocaster-style oil-finished Blazer, soon altered to feature slightly "hooked" body horns. The Blazer became popular and would help to set the pattern for Ibanez's upcoming Roadstar II series.

Ibanez reintroduced in 1981 a version of its Explorer-style guitar, the Destroyer II, this time with a rather more stylized, "pointy" body shape. Some models sported fancy tops. Two more endorsement guitars appeared, the LR10 Lee Ritenour Model, an equal-double-cutaway thinline semi-hollowbody in ES-335 style, and a full-size single-cutaway archtop hollowbody, the JP20 Joe Pass Model. In 1982 Ibanez revived its Flying V-style model as the Rocket Roll II, along with the Iceman II, some with flamed-

One of the signature models for George Benson, this is a small-body GB-10 (far left) made in 1978. Ibanez's Musician series was Alembic-influenced, as can be seen on this Musician MC500 (center) made in 1978. The Professional 2617 shown here (near left, made in 1978) is another limited edition, but exemplifies the company's new and popular Artist double-cutaway style.

Paul Stanley's PS10 model was revived in the 90s, with this 1995 ad (left) promoting the PS10II as well as a limited-edition version.

maple tops. Also during 1982 the Blazers were replaced with what would become the enormously successful Roadstar II series, hitting the market as both Strat-style guitars and heavy metal pyrotechnics enjoyed a popular revival.

By 1983 Roadstar IIs ranged from the ash-bodied RS-100, a three-single-coil descendent of the Roadster, to the RS-1000 with carved birdseye-maple top, plus two through-neck models with twin humbuckers or three single-coils. Locking vibrato systems appeared in 1984, as did the company's first model with a humbucker/single-coil/single-coil pickup layout, the RS-440.

Steve Lukather endorsed a Roadstar, the basswood-and-maple RS-1010SL, launched in 1985. This model had two special humbuckers and a Pro Rocker locking vibrato system. Jazz-fusion legend Allan Holdsworth also helped to design his own Roadstar: the twin-humbucker AH10 and AH20 appeared briefly from 1985. The Roadstar II shape continued through 1986, although at the end the prefix changed to RG – which is confusing, because subsequent RGs had different styling. The birdseye models were gone, but the hardtail RG-600 still sported a bound flamed-maple top as well as low-impedance active pickups.

The V-shaped Rocket Roll was rolled into a new X series of heavy-metal-style guitars in 1983. These included a new Destroyer, combining the V and Explorer shapes into a model similar to a Dean ML, and the dramatic stretched-x-shape X-500. Ibanez

Steve Miller (above) was one of the most visible players of Ibanez's Artist models in the late 1970s and early 1980s. One of the best-known Ibanez guitars from the late 1970s is the odd-shape Iceman, snd this IC210 (main guitar) dates from 1979. Ibanez shifted from Gibson influence to Fender flavors with the Roadster series, new in 1979; this Roadster RS100 (far right) was made that year.

launched a brief foray into synth-access guitars in 1985-86 with the IMG-2010 guitar (sometimes referred to as a "controller") that had a space-age minimalist shape. The IMG featured a clever electronic vibrato system that reproduced the analog effect without tracking problems.

The move away from the Roadstar II era began in 1985 as Ibanez introduced the Pro-Line series, which had old Roadstar styling but new "superstrat" features. The guitars had the now ubiquitous superstrat appointments – that is, humbucker/single-coil/single-coil pickup layouts and locking vibrato systems – plus a row of small pushbuttons for recalling pickup settings.

Also debuting in 1985 was the RG series, distinct from the renamed Roadstar-style RGs by virtue of a more modern superstrat design with deep, pointed double cutaways. These guitars came in a wide array of pickup and trim configurations, in vibrato or stop-tail versions, with or without pickguards, and some with flamed-maple tops. They had a remarkable run and would anchor the Ibanez solidbody line right throughout the 1990s. The RG7620 (vibrato) and RG7621 (fixed bridge) seven-strings catered to the late-1990s rage for the extra low-tuned string, with the cheaper 7420 and 7421 models following in 2000.

Four new guitars appeared in 1987 – three basic bolt-on-neck Pro-Line models and the shortlived, more radical looking Maxxas line. The Pro-Lines included the Pro-

540R Radius, a pointy-horned offset-double-cutaway instrument with a wedge-shape cross-section, quickly adopted by solo virtuoso Joe Satriani, and the Pro-540S Saber. This had a similar shape but featured a wafer-thin contoured body. Both would achieve considerable success in the 1990s.

Ibanez's involvement with endorsers had accelerated and expanded during the 1980s. By the end of the decade the redesigned Pro-Line Power model was endorsed by fusion ace Frank Gambale, and the JEM series appeared in 1988, designed in conjunction with former Frank Zappa guitarist Steve Vai. The JEM77 had deeply offset, sharp double-cutaways, vine-pattern inlays, humbucker/single-coil/humbucker pickup layout, locking vibrato system, floral pattern finish and a "monkey grip" cut-out body handle. A number of colorful versions, some with aluminum pickguards, subsequently appeared. A celebratory 10th Anniversary JEM with engraved pickguard and fancy trim was issued by Ibanez during the late 1990s.

The technically brilliant Vai had first come to notice in terms of his choice of instrument when he opted for a custom-made Charvel in the mid 1980s, a guitar known as the Green Meanie. Vai modified the instrument regularly. His tool-kit-assisted changes included the addition of a rout beneath the vibrato plate to allow for upbends as well as downward travel, much further chamfering of the cutaways to allow yet more access to the upper frets, and the inclusion of the influential pickup combination of

Three Ibanez models made in the 1980s are pictured on this page: an Artist 2618 (far left) from 1981, and the Ferocious ad next to it from '83 shows the series continuing to exude style; an Axstar AX45 (center) made in 1985; and a Rocket Roll II (near left) produced in 1982.

humbucker/single-coil/humbucker. When the Meanie was stolen, Vai remembered a Maxxas model that Ibanez had sent to him as a Christmas gift, and got in touch with the Japanese company. A prototype Vai model followed, based on drawings of the old Charvel, and along came the JEM series.

The JEM777 was first issued in a limited run of 777 examples, each in Loch Ness green and signed by Vai. The JEMs were often wildly finished, sometimes with vibrant color schemes and strange fingerboard inlays, as well as a floral version of the JEM77 that had a "tree-of-life" inlay.

Ibanez faced a dilemma common to other Japanese makers in the late 1980s. Successful marketing had made the company one of the largest guitar producers in the world, but inherent costs and currency exchange rates made it increasingly difficult to market guitars manufactured in Japan at the lower price points customers had come to expect. In order to continue offering high-end options, in 1988 Ibanez opened a US custom shop operation in Los Angeles, California. At first the shop dealt with custom graphics, but by 1989 had introduced the American Master Series, high-end through-neck versions of regular models, including the basswood MA2HSH and maple-topped-mahogany MA3HH, which lasted to 1991.

In 1990 the US shop began making the Exotic Wood series with fancy, unusual timbers. Two years later the USA Custom Graphic series appeared with colorful

More 1980s Ibanez guitars on this page: a Destroyer II DT555 (near right) from 1984 (another model from the DT line was endorsed by Def Leppard's Phil Collen – see 1984 ad, above); a highly sculpted X Series XV500 (center) made in 1985; and the instrument part of Ibanez's shortlived IMG2010 guitar synthesizer (far right) from 1986.

John Petrucci of Dream Theater (1992 album, left) used a number of American-made Ibanez USA Custom models in the 1990s (pictured, right). Later in the decade a signature Petrucci model would appear, the JPM100.

imaginary painted landscapes. Custom models can feature highly figured woods and extremely elaborate PRS-style multi-color inlays.

By 1994 Ibanez had moved its American production to the PBS factory in Pennsylvania operated by innovative luthier Dave Bunker. This lasted until about 1997, when PBS folded. Ibanez began producing the low-end bolt-on-neck EX series in Korea from 1989 to 1994. These EXs were superstrats – with deep, sharp double-cutaways – and reflected Ibanez's well-known RG series. The better EX models came with special touches such as bound fingerboards and triangular-shape fingerboard inlays.

At the start of the 1990s Ibanez introduced a new Artist series of set-neck double-cutaway electrics, twin-humbucker guitars only vaguely reminiscent of the old Artists. They included the semi-hollow f-hole AM200, the all-mahogany solidbody AR200, and maple-capped AR300, all lasting until mid-decade.

In 1990 Ibanez began to shuffle its Japanese solidbody lines. The wedge-cross-section Radius was endorsed by Satriani and transformed into the JS Joe Satriani Signature series, a variety of twin-humbucker models in finishes ranging from oiled mahogany to custom graphics. In 1998 came the JS 10th Anniversary Chrome Limited Edition, made of synthetic "luthite" material and finished in chrome. Ibanez's relationship with Steve Vai yielded the seven-string Universe series in 1990, essentially a JEM without the "monkey grip" handle. By 1992 the UV77 was available with pyramid

inlays and swirled, multi-colored "bowling ball" finishes. Yet more changes occurred in the Ibanez catalog during 1991. The thin-bodied Saber guitars were renamed the S-series, adding a seven-string model and proliferating as the decade progressed. By 1997 variants included the S Classic SC620 with a bound, flamed-maple top, and the S Prestige S2540 NT made of figured sapelle mahogany.

Frank Gambale got his own Signature FGM series in 1991, a version of the thin Saber with humbucker/single-coil/humbucker pickups, locking vibrato system and "sharktooth" inlays. In 1994 the Gambale line split into vibrato and stop-tail models, and three years later these were replaced by the FGM400, a high-end version with a quilted maple top and block inlays that lasted until 1998.

Reb Beach helped design the Voyager model, offered from 1991 until 1996. Behind its vibrato was a wide, wedge-shaped cutout designed to make extreme double-action

This Roadstar II RG240 (far left) dates from 1986; the Pro Line PL2550 shown here (center) was made in 1987; and this Maxxas MX3 (right) dates from 1989. The 1984 ad (above) reveals the Comet color options for the Roadstar II series.

209

Steve Vai played a custom Charvel, the "Green Meanie," before collaborating with Ibanez for the JEM (see below) and the seven-string Universe series. On this 1995 cover (right) an alienized JEM promotes his Alien Love Secrets album.

vibrato work easier. The RBM1 had a maple neck; the RBM2 had a koa top and Bolivian rosewood neck. These were replaced in 1994 by the mahogany-bodied RBM10 and oil-finish RBM400, available through 1996.

Ibanez's respected Benson electric archtops were joined by the Artstar series, beginning with the AF2000 in 1991. These were conceptually related to the late-1980s Artist line, with full-size hollow bodies and a single rounded cutaway, twin humbuckers, a headstock shaped somewhat like the old Artist "castle," and a trapeze tailpiece. A new Artstar AS200 semi-hollowbody thinline also debuted in 1991, with a larger body than the contemporary Artist AM200. These too would continue to be available in various versions through the following decade.

While the Radius guitars had earlier been transformed into the Satriani Signatures, their success inspired the less expensive R series in 1992. These lasted only a year, except for the R540 LTD which, with its humbucker/single-coil/humbucker pickups and sharktooth inlays, lasted to 1996.

By the early 1990s guitar manufacturers with any longevity had begun to realize that they were not only competing with other makers, but with their own "vintage" models which were increasingly prized by players and collectors alike. This resulted in two trends: the introduction of "retro" guitars with pseudo-1960s styling; and the reissuing of the company's own vintage classics. For Ibanez this was reflected in 1994

with the retro Talman series and the reissue of its radical Iceman guitars. The Talman had an offset cutaway shape, like a lumpy Jazzmaster. The initial line was made in Japan and featured synthetic Resoncast (MDF) bodies. Some had Sky "lipstick" single-coil pickups and photogravure pseudo-figured-maple on bodies and necks. In 1995 the line expanded to include models with pearloid pickguards, metallic finishes and retro-looking fulcrum vibratos. In 1996 Talman production was shifted to Korea where the line changed to wood-body construction. The Talmans were gone by 1999.

The 1994 Iceman series included two bolt-on-neck reissues, the IC300 with a bound body and fingerboard, and the IC500 with fancier pearloid binding. In 1995 Ibanez added the limited-edition Paul Stanley PS10LTD, with a carved maple top and set-neck, and the general-production PS10II. In 1996 the Paul Stanley PS10CL replaced the IC500, and a year later the glued-neck ICJ100 WZ with abalone binding supplanted the Stanley-endorsed models.

The Ghostrider was new in 1994. An equal-double-cutaway solidbody with a bound top, two humbuckers and three-tuners-a-side headstock, it provided an early-to-mid-1980s feel with a late-1950s name, and lasted two years. While pointy-double-cutaway superstrats were still the principal fare for Ibanez, the retro vibe brought back traditional Strat-shaped guitars in 1994 with the RX series. These ranged from the RX750 with a padauk/mahogany/padauk sandwich body and the RX650 with a

Steve Vai's JEM marked a big breakthrough for Ibanez (Vai with JEM on-stage, above) and as this 1987 JEM777LG shows (near right), it was a distinctive instrument. The JEM90HAM (far right) was a limited edition to mark the 90th anniversary in 1998 of Ibanez's parent company Hoshino. This 1990 ad (left) features Vai's later creation, the seven-string Universe, here a UV77MC in multicolored swirl finish.

Guitar virtuoso Joe Satriani (below) is a long-time Ibanez player. This 1987 ad (right) is from around the start of their association, when Satriani endorsed the Radius 540R model – which formed the basis for signature models in the later JS series. This special JS10th anniversary guitar (left) dates from 1998, its synthetic "luthite" body finished in chrome.

figured-maple top, to models with Strat-style pickguards – all in various pickup configurations. The RX series continued through 1998 when it was renamed the GRX series and downsized. In 1999 the series was augmented with a beginner-level equal-double-cutaway guitar, the twin-humbucker GAX70.

Ibanez added yet another pro endorsement in 1994 with the Paul Gilbert series. The first guitar was the PGM500, basically a deep-cutaway RG with a reverse headstock, humbucker/single-coil/humbucker pickup layout and fixed bridge assembly. The most distinctive decorative feature was its white finish with painted-on black f-holes. This was available for two years.

The first Gilbert model was joined by the PGM30 in 1995, the same guitar except for the addition of a double-locking vibrato system. This guitar would become the principal Gilbert model. In 1998 the Gilbert line was briefly enhanced for about a year by the transparent red PGM900 PMTC, essentially a Talman with twin humbuckers, stop tailpiece and the distinctive fake f-holes.

Another celebrity series was introduced in 1996, endorsed by jazz guitarist Pat Metheny, a long-time Ibanez player. The first model was the fancy PM100, a uniquely shaped offset-double-cutaway f-hole hollowbody archtop with a small pointed cutaway on the bass side and a deeper, pointed cutaway on the treble side. It was joined in 1997 by the PM20, a more traditional single-rounded-cutaway archtop with a

211

rosewood fingerboard and ivoroid trim, still with one neck humbucker. In 1997 Ibanez brought back the Blazer, its Fender-influenced double-cutaway of 1980. The new Blazers revived the "hooked-horn" body, "blade" headstock, pearloid pickguard and a humbucker/single-coil/humbucker pickup arrangement. The BL1025 had a Wilkinson vibrato; the BL850 had a Gotoh unit. These late-era Blazers were available until 1999.

The last new endorsement of the 1990s came from another long-time Ibanez player, John Petrucci. The JPM100 of 1998 was another pointy deep-double-cutaway guitar with the RG profile, but finished in a camouflage pattern.

A line of mid-priced hollowbody Artcore models was introduced in 2002, made in northern China by a specialist producer. Fritz Katoh, the designer responsible for many of Ibanez's finest moments, left Hoshino in 1995, setting up his own Fritz International Associates three years later. There were also changes upstairs in Ibanez management. In 1998, the long-serving Hoshino USA vice-president, Roy Miyahara, became president, taking over from Tom Tanaka. Miyahara left in 2002, when Bill Reim became president of the US operation, the first American to hold the post. In Japan, Tom Tanaka became president of the main Hoshino Gakki company in 2005, and ten years later he was succeeded by Ken Hoshino as president, while in 2009, Shinichi Kubo took over from Hiroshi Ando as president of Hoshino Gakki Hanbai, the domestic sales firm. With seven-string guitars established in the line, in 2007 Ibanez introduced an eight-string

guitar, the RG2228, with a necessarily ultra-wide neck (about two inches at the nut and three at the body), custom hardware, including a fine-tuning fixed bridge, a 27-inch scale, with an extra F-sharp and B below a regular six-string set, and then everything down a half-step. A Meshuggah signature eight-string, the M8M, was added to the Ibanez multi-string line in 2012.

In 2006, a signature model appeared for Mick Thomson of Slipknot, the masked nine-piece from Des Moines. The six-string MTM1BR was specifically designed to cater for Thomson's low tuning, down three half-steps from regular and with the low C-sharp dropped to B.

In 2007, Hoshino established the Ibanez Guitar Design Center in Nagoya, Japan, with two designers and a woodworking specialist. The first model from the new Center was the FR, introduced in 2008, another Talman-like retro guitar, but more like a two-humbucker Telecaster. The Darkstone DN models followed a year later, also born in the Design Center. Some ideas came from Ibanez's international distributors, such as the new-for-2012 Roadcore RC320, developed and named with help from Headstock, Ibanez's British distributor since 1996.

A result of old-Ibanez influence came with a guitar that Paul Gilbert asked the firm's LA custom shop to make. The Iceman had always been one of his favorite pointy guitars, and he'd been revisiting some favorite old players, too, and remembered Frank

Three more Ibanez models are shown on this page: an S Classic SC420 (near right), updating the Saber series, from 1999; a star-studded signature Iceman ICJ100 for J from White Zombie (center, 1998); and Paul Gilbert's FRM1 (right) from 2009, a sort of retro reversed Iceman. Korn were among the bands who brought a new metallic popularity to seven-string guitars, seen in this 1999 ad (right).

Marino's SG with multiple single-coils, so he had DiMarzio make him a new single-coil pickup. Marino had angled one of his pickups: Gilbert tried that, and ended up with all three single-coils angled. He received his custom guitar in 2007. But what to call it? A Fireman! Ibanez released two Japan-only limited edition models in 2009, the FRM1 and 2, followed later by the FRM100 and FRM150 production models.

By 2017, Ibanez's electric lines still proudly displayed five JEM models, and the by-product RG guitars took pole position. The RG line still provided Ibanez's metal heart, from top end Prestiges and Premiums, through guitars with and without vibrato, straightahead Iron Labels, RGD multi-stringers and long-scale down-tuners, and the curvier RGAs. Vai's seven-string Universe series still boasted a couple of models, too. The various S models formed an equal tier of solid Ibanez achievement in the line. There was also a single classic Ibanez double-cut AR and 24-fret Les Paul-like ARZ, retro-flavored FRs, Talmans and Roadcores, budget GRGs, GRXs, GAXs and a GSA, plus plenty of Artcore and Artstar hollows and semis. An impressive team of artists lined up, too, for the various Ibanez signature models: Tosin Abasi, George Benson, Jake Bowen, JB Brubaker, Dino Cazares, Paul Gilbert, Eric Krasno, Herman Li, Kiko Loureiro, Marlen Hagstrom, Pat Metheny, Chris Miller, Munky, Noodles, Joe Satriani, John Scofield, Paul Stanley, Marco Stogli, Fredrik Thordendal, Andy Timmons, Sam Totman, Steve Vai, Paul Waggoner, and Bob Weir.

Here we see a 2012 MTM100 ultra-pointy signature model (left) for Slipknot's Mick Thomson; a re-creation of Steve Vai's fave working guitar, the limited-edition JEMEVO (center) from 2012; and a 2012 RC230 (far right), part of Ibanez's recent retro-new-oldie Roadcore series of models.

JACKSON

Grover Jackson's brand came to symbolize the "superstrat" rock guitar of the 1980s. His update of Fender's classic Stratocaster design offered more frets, deeper cutaways, a drooped "pointy" headstock, altered pickup layouts and a high-performance vibrato system. Jackson attracted many of the emerging fast-gun players like Randy Rhoads, George Lynch and Vivian Campbell, as well as more mainstream guitarists such as Jeff Beck, Gary Moore and Frank Stepanek.

Guitarist Jackson liked to tinker with guitars, and he joined Wayne Charvel's guitar-parts supply operation in San Dimas, California, in September 1977. However, the company was experiencing some financial problems, and in November 1978 Jackson bought the outfit for almost $40,000. Initially the small three-man workshop continued making necks, bodies and other components, as well as repairing and modifying instruments. Charvel-brand bolt-on-neck instruments debuted in 1979 (see Charvel).

In late 1980, Grover Jackson met a 24-year-old up-and-coming guitarist called Randy Rhoads. Together they designed a custom guitar that was based on the overall design of Gibson's Flying V. In 1981 they collaborated again on a more radical variant of the original design, this time with an offset body style. For these clear departures from the Charvels, Jackson began to use his own name as a brand. In fact, the two brands would remain clearly distinct from one another until early 1986. Charvels were made mostly in a Fender-like style, and had bolt-on-necks. Jacksons, however, were more original, and featured through-neck construction. Guitars from either brand made a feature of flashy graphics and custom paint-jobs.

With the tragic death of Rhoads in 1982 and the subsequent interest in his unusual Jacksons, the value of player-association was underlined. So it was that early in 1983 the first Jackson-brand production model appeared, the Randy Rhoads.

More exaggerated-shape custom designs were built especially for players such as Australian band Heaven's guitarist Kelly (a curved Explorer-style design) and Dave Linsk of Overkill (a Flying V-like "Double Rhoads"). At first, Jackson would reserve his own brandname for these custom instruments built to the various designs of the individual musicians concerned. Gradually, however, favorites emerged, and all Jackson's significant body styles – which would later be given specific model names – were developed at the company's San Dimas workshop between 1983 and 1986.

These were: the Randy Rhoads (offset V, from 1983); the Soloist (superstrat, from 1983); the Kelly ("curved" Explorer-style, from 1984); the Double Rhoads and later King V (Flying V-style, from 1985). More or less from the start, these models were offered with two levels of trim – Student (with rosewood fingerboard, dot markers, unbound neck/headstock) and Custom (with ebony fingerboard, "sharkfin" markers, bound neck/headstock) – although variations often appeared. Jackson gradually

Two early Jackson guitars are shown here. The earliest guitar (right) was probably the first Jackson Strat-style instrument, made in 1982 for Mark St John, then a member of Kiss. Note the early freehand Jackson logo. The other guitar (left, from 1983) is the first Jackson Soloist, and the first Jackson with a graphic finish. It marks the birth of the superstrat design that defined the look of rock guitars in the 1980s, achieving wide acclaim for Jackson in the process and spurring many makers to adopt the style.

Randy Rhoads is pictured on-stage during an Ozzy Osbourne tour (above) with one of the custom guitars made for him by Grover Jackson. It became the Jackson Randy Rhoads model of 1983. This example (right) from that first year was the 30th built, and the first to be equipped with a Floyd Rose vibrato.

A motley crew of Jackson/Charvel endorsers lined up for this ad published in 1985 (left), with the accent on the graphic finishes that the joint company pioneered. Steve Vai is there, fourth from the right.

humbucker, partnered by a locking heavy-duty vibrato system. Jackson also instigated the drooped "pointy" headstock. So was the superstrat born: a new tool for high-speed, high-gain guitarists, able to meet, match and foster their athletic excesses.

The Charvel logo was transferred to a Japan-built line in 1986, with the Jackson brand retained for the high-end US-made line. By 1987 production of the US Jacksons switched to a large new facility at Ontario, California. By late 1987 the King V was a production model. Two years on, the Strat Body's name was changed to the less contentious Vintage Style, while the line expanded to include the Dinky.

Also new in the Jackson line at this time was the strange Phil Collen signature six-string, its radically carved and contoured body far removed from the established idea of a rock guitar. A more affordable Collen model, the PC3, appeared in 1997.

In 1985 Jackson himself had started a joint venture with Texas-based distributor International Music Corporation. Jackson left in 1989. He later went on to design a number of instruments for Washburn and others. After Jackson's departure, three different Jackson lines emerged: Custom Shop; US series; and Jackson Professional. The Custom Shop editions were US-made special pieces at prices too rarefied for most mortals to even consider. The limited-production US series models each came with the option of ten different hand-painted airbrush graphic finishes. The Japanese-made Jackson Professional line was intended to bring Jackson to a wider market with high-

developed and modified the original Strat-style guitars he'd made with the Charvel brandname, at first as the blatantly-named Strat Body, but more importantly as the Jackson Soloist. From about 1983 the Soloist came to define what we now know as the superstrat, the most influential electric guitar design of the 1980s. With input from players regularly shaping the changing design, Jackson built on the classic Strat-style guitar, squaring the body's sides while making the contouring bolder and overall shape slimmer, and "stretching" the horns.

While his early superstrat-inclined guitars continued with 22 frets, Jackson began to capitalize on the extra upper-fret access provided by his through-neck and deeper cutaways by increasing the number of frets to 24, giving players a wider range. The revamped body carried powerful combinations of single-coil and humbucker pickups, evolving to the "standard" superstrat combination of two single-coils plus bridge

This Double Rhoads Custom (far left, from 1984) was named for its two Rhoads "wings," and later in scaled-down form it became the King V series. The custom-made reverse-Firebird-style guitar (center) was called Instant Sex, built in 1988 for Robin Crosby of Ratt. This PC3 (near right) is from 1998. Joey Z is seen promoting the US-made JJP model in this 1997 Jackson ad (above).

215

You won't go blind playing with this

A 1998 Jackson ad (left) highlights the JJ1, a signature model for Scott Ian of Anthrax, with a distinctive hot rod flame finish.

The Jacksons pictured here are a Custom Shop Soloist from 2006 (main guitar, left) with Iommi-style cross fingerboard inalys; a Phil Collen PC1 (center) from 2008; and a 2009 USA Custom Soloist SL2H with its flame maple top visible through the green trans finish (far right).

quality versions of the American originals. These included the unusual Phil Collen model, along with the new Fusion Pro and ultra-pointy Warrior Pro. Prices of the Professional line were relatively elevated for Japanese factory-built instruments.

Despite such variation in list prices, the choice of models remained limited, although the company wasn't slow to pick up on what was happening and to exploit the changing musical trends. As part of the 1992 Professional series, the Infinity model, despite being in a modern PRS-style, insisted on retaining Jackson's most distinctive features: namely, the pointy headstock and the heavy-duty vibrato system. The retro-influenced JIX model appeared in the Jackson catalog during 1993, as did the Kelly Standard version of a Custom Shop line. High-end limited editions and variations on continuing themes appeared throughout the 1990s.

Grover Jackson left Jackson/Charvel in 1989, and he stayed out of the guitar business until '92, when he went to Washburn for three years. In more recent years, he has been making guitars for his own new brand, GJ2, in Orange County, California.

One of the first signs of the impending retro fashion in the guitar world came in 1991 when the Jackson-related Charvel brand introduced the Surfcaster, a heady mix of design influences from the 1950s that included lipstick pickups, which recalled Danelectro, and a Rickenbacker-like soundhole and fingerboard inlays. The acquisition of Jackson by the Japanese electronic musical instrument company Akai in 1997 saw (for now) the demise of the Charvel brand. The Surfcaster then moved to Jackson, from 1998 as a production instrument. Many other non-US and US-based firms took note of this indication that retro could not only look good but also, promoted by a leading brand such as Charvel and then Jackson, could sound good and attract players.

Jackson was concentrating on established strengths while continuing to expand into lower-price markets. The Concept series launched in 1993 featured relatively affordable Japanese-built versions of the best-known Jackson designs, while the Performer line of 1994 was manufactured in Korea in an effort to achieve even cheaper prices. By 2000 the X Series was made in India. Jackson continued to refine its body shapes, for example in 2000 when it melded the Kelly and Rhoads styles to create the Kelly Star KS2 model.

At the end of 2002, Fender acquired the Jackson/Charvel guitar line from Akai. The deal meant that Fender purchased all Jackson/Charvel inventory, trademarks and designs, and also it acquired the Jackson/Charvel manufacturing operation in Ontario, California, which produced custom and limited edition guitars. By 2017, the Jackson line consisted of US-made and import guitars, including pointy models such as the Demmelition, Kelly, King V, Rhoads, Star and Warrior series, alongside superstrat models such as the Dinky, Juggernaut and Soloist series, plus a good showing of signature models, from Adrian Smith to Misha Mansoor.

Three more Jacksons are pictured on this page: a 2012 Pro Series Dinky DK2M (far left); a 2014 USA Signature Misha Mansoor Juggernaut HT6 (center); and another Pro Series DK2M (main guitar, right), this one a 2015 limited edition in slime green swirl finish. The 2009 ad (right) is for Matt Tuck of Bullet For My Valentine and his signature Rhoads model.

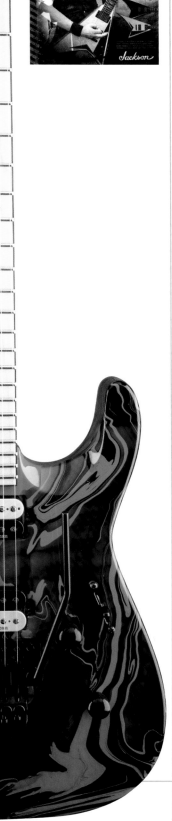

217

JAMES TYLER

These high-end instruments are held in high esteem by many LA and Nashville sessionmen, and typify the virtuoso rock-style guitar. They are high-class, high-performance mostly Stratocaster-like guitars, available in spectacular custom colors including "psychedelic vomit" and even "haz-mat-sewage-fiasco shmear."

Tyler is virtually a custom maker, heading a team of three other builders based in Van Nuys, California. There is a line of firm models available too that includes the superstrat-style and Telecaster-like Studio Elites, the Stratocaster-style Classic (also with Michael Landau and Dan Huff signature versions), the Les Paul-based top-of-the-line Mongoose model, and the rather more originally styled Ultimate Weapon. By 1999 the operation was producing some 150 instruments a year.

JOHN BIRCH

During the 1970s this UK maker produced a line of solidbodies demonstrating individual ideas. Models such as the J1 and J2 employed through-neck construction, distinctive multi-pole pickups and often comprehensive circuitry. Styling, however, seldom strayed beyond conventional designs.

Custom requirements were also accommodated at the Birch workshop and many famous British names employed him to build what often amounted to some very unusual instruments. Such customers have included Tony Iommi, Roy Wood, Ritchie Blackmore and Dave Hill. This became Birch's best known work, often providing the most bizarre creations to bear the maker's brand. Birch quit the guitar business in the mid 1980s, but returned during the early 1990s with new instruments, pickups and synth-access systems. Birch died in 2000 and John Carling continued the business.

KAPA

Capitalizing on the early-1960s guitar boom, Kapa guitars were the brainchild of Dutch immigrant Kope Veneman of Hyattsville, Maryland, and were launched around 1963. Known for ultra-thin necks and an unusual 12-string vibrato, Kapa launched its first offset-shape solidbodies with the Challenger model name.

Thinner-body Continental models appeared in 1966. However, names were used indiscriminately on many models. The Hofner-style pickups were mostly made by Kapa itself. Kapa's popular Minstrel teardrop-shape guitars were introduced in 1968, and Japanese thinlines and solidbodies (plus oriental hardware) began to appear in 1969. A very few all-Japanese guitars appeared near Kapa's end, in 1970, when parts and equipment were sold to Micro-Frets and Mosrite.

KAWAI

This Japanese manufacturer is best known for pianos, keyboards and synthesizers. Its electric guitars started in the 1960s, targeting the lower end of the market and often attempting to impress with chromed control panels, banks of multiple switches and

A conservatively-finished James Tyler Studio Elite (near right) made in 1999; a fine example of John Birch's often bizarre custom work: this 1976 AJS Custom (center) was named for the initials of its original bat-obsessed owner; and a Kapa Continental 12-string made in Maryland in 1966.

eye-catching body shapes. The late 1970s brought much improved quality, and the KS series from that period featured a distinctive slotted headstock. Other models aped Alembic's multi-laminated through-neck style, but the crescent-shaped Moon Sault solidbody was a design clearly out on its own.

The early-1980s Aquarius line from Kawai was rather more Fender-orientated. The company later catered mainly for domestic customers in Japan, and it reissued the Moon Sault and some other oldies.

KAY

Of the huge Chicago-based guitar power-houses, only Kay approached the size and influence of Harmony on the lower to middle ranges of the mass market. Kay was founded in 1890 as the Groehsl Company, a mandolin manufacturer, adding guitars and banjos around 1918.

In 1921 the company name was changed to Stromberg-Voisinet and two years later Henry Kay "Hank" Kuhrmeyer joined the company. The guitars themselves were called Strombergs, while the company was referred to as Voisinet (thus distinguishing it from a Boston company that was producing Stromberg-brand archtop acoustics).

By the mid 1920s Voisinet was supplying some of mail-order company Montgomery Ward's fancier instruments, often using pearloid, a popular Kay material. Voisinet (Kay) also supplied many guitars for the Spiegel catalog and other distributors, including

The Kawai Concert shown (far left) dates from around 1968. The Japanese Kawai company built instruments for a number of other brands, including the obscure Telestar, whose 1960s catalog (above, left) has a painfully hip cover. Two Kays are shown on this page: a 1954 Thin Twin K161 (center, with 1953 ad), known as the Jimmy Reed model after its use by the bluesman, and a monstrous Solo King (near left) from about 1958.

Continental, Chicago Musical Instruments (CMI) and Oahu. In 1928 Voisinet introduced some very early production "electric" guitars, the Stromberg Electros. Despite their ground-breaking status, they were not what we think of now as electric guitars: crucial electro-magnetic pickups were still a few years away. The Stromberg Electros were in fact acoustic flat-top instruments fitted with a transducer to pick up the vibrations of the body's top (but not the strings). They were supplied with a primitive amplifier. The unusual Electro models were nonetheless greeted with some enthusiasm, especially among Chicago's hillbilly radio performers. But few were made, and with the onset of the Depression they disappeared from the market.

Stromberg-brand instruments, often with a decal decoration, continued to be sold until around 1932. In 1931 Kuhrmeyer became president. The KayKraft brand debuted on both regular Spanish and distinctive two-point Venetian guitars. Through the 1930s the line was anchored by KayKrafts, cheaper Arch Krafts, and small-bodied guitars often of plywood. By 1934 the company was known as the Kay Musical Instrument Company. The Kay brand began to appear around 1936.

Kay resumed making electrics in 1936 with a pickup-equipped flat-top for Ward. Unique violin-shaped guitars were made in 1938, and in 1939 the high-end Television archtop appeared. Kay also made a few guitar models for National and Gretsch during the 1930s. In 1940 Sears' new Silvertone brandname was first applied to a Kay-made

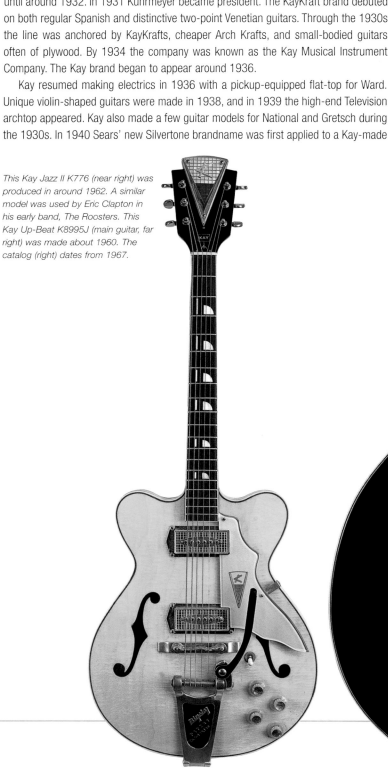

This Kay Jazz II K776 (near right) was produced in around 1962. A similar model was used by Eric Clapton in his early band, The Roosters. This Kay Up-Beat K8995J (main guitar, far right) was made about 1960. The catalog (right) dates from 1967.

KAY
INSTRUMENTS
1967-68 EDITION

GUITARS, ELECTRIC GUIT... ...S, MANDOLINS, BANJOS, UKULELES, STRINGS, CASES

Introducing

THE SUPERLATIVE NEW KAY LINE

ONLY KAY offers you so complete a line—ranging from a $22.95 student model to a $400 professional electric

ONLY KAY boasts slim, steel-reinforced necks on every guitar

ONLY KAY gives you life time laminated construction on every guitar

The Ultimate in Professional Electric Guitars...
...The Gold "K" Line

Sensitive instruments with action... sound... and style for the fine guitarist.

The Gold "K" guitars feature "planned electronics". Power, balance, sensitivity and style are perfectly united. Separate tone and volume controls. Each string has its own output adjusting post.

The Gold "K" guitar necks are perfect in their slimness... steel reinforced, adjustable, too... and fully guaranteed.

The Gold "K" guitars feature highly figured curly maple and super-selected seasoned spruce... and the luxurious, hand finish you deserve.

KESSEL JAZZ SPECIAL. Barney's choice features a Melita bridge for absolutely perfect intonation. Maximum Fidelity sound reproduction assured by new Gold "K" pickups. Pearl inlaid Ebony fingerboard. New style THIN master size — the finest strings, hardware and styling.

8700S Double pickup, shaded finish, sunburst....$400.00
8700S Double pickup, gleaming natural blonde.. 400.00
8701S Single pickup, shaded finish, sunburst.... 350.00
8701S Single pickup, gleaming natural blonde.. 350.00
8000C Hard-shell, plush-lined case for above.... $2.50

KAY

KEN BRADER & SON
The Musician's Department Store
359 FERRY STREET
EASTON, PA.   PHONE 3-652

MUSICAL INSTRUMENT COMPANY
1640 WALNUT ST., CHICAGO 12, ILL.

Kay's Barney Kessel series of the late 1950s improved the image of the Chicago-based maker of bargain guitars. Cheapest of the three Barney Kessel models was the semi-solid Pro (main guitar). It was made around 1958, as was the hollowbody Artist (far right). The catalogs detail the top-of-the-line Special (above) as well as the Artist (below).

archtop. More serious involvement with electric guitars began in 1947 when Kay began putting pickups on its archtops, which continued through the 1960s. In 1952 Kay introduced its first cutaway archtop, the K-1.

That year also saw the first appearance of the Thin Twin, a flat-topped single-cutaway semi-hollowbody guitar with two pickups, known popularly as the Jimmy Reed for his use of the model. Kay's first solidbody electric, the K-125, was a small Les-Paul-shaped guitar, also debuting during 1952. The similar one-pickup K-136 and two-pickup K-142 replaced the K-125 and was made between 1955 and 1957, while a more exaggerated version called the Sizzler was offered from 1956 to 1958. The bizarre and shortlived "map of Ohio" Solo King appeared in 1960, and may well be the ugliest solidbody guitar ever made.

In 1955 Kuhrmeyer retired and was succeeded by Sidney M. Katz. In 1956 Kay picked up its first professional endorsement when jazz guitarist Barney Kessel put his name on three better-grade electric archtops, the Jazz Special, Artist and Pro, part of the Gold K line with plastic-covered "Kleenex box" pickups and elaborate extruded-plastic headstock facings (known among collectors as "Kelvinators" because of their resemblance to the Sears appliance logo).

Kay was especially pleased that this association with Kessel went some way to counter the brand's generally low-end image. Almost beside itself with pride, Kay announced in advertising material in 1957: "Kay and the nation's number one jazz guitarist Barney Kessel, winner of the *Down Beat*, *Metronome* and *Playboy* polls, have together developed a professional guitar which will establish new standards in quality of sound, workmanship and design."

Unfortunately, the liaison did not last. Kessel's name was dropped from the instruments during 1960, but the guitars continued with abridged headstock designs. Other popular Kay electrics of the time included the mid-size Upbeat and thinline single-cutaway Swing Master. In 1960 the hollowbody Les-Paul-shaped thinline Value Leader, Style Leader and Pro arrived in various finishes and pickup configurations, with metal "Art Deco" pickguards.

Versions without the metal were offered by St. Louis Music with their own Custom Kraft brandname. From this point onwards, Kay increasingly employed bolt-on necks on most of its electric guitars.

The Vanguard line of solidbodies followed in 1961. These had slab bodies shaped something like a Fender Jazzmaster. A more attractive solidbody was introduced the following year, the Strat-style K-300. Three new electric thinline hollowbodies also joined the Kay line in 1961: the pointy single-cutaway Speed Demon and Galaxie, and double-cutaway Jazz II. In 1965 the Vanguards were redesigned with a "German carve." Kay's six-tuners-in-line "bushwhacker" headstock also debuted in 1965. In

1964 Kay had relocated to a huge ultra-efficient factory in suburban Elk Grove Village, Illinois. Three more solidbodies were introduced during 1965 – the Artiste, Titan I, and Apollo – with the new bushwhacker head, short cutaways, heavy contouring and a shape that crossed a Strat with a Jazzmaster.

In 1966 Kay was purchased by Louis J. Nicastro's Seeburg Corporation, best known for its juke boxes. Katz remained in control of the new musical instrument division. Most of the guitars from the early 1960s were eliminated, but the frumpy early Vanguards became the budget Value Leader line. The mid-1960s models expanded. The somewhat high-end K400 Series Professional solidbodies were introduced, with equal cutaways similar to a Gibson SG and a tapered lower bout like a Strat. The Speed Demon name was applied to a couple more similarly-shaped solidbodies.

Seeburg's tenure as a guitar-maker was brief. In 1967 Kay changed hands again, purchased by long-time competitor Valco (formerly National and National-Dobro), headed by Robert Engelhardt who was keen to obtain the new manufacturing capacity.

The Kay line remained unaffected, although a number of hybrid Supro-brand guitars including the solidbody Lexington began sporting Kay components and Japanese-made parts. The Valco-Kay marriage was also shortlived. In 1968 the market for electric guitars collapsed. It was in that year that the Valco-Kay operation declared bankruptcy and closed its doors. During 1969 Valco-Kay's assets were auctioned off

Three more Kay guitars are shown on this page: a Double Cutaway K592 (near right) made around 1964; a K30 (center) from about 1976; and a Busker (far right) with built-in amp and speaker, dating from 1986.

The shortlived Kent brand was applied to Japanese-made guitars sold in the US. This model 742 (main guitar) was made around 1968, probably by Kawai. The surf ad (above) was published in the early 1960s, before the dangers of electric guitars and large expanses of water were fully understood.

This Kent ad from 1965 (below) features instruments made for the US-marketed brand by Japanese companies Guyatone and Teisco.

and rights to the Kay name passed to Sol Weindling and Barry Hornstein of WMI, importer to the US of Teisco Del Rey guitars from Japan. In the early 1970s both the Teisco Del Ray and Kay brands appeared on Teisco-made instruments, but by about 1973 WMI was using only the Kay brand. The bolt-neck K-20T Gibson SG "copy" appeared that year, and most 1970s Kay guitars were low-end copies of popular American models. In 1980 the Kay name was sold to Tony Blair of AR Musical Enterprises of Indianapolis, Indiana. From that point on the Kay name was used on guitars for the beginner market. Guitar maker Roger Fritz came on board in 2010 to help produce a number of reissues of classic Kay models.

KENT

The Kent brandname appeared on some of the earliest Japanese-made musical equipment imported to the US. New York distributor Buegeleisen & Jacobson used it on microphones and pickups in the late 1950s, and around 1962 on beginner-level solidbody guitars made by Guyatone and Teisco with small slab bodies and up to four pickups. The Kent line eventually included guitars, basses, amps, mandolins and banjos. The most interesting Kents came in 1967, symmetrical and asymmetrical hollowbodies and solidbodies with burled-maple tops and wide, almost baroque black-and-white plastic strips covering the sides. Kent-brand guitars do not appear to have survived the 1960s.

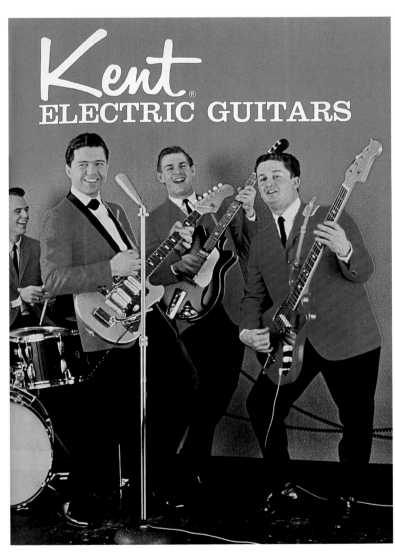

KLEIN

Steve Klein is best known to electric guitarists for his unusual ergonomic "Kleinberger" headless-guitar design. As well as the normal requirements to provide a fine, playable instrument with a good sound, the Klein electric is also intended to enable correct posture for the seated player.

Klein himself continues to market acoustic guitars made in Lafayette, California, but is no longer associated with the electric guitar company, having sold out to employee Lorenzo German in 1995. German's Klein Electric Guitars operation is now located in Byron, California, north-east of San Francisco.

The Steinberger-style headless one-piece rosewood neck of the Klein electric instrument is joined to an unusually-shaped and distinctive curving body. It was originally devised by Klein with the help of Carl Margolis, musician Ronnie Montrose and designer Ned Steinberger.

The Klein electric is at the time of writing available in two three-pickup versions: the solidbody basswood or alder DT; and the swamp ash or alder BF with hollowed body chambers. The chambered model is a new development since Klein's own involvement ceased. Pickups are by Seymour Duncan, or optionally Joe Barden.

Both models come as standard fitted with either a Steinberger S-trem or Transtrem vibrato bridge, although they are also available with a DeLorenzo vibrato or hardtail

This Klein (main guitar) is a BF model, with "chambered" swamp ash body, made in 1998. Pickups are Kent Armstrong lipsticks plus a DiMarzio, and the bridge is equipped with an RMC piezo pickup.

Klein has attracted a number of name players to its distinctive instruments. This 1990s ad (below) features two: ex-Police guitarist Andy Summers (left) and avant-garde stylist David Torn.

TWO INNOVATIVE PLAYERS
TWO INNOVATIVE PRODUCT

ANDY SUMMERS

PEARCE
AMPLIFIER SYSTEMS

KLEIN
ELECTRIC GUITARS

AVAILABLE DIRECT

DAVID TORN

BLAKE BOGDANOVICH

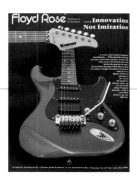

bridge. Klein also offers limited production of a four- and five-string bass in the same general design. The "ergonomic" qualities of the Klein guitar stem from the unusual body shape. The whole object is designed so that when the player sits with the guitar, the neck will be situated at an optimum angle and in a way that allows the fretting hand to access the fingerboard easily and comfortably.

This contrasts with a regular electric guitar where the player's fretting hand is moved away from his body to play on the lower frets, and into his body to reach the upper frets. With the Klein, it is claimed, the player's hand and arm moves freely and travels the minimum distance to reach any particular fret on the fingerboard.

Klein guitars have been used by an impressive array of artists that includes Bill Frisell, Joni Mitchell, Lou Reed, Andy Summers, David Torn and Joe Walsh. Custom-built oddities have included an electric harp-guitar for the late Michael Hedges and an electric sitar for Steve Miller.

KLIRA

This German maker provided value-for-money electrics during four decades. Klira was established in Schoenbach, West Germany, in 1887 by violin maker Johannes Klier, succeeded by his son Otto Josef in 1914. The company relocated in 1950 to Bubenreuth (also the base for Hofner and Framus), the emphasis shifting from violins to guitars. Klira first offered electrics in 1958 with a line of amplified archtops with

unusually shaped soundholes. Most Klira electrics were designed by Heinrich Weidner. Solidbodies debuted in 1960, budget Fender-influenced models often covered in sparkle plastic or textured vinyl. The mid 1960s represented the peak of Klira's electric production, with many exports.

Klira also made very cheap Triumphator-brand instruments, which were sold in Germany only through the Quelle mail-order operation. In the 1970s Klira offered mainly copies, although there was some retention of individual character. However, electric guitar production slipped dramatically, and by the end of the 1980s Klira guitar manufacturing had ceased.

KRAMER

Kramer began in the late 1970s as part of the movement to improve guitar technology with aluminum necks, but before its demise at the end of the 1980s it had become one of the largest guitar companies in the United States.

Kramer guitars were made by the BKL Corporation, founded in 1976 in Neptune City, New Jersey, by former Travis Bean associate Gary Kramer, music retailer Dennis Berardi and ex-Norlin executive Peter LaPlaca. Financial backing came from real-estate developer Henry Vaccaro. Kramer himself, however, left the company shortly after it was originally set up. The first Kramer guitars – the 450G model and the 350G model – were designed in conjunction with luthier Phil Petillo and featured fancy

A Klira 320 Star Club (far left) made around 1965; a Kramer 450 (center) from 1977; and a Kramer 650, also made around 1977. This 1981 ad (left) gets its grand claim pretty much right: the 80s would indeed belong largely to Kramer... but not, however, its metal-neck guitars.

In the 50's it was Fender...
the 60's it was Gibson...
the 80's it's...

Kramer
BKL

Kramer's most famous and valuable endorsee, Edward Van Halen, is pictured in this 1984 ad (left) with a guitar he made from a Kramer Baretta body and a Kramer neck. It could easily be described as highly modified. Edward is also seen (below, left) on-stage with the Kramer.

hardwood bodies with slightly offset double-cutaways and bolt-on "T-bar" aluminum necks. These necks had wooden inserts in the back, synthetic ebonol fingerboards and "tuning fork"-shape headstocks.

Kramer switched from its own pickups to DiMarzio-made units with the DMZ series beginning in 1978. In 1980 Kramer briefly launched a series of exotic shapes, including the B.C.-Rich-inspired XL series, the V-shaped XKG models, and the legendary battle-axe-shaped Gene Simmons Axe.

During 1979 Kramer ran into financial problems and until 1982 management was assumed by Guitar Center of Los Angeles. They recommended a switch to more economical wooden necks, and these were introduced as an option in 1981.

This was another big year for Kramer, seeing the introduction of the popular minimalist aluminum-necked headless Duke model, somewhat similar to a Steinberger, the "pointy" Voyager series, which was more in the style of Dean's influential ML guitar, and the first series of Kramer's Stratocaster-style Pacers and the high-end Stagemaster models. German-made Rockinger vibratos also began to be offered that year on Kramer guitars. Aluminum necks were losing popularity in the early 1980s, and the last few Kramers with these were produced in 1985.

In 1982 Kramer began a long-time association with locking-vibrato innovator Floyd Rose, becoming the exclusive distributor while introducing the asymmetrical pointy Floyd Rose Signature model. The link with Rose brought Edward Van Halen into the Kramer camp, the brand's most important endorser who further boosted Kramer's success. In 1983 the Pacer series was slimmed down, with the Deluxe model becoming one of the first guitars to feature the "superstrat" pickup layout of humbucker/single-coil/single-coil. This became a very popular configuration and, along with Stratocaster-based body shapes and drooped "pointy" headstocks, would dominate the rest of the 1980s.

In 1984 the popular single-slanted-humbucker Baretta with "banana" headstock debuted. That year Kramer also introduced the Ripley Stereo, with electronics by luthier Steve Ripley that had individual volume and stereo fader controls for each string. In 1985 a revised Voyager, the Vanguard (reminiscent of the Jackson Randy Rhoads) and the Explorer-like Condor appeared.

A sign of Kramer's growing muscle were the company's 1985 endorsers Brad Gillis, Jeff Golub, John McCarry, Ed Ojeda and Neal Schon. Also that year Kramer purchased Spector Guitars & Basses, instruments designed by Stuart Spector and Alan Charney and available in American- and Japanese-made versions.

Along with other major US guitar companies, Kramer began importing its own budget versions of its main designs, starting with the Japanese-made Focus line in 1984, followed by the Korean-made Striker series in 1985 and Korean Aero-Stars in

Two Kramer guitars are pictured on the opposite page: a Duke Special (far left) from 1982, and a DMZ-2000 Custom (near left) made in 1979. Meanwhile, this 2010 ad (right) was published by Gary Kramer Guitars, a revival begun by the brand's original founder in 2005.

Three more Kramers are shown here: a Voyager Imperial (main guitar) from 1982; an RSG-1 Ripley Stereo (center) dating from 1984; and an American Sustainer (far right) made in 1989, with a Floyd Rose Sustainer pickup in the neck position. This 1989 ad (below) highlights the Kramer Nightswan, endorsed by Vivian Campbell, who would later join Def Leppard.

1986. Kramer's strangest models, the spaceship-shaped Enterprize and Triaxe, appeared in 1986 only. That year also saw the limited-edition through-neck Paul Dean Signature. By the end of 1986 Kramer was the largest American guitar company.

By 1987 Kramer's golden age of superstrats had begun, with revamped Pacers, Baretta models and luxurious carved-top, through-neck Stagemasters, plus a host of other broadly similar models.

Elliot Easton joined the ranks of Kramer endorsers with the release of the EE Pro guitars, Vivian Campbell began his endorsement of the NightSwan models, and during 1988 Richie Sambora got his own Kramer model too.

The Kramer Sustainer with the Floyd Rose distortion-generating pickup also appeared in 1988. It was around this time that Kramer founder Dennis Berardi started a management company that handled a Russian band, Gorky Park. Kramer introduced a Korean-made balalaika-shaped Gorky Park model in 1989.

Following the introduction in 1989 of the Metalist and Showster lines that used some metal parts to improve sustain, the Kramer empire suddenly collapsed in bankruptcy. New management under James Liati took over, but by late 1990 Kramer was gone. In 1995 Henry Vaccaro (see Vaccaro) intended a revival of the aluminum-neck models, but in 1997 the rights to the Kramer name and most of its model designations were sold to Gibson, which offered a line of Kramer guitars.

The LaBaye 2-By-4 guitar and a band called The Robbs feature in this ad. Its publication in 1967 appears to have marked the one big moment both for the guitar and for the band.

This bizarre Krundaal Bikini (main guitar) was made by Wandre in Italy around 1962. It was one of the first self-contained electric guitars: the pod attached to the body contains a built-in amp and speaker.

Another oddity from the 1960s was this LaBaye 2-By-4 Six (below right), made in 1967 and with a bare minimum body, many years before Steinberger. Vox launched its own small-body guitar, the Winchester, the same year, seen with bearded designer Dick Denney in the picture.

KRUNDAAL

Wandre Pioli of Cavriago, Italy, made guitars in the 1960s, including a number of eccentric models, and with a variety of brandnames (see Wandre).

Some of Pioli's instruments even had two or three different names spread across them, which makes for even more confusion when attempting to map this maker's history. Foremost of Pioli's brandnames was Wandre, but other brands appearing on his guitars included Avalon, Krundaal, Noble and Orpheum. Any of these US importers' names indicate a Pioli instrument. Krundaal may have been the parent company of Davoli, Pioli's Italian pickup supplier, and seems to have appeared only on a very unusual amp-in-guitar model called the Bikini, produced around 1960.

LABAYE

LaBaye inventor Dan Helland reasoned that a guitar is just pickups and strings… so if you put those on a 2x4 block of wood, that would be a guitar.

Helland, a guitar teacher and photographer living in Green Bay, Wisconsin, decided to turn that idea into a reality. He was financed by music store owner Henry Czachor and decided to hook up with the Holman-Woodell guitar factory in Neodesha, Kansas. Holman-Woodell also made Wurlitzer-brand guitars.

The new company produced around 45 of the now-legendary LaBaye 2-By-4 Six, Twelve and Four guitars and basses for display at the 1967 NAMM music trade show in Chicago, Illinois. Finished either in solid colors or sunburst, the instruments had a standard Holman neck attached to a 2x4 log with two Holman pickups, thumbwheel controls and a Wurlitzer vibrato.

Some samples were put into the hands of the guitarist and bassist for Tommy James & The Shondels, who used them briefly on tour. A local Milwaukee band called The Robbs also performed with LaBayes.

Despite high hopes and an ad in *Guitar Player* magazine, no orders were received, and the LaBaye 2-By-4s became history... almost. Holman-Woodell apparently had hoped for a larger contract and was left with some 2-By-4 bodies which it released around 1968 with the 21st Century brand – and achieved hardly any more success than LaBaye. In the 1980s Mark Mothersbaugh of Devo was pictured with a LaBaye on an album sleeve, though it's unclear if he actually played it.

MAGNATONE

Best known for amplifiers that propelled Buddy Holly's glassy rhythms and Lonnie Mack's pulsing sound in the 1950s, Magnatone also made a series of unusual electric guitars. The amps descended from a line introduced around 1937 by Dickerson Brothers of Los Angeles. Dickerson evolved into Magna Electronics and, in turn, the Magnatone brand, run by Art Duhamell in Inglewood, California, from about 1947. Innovative steel guitars of the early 1950s with stamped metal and chrome-and-

colored-Lucite bodies led to Magnatone's first single-cutaway Spanish Mark III solidbody in 1956, followed by the hollowed-out, set-neck, double-cutaway Mark IV and Mark V, professional-grade guitars designed by Paul Bigsby in 1957.

Following a merger with Estey organs in 1959, the Mark models were succeeded by the bolt-on-neck double-cutaway Artist Series, which were similar to Rickenbacker's 600 model and were thus probably designed by Paul Barth, who had formerly been an executive with National and then Rickenbacker.

In 1961 Barth certainly contributed Magnatone's "golden-voiced Magna-Touch" line. These instruments were Telecaster-like in body shape, and had a hollow-core construction similar to that employed by Danelectro. These models lasted until 1965 when the best-known Magnatones debuted, the Starstream Series of Zephyr, Tornado and Typhoon. These guitars were small offset-double-cutaway beginners' solidbodies (some with metalflake finishes) inspired by Fender's Stratocaster.

In 1966 the Starstreams were redesigned with a hooked three-tuners-each-side headstock, endorsed by country legend Jimmy Bryant, and joined by the pointy-horned double-cutaway Semi-Acoustic Thinbody guitars. That same year Magna relocated to Harmony, Pennsylvania, making huge solid-state amps. A few Italian-made Magnatone hollowbodies appeared following the move, but guitars faded away. The end came in 1971 when Magna was purchased by a toy company.

Two Magnatone guitars are pictured on this page: a Mark V from around 1959 (far left, with a 1959 ad) and a Zephyr X-5 (near left), this one made in about 1965.

SOLID BODY GUITARS

Maton (logo, left) has been one of the few Australian makers of electric guitars. Martin (ad, right) is better known for flat-top acoustics, but it made some attempts at the production of electrics.

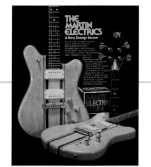

MARTIN

Starting in the early 1830s, the C.F. Martin company has established itself as the producer of some of the finest flat-top acoustic guitars in the world.

Based in Nazareth, Pennsylvania, Martin has dominated the American flat-top scene, but interestingly made a couple of brief – and ultimately unsuccessful – forays into the electric guitar market.

At the end of the 1950s Martin decided to add single-coil DeArmond pickups and associated controls to its existing 00-18, D-18 and D-28 flat-top guitars in order to create the "electric-acoustic" 00-18E, D-18E and D-28E models. Unfortunately the results were not good, whether played electrically or acoustically, and this now seems like an example of an idea before its time.

Martin's next attempt at electric guitars went further into competitors' territory. In 1961 the company launched its thinline f-hole hollowbody F-50, F-55 (both single-cutaway) and F-65 (equal-double-cutaway), aping successful models of the period by Gibson and Gretsch. Martin found little success, however, even when it revised the headstock shape for the similar GT series in 1965.

The last stab at electrics came in 1979 with the E series, Martin's first and equally unsuccessful attempt at producing solidbody electrics. The blockish E-18, EM-18 and E-28 ended Martin's electric experiments when they were dropped in 1983.

MATON

One of the few high-profile Australian makers, Maton for years offered viable alternatives to imports. Bill May set up as a guitar-maker in 1944, joined later by his brother Reg, in Canterbury, Victoria. Their first electrics appeared in 1949, with solidbodies added by 1959 and thinline semis in the 1960s. Maton boldly promoted such features as Magnametle pickups and Break-Thru Sound Barrier switching. By the 1980s acoustic guitars dominated. May, who retired in 1986, died in the early 1990s. Maton returned to electrics in 1999 with the Mastersound, reviving a 1960s model used briefly by George Harrison and various other models.

MELOBAR

Walt Smith from Sweet, Idaho, thought slide-guitar players should abandon their "lap" instruments and stand up. So he invented the Melobar guitar with a neck mounted at 45-degrees to the top.

The first Melobars were metal ten-string acoustics introduced in 1964, made in the California workshop of Ed and Rudy Dopyera of Dobro. Solidbody electric Melobars debuted in 1967, double-cutaway guitars with an extended lower horn. The first 400 were made by Semie Moseley featuring Mosrite pickups.

Early Melobars were played on Jefferson Airplane's *Crown Of Creation* LP and by Poco's Rusty Young. Other guitarists favoring Melobars have included Brian Jones,

A Martin GT-75 (near right) made in 1967, this one with a non-standard red finish; a Martin EM-18 (center) from 1981; and a Maton Wedgetail (far right) produced around 1968.

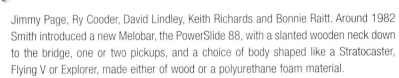

Jimmy Page, Ry Cooder, David Lindley, Keith Richards and Bonnie Raitt. Around 1982 Smith introduced a new Melobar, the PowerSlide 88, with a slanted wooden neck down to the bridge, one or two pickups, and a choice of body shaped like a Stratocaster, Flying V or Explorer, made either of wood or a polyurethane foam material.

Smith died in 1990 and was succeeded by his son Ted. By the late 1990s Melobar models included the birch or fiberglass acoustic resonator Melobro, the Steel Gitr Double-Neck (slide and regular necks), six- and eight-string Lap Steel Guitars, and the Skreemer (Flying V-style).

MESSENGER

Among the more mysterious and interesting guitars produced during the 1960s were the aluminum-through-neck Messengers. They were built by Bert T. Casey and Arnold B. Curtis of Musicraft Inc, originally based in San Francisco, California.

Beginning in 1967, the six- and 12-string guitars (and basses) had medium-depth hollow bodies with "cats-eye" f-holes, colorful translucent finishes and sometimes fancy timbers. Oddly, the expensive Messenger instruments featured inexpensive DeArmond single-coil pickups, which were wired for mono or stereo output (one pickup per channel) at the flick of a switch.

By early 1968 the company had relocated to Astoria, Oregon, and were busily touting an "improved" magnesium neck – before promptly disappearing from sight.

The strange Melobar (main guitar, made around 1973) was an electric-guitar-shaped instrument for steel players. Rusty Young of country-rockers Poco is seen attacking one in the picture (above) around 1978. Another unusual guitar was the Messenger ME-11 (far right, made in 1967) which had a structural "backbone" of magnesium alloy.

During the late 1960s, increasing attention began to be paid to the methods which could be adopted to improve electric guitar technology. Among the more curious results were Micro-Frets guitars, the brainchild of self-educated genius Ralph J. Jones. After working on various prototypes, Jones put Micro-Frets instruments into production in Frederick, Maryland, during 1967.

Micro-Frets guitars featured three curious patented innovations. First, the front and back of the instrument were made of two hollowed-out pieces of wood joined at the side, a technique that Jones dubbed "Tonesponder."

Second, the (very thin) bolt-on necks proudly sported the Micro-Nut, a metal device that allowed for the adjustment of the length of each individual string at the nut as well as the tail, theoretically providing more accurate intonation.

Third, from 1968 or so Micro-Fret guitars could be outfitted with a Calibrato vibrato, which was specially designed by Jones to keep all six strings harmonically in tune during use, even after taking into account the different string gauges. It was also intended to be less likely to render the guitar out of tune after use.

Most Micro-Frets guitars were frumpy-shaped variations on two basic designs: equal-double-cutaway (such as Spacetone and Signature models) or offset-double-cutaway (Wanderer, Golden Melody). The earliest Micro-Frets guitars had a side gasket

There are four Micro-Frets guitars pictured on these pages: an Orbiter (this page, main guitar) made in about 1968, with onboard wireless transmitter and Calibrato vibrato; a Golden Melody (this page, far right) from around 1970; a Huntington (opposite page, near right) made about 1971; and a Signature (opposite page, center) that dates from around 1968. The Micro-Frets catalog (above) details a number of other models in the line.

where the body halves joined, DeArmond-like pickups, an early-Bigsby-style vibrato design, and a bi-level pickguard with thumbwheel controls built into a scalloped edge on the top portion.

Other early guitar models included the Huntington (with a scrolled upper horn), Covington, Golden Comet, Orbiter (extended upper horn and pointed lower bout) and Plainsman. In 1968 Micro-Frets announced one of the earliest wireless systems, using an FM transmitter. Jones apparently got the idea from newly-invented garage door openers. Wireless became a shortlived option on most models, with an antenna protruding from the upper horn.

By around 1970 the side gasket had disappeared and a variety of Jones-designed pickups were used. The bi-level pickguards now had regular knobs mounted on the lower portion. Models from this era include the Calibra I, Signature and Stage II. By 1971 Micro-Frets also offered its first true solidbody, the Swinger, plus the Signature Baritone and Stage II Baritone.

While most Micro-Frets finishes were reasonably conventional, a wild green-to-yellow "Martian sunburst" was also offered. Oddly, some models came with plastic decals of cats or pumpkins affixed. Jones died around 1973, and by 1974 the brand was gone. A very few guitars with the Diamond S brand were subsequently assembled in Virginia using leftover Micro-Frets parts.

MIGHTY MITE

Mighty Mite was involved in the "replacement parts" phenomenon that began in the mid 1970s. Guitar players increasingly wanted to improve their guitars by replacing stock factory parts such as pickups, tuners and bridges with "retrofit" or "aftermarket" units provided by independent manufacturers.

Mighty Mite was started in Santa Monica, California, by Randy Zacuto, who at the time was the west-coast distributor of DiMarzio pickups. By 1976, Mighty Mite had a full line of replacement parts that included Screamer humbucking pickups, Matchatone guitar tuners and Metrognome metronomes, and brass knobs, bridge parts, pickguards and jack plates.

About a year later Mighty Mite relocated to Camarillo, California, and increased its offerings. By 1978 the products were being distributed internationally and included full pickguard assemblies, and pickups with colored bobbins. At the end of the 1970s the company was providing unfinished bodies, necks and complete guitar kits.

Mighty Mite's line eventually expanded to include its most famous pickup, a three-coil monster called a Motherbucker, and some exotically-shaped, finished mahogany bodies (Mercury, Buick etc) with fancy figured flat caps routed to house the Mother. Mighty Mite faded from the scene in the early 1980s, but the tradename is still actively used on parts distributed by Cort/Westheimer in Illinois.

Mighty Mite started as a supplier of guitar parts (1979 ad, above) but also provided complete guitar kits. This parts-guitar (near left) from around 1980 has a Mighty Mite Mercury body, Mighty Mite three-coil Motherbucker pickup, and a Warmoth neck.

MODULUS GUITARS

Modulus is a pioneer of composite "carbon-graphite" materials for guitar-making, and an active proponent of the ecologically responsible use of timber. The original company was called Modulus Graphite and was started by Geoff Gould in 1978 with the intention of making composite necks in California.

Geoff Gould and Rick Turner while still at Alembic had come up with the idea of molded carbon-graphite fiber-and-resin necks, primarily intended for use on Alembic and Music Man basses.

By the early 1980s Modulus Graphite began producing basses, then guitars. These graphite-neck high-end instruments were generally allied to classic-style US solidbody designs, aimed at players who realized that the new material offered an even sustain across the range as well as a road-friendly resistance to environmental change.

These instruments continued to appear from the Modulus Graphite workshop in San Francisco, California, in a low-key manner until late 1995 when Rich Lasner bought the Modulus name from founder Geoff Gould. Lasner, who dropped the "Graphite" suffix to rename the new operation Modulus Guitars, had previously worked as an instrument designer for Yamaha, Ibanez and Peavey.

Lasner took the Modulus legacy of carbon-graphite construction to produce new Genesis models, with a wood-shrouded graphite-spined neck construction. Like a

Mosrite's Mark I Ventures model (this example, main guitar, made around 1966) was built in collaboration with the American instrumental group (sleeves featuring Mosrites, above). The two other guitars on this page are a Modulus Graphite Flight 6 Monocoque (below, left) made in 1983, and a Modulus Guitars Genesis from 1998 (below, right).

number of modern makers, Modulus recognized the combined virtues of graphite's strength and wood's tonal qualities. Modulus relocated to Novato, California, in 1997.

Modulus was concerned about the ecologically responsible use of timber. The company emphasized the need for sustainable timbers and employed non-traditional alternative woods such as granadillo, chechen, red cedar and soma. Modulus said its goal was that all the wood it used should be "earth-friendly and properly harvested," and it cooperated with pressure groups such as SoundWood and Eco Timber.

The original company ceased trading in 2013. A new firm was started by Joe Perman, and it produced only basses.

MOSRITE

One of the most colorful American guitar-makers, Semie Moseley enjoyed an erratic career producing distinctive, boldly-designed instruments. Moseley was born in Durant, Oklahoma, in 1935, and later moved to Bakersfield, California. At age 13 he was playing guitar with an evangelical music group.

Moseley joined Rickenbacker in the late 1950s, but soon formed his own guitar-making business, encouraged and assisted by the Reverend Ray Boatright. Their combined surnames, with a little modification in the spelling, provided the name for their new Los Angeles-based Mosrite company. From the outset Mosrites had unusual features, including a distinctive "M"-topped headstock. Moseley soon produced what

The ad for Mosrite's original Ventures model (above left) dates from 1966. Johnny Ramone of The Ramones is pictured (left) playing his Mosrite Ventures around 1979. The two unusual Mosrite instruments on this page – a six-string (far left) and 12-string (near left) – were custom-made by Semie Moseley for the Strawberry Alarm Clock group in 1967. The painting was done by California artist Von Dutch, well known in the hot-rod and custom-bike worlds at the time.

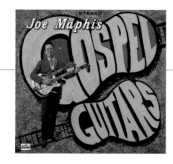

was to become the definitive Mosrite design, essentially a reversed Stratocaster-like body with stylistic and dimensional changes that gave a wholly new and refreshing outline. The design was streamlined and full of visual "movement," but still managed to be comfortable and well-balanced.

This radical design was noticed by Nokie Edwards, guitarist with The Ventures, America's leading instrumental group of the time. Production of the Mosrite Ventures models commenced during 1963 at a new factory in Bakersfield, funded by the band in return for exclusive distribution. The new Mk I guitars each carried a Ventures logo on the headstock. Output soon increased from 35 to 300 instruments per month. None of the subsequent models achieved the popularity of the Ventures guitars, which are now the most collectable. Mosrite closed in 1969.

The next 20 years saw false starts and financial setbacks for Moseley. In 1976 his unsuccessful Brass Rail model had a brass fingerboard for extra sustain.

Demand increased in Japan for original Ventures models, and a dealer there commissioned recreations, but it wasn't until 1984 that Moseley was able to establish a production facility in Jonas Ridge, North Carolina, making reissues and other models. His last production instrument was the 40th Anniversary model of 1992. Moseley died that year; his widow Loretta continued the business. By 2017 Ed Roman offered new Mosrites, and Eastwood had its Mosrite-influenced Sidejack models.

Mosrite guitars have always been extremely popular in Japan – as have The Ventures – and Japanese copies of Mosrites flourished, none more blatant than those of Firstman (catalog from about 1967, above). A real Mosrite ad from the same year (right) features "Mr & Mrs Country Music": Joe Maphis and Rosa Lee Maphis with Joe's famous double-neck Mosrite. Three more Mosrite guitars are pictured on this page: a remarkably crafted custom-made instrument (near right) built by Semie Moseley in 1980 for a business partner; a Ventures-like Model 88 (center) made in 1988; and a Ventures reissue, the Japanese-made Excellent 65 (far right), this one produced during 1998.

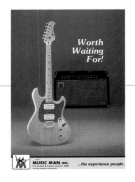

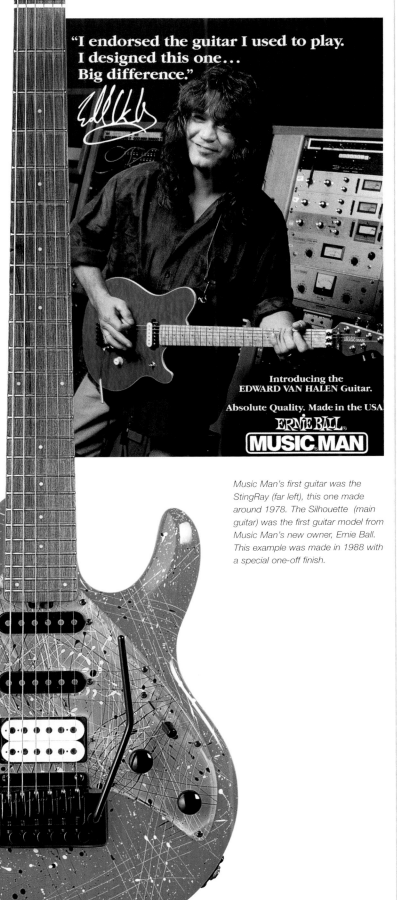

Two promos from Music Man's different eras are shown here. This 1977 ad (left) announces the company's first guitar, the StingRay, while the 1991 ad (below) highlights Edward Van Halen's involvement with the design of a new EVH model.

MUSIC MAN

Originally connected with Leo Fender, US-made Music Man guitars are now among the leading alternatives to the "big two" brands, Fender and Gibson.

Two ex-Fender employees, Forrest White and Tom Walker, together with Leo Fender, set up a new company in Fullerton, California, in 1972, naming it Music Man two years later. At first production concentrated on a line of amplifiers based on designs by Walker, but a move into instruments followed in 1976. The distinctive Music Man logo had two guitarists whose legs formed a large "M."

When CBS purchased the Fender companies it had given Leo a contract with a ten-year non-competition clause. This expired in 1975. In April of that year Leo was announced as president of Music Man Inc. The first guitar to appear was the StingRay, introduced in mid 1976, along with a fine bass guitar with the same model name. They reflected typical Fender styling, but displayed significant and subtle refinements of construction and components. A three-bolt neck/body joint was successfully employed, contradicting the poor reputation it had gained when Fender used it amid inferior manufacturing standards in the 1970s.

The StingRay followed trends of the time, favoring twin humbuckers and a fixed bridge, while active circuitry was optional. The instrument was not necessarily what was expected of Leo Fender, and the notorious resistance of guitarists to anything new

"I endorsed the guitar I used to play. I designed this one... Big difference."

Introducing the **EDWARD VAN HALEN Guitar.**

Absolute Quality. Made in the USA.

ERNIE BALL
MUSIC MAN

Music Man's first guitar was the StingRay (far left), this one made around 1978. The Silhouette (main guitar) was the first guitar model from Music Man's new owner, Ernie Ball. This example was made in 1988 with a special one-off finish.

237

Albert Lee is a fine player whose work includes his own band Heads Hands & Feet (1972 album, far left) and many sessions, including contributions to Emmylou Harris's Quarter Moon In A Ten Cent Town (1978, sleeve near left). Lee is pictured (below) playing his signature Music Man model.

meant that it never enjoyed much more than a low-key reaction. But Leo, typically, saw little point in merely reworking his past achievements, and aimed to offer genuine improvements in quality, consistency and performance.

The Sabre guitar was added two years later with a body outline slightly different to that of the StingRay. It shared the large, six-tuners-on-one-side headstock and one-piece maple neck construction, and likewise came in two versions – I or II – the former with a 12″-radius fingerboard and jumbo frets, the latter employing a more "vintage" 7.5″ radius and standard-size frets. Once more, neither single-coil pickups nor a vibrato unit were present, while active electrics came as standard, together with more comprehensive circuitry and refinements to hardware. Regardless of such changes and the more streamlined image, the Sabre fared no better with players.

Behind the scenes, all was not well. Part of the business arrangements of the operation meant that Music Man instruments were manufactured by Leo's CLF Research company, but after Music Man tried unsuccessfully to buy CLF in 1978 Leo decided to break away and set up his own guitar-making business, G&L, in 1979. The first instruments bearing his new brandname appeared in 1980.

Music Man continued to manufacture instruments in Fullerton for a time after this upheaval, but later other production sources were used, including Jackson. Despite such turmoil, a limited model selection continued until 1980 when the StingRay guitar

"Somebody finally got it right!"

ERNIE BALL
Introducing the MUSIC MAN Steve Morse Guitar
with
ERNIE BALL RPS Strings:
.010 .013 .016 .026 .032 .042

Photo by La Ferman

Albert Lee
Now with dual DiMarzio humbuckers, African mahogany body, and a full rosewood neck.
ERNIE BALL
MUSIC MAN
www.ernieball.com • www.music-man.com

Music Man has marketed some impressive signature guitars. These have included Steve Lukather's model, the Luke (1998 example, far left), and the odd-shape Albert Lee (the guitar, not our Albert). This Lee model (main guitar) dates from 1994 and the ad (left) from 2011. The 1998 ad (above) shows Steve Morse with his signature Music Man guitar.

MUSIC MAN

disappeared from the catalog, the remainder lasting into the early 1980s. However, in March 1984 Music Man was acquired by the Ernie Ball company, production being transferred north, near to Ball's string and accessory works in San Luis Obispo, California, and the second chapter in the Music Man story began.

Music Man's basses had been more popular than the guitars thus far, so it was the four-string models that first went into production with the new owner.

The prototype of an all-new guitar, the Silhouette, was previewed in 1986, and production commenced the following year. Designed in 1985 by ex-Valley Arts man Dudley Gimpel, with the help of country-rock guitarist Albert Lee, this solidbody was Fender-inspired. But other features included a compact, stylishly-contoured body and a headstock that echoed the Music Man bass design, the tuners now arranged in a convenient four-and-two formation.

Options included the 24-fret maple neck with rosewood or maple fingerboard, a fixed bridge or locking vibrato system, and various pickup formats. The most recent variant is the Silhouette Special, launched in 1995, its 22-fret neck and Wilkinson vibrato unit being the most obvious of a number of changes made to the (continuing) standard model. Among the high-profile players of the Silhouette have been Ron Wood and Keith Richards in what appears to be a rare example of these two favoring contemporary new-design guitars rather than vintage-style oldies.

Back in the 1980s, the Silhouette was joined by the Steve Morse signature model in 1987. The model employed a novel four-pickup configuration favored by this players' player. A very popular Music Man six-string model was the EVH, offered for a few years from 1991 and designed in close collaboration with the influential high-speed guitarist Edward Van Halen.

Features of the EVH included Van Halen's own-design body, a custom-profile neck and specially devised DiMarzio-made humbuckers. The original Floyd Rose-equipped model was joined by a fixed-bridge option, reflecting Van Halen's changing requirements. However, in the mid 1990s the guitarist changed allegiance to Peavey for a new signature model, and so Music Man subsequently altered the name of its EVH model to the Axis. Since then the original Music Man EVHs have become quite collectable, especially examples with pretty woods.

Causing some confusion in retrospect, Music Man had used the Axis model name earlier for a number of prototypes of what would become the Albert Lee model. One of these angular prototypes was made for Paul McCartney, enjoying the distinction of being the first left-handed solidbody six-string instrument made by the new Music Man operation. The remarkable Nigel Tufnel had a typically more refined version, too, that featured no less than four humbuckers, a rev counter, tailpipes, Woody Woodpecker logo and, rather subtly, note names inlaid into the fingerboard to increase Tufnel's

Three more Music Man guitars are pictured on this page: an EVH (near right) made in 1992, as endorsed by Edward Van Halen; a hybrid Axis Super Sport (center) from 2000; and a Silhouette Special (far right) made in 1998. This 2013 ad (right) features the Armada model, the company's first neck-through guitar.

already frightening speed. Other 1990s additions to the Music Man guitar line included two more signature editions that were added during 1993, the Luke and the Albert Lee.

The Luke was designed to the specifications of Steve Lukather, while the Albert Lee had that odd-looking, angular body shape. New in 1997 at Music Man was a cheaper Axis variant, the Axis Sport, which had the P-90-like MM90 pickups, the first pickups to be made in-house at Music Man. In 2011 Music Man added the Armada model to its lines, the firm's first guitar constructed in the neck-through-body style.

While the choice is far from vast, the Music Man line offers a high-quality, top-performance selection that represents some of the best of the new generation of American-made instruments.

NATIONAL

The National brand appeared on some early electric guitars of the 1930s, but the company is especially remembered for its unusual "map shape" electrics of the 1960s.

John Dopyera and his brothers Rudy and Ed emigrated from what was then Czechoslovakia and set up the National String Instrument Corporation in Los Angeles, California, in the mid 1920s, at first to produce a metal-body tenor banjo that John had invented. In 1927, National launched its now-famous acoustic "tricone" resonator guitar. Suspended inside its metal body were three resonating aluminum cones that acted a little like loudspeakers. The result was a loud, distinctive instrument. A few rare

Two classic fiberglass-body National guitars are shown here: an Art Deco-inspired Studio 66 (far left) from 1961, and a Varsity 66 (main guitar) made in 1964. The two pictures at the top of the page are views of Nationals being made at the Valco factory in 1962, and the catalogs also date from the 1960s.

examples were fitted with pickups. A complicated set of business maneuvers followed, during which the Dopyera brothers split from National after an argument and formed the Dobro Corporation in 1929 ("Dobro" derives from the first syllables of "Dopyera brothers"). Dobro then started to make single-cone resonator guitars.

Dobro and National were merged again in 1935, and it was at this time that National-Dobro marketed a National electric guitar, the Electric Spanish f-hole archtop model (along with a similar Dobro-brand version, plus cheaper Supro-brand electrics). The magnetic pickups on these early electrics were designed by Victor Smith.

In 1936 the company relocated to Chicago. It continued to make a number of National archtop electrics, unusually including some that were without f-holes, as well as one of the earliest guitars with two pickups, the Sonora model of 1939.

During 1942 Victor Smith, Al Frost and Louis Dopyera (another of the Dopyera brothers) bought the National-Dobro company and changed the name to the Valco Manufacturing Company.

After World War II, more Valco electrics appeared bearing the National brand, as well as low-end Supro-brand models and catalog-company contracted brands such as Airline. Post-war National archtop electric models included the Aristocrat – at first with an unusual arrangement of control knobs and jack either side of the large bridge/pickup unit, and later with bodies supplied by Gibson – and the single-cutaway

VERSATILITY · BEAU~~ ~~ ~~EGANCE~~

The Kim Sisters and ~~N~~ ~~ric G~~

EXCLUSIVE DISTI~~ ~~
FRED GRETSCH MFG. CO. — 60 BROADWAY, BROOK~~ ~~
L. D. HEATER MUSIC CO.—1930 W. IRVING ST., PORTL~~ ~~
TURNER MUSICAL INSTRUMENTS, LTD.—51 NANTUCKE~~ ~~

Write For Free Color Catalog Add~~ ~~

The two Nationals on this page both have fiberglass bodies. This Newport 84 (main guitar) was made in 1964 and has a regular magnetic pickup plus a bridge-mounted "contact" pickup (the connecting wire is visible). The Glenwood 95 (right) was also made in 1964. The glamorous Kim Sisters (above) model some National Glenwoods in an ad published during 1966.

National made some early and significant electric guitars in the 1930s (catalog, right), but the brand is best known for its "map shape" fiberglass-body and wood-body guitars of the 1960s, some examples of which are pictured below.

Club Combo introduced in 1952. Valco then started its experiments with materials. It was not the first brand to offer guitars built from synthetic materials, earlier innovations including Rickenbacker's Bakelite models of the 1930s. But the brightly colored and unusually shaped fiberglass Valco-made guitars of the 1960s were without doubt among the most eye-catchingly different instruments of the era.

Valco was never short of impressive sounding names for its guitar innovations, and came up with "Res-O-Glas" and "Hollow-Glas" for the material used in its new line of non-wood instruments, introduced in 1962. This was in fact one of the first composite materials used for guitar manufacturing, a technique that would in later decades become more prevalent with the advent of "carbon-graphite."

The material used for the National (and Supro) guitars of the 1960s was described at the time by Valco in advertising material as "polyester resins with threads of pure glass." More simply, this was fiberglass. Valco intended that the material, which it trumpeted as "more adaptable and workable than conventional wood," would provide a longer lasting instrument. Two molded body halves were joined together with a strip of white vinyl binding around the edge.

Valco also produced wood-body National models alongside the Res-O-Glas guitars. The various plastic Newport and Glenwood models and wood-body Westwood guitars have become known as "map shape" Nationals among collectors, because the body

suggests a stylized outline of part of the map of the United States. By 1964 National had nine map-shape guitars in its catalog, ranging from the wood-body Westwood 72 to the most expensive model in that line, the plastic-body Glenwood 99.

Like some contemporary Supro models, a number of National guitars, including map-shapes, had in addition to the conventional magnetic pickup(s) an innovative "contact" pickup built into the bridge. The facility was also included on non-map-shape Nationals, including the various Val-Trol models introduced in the late 1950s. The bridge-pickup scheme was another National idea before its time; similar piezo bridge pickups would find success in the "hybrid" guitars of the late 1990s.

However, these brave plastic and pickup experiments ended with Valco itself in the late 1960s. Control in Valco had passed to one Robert Engelhardt, who went on to buy its competitor, the Kay guitar company, in 1967. When Kay went out of business during the following year, Valco – and its National and Supro brands – went down with it.

The National brand has resurfaced since, including a 1970s line of unremarkable imported electrics. In 1988 National Reso-phonic Guitars was founded in San Luis Obispo, California, and began producing resonator guitars, with a line of ResoLectric electric models following in the 1990s. Meanwhile, National's "map shape" design was revived in 1996 for wood-body guitars with the Metropolitan brandname, made by Robin in Houston, Texas, and marketed by Alamo Music Products.

Three more National "map shape" guitars are pictured on this page: a fiberglass-body Newport 82 (far left) made in 1964; a wood-body Westwood 75 (center) made in 1963; and a 1962 wood-body Westwood 77 (near left), another model that had Valco's extra bridge pickup.

O V A T I O N

Known for revolutionizing electric-acoustic guitars with "Lyracord" fiberglass bowl-back instruments in 1966, Ovation tried for years to market innovative solidbody electric guitar designs, but with little success.

Ovation was founded by aeronautical engineer and helicopter manufacturer Charles H. Kaman in Bloomfield, Connecticut (relocating to New Hartford in 1967). The guitar company used aeronautical materials to solve what they considered as problems with the instability of natural wood. Ovation acoustics got an early push when played by Josh White and Charlie Byrd, but it was Glen Campbell's TV show *Goodtime Hour* in 1969 that made the brand.

It was on that show that Ovation's first under-bridge-saddle transducer was introduced. This device paved the way for a revolution in "amplified acoustic" or "electro-acoustic" guitars, as well as the later trend toward "hybrid" instruments that mixed bridge transducers and conventional magnetic pickups.

While waiting for the bowl-backs to catch on, Ovation had in 1968 introduced its first semi-hollow thinline electrics, the Electric Storm series: Thunderhead, Tornado and Hurricane 12-string. They had German Framus-made bodies, Schaller hardware and pickups, and Ovation necks. In 1971 a low-end black Eclipse model was added. These were all discontinued by 1973. Ovation entered the solidbody electric guitar market

Ovation went into battle with these two odd-shape solidbodies: the Breadwinner (1975 example, far left) and the higher-end Deacon (main guitar, also made in 1975). Steve Marriott is seen with a Deacon in this 1976 (ad), a year after Marriott's band Humble Pie had finally split.

with its battle-axe-shape Breadwinner model in 1972, followed by the more high-end Deacon with high gloss finish, neck binding and fancier inlays.

Featuring onboard FET pre-amps, the Breadwinner and Deacon were among the earliest American production guitars with active electronics. A 12-string model was available by 1976. While the Breadwinner lasted until 1979 and the Deacon to 1980, they never achieved much popularity. Toward the end of its life the Deacon had extra contouring added to its body, but this didn't help sales.

Meanwhile, the company's various acoustic guitar models continued to mature and evolve, most notably with the introduction in 1976 of the graphite-topped Adamas series, which had a multiple series of soundholes in the body. Ovation's successful Collector Series debuted in 1982, and its domestic and imported electro-acoustic lines continued to proliferate and thrive.

During 1975 Ovation introduced more solidbodies, this time the more conventional-looking double-cutaway Preacher, Preacher Deluxe and single-cutaway Viper models. The Preacher had passive electrics, while the Preacher Deluxe featured active circuitry and fancier appointments. A 12-string version of the Deluxe was also offered. The Viper came with two or three pickups.

In 1979 the curious Ultra Kaman, or UK II, made its debut. This single-cutaway guitar featured an aluminum-framed body that was filled out with lightweight urethane foam. It boasted precise tone and volume control. The aluminum/foam concept was derived from the necks of Ovation's low-end Applause acoustics. Alas, none of these efforts caught on with the market and in 1983 Ovation's American-made solidbodies ceased production. The only "stars" to play Ovation solidbodies briefly were Jim Messina, Roy Clark and Glen Campbell.

Around 1985 Ovation attempted solidbodies one more time with the introduction of its Hard Body series, consisting of Korean-made necks and bodies assembled and finished in the US using Schaller hardware and DiMarzio pickups. The GP was a flame-top, equal-double-cutaway with a set-0neck; the GS a bolt-on-neck Strat-style guitar, with one or two humbuckers or humbucker/single-coil/single-coil pickup layout. These lasted only a year or so.

A few hundred more solidbody guitars were briefly imported from Japan, and a shortlived, entry-level, Korean-made Celebrity By Ovation line of superstrats was offered around 1987. None of the various models was successful. A few experimental guitars that were fitted with Steve Ripley's "stereo" electronics were tried (as on Kramer's Ripley Stereo) but the project went nowhere.

Giving up on its own efforts, Kaman purchased Hamer Guitars of Chicago in 1988. Kaman Music Corp was in turn bought by Fender in 2007, and in 2015 Drum Workshop bought the Ovation brand.

Three more Ovation solidbodies are pictured on this page: a Preacher (far left) from around 1976; a UK II (center) made in 1979; and a Viper III (near left) from about 1978.

PARKER

In the mid 1990s Parker popularized the "hybrid" guitar – an instrument fitted with piezo as well as magnetic pickups – and revolutionized the way in which electric guitars can be built.

Parker is a partnership between guitar-maker Ken Parker and electronics expert Larry Fishman. The project required considerable finance, provided primarily by Korg USA, a company better known for its electronic musical instruments.

A purpose-built factory was established near Boston, Massachusetts, to manufacture the unusually-shaped Parker Fly. The facility was designed to make Parkers in an entirely different way to any other electric guitars. Every part of the Fly, with the exception of its Sperzel locking tuners, is unique to Parker, including the tangless stainless-steel frets which are glued into the fingerboard, and the unusual "flat-spring" vibrato with built-in piezo-electric pickups.

Parker said that all this was intended to make its new Fly a more versatile guitar – not merely something that looked different from the rest. The theory involved in the new design was that the only reason for a guitar's solid wooden body is strength, and that the wood's effect on the sound of the instrument is secondary.

However, Parker knew that acoustic guitars depend much more for their sound on the timbers used, especially that employed for the body's top. So the company intended

Two guitars from the Parker lines are shown on this page: a Fly Artist (far right) from 1997 with Parker's revolutionary wood/composite construction; and a less expensive bolt-on-neck wood-body NiteFly (main guitar) made in 1996. Reeves Gabrels, whose credits include work with David Bowie, and an enthusiastic Parker player, is seen in this 1997 ad (above) with a NiteFly.

246

Ken Parker, co-founder of Parker Guitars, is pictured in this ad published in 1998.

that its Fly models would have thin, lightweight but highly resonant wooden bodies strengthened by a composite material (glass and carbon fibers in an epoxy matrix) that forms a very thin "external skeleton" around the wood. The necks are constructed in a similar fashion. It's almost as if the body of a Parker instrument is just the top of an acoustic guitar, specially strengthened.

Most Fly guitars have two different kinds of pickup fitted. The first is recognizable as a traditional magnetic type that provides normal electric-guitar sounds, while piezo elements in the bridge give the instrument "acoustic"-like tones.

While these two different types of pickup had been offered on individual guitars before, no previous instrument had provided the player with a means to combine magnetic and piezo pickups in a way that allowed the use of either type independently or both mixed together.

The Parker's Fishman-designed pickup-mix facility effectively provides musicians with two guitars in one, merging electric and electro-acoustic sounds. Many other makers have subsequently emulated this "hybrid" style, and some guitar-industry people are arguing that it provides one of the most exciting possible future directions for the electric guitar.

The first Parker introduced was the poplar-body Fly Vibrato Deluxe, in 1993, followed by the mahogany Fly Classic (introduced 1996), the spruce Fly Artist (1997),

the rare figured-maple Supreme (1998) and a nylon-string version, the Spanish Fly (1999). The Concert model (1997) is a piezo-only guitar without vibrato. The MIDI Fly (1999) uses a sophisticated synth-access system, while the lower-price NiteFly (1996) has many of the regular Fly's attributes but with a bolt-on reinforced-wood neck and a more conventional soft maple body (ash and mahogany from '99).

New non-vibrato Parker guitars appeared in 2000. These included the basswood-body black-hardware Hardtail model, which includes a Sperzel D-Tuner on the D-string and is aimed at the modern rock market, as well as the Jazz model that has gold-plated hardware and a mahogany body.

Korg pulled out in 2011, and U.S. Music Corp, which owned Washburn among other brands, bought Parker Guitars three years later. Ken Parker and Larry Fishman left, and U.S. Music designed new Parkers. Ken Parker now makes acoustic archtops.

PEAVEY

Beginning as an amplifier manufacturer founded in 1965 by Hartley Peavey in Meridian, Mississippi, Peavey Electronics was notable in pioneering new construction techniques for electric guitars in the late 1970s, and has offered a large, varied and mostly mid-priced line of instruments ever since.

Peavey guitars originated with Hartley's idea that he could create a relatively inexpensive alternative to Gibson and Fender offerings. Working with Chip Todd, he

A Parker synth-access MIDI Fly (near right) made in 1999, alongside a 2000 ad featuring Orgy's Amir Derakh. The 2006 ad (right) features Adrian Belew with his signature Parker Fly. This Peavey T-60 (far right) was produced during 1979.

devised the T-60 guitar ("T" for Todd). This instrument effectively combined a Gibson-like rounded body shape and twin humbuckers with a Fender-style maple fingerboard and slightly offset double-cutaways.

The T-60 debuted in 1978, lasted a decade and was notable for three innovations. First was a tone control that doubled as a coil-tap, devised for Peavey by the Los Angeles-based pedal-steel guitarist Orville "Red" Rhodes. The second development was a patented "bi-laminated" maple neck that had opposing grain directions to provide extra stability. Finally, this was the first guitar constructed using computer-controlled carving machines, a technique borrowed from gun-stock-making that is now standard practice among mass-production guitar-makers.

The 1980s were exceptionally fertile for Peavey guitars. The T Series had a facelift in 1982, including a new T-25 Special with a phenolic fingerboard. The profile was slightly reshaped and Super Ferrite blade-style pickups were added; these lasted only about a year. Peavey's first traditional-style vibratos debuted in 1983, and the company flirted with "pointy" body shapes in the mid 1980s with the electric-shaver-shaped Razer, B.C. Rich-style Mystic and V-shaped Mantis.

Peavey also began to introduce more conventionally shaped offset-double-cutaway models between 1983 and 1986. These included the Horizon, Milestone and Patriot series, the latter with a solid-state amp included in the instrument's molded plastic case, a tribute to Danelectro. Peavey's Hydra double-neck debuted in 1984, and a Kahler-equipped Jeff Cook model appeared the following year. Peavey began using Kahler locking vibratos on other models in 1985.

The popular Stratocaster-style Predator series was introduced by Peavey during 1985. (The line was revived in 1990, and a seven-string version was added to the series in 2000.) An Explorer-inspired "pointy" Vortex model also appeared in 1985, and the Stratocaster-style Impact series debuted the following year. All these had disappeared from the line by the late 1990s, although the Impact was briefly revived as the figured-top Impact Milano and Torino models during 1994.

Peavey guitars always offered high quality at their respective price points, but in the late 1980s the company began markedly improving the quality of its instruments. During 1987 the popular Nitro series of superstrats and the active and passive Falcon series of near-Strats appeared (both with versions lasting until 1990), as well as Peavey's first venture into through-neck construction, the Impact Unity model. In 1988 Peavey began using Alnico pickups and unveiled the superstrat Tracer series, some models of which survived to 1994.

In 1988 Peavey began working with another celebrity, introducing the violin-waisted Vandenberg Signature model that had been designed with Dutch guitar-slinger Adrian Vandenberg. During the following year the company introduced the high-end Destiny

Three more Peavey guitars are pictured here: a T-25 Special (near right) with plastic fingerboard, this example dating from 1982; a Razer model (center) made in 1984; and a Vandenberg Signature (far right) from 1989, this one in rock-it pink, which was designed in collaboration with Adrian Vandenberg, who at the time played with Whitesnake. Vandenberg is featured in this 1990 ad (right) with the later Custom version, this one with puzzle-pattern graphics.

VANDENBERG CUSTOM

By Peavey

superstrat as well as the Generation Telecaster-style model, both of which came with carved figured maple caps. These were offered until 1994.

In 1990 Peavey introduced its first Les-Paul-inspired model, the single-cutaway Odyssey, available until 1994 and including a quilt-top version. The 1990s saw the continuation of the offset-double-cutaway style – Axecellerator, Defender, Detonator, Firenza (formerly Impact), G-90 and Raptor – and the Tele-style designs – Cropper Classic, for Memphis great Steve Cropper, and Reactor. A PRS-style guitar, the Ltd model, appeared in the Peavey line during 2000.

Many felt Peavey guitars finally arrived with the landing of the Eddie Van Halen EVH Wolfgang series in 1996, the acclaimed guitarist having transferred his allegiance to Peavey from Music Man. Van Halen had already worked with Peavey on the 5150 amplifier series (the 5150 name coming from the title that Van Halen then used for his own recording studio). Peavey's various offset-double-cutaway Peavey Van Halen models, with their distinctive chunky upper horn, were high-end, desirable guitars that lasted until Van Halen's relationship with Peavey ended in 2004.

By 2017 the Peavey electric line was down to five series: the Jazz Fusion JF-1, an Indonesian hollowbody; the through-body AT-200 AutoTune Guitar; the SC Les Paul-like models; the Raptor Stratocaster-like models; and the Powerslide stand-up slide guitar that recalled the old Melobar.

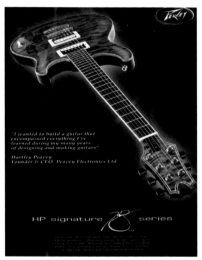

A Peavey EVH Wolfgang (left) produced in collaboration with Eddie Van Halen, this one made in 1997, and a Peavey Cropper Classic (right) from 2000. The ad for the EVH Wolfgang (left) dates from 2002, while the other two ads here are for endorsers Soundgarden (1994, top right) and for Hartley Peavey's HP Signature series (2008, bottom right).

PRS

P R S

Back in the mid 1970s, few would have imagined that a lanky, big-haired kid repairing guitars in an impossibly small workshop in Annapolis, Maryland, would one day be running the number-three guitar company behind Fender and Gibson. Yet that is the remarkable story of Paul Reed Smith, "the Stradivari of the electric guitar" as one satisfied customer would later call him.

The details of this ascent are more fabulous still. Coming from a musical family, Smith started both his musical and guitar-making career during high school. Initially playing bass before moving on to guitar, Smith built his first instrument toward the end of senior high school by fixing the neck of a Japanese "Beatle bass" copy to a strangely-shaped solid body.

Smith then managed to get a job repairing guitars at the Washington Music Center before deciding to go to St. Mary's College in Maryland to study mathematics. The opportunity in the second half of his first year to undertake an independent study project proved to be a turning point. Smith made his first proper guitar, a single-cutaway solidbody in the style of Gibson's Les Paul Junior, which earned him credits and respect from his teachers.

In that summer of 1975 he turned the top floor of his parents' house into a workshop and, with the help of his brother, set about making more guitars. The bug

Two early PRS Custom guitars are pictured on this page: number 0002 (far left) and 0005 (main guitar). The company's ads have continually stressed the importance of name players, including Dickie Betts of The Allman Brothers (above) and Brad Whitford of Aerosmith (below).

had bitten, and Smith's return to college proved to be shortlived. By the start of 1976 he had left and moved into his first workshop in West Street, Annapolis.

Smith made his first electric guitar at his new shop, a solidbody Gibson Byrdland-style instrument for Ted Nugent. This was quickly followed by a guitar for British rocker Peter Frampton. The all-mahogany guitar for Frampton was an interesting instrument which, although built in early 1976, set the foundation for Smith's future.

Its double-cutaway outline apes Gibson's post-1958 Les Paul Special, but features the arched, carved top of a Les Paul Standard. For the first time on a Smith guitar there were mother-of-pearl birds inlaid by hand down the fingerboard, a distinctive feature that would later help to shift a lot of PRS guitars. But why birds? Smith's mother was a keen bird-watcher, and he says that he simply grabbed one of her bird-watching guides and stole the pictures out of it, drawing a couple of others with friends Billy Armiger and Tim Campbell.

Along with the motif of an eagle landing that was inlaid into the headstock – a feature that would return to PRS guitars some years later – Frampton's guitar also featured the combination of a 24-fret-neck and twin humbucking pickups that would be the basis of Smith's instruments until the beginning of the 1990s.

Smith's dream, however, was to make a guitar for Carlos Santana, one of his guitar-playing idols. Getting to meet players like Santana proved one of Smith's hidden talents. He achieved this by hanging out backstage at the local arenas, begging roadies to let their employer see his instruments. The deal was simple: if you don't fall in love with the instrument, you get your money back. It worked.

Apart from Nugent and Frampton, Smith got orders from Al DiMeola (a 12-string with a built-in phase shifter), and from Frampton's and Bruce Springsteen's bass players, not to mention many local musicians. It also became apparent to Smith from a very early point that big-name guitar players sell guitars to others. DiMeola said after owning a PRS that he felt Smith had the ability to custom-make the guitar of anyone's dreams. Slowly, the word was beginning to spread.

In 1980, after selling his first maple-topped hand-made guitar to Heart guitarist Howard Leese, Smith got to make an instrument for Carlos Santana. This would be the first of four hand-made Smith guitars that Santana used in the coming years.

The association with Santana, and the maple-topped instruments themselves, proved to be vastly important turning points – although as is so often the case that is not how they appeared at the time.

The figured "curly" maple that Smith used for these early maple-top guitars originally came from the drawer-fronts of a friend's dresser. This crucial timber helped to summon up visions of those late-1950s Les Pauls that have influenced so many players and makers. By the time Carlos Santana owned a Smith guitar he was already

This PRS Guitar (far left; the all-mahogany-body model was soon renamed as the Standard) dates from 1986 and is finished in a striking Magenta Pearl. The Metal (1985 example, center) was a shortlived graphic-finish Standard. The Signature (1986 prototype, near left) was PRS's first ultra-high-end model, with hand-signed logo and outrageously flamed maple top.

on his first comeback. Nearly 20 years later, still playing a PRS guitar, he would be topping the *Billboard* charts again with *Supernatural*, another comeback album. Smith said in 1999 that he couldn't have been successful without Santana's support, because the guitarist gave his instruments instant credibility.

Musicians such as Santana, Howard Leese and Al DiMeola all disregarded the overwhelming opinion of the time about which guitars pro players should be using. Their mark of approval was crucial to Smith's early operation. Smith knew that by successfully building a guitar that Santana liked, he had a shot at starting a professional guitar-making operation.

However, building Santana's guitar nearly didn't happen at all. But when, eventually, Santana received his first instrument, the guitar player remarked that its special quality was "an accident of God" and that Smith would never be able to do it again. Santana then said the second guitar Smith made for him was, too, an accident of God. There was a third one, and then a double-neck. When he finally got that, Santana said that maybe this wasn't an accident of God. Finally it seems Santana concluded that Smith might actually be a guitar-maker.

But by 1984 Smith was struggling to survive. He still held some ambition to become a professional guitar player, but with the counsel of his close friends and loyal assistant John Ingram, Smith realized that it was his guitar-building that was making headway,

not his playing. He'd set about designing what we know today as the PRS Custom, and after trying unsuccessfully to persuade various big-name manufacturers to make his design under license, he realized he'd have to do it himself.

Armed with a couple of prototypes, Smith headed out on the road and raised orders worth nearly $300,000. Making the guitars to fulfill these orders was another matter. But by the fall of 1985 Smith and his wife Barbara, guided by the business know-how of Warren Esanu, had set up a limited partnership to raise the capital necessary to start a factory in Virginia Avenue, Annapolis. At last, just about a decade after making his first electric guitar, Smith had his production company, PRS Guitars, up and running and in business.

Apart from a few lucky musicians and their fans, nobody knew Paul Reed Smith when the company first displayed its wares at the important American NAMM trade-shows held during 1985. It was a time of hi-tech musical fashion. The major trends swirling around the guitar industry during that period mainly involved aggressive, futuristic-looking, modern rock guitar designs. In those surroundings, the PRS Custom must have seemed very out of place.

With the Custom, here was an instrument clearly inspired by classic 1950s Gibson and Fender guitars. Often called evolutionary rather than revolutionary, the PRS guitar was substantially more expensive than the high-line Gibson or Fender instruments, but

A Studio Maple Top from 1990 (near right), with humbucker/single/single pickup layout, and a bolt-on-neck Classic Electric (far right, with ad) made in 1988. The Classic Electric was soon renamed the CE.

This PRS semi-solidbody Limited Edition (near right) was made in 1989, one of only 300 examples, each of which had an unusual figured cedar top.

The Artist I (1991 example, far right, with original flyer) continued the Signature theme as a high-end model using exclusive, top-grade materials, but also it had new pickups and a changed neck/heel.

ARTIST SERIES

"Occasionally a mahogany board comes into our shop that is extra dense and resonant. Sometimes the figure and curl in a particular block of curly maple is absolutely exceptional. These rare pieces become the Artist Series. My favorite stains...violin glues...Abalone inlays...vintage tones...Our Very Best."

- Exceptionally figured Curly Maple top
- One-piece Mahogany body and neck
- Select Rosewood fingerboard
- Wide-Fat ARTIST SERIES neck
- Inlaid Signature Headstock and Abalone birds
- 25 inch scale
- Thin finish for enhanced resonance
- PRS ARTIST SERIES pickups
- Five-position Rotary, Volume and Tone
- PRS Tremolo System
- Certificate of Authenticity
- Options: Semi-hollowbody, Gold hardware, PRS Stop-tail, Quilted Maple top, Studio package, Hum/Single/Hum pickups

AVAILABLE COLORS: Amber, Teal Black, Indigo, Dark Cherry Sunburst.

PRS PAUL REED SMITH GUITARS

Made in the USA

© 1992 PRS

it began to gain interest from players and press. The fabulously-colored carved-maple tops harked back to the classic late-1950s Gibson Les Paul, while the guitar's outline melded the double-cutaway shape of Smith's earlier instruments with elements of a Fender Stratocaster-style shape, creating a unique hybrid design that was both classic-looking yet original enough to be noticed.

This mix of Gibson and Fender – effectively the two major cornerstones of electric guitar design – was crucial to the concept.

PRS's scale-length of 25″ (635mm) sat half-way between Gibson's shorter 24.56″ (626mm) scale and Fender's longer 25.5″ (648mm). The 10″ (254mm) fingerboard radius also sat between Gibson's flatter 12″ (305mm) camber and the smaller 7.25″ (184mm) radius of vintage Fenders. That wasn't all. With an unusual rotary pickup selector switch, the twin PRS humbuckers created five distinct sounds: a combination of thick humbucking Gibson-like tones and thinner single-coil mixes that approximated some of the Stratocaster's key voices.

Augmenting the pickup switch was a master volume control and, instead of a conventional tone control, a "sweet switch" which rounded off the guitar's upper frequencies. (By 1991 the sweet switch had been replaced on all models in favor of a standard tone control.) The early 1980s had seen the double-locking Floyd Rose vibrato become one of the most popular design features used on contemporary electric

guitars. However, as a working musician Smith didn't like the fact that you needed a set of Allen wrenches to change strings.

So, with the help of local guitar-playing engineer John Mann, Smith designed his own vibrato system that updated the classic Fender vibrato and employed unique cam-locking tuners, yet still offered fashionable "wide-travel" pitch-bending with near perfect tuning stability.

The Custom used classic "tonewoods," including top-quality curly maple for the distinctly carved top, mahogany for the back and set-neck, and Brazilian rosewood for the fingerboard. The instrument also brought some innovations. Instead of employing conventional plastic binding, the edge of the maple top was left natural-colored, contrasting the colored finish of the guitar's top. Along with all this detail, the guitar's double-octave, 24-fret fingerboard was made to feel "as comfortable as an old T-shirt," like a guitar that had been played in.

It was a design that embodied all of Smith's experience to date, made by a guitar player for other guitar players. Although there have been numerous design changes over the years, the PRS Custom is one of the few electric guitars designed outside the 1950s that can genuinely lay claim to the term "design classic."

Launched at the same time as the Custom was the Standard. Originally just called the PRS, it featured an all-mahogany body, and as such was the workingman's PRS,

Three examples of PRS's EG models, the company's first attempt at "affordable" guitars, are shown on this page, all made during 1991: an EG 3 (near right); an EG 4 (center); and an EG II (far right).

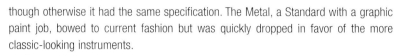

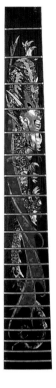

though otherwise it had the same specification. The Metal, a Standard with a graphic paint job, bowed to current fashion but was quickly dropped in favor of the more classic-looking instruments.

Further models followed that only subtly changed the specification of the main pair of PRS models. The Special, which first appeared during 1987, pandered more to contemporary heavy-rock playing trends, while the Studio, which debuted in the PRS line in 1988, offered a pickup layout that featured a humbucker and two single-coils, and came with or without a maple top.

These early years were fraught with the problems of production. Smith had a decade of experience in custom one-off building and repairing, but the production of a number of instruments to the high quality of his pre-factory hand-made guitars provided a steep learning curve. Yet apart from the guitars themselves, Paul Reed Smith became a natural figurehead. His own playing experience enabled easy communication with top-line players – he would sometimes guest with name bands – and early on his in-store clinics became a successful if time-consuming part of his job. For many years PRS was quite happy to let people believe that it was Paul Reed Smith himself who made every guitar.

To support these high-end instruments a sequence of simple and distinguished advertisements became another hallmark of the brand. This parallel invention did not

The fabulous fingerboard inlay work by Pearl Works on the Dragon I overshadowed the developments made at PRS for the guitar's design. Changes included the Stop-Tail bridge and the first set-neck 22-fret fingerboard. The 1992 Dragon I was produced in a limited run of 50 instruments; this one (main guitar) is number 31. The Dragon II (far right, 1993, limited run of 100) had a more elaborate inlay. The four fingerboards pictured above show (left to right): Dragon I inlay with pearl wings; Dragon III inlay; Dragon I inlay with blue wings; Dragon II inlay.

go unnoticed: the ads' designer Dennis Voss and photographer Michael Ward won an Award of Merit for Graphic Excellence in 1985.

Smith seemed on every level to surround himself with mentors and teachers. Early on in PRS's history, Eric Pritchard had given Smith valuable advice on numerous engineering and technical matters. Pritchard not only helped to design the locking PRS tuners but also many of the production tools that were used to fabricate PRS guitars for years. Many friends remarked how Smith possessed an uncanny ability to absorb information, like a sponge.

In 1987 Smith introduced a theme that has since become an important part of PRS Guitars: the limited-edition "ultimate quality" guitar. A friend had remarked to Smith that he didn't charge enough for his work. The result was the Signature, basically a Custom but with absolutely top quality woods and maple tops.

In all, some 1,000 Signature models were made. Each was hand-signed on the headstock by Smith himself, before the Artist Series took over the top-of-the-line position in 1991. Smith would at this time go on long sales tours, away from the factory, and obviously wasn't available then to sign the Signature models. An interim solution was to have Smith sign decals which could go under the finish, and Smith says the production team even threatened to sign the guitars themselves. So the Signature came to an end. Nonetheless, the new Limited Edition model appeared during 1989,

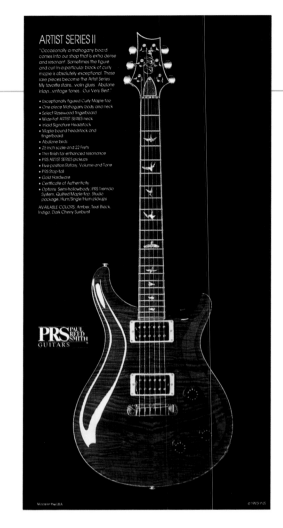

Two more high-end Artist models appeared from PRS: the Artist II (far left, and original flyer, above), this one from 1995; and the Artist Limited (main guitar), this one produced in 1994. Both the Artists shown here have fabulous examples of the optional "quilted" maple top.

One of Paul Reed Smith's original customers from the pre-factory days, Ted Nugent stayed faithful to the new PRS instruments, as this 1994 ad (right) demonstrates.

the first production PRS to feature as standard a non-vibrato, tune-o-matic bridge and stud tailpiece. The guitar also featured hollow tone chambers, although the top was sealed, without any f-holes. Along with curly maple, unusual but highly-figured woods for tops such as cedar and redwood created one of the most unusual PRS guitars from this period. Of Signature quality and price, the Limited Edition was only planned as a small 300-piece run, though fewer were actually made. Both the Signature and Limited Edition proved that there was a highly lucrative market for limited-edition PRS guitars.

By 1988 some dealers, not to mention new export markets like the UK, were calling for PRS to make a less expensive guitar. The result was the first PRS bolt-on-neck instrument, the Classic Electric (quickly abbreviated to CE after Peavey objected to the use of "their" word Classic).

Originally the CE, with its alder body and maple neck and fingerboard, brought a more Fender-like style to the PRS line which up to that point had exclusively featured set-neck guitars. Initially the market was confused, and the company realized that players wanted a cheaper PRS Custom, not a different-sounding instrument. So a black-face headstock quickly followed, as did a maple-top option and, of course, the majority of PRS options such as bird inlays.

The CE evolved into a highly successful guitar. Its body changed to mahogany in 1995, a year after 22-fret versions had been added. It wasn't until 2000 that the standard, non-maple-top CE 22 and CE 24 were phased out, not for lack of popularity or sales, but for simple economic reasons. The start-up CE made little profit for the company and, with pressures on production space caused by increased demand, the CE was an obvious candidate for shelving.

Yet especially in the UK and Europe the CE didn't really satisfy the demand for a lower-priced PRS. This market pressure led the company to produce the bolt-on-neck EG, the first flat-fronted PRS guitar and the first with a 22-fret fingerboard. However, the company soon realized that they were losing money on every EG that was shipped. Smith has said in retrospect that he was unhappy with the sound of the original EGs.

In 1991 a new version appeared, again with a flat front but a rounder, more PRS-like outline. This new EG line was quite a departure. The bodies were crafted on computerized routers by a Baltimore engineering company, Excel (who would manufacture the majority of PRS's hardware parts during the 1990s). However, by 1995 the EG line was discontinued, and at the time of writing they mark the final attempt at a cheaper PRS guitar. There are rumored plans of a PRS guitar that is to be made outside the US ("offshore" in business-speak), as well as another attempt at producing a low-cost US-made electric guitar.

Wood quality was paramount from the start of PRS Guitars, as it had been in Smith's "apprentice" days making one-off custom instruments. Early on, Smith had

The first major change to the Custom model was its move in 1993, inspired by the Dragon I, to 22 frets as the Custom 22 (1994 example, far left). Other models were also made available with 22 frets at this time, including the CE. This CE 22 Maple Top (near left) was made in 1998.

The CE models widened the appeal of PRSs to some players, as these 1990s ads show. They feature Alex Lifeson of Rush (top) and Brian "Damage" Forsyth of Kix.

PRS's McCarty models were developed with Ted McCarty, Gibson president from 1950 to 1966. McCarty is pictured (right) with Paul Reed Smith at the PRS factory. The PRS McCarty solidbodies were endorsed by players such as Larry Lalonde of Primus (centre right) and Ross Childress of Collective Soul (far right).

drawn the conclusion that the better the quality of the raw material, in terms of its weight and condition, the better the guitar would sound.

Unlike many makers at the time, Smith believed that an electric guitar's tone was not all derived from its pickups and electronics. His feeling was that the electric guitar was an acoustic structure, and that the pickups and signal chain could not amplify what wasn't there in the first place. It led him on a quest for the finest woods and knowledgeable timber suppliers, such as Michael Reid whom Smith had first met in 1980. Reid became a valued part of PRS's production chain.

The fabulously curly and quilted maple tops were especially important to PRS Guitars. The company set up a grading system: the Classic grade, used for the CE Maple Top guitars, is about a "7" on PRS's 1-to-10 rating system. The set-neck guitars use a Regular grade – now more commonly known as a Custom grade – of around 7 to 9 on the system.

PRS's "10-tops" are an option on certain production guitars like the Custom, and are obviously 10 on that scale. The Signature series and subsequent limited-edition models use what Smith describes as "something spectacular."

Curly maple is a highly "figured," or patterned, timber. Under the vibrant, stained and colored finishes used by PRS, it helps to create a guitar that for many is as much a work of art as a working musical tool. Conversely, the opulent appearance of a PRS

curly maple top has drawn many a derogatory phrase, from "over-pretty" to "furniture guitar." Although curly maple has been synonymous with guitars such as the Gibson Les Paul since the late 1950s, PRS refueled the demand almost as soon as its guitars appeared in the mid 1980s.

Once a curly log is discovered it needs to be correctly processed before it gets close to being part of a PRS guitar. Imagine a rectangular block of maple. Along the sides run "wave" shapes. By slicing the blank in two – as you would to cut a bun before buttering it – you slice through the wave, and open the blank like a book. You then see the curl, like lines across a page.

The type of wave, and the extremes of width and distance between its "peaks" and "troughs," will influence the look of the curl. A slightly curved wave will result in a mild curl; a triangular wave will be more spectacular; and a square wave will be the strongest. Because the relative hardness between the peaks and the troughs of the curl differs, certain color-staining and sanding techniques can emphasize the curl.

The way in which a log is cut will also affect the final look of the curl. A quarter-sawn rectangular blank, with grain running parallel to the long sides, creates a pronounced and symmetrical curl. If the blank is slab-sawn, with grain running parallel to the shorter top face of a rectangular blank, the curl twists and looks more diverse – and the grain will not be symmetrical across the halves of the bookmatched top, unlike

The Dragon III (1994 prototype, near right) had another highly detailed fingerboard inlay. PRS's two new McCarty guitars marked a distinct development: shown here are a McCarty Model (center, from 1994) and a McCarty Standard (far right, made in 1998).

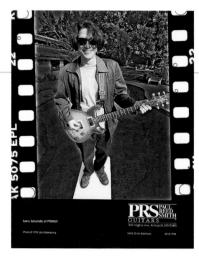

This PRS 10th Anniversary model (main guitar, 1994 prototype) was issued in 1995 to mark ten years since the first PRS factory had been set up in Annapolis, Maryland. The PRS 10th Anniversary had a special "scrimshaw" engraved eagle and suitable inscription on the headstock.

the curl. The curl of a slab-sawn example will be less curly and more "wiggly." The look of a curly-maple top will be further altered by the type of maple used. PRS use two main types of maple for guitar tops: West Coast and East Coast. East Coast maple, also known as red maple, is what PRS started with. Later they added West Coast maple, also known as big-leaf maple, which can be had from a variety of sources including British Columbia, Washington state, Oregon and Southern California.

In 1991 PRS announced the Artist I, which outwardly seemed a continuation of the Signature series. In fact, the Artist I signaled a fundamental change in the design of PRS guitars. Many of the top pros who'd been attracted to PRS guitars loved the look and feel of the instruments but felt there was room for tonal improvement.

It seemed clear to some that PRS provided a natural progression beyond vintage Gibson Les Paul instruments – but the sound lacked the low-end associated with those classic guitars. So, along with its ultimate-grade timbers, the Artist I introduced a stronger neck construction and many different production techniques, primarily

A further example of PRS's CE 22 Maple Top model, this one (far left) made in 1998. The superb quilted maple top of this example is enhanced with a Grey Black finish.

PRS

Carlos Santana (below; 1999 Supernatural album, right) has been a long-time PRS player. The main guitar pictured here is the first instrument that Paul Reed Smith built for Santana in 1980 at the guitar-maker's West Street, Annapolis, workshop.

intended to improve the "acoustic" tone of PRS guitars. While the Artist got Smith closer to the sound he and a significant number of his top-flight customers were looking for, it still wasn't close enough. Yet PRS's next sonic development was virtually missed by the guitar-playing public.

When the Dragon I was launched in 1992 in a limited edition of just 50 pieces, the market was staggered by the exquisite computer-cut inlay down the fingerboard. But this feature, which brought the company a good deal of media interest, disguised the fact that the guitar featured a shorter 22-fret neck with a "wide-fat" profile, a new non-vibrato Stop-Tail bridge, and new pickups.

While the Dragon I was heading for guitar collections around the world, those lucky enough to own and play one realized the tonal improvement. This led the following year to the introduction of the PRS Custom 22, basically a Dragon without the inlay. Indeed, while 24-fret options still remain on the Custom, Standard and CE, the majority of future PRS guitars would follow the shorter and fatter neck concept. Smith says that a big neck equals big tone, and few players would disagree. As a consequence, PRS's other major models of the time – the Standard and CE lines – were also offered in 22-fret formats from 1994.

These gradual changes in specification are typical of PRS. With a couple of exceptions the guitars have always used pickups designed and made by PRS.

Originally, the Custom, Standard and Signature used what PRS called the Standard Treble and Standard Bass humbuckers.

These pickups looked like any other uncovered humbucker, but actually used magnetic "slug" polepieces in the non-adjustable inner coil, as well as a rear-placed feeder magnet. This helped to achieve a more accurate single-coil tone when split by the company's five-position rotary switch.

Catering for the more aggressive rock market, PRS developed pickups such as the Chainsaw, and the HFS ("Hot, Fat and Screams") as used initially on the Special. The Vintage Treble and Vintage Bass humbuckers first appeared on the Classic Electric, and the pairing of an HFS at bridge and Vintage Bass in neck position endures today on the 24-fret CE Maple Top, Standard and Custom. The first Dragon guitar featured the Dragon Treble and Dragon Bass pickups (which also appeared on the Custom 22), but since the McCarty Model and its new McCarty pickups the 22-fret PRSs have featured covered pickups which, tonally, chase a more "classic" sound.

In 1988 PRS launched the unique Electronics Upgrade Kit designed to improve the "fatness" and midrange definition of pre-1993 PRS instruments. It could have been called the "all we've learned since we started" kit as it reflected changes made over the years to minor components, such as lighter-weight tuner buttons and thumb screws, nickel-plated-brass screws for saddles and intonation, a simulated tone

Three more PRS guitars are illustrated on this page: a Fender-flavored Swamp Ash Special (far left) from 1997; an Artist III (center) made in 1997; and an Artist IV prototype (near left) produced in 1995.

control for early switch-equipped guitars, and high-capacitance hook-up wire. The Dragon I, meanwhile, had been a risk that worked. The Dragon II followed in 1993 (along with the 22-fret Artist II) and the Dragon III in 1994 (joined by the Artist Ltd). Both new Dragons were limited to just 100 pieces and each featured along the fingerboard a more flamboyant dragon inlay than the last.

Announced in 1999, the most fabulous Dragon guitar was unleashed with a "three-dimensional" inlay, this time over the complex curves of the body. The Dragon 2000, limited to 50 pieces, may for some have been just another collectors' guitar, but it illustrates the desire of PRS to stretch the boundaries of guitar-making in their ultra-high-end models.

Little known until 1994 was the involvement with PRS of Ted McCarty. He had been president of Gibson between 1950 and 1965, the period that many considered as the company's golden years. Smith says he "discovered" McCarty's name when doing some research in the local patent office. Just after starting his production company, Smith cold-called McCarty for advice. With great foresight, Smith subsequently enlisted him as a consultant. McCarty, meanwhile, "downloaded the hard disk" for Smith, explaining how Gibson made its instruments back in the 1950s.

But when it came to PRS's next landmark guitar, it was again player pressure that spurred the idea onward, notably from Texas guitar-slinger David Grissom. Leaving the

Ted McCarty collaborated with PRS for two new hollowbodys, the deep-body Archtop and shallower Hollowbody. McCarty is pictured (below) with Paul Reed Smith at the launch of the models in 1998. Pictured are a 1997 prototype of the spruce-top Archtop (below, far left); Private Stock #62 (center), which was a 1998 Hollowbody with figured one-piece maple top; and a flame-maple Hollowbody II (right), a guitar also made in 1998.

opulence of the Dragon and Artist guitars behind, 1994's McCarty Model changed the formula in a seemingly subtle way, creating a PRS guitar that got closer still to the sound and feel of Gibson's classic late-1950s Les Paul.

PRS said the McCarty Model was essentially a Dragon with a thicker body, thinner headstock, lighter tuners and different pickups. In reality it was much more than that. It proved a turning point for PRS Guitars.

The company had grown up and the McCarty Model quite quickly became the "player's PRS." Certainly when compared side-by-side with a mid-1980s Custom, the differences in sound and feel were startlingly obvious. Physically, the McCarty had a shorter, fatter neck, while the difference in body thickness, while subtle, is there: the McCarty feels slightly less petite. Generally speaking, the McCarty has more of a Gibson-like, "vintage" vibe to it. It has a broader sound than an early Custom's typically aggressive, thinner tone, but still with plenty of PRS character, particularly a focused midrange and a chunkier feel.

The McCarty Model also featured for the first time on a major PRS guitar a three-way Gibson-style pickup-selecting toggle switch instead of PRS's unique five-way rotary switch. (Later, a pull/push switch was added to the tone control in order to coil-split the humbuckers.) Mirroring the Custom/Standard relationship in the PRS line, the mahogany McCarty Standard without a maple cap was introduced at the same time as

the maple-top McCarty Model. In 1998 the McCarty Model was offered with twin Seymour Duncan P-90-style "soapbar" single-coil pickups as the McCarty Soapbar, cashing in on the popularity of P-90s toward the end of the decade. The all-mahogany McCarty Soapbar returns to the construction and style of Smith's early pre-factory pre-maple-top guitars which usually favored mahogany construction and P-90 pickups.

Another "soapbar" guitar, the Custom 22 Soapbar, appeared in 1998, unusually for a PRS featuring a maple set-neck and three soapbar pickups controlled by a five-way lever switch, giving a unique "hot" Strat-style tone. Ten years old as a production company in 1995, PRS Guitars released the 10th Anniversary model that year which featured "scrimshaw" engraved bird inlays and headstock eagle.

After many, many requests, PRS also started making in 1995 a reproduction of the pre-factory Santana guitar, with its old-style double-cutaway outline, 24.5″ (622mm) scale-length and flatter 11.5″ (292mm) fingerboard radius. Ironically, although this seemed a backward design step, it was among the first PRS guitars to be made using the company's recently installed computer-assisted routing machines. These began to replace the innovative jigs and tools that had helped to fabricate PRS guitars for the previous decade.

Santana always liked his pre-factory PRS guitars, although Smith says that the guitarist tried "really hard" to like the new, modern PRS design. Eventually, PRS made

There was little doubt about the inspiration for PRS's Singlecut, which appeared in 2000. Pictured here are a 2001 Tremonti Model (near left); a 2001 Singlecut Brazilian Rosewood (center); and a 2001 Singlecut (far right). Mark Tremonti was only the second artist with a PRS signature model, after Carlos Santana. A dispute with Gibson over the Singlecut was finally settled in 2006 with a win for PRS.

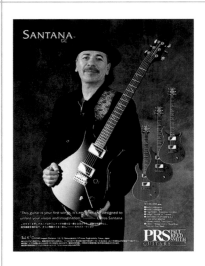

The SEs were PRS's first guitars made in Korea. Shown here are a 2002 Santana SE (near right) and a 2004 SE Billy Martin Model (far right). Billy Martin of Good Charlotte is pictured with his PRS in this 2004 ad (above), and Carlos Santana, who wanted a guitar a student could buy, in the 2001 ad (top).

Santana some replicas of his now well-used originals. PRS wanted to make its new Santana guitar a production model, and to use Santana's name. A deal was subsequently arranged, and a large percentage of Santana's royalties go to charity. Santana remains the only guitar player to have a "signature" PRS guitar.

The growth of PRS guitars is aptly reflected by its expanding workshop space. Compared to Smith's tiny West Street rooms in Annapolis, the first Virginia Avenue factory must have seemed massive to the handful of staff who manned it in early 1985. At first there were just eight people working there. PRS had one-third of the building to start with, sharing with a furniture-stripping shop, a brass business and a sail-maker, but after three or four years PRS had taken over most of the premises. As time progressed a separate woodshop was added, a short walk from the main facility.

This was all certainly a far cry from the beginnings of PRS Guitars. During the ten years preceding the move in 1985 to Virginia Avenue, it was taking Smith and his co-workers on average a little over a month to produce every guitar. By 1988, a crew of 45 people were making around 15 guitars every day, and by 1995 Virginia Avenue housed about 80 workers who were crafting between 25 and 30 guitars daily. The last PRS guitar was shipped from the Virginia Avenue plant at the end of December 1995. The company estimates that in its first ten years it produced around 23,000 set-neck guitars and about 14,000 bolt-on-neck models. PRS relocated to its brand new

manufacturing base at Stevensville, on Kent Island, just across the Chesapeake bridge from Annapolis, and production resumed in the first week of January 1996. With some 25,000 square feet now at the company's disposal – which was nearly double that of the Virginia Avenue facility and its outbuildings – PRS employed around 110 staff by the end of 1998 and aimed to produce around 700 guitars every month.

Having invested in computer-assisted routing machines in 1995, more were installed at the new factory to bring a higher level of consistency to guitars that were already renowned for their craftsmanship. Pushing production efficiency further forward, robotic buffing machines appeared soon after the factory move. But even with these new tools, PRS guitars still felt "hand-made," comfortable instruments rather than sterile, machine-made items. Even with the high-tech equipment, there is more hand-work in the sanding, coloring and finishing of a PRS guitar than most other production instruments.

The first new models to come off the line in 1996 were the Rosewood Ltd and the Swamp Ash Special. The former continued Smith's pursuit of the ultimate tonewood for necks, featuring a solid East Indian rosewood neck with Brazilian rosewood fingerboard, the latter inlaid with a fantastically detailed tree-of-life design.

Although mahogany is used for the majority of PRS's set-neck guitars, there's little doubt that Paul Reed Smith would choose rosewood if the cost was not prohibitive.

Smith's personal "number one" guitar – an amber-colored Dragon I – was the first PRS to feature a rosewood neck, and the option of an Indian rosewood neck was subsequently offered for the McCarty. During 1999, a limited run of McCartys with expensive Brazilian rosewood necks was made.

While the Rosewood Ltd was a limited edition of 100 pieces, it was dramatically different to the Swamp Ash Special, which was intended like the original Classic Electric and Studio to bring a more Fender-like tone to the PRS line. The 22-fret Swamp Ash Special, as its name implies, uses a lightweight ash body with bolt-on maple neck and fingerboard, and pairs two McCarty humbuckers with a centrally-placed single-coil-size humbucker.

Also launched by PRS during 1996 were two more luxurious Artist models, the III and IV. These were intended to replace the previous Artist II and Artist Limited.

PRS's custom shop, producing what the company calls Private Stock guitars, was established in 1996. It aimed to recreate the circumstances of Smith's old workshop: almost anything a customer wants, PRS will make as a Private Stock instrument – at a price. While some guitars are based on existing production techniques, others need to be built fully or partially from the ground up. PRS estimates the ratio of hand-work to machine-work on a Private Stock guitar is around 50/50 in the initial stages, but a double-neck, for example, would be all hand-made. For many customers the starting

Three more PRS guitars: a 2004 513 Rosewood (left), a redesign of the original Custom that included five pickups; a 2005 20th Anniversary Custom 24 (center), which marked a birthday for the PRS company; and a 2006 Private Stock 10th Anniversary Singlecut (far right), which marked a particular birthday for PRS's Private Stock scheme. This 2005 ad (right) shows Dave Navarro with his all-white Custom 24 signature model.

PRS

A page from PRS's luxurious 1998 catalog highlights the McCarty Soapbar model launched that year.

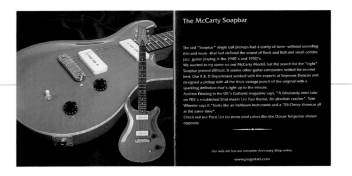

The McCarty Soapbar

The old "Soapbar" single coil pickups had a clarity of tone—without sounding thin and weak—that had defined the sound of Rock and Roll and small combo jazz guitar playing in the 1940's and 1950's.
We wanted to try some on our McCarty Model, but the search for the "right" Soapbar proved difficult. It seems other guitar companies settled for second best. Our R & D Department worked with the experts at Seymour Duncan and designed a pickup with all the thick vintage punch of the original with a sparkling definition that's right up to the minute.
Andrew Fleming in the UK's Guitarist magazine says, "A fabulously retro take on PRS's established Strat meets Les Paul theme. An absolute cracker". Tom Wheeler says it "looks like an heirloom instrument and a '55 Chevy showcar all at the same time".
Check out our Price List for more cool colors like the Ocean Turquoise shown opposite.

Our web site has our complete Accessory Shop online.
www.prsguitars.com

point for a Private Stock has tended to be a McCarty with custom bird inlays, Brazilian rosewood fingerboard and double-stained "killer" top.

The first Private Stock guitar was completed in April 1996. By the spring of 1999 some 87 pieces had been built, each carrying a sequential Private Stock number as well as a standard serial number. Around half have been high-end McCartys, but there have been Archtops, double-necks, 12-strings and others. As with the Guitars Of The Month that prompted the Private Stock scheme, new ideas and designs that come up can effectively provide prototypes for future PRS production models. A bass design was unveiled at a trade show during 1998, for example, and positive reaction led to a new PRS bass joining the line in 2000.

A Private Stock example of a hollowbody archtop PRS guitar was shown at another trade show, this time in 1997, and the following year PRS brought out a new line of hollowbody McCarty guitars, marking a company well into its stride.

The Archtop looked like any other PRS, save for the twin f-holes and substantially deeper body. A guitar like this would not have been commercially possible if it wasn't for PRS's use of computer-assisted machinery. This hollows out the central mahogany block, leaving thin sides, a pocket for the neck and, importantly, a block under the bridge. Not only was the front carved but the back too and, like a violin, the top and back were carved on the inside as well. Launched at the same time, the PRS

Hollowbody used the same construction as the Archtop, except that the body was less deep: about three inches at its center as opposed to four inches. The majority of production-built semi-solidbody or fully hollow guitars from other makers tend to use laminated maple tops, back and sides. PRS's use of solid timbers matches the kinds of specification usually limited to hand-carved (and more expensive) guitars.

The Archtop featured a new version of the PRS Stop-Tail tailpiece with adjustable saddles to cater for the larger string gauges used by the jazz players for whom the instrument was intended. Also, new pickups were developed for these instruments' more "classic" tones. The basic models came with spruce front and mahogany back and sides. The Archtop II and Hollowbody II added figured maple tops and backs, while the Archtop Artist was an ultimate high-end model – PRS called it "a piece of art that doubles as a musical instrument."

This hollow guitar line had been developed by Joe Knaggs, PRS's master luthier who builds the majority of the company's custom one-off Private Stock line. The Archtop in particular was intended to enable PRS to offer a more jazz-oriented instrument. However, it quickly appeared that the more Gibson ES-335-like Hollowbody was the most popular of the new line, and by late 1998 it accounted for nearly half of PRS's total production. All the Hollowbody and Archtop models are offered with an optional piezo-pickup bridge system, developed in conjunction with noted US acoustic

The SE line continued to flourish, and among the new signatures was this SE Paul Allender Model (2007 example, near right) for the Cradle Of Filth man, the first 24-fret SE. Shown next to that is a 2007 SE Custom Semi-Hollow (center), with its "slash" soundhole inspired by Rickenbacker. The 2011 Mira (far right), along with the accompanying Starla, was the latest of PRS's attempts to produce an affordable US-made guitar.

The shortlived Mira X (2009 ad, left) was intended to be an even more affordable take on the earlier Mira.

pickup manufacturer L.R. Baggs. The extremely efficient piezo system allows these guitars to sound like amplified acoustic instruments as well as offering all the usual magnetic pickup tones. By 2000 the Hollowbody craze had settled, while the Archtop had become a minor part of PRS sales.

The introduction of left-handed PRS models came in 1999 for the McCarty and Custom 22 (with Stop-Tail or vibrato bridge). Typically, these were carefully detailed models with every feature properly left-handed, from the positioning of the headstock logo right down to the labeling of the control knobs.

Some 25 years after Smith built his first proper electric – that single-cutaway flat-front Les Paul-alike – PRS launched the Singlecut, the closest the company had got to both the look and tone of those classic vintage Les Pauls. The company's first ads for the new-for-2000 model, which wasn't in the McCarty line, featured a profile picture of Ted McCarty and the caption, "Ted McCarty introduced the single cutaway, carved-top solidbody to the world in 1952. We learned a lot from Ted while we were working on ours." This illustrated where PRS was heading.

Over the years many companies have either blatantly copied the Les Paul or used it as clear inspiration. Yet the PRS Singlecut will be seen by many as the closest anyone has come to the hallowed tone of Gibson's late-1950s Les Paul without actually breaching any trademarked design features. Apart from the single-cutaway shape, the

PRS's piezo pickup system became standard on the Hollowbody II in 2011, and it's included on this 2012 example (main guitar, far left). PRS celebrated its 25th birthday with many special models, including this 2010 25th Anniversary 305 (left), about as close as PRS had come to a Fender vibe. The limited-edition Bigsby-equipped SCJ (2008 ad, above) was a shortlived addition to the hollowbody lines.

*The Signature Limited (2012
example, main guitar, left) had new
pickups and was limited to 400
pieces. A new signature model
added to the line was the SE Bernie
Marsden (2012, center), and this S2
Custom 24 (2013, far right) was part
of PRS's S2 line, a further attempt at
affordable US-made guitars.*

guitar followed the specification of PRS's McCarty model with, typically, many subtle changes. These included a slightly thicker body and new covered pickups simply called PRS 7s. Smith believed these were the closest yet to the tone of original Gibson PAFs, but with modern-day performance standards. On the Singlecut's launch early in 2000, initial sales were strong, and in a number of guises the design would remain in the PRS line for many years.

The Santana SE of 2001 was the first PRS guitar to be made overseas, in Korea. Rather than a copy of the Custom, the simple all-mahogany flat-top SE harked back to the second-series EG models. In 2003, the Tremonti SE appeared, based on the USA model but with a thinner all-mahogany body and a contoured rather than carved top. The following year saw the second Singlecut design, the SE Soapbar, like the Tremonti but without the bound fingerboard or body and with a pair of Korean-made soapbar single-coils.

A new double-cut guitar for 2004 was the 513 Rosewood, in effect a complete redesign of the PRS guitar. Fundamental changes included the scale length, increased a quarter of an inch from 25 inches, a stronger neck-to-body joint, a model-specific neck profile, and most obviously new pickup-switching. It had five single-coil pickups, the outer four grouped in humbucking pairs, and two blade-style pickup selector switches. One of the blades was a five-way type that selected pickups in Strat-like

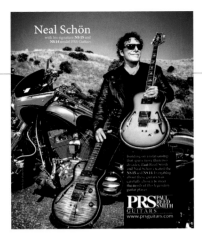

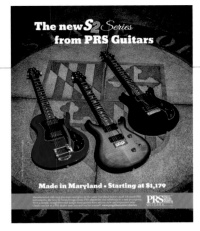

Ads here are for Neal Schon, pictured with his NS-14 and NS-15 signature models (2013, far left), and the S2 affordable made-in-USA guitars (2013, near left).

selections, while the other was a three-way blade that selected both coils; both coils with tapped output; or single-coil.

In September 2005, PRS announced that in a long-running trademark dispute between PRS Guitars and Gibson Guitar Corp over the Singlecut design, the US Court of Appeals had reversed a lower court decision and ordered the dismissal of Gibson's suit against PRS. A further legal twist resulted in a further announcement in June 2006, stating that the US Supreme Court had denied Gibson's final appeal. PRS said in conclusion that the Supreme Court's decision left the Sixth Court opinion in place and that this therefore put an end to the dispute.

The new-for-2007 Mira was the most affordable USA-made PRS so far, with a purposeful retro vibe, and at the time it bridged the gap in style and price between the SE line and the full-blown maple-topped classic models.

In 2009 the single-cut Starla was added to the Mira, plus the shortlived Mira X, the most affordable USA model so far. A further SE signature model appeared in 2007, the maple-topped SE Paul Allender model, designed with the Cradle Of Filth guitarist. It

was the first of PRS's SE models to feature a 24-fret neck and a wide-thin type neck-carve on a glued-in maple neck.

The signature David Grissom Trem (DGT) of 2008 was based on a McCarty. Grissom, a Texan musician best known as guitarist and band-leader of Dixie Chicks, was a prime mover in the development of the original PRS McCarty, which had first appeared back in 1994. It was clear, therefore, that he was well-placed to help create an "improved" model. New pickups were built from the ground up, and Grissom spent over a year using a special test guitar to try out prototype units. More visibly, the DGT was the only PRS guitar with two volume controls and one master tone (with a push/pull for the coil-splits). A further Grissom model appeared in 2012, the similar, limited all-mahogany DGT Standard.

PRS launched its new Sunburst Series in 2009, which consisted of the Sunburst 22, the Sunburst 245 and the Smokeburst McCarty. Their nitrocellulose gloss finishes were a first for PRS on a non-limited guitar. Further vintage elements came with the pickups, which were 57/08 humbuckers, and the Smokeburst finish of the McCarty, which gave it an aged look on the edge.

The new Narrowfield 25th anniversary models of 2010 – McCarty Narrowfield, Modern Eagle III Narrowfield and Swamp Ash Narrowfield – referred to a new Narrowfield (NF) humbucker, the third in the 57/08 series of pickups. It was a narrower

Three more PRS guitars: a 2013 Brent Mason Signature (near right), a signature model for Tele fan Mason; an Experience PRS 2013 408 Semi-Hollow (center), available at PRS's open-house event that year; and a 2013 Paul's Guitar, based on a 408 Maple Top and intended to be as close as a production PRS could get to the Private Stock guitar that Smith himself played.

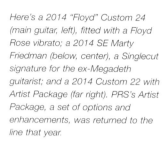

Here's a 2014 "Floyd" Custom 24 (main guitar, left), fitted with a Floyd Rose vibrato; a 2014 SE Marty Friedman (below, center), a Singlecut signature for the ex-Megadeth guitarist; and a 2014 Custom 22 with Artist Package (far right). PRS's Artist Package, a set of options and enhancements, was returned to the line that year.

and taller humbucker, and therefore it saw less of the string, coming on as more of a single-coil in tonality but without the associated hum.

The 305, introduced in 2010, seemed like PRS trying to nail a more accurate Strat-like single-coil sound. On paper, the guitar looked like a simplified version of the 513, but that instrument's five single-coils were trimmed to three, and there was just the one five-way blade pickup switch. The scale length was increased, too. With its slightly thicker alder body with maple neck, the 305 was already more Fender-like, a vibe increased by the steel blocked vibrato, unique to this shortlived PRS model.

The same year saw the introduction of the very expensive 50-only Private Stock Violin (McCarty) Guitar, the latest of Smith's visions of how good a solidbody electric guitar could be. There were a pair of new three-pickup solidbodys in 2011, the Strat-flavored DC3 and the Narrowfield-equipped NF3, each featuring PRS's new ultra-thin V12 finish and a vibrato with steel components.

The SE line had some newcomers, too, including the straightforward short-scale single-cut SE 245, as well as signature models for Mikael Åkerfeldt (Opeth), Nick Catnese (Black Label Society), Tim Mahoney (311), and Zach Myers (Shinedown), plus a new Santana model with the original body style.

The new-for-2012 P22 and P24 were the first PRS solidbody models fitted with piezo electronics, the system designed to produce acoustic-like sounds when

amplified. PRS's take on the system dated back over a decade, and it had been an option or a standard feature on PRS's double- and single-cut Hollowbody guitars since the early 2000s. The smaller size of its new piezo system allowed PRS to fit it into a slightly extended cavity in a regular solidbody.

In summer 2013 PRS announced a new line, called the S2. The instruments were made on a new second production line in Maryland, but the list prices of the new guitars were around a third of the regular US-made instruments. The Korean-made SE guitars had been a success and for many years outsold the US-made guitars in terms of numbers. But there was still a large gap in price, quality and feel between the US instruments and the Korean SEs. The Mira and the Starla had hinted at something of a more retro, simplistic style, but even the newer bolt-on guitars such as the DC3 and NF3, introduced in 2011, seemed to be simply too high-priced to sell in anything other than relatively small numbers. The new S2 line at first consisted of three guitars: there were new versions of the Mira and Starla, and also a new streamlined version of PRS's venerable Custom design.

The 408s, launched in 2013, had an interesting pickup system. Following on from the 513 pickups and the Narrowfield mini-humbuckers, the 408 pickups – which used the same wire and magnet type as the 57/08 humbuckers – were designed in essence to extend and enhance the guitar's tonal spectrum. The 408's three-way blade switch selected either pickup, or both in combination, while the instrument's two low-profile mini-toggle switches voiced either the full humbucking modes or the "slug" single-coils. This particular combination of four coils and eight sounds was what provided the model with its 408 name.

The US-made PRS line in 2017 had the current incarnations of the classic Custom 22 and 24, McCarty, and Hollowbody II models, along with the new-for-2016 McCarty 594. There were 12-string and Piezo versions of the Hollowbody II, baritone versions of a few models, and the 408 and 509, with bolt-on models confined to the CE24. The S2 electric lines had developed since their introduction four years earlier and now consisted of a Custom 22 and 24, Standard 22 and 24, various Singlecuts, including a Semi-Hollow, and the Mira, Starla and Vela.

The imported SE line boasted a Custom 22 and 24, Standard 22, 24 and singlecut 245, plus the regular maple-top 245. Signature models (US-made or imported) included guitars named for David Grissom, Mark Holcomb, Zach Myers, Carlos Santana and Mark Tremonti. There was also the continuing high-end Private Stock, PRS's name for its custom shop. Meanwhile, as a summary of PRS's appeal, it's hard for once to beat a sentence from the company's own mission statement: "We are devoted to the guitar's rich heritage," PRS said, "while committed to new technologies that will enrich our products with uncompromised tone, playability and beauty."

Three more PRS models: a 2015 SE Zach Myers Signature (far left); a 2014 Violin II prototype (center); and a 2015 S2 Singlecut (near left). The 2015 Custom ad (above) showed that the company's original and still bestselling models and designs were continuing to thrive.

RICKENBACKER

The cover of this 1956 catalog (right) commemorates the 25th anniversary of Rickenbacker's first electric guitar, the prototype "Frying Pan" lap-steel.

R I C K E N B A C K E R

Rickenbacker is best known for some great designs devised in the 1950s, as well as its popularization of the electric 12-string guitar through prominent use by acts such as The Beatles and The Byrds during the 1960s.

Adolph Rickenbacker was born near Basel, Switzerland, in 1886, but while still young was brought to the United States. Around 1918 he moved to Los Angeles, California, and in the 1920s established a successful tool-and-die operation there, stamping out metal and plastic parts. One especially enthusiastic customer for these was the National guitar company of Los Angeles.

At National, George Beauchamp and Paul Barth put together a basic magnetic pickup for guitars. Their experiments culminated in a pickup with a pair of horseshoe-shape magnets enclosing the pickup coil and surrounding the strings. Beauchamp and Barth had a working version in mid 1931. Another National man, Harry Watson, built a one-piece maple lap-steel guitar on which the prototype pickup could be mounted. This was the famous wooden "Frying Pan" guitar, so-called because of its small round body and long neck. It was the first guitar to feature an electro-magnetic pickup, and in that sense the basis for virtually all modern electric guitars.

Beauchamp, Barth and Adolph Rickenbacker teamed up to put the ideas of this exciting prototype electric guitar into production. They formed the curiously named Ro-

The Combo 800 (1955 example, near right) was Rickenbacker's first relatively conventional-looking solidbody electric, launched in 1954. The Model 1000 (1957 example, main guitar) was the cheapest in a trio of short-scale "student" guitars of the time. The through-neck construction used by Rickenbacker on many of its models is clearly visible at the bottom of the body. This 1957 catalog (above right) features the Model 900, 950 and 1000 "three-quarter Spanish guitars."

ACCORDION and GUITAR
WORLD

JAZZ issue · APRIL, 1960

Jean "Toots" Thielemans (left), guitarist with the George Shearing Quintet, on a 1960 magazine cover. It was at this time that John Lennon saw Thielemans's Rickenbacker and became interested in owning one.

Pat-In company at the end of 1931 – just before Beauchamp and Barth were fired by National. In summer 1932 Ro-Pat-In started manufacturing cast aluminum production versions of the Frying Pan electric lap-steel guitar, complete with horseshoe electro-magnetic pickups. Ro-Pat-In's Frying Pans were effectively the first electric guitars with electro-magnetic pickups put into general production.

Early examples of the Frying Pan lap-steels tend to have the Electro brandname on the headstock, and so are usually referred to by players and collectors today as the Electro Hawaiian models. By 1934 "Rickenbacker" had been added to the headstock logo (sometimes the name is spelled "Rickenbacher"). Also that year the name of the manufacturing company was changed from the bizarre Ro-Pat-In to the more logical Electro String Instrument Corporation.

Around this time Electro also produced some Spanish wood-body archtop electrics. The Electro Spanish appeared around 1932 – among the earliest of its kind – and the Ken Roberts model, named for a session guitarist, followed about three years later. Bakelite was the first synthetic plastic, and Electro started using it in 1935 for its Model B Hawaiian lap-steel and the Electro Spanish (also called the Model B). The latter was arguably the first "solidbody" electric guitar.

During World War II Electro worked for the government, extending the Los Angeles factory in the process. After the war Adolph Rickenbacker decided not to continue

Three more early Rickenbackers are shown on this page: a "tulip" shape Combo 450 (far left) from 1957 with classic "cooker" knobs; a Combo 850 (center) made in 1957 with the new "crescent" shape cutaways; and a 460 (near left) from 1961, with the new five-knob control layout and "cresting wave" body shape.

Two early examples of the best-known of Rickenbacker's designs: a 360 (main guitar) made in 1959, and a 330 (far right) from 1958. The 1960s ad (below) promoted Rickenbacker's 21-fret neck with "easier, faster reach." The 1989 catalog (above) shows a 381.

many of his musical instruments, including most of the poorly-received Spanish electrics. During 1946 he turned 60, and began to think about selling the musical instrument part of his business.

The eventual buyer was Francis Cary Hall, who had moved with his family to California when he was around 11 years old. He'd opened a radio repair store, Hall's Radio Service, in the 1920s. This led logically to a wholesale company distributing electronic parts, the Radio & Television Equipment Co (Radio-Tel), which F.C. Hall set up in Santa Ana, Orange County, in 1936.

After distributing Fender guitars and amplifiers for a time, Hall began to reconsider his position. Given his experience, Hall could see the potential for an instrument business where he not only distributed the product but also manufactured it. So in late 1953 Hall bought the Electro String Music Corporation from Adolph, with its guitar factory still at South Western Avenue, Los Angeles.

Around the beginning of 1954 German-born guitar-maker Roger Rossmeisl, previously at Gibson, was hired by Electro to come up with new designs for Rickenbacker electric guitars. That same year Electro launched its first "modern" electrics, the double-cutaway carved-top Rickenbacker Combo 600 and Combo 800. They were aptly named, combining the horseshoe pickup and almost square neck of the earlier Hawaiian lap-steels with the up-and-coming solidbody electric Spanish

style. The first Combo models began to feature on the headstocks a brand new "underlined" Rickenbacker logo of the type still in use today.

Electro's next move was to abandon the clumsy horseshoe pickup and apply a more suitable pickup to its Spanish electrics. First to receive the new pickup was the Combo 400, launched in 1956. Another first was its through-neck construction, a feature that would become a familiar aspect of many of Rickenbacker's solidbody instruments.

New Combo 650 and Combo 850 models appeared in 1957, introducing a body shape with a "sweeping crescent"-shape across the two cutaways. In various incarnations and dimensions this has been in continual use by Rickenbacker to the present day.

In 1958 a series of new models was introduced that formed the basis for Rickenbacker's success during the 1960s and onwards. The thin-hollowbody designs were largely the responsibility of Rossmeisl.

For these new electric hollowbody Capri guitars he further developed an unusual "scooped-out" construction. Rather than make a hollow guitar in the traditional method he would start with a semi-solid block of wood – usually two halves of maple joined together – and cut it to a rough body shape, partially hollowing it out from the rear. A separate wooden back was added once all the electric fittings had been secured, and the neck was glued into place. The first new Rickenbacker Capri was the small-body

short-scale three-pickup 325 model, a guitar that would have a great effect on the company's success when it was taken up a few years later by John Lennon.

A full 12-model Capri line-up was launched during 1958, though the Capri name itself was soon dropped. There were four short-scale models: 310 (two pickups), 315 (plus vibrato), 320 (three pickups) and 325 (plus vibrato); four full-scale models: 330 (two pickups), 335 (plus vibrato), 340 (three pickups) and 345 (plus vibrato); and four "deluxe" full-scale models with triangle-shape fingerboard inlays: 360 (two pickups), 365 (plus vibrato), 370 (three pickups) and 375 (plus vibrato).

Two classic Rickenbacker design elements began to appear at this time. New "toaster-top" pickups were devised, nicknamed for their split chrome look, and unusual two-tier pickguards, made at first in an arresting gold-colored plastic. These comprised

A relatively conventional hollowbody, this 375F (far left, 1964) was top of the Thin Full-Body line, and a heavily-carved Thick-body 381V69 (near left) from 1990. Steppenwolf guitarist John Kay (above) with his 1988 signature model, the 381JK.

George Harrison received the 12-string Rickenbacker 360/12 pictured here (main guitar) in 1964 during The Beatles' first US tour. The chiming 12-string soon became an important part of the Beatle sound, notably marking the dramatic opening of the group's 'Hard Day's Night' single.

a base plate flush to the guitar's body carrying the controls, plus a second level raised on three short pillars, intended as a finger-rest. Another idiosyncratic touch was the shortlived "cooker" control knobs with distinctive diamond-shaped pointers on top.

In 1960 a new stereo feature called Rick-O-Sound was added to some guitars. The system simply separated the output from neck and bridge pickups so that a special split cord would feed the individual signals to two amplifiers (or two channels), made possible by a special double jack offering mono or stereo output from Rick-O-Sound-equipped Rickenbackers. In summer 1962 the factory moved from South Western Avenue, Los Angeles, to Kilson Drive, Santa Ana, not far from the Radio-Tel HQ. Soon afterwards Roger Rossmeisl left to work for Fender.

During 1963 the company started to develop an electric 12-string guitar. Acoustic 12-strings had been around for some time, and the folk craze in the early 1960s had given a boost to their appeal. Electric 12s were far less common. The first had been made around 1955 by the small Stratosphere company, while Danelectro's Bellzouki model had been launched in 1961. The glorious electric 12-string sound derived from octave and unison doubling of paired strings to produce a wonderful "jangling" sound, almost as if two guitars were playing together.

Dick Burke came up with a brilliant headstock modification for the new Rickenbacker 12 that kept the existing six tuners where they normally were – three on

John Lennon regularly played a Rickenbacker 325, as on the 1965 magazine (top) and ad (below). Rick's UK distributor Rose-Morris imported models with soundholes in an "f" shape, not the usual "slash" shape. These included the Lennon-associated 325, which they called a model 1996 (main guitar, left, made in 1964). This Lennon signature 325/12 (right) dates from 1985.

Rickenbackers became popular in Britain in the 1960s as a result of The Beatles' use of the instruments. Importer Rose-Morris gave its special f-hole guitars different numbers: for example, this 360/12 (near right) made in 1964 was known in the UK as a model 1993. Pete Townshend of The Who was an enthusiastic user (and abuser) of Rickenbackers. Pete's influence lives on. This 1998PT signature model (main guitar, far right) was made in 1988. Paul Weller's debt to 1960s music in general and Townshend's in particular was underlined by The Jam guitarist's prominent use of Rickenbacker guitars (above).

*One of the most influential
Rickenbacker players in the 1980s
and beyond was Peter Buck of REM,
seen on-stage here (left) with 12
strings at his disposal.*

each side – but added two parallel channels into the face, as if the slots of a classical guitar had been cut only half-way through. Burke attached the second set of six tuners at 90 degrees to the first set, the keys facing "backwards" – again, like a classical guitar, with strings attached into the tuners' spindles in the channels. The design overcame the problems that many makers of 12-string guitars have discovered, not least the unbalancing effect of a heavy long head with six tuners each side.

Rickenbacker made at least three experimental 12-string guitars in 1963. The first model went to showband singer, fiddle-player and guitarist Suzi Arden, whose Suzi Arden Show, a regular at the Golden Nugget in Las Vegas, was kitted out with Rickenbacker equipment.

Rickenbacker set up a special display at the Savoy Hilton hotel in New York City in February 1964 to show some equipment to The Beatles. The group's arrival in the US to play Ed Sullivan's TV show and three concerts had caused unrivaled scenes of fan

mania. Despite missing the display due to illness, George Harrison ended up with a great prize, one of the company's experimental 12-string electrics, in model 360 style.

John Lennon also came away with a new guitar, a black 325 model with new five-control layout, replacing the somewhat road-weary 325 that he'd used for most of the group's early career. The company also promised to send to Lennon a special one-off 12-string version of the 325, just as soon as they'd made it. And Beatles manager Brian Epstein requested a second 360-style 12-string for another of his now famous charges, Gerry Marsden of Gerry & The Pacemakers.

For the two *Ed Sullivan Show* appearances in New York Lennon used his old 325, but for a further appearance, broadcast from Miami, Lennon gave his new five-knob 325 its public debut. The Sullivan shows were outrageously popular, each receiving an unprecedented American TV audience of some 70 million viewers. No doubt Rickenbacker boss F.C. Hall allowed himself a smile as he watched the group perform in the New York TV studio.

After their thoroughly successful invasion of the United States, The Beatles returned to Britain, and Harrison used his 12-string to great effect on some new recordings, including the distinctive opening chord of the title song from *A Hard Day's Night*, ringing out in typically jangling fashion. A rush for Rickenbacker 12-strings followed. Rickenbackers proved popular with other British pop guitarists during the second half

*Rickenbacker's "deluxe" large-body
models were redesigned in 1964
with a more rounded body shape,
the lack of binding on the front
softening the outline still further. This
360 (near right) from 1975 shows the
new look. Roger McGuinn (right) of
The Byrds did much to promote the
jingle-jangle Rickenbacker 12-string
sound in the 1960s. The company
issued this signature 370/12RM
model (far right) in 1988.*

of the 1960s, including such influential guitarists as Denny Laine, Hilton Valentine and, with most notable effect, Pete Townshend.

During 1964 Rickenbacker officially added three 12-strings to its line, the 360/12 (two-pickup 360-style), 370/12 (three pickups) and 450/12 (two-pickup solidbody). The company also began at this time to supply export versions of certain models to distributor Rose-Morris in the UK, lasting until 1969. This would be unremarkable but for the fact that the British company requested instruments with real f-holes rather than Rickenbacker's customary "slash"-shape soundholes, and models with this feature have since become collectable.

From 1964 Rickenbacker introduced an alternative body style for the "deluxe" models (360, 360/12, 365, 370, 370/12 and 375) with a streamlined, less angular look to the front of the body, as well as binding on the soundhole and, now, only on the back edge of the body. Designed to be more comfortable for the player, the new streamlined design was the main production style used for the models mentioned from 1964. Old-style versions (body bound front and back, "sharp" edges) remained available on special order. A year earlier Rickenbacker had also introduced a striking new tailpiece, in the shape of a large "R."

The name of the sales/distribution company was changed in 1965 from the old Radio & Television Equipment Co to the more appropriate Rickenbacker Inc, and the sales office moved within Santa Ana in 1966. The name of the manufacturing company remained as Electro String.

A "light-show" guitar was introduced in 1970 with a clear plastic top through which a psychedelic array of colored lights would shine, flashing in response to the frequencies of the notes being played. Roger McGuinn had a special 12-string light-show Rickenbacker built with slanted frets and three pickups, which he used for 'Eight Miles High' at the end of Byrds shows in the early 1970s. It was perhaps the most bizarre Rickenbacker ever made – which makes it a rare beast indeed, given the number of odd and peculiar instruments that were made at and escaped from Rickenbacker's Santa Ana factory.

Around this time demand for Rickenbackers began to decline. Fortunately for Rickenbacker, its bass guitars gained in popularity in the early 1970s. Production began to pick up again at Santa Ana, concentrating on four-string models.

A new body shape appeared in 1973, although it was really only new to Rickenbacker's six-string guitar lines. The 480 used the body styling made famous by the company's electric bass guitars, which had first appeared in 1957, with a distinctive elongated upper horn.

A few custom double-neck guitars had been made for individual Rickenbacker customers in the 1960s, but in 1975 the company's first production double-necks

Three Rickenbackers are pictured on this page: an Astro kit guitar (near right) from 1964, sold as a self-assembly pack of parts; a 336/12 Convertible (center) made in 1967, with a Converter "comb" to switch between six-string and 12-string operation; and a 331 "light show" guitar (far right) from 1971, with sound-triggered lights visible through the transparent plastic top. Whatever it was that Rickenbacker's team was on at the time, modern guitar designers surely need a dose or two.

appeared. There were two types: the 4080 also used the electric bass body, while the 362 enlarged upon the familiar 360 style.

In 1983 Rickenbacker made a low-key attempt to recreate some of its older models, which the company noticed were increasingly popular among "vintage" collectors. A new generation of guitarists had also started to take up Rickenbackers, and this helped the company's climb back to popularity during the 1980s. Among the most notable and visible players of Rickenbackers at the time were Peter Buck and Johnny Marr. The jangling, rhythmic thrust of Rickenbackers was once more to be heard at the heart of some of pop's most vibrant offerings.

The business operation of Rickenbacker was changed in 1984 when F.C. Hall's son John, who'd worked at Rickenbacker since 1969, officially took control. He formed a new company, Rickenbacker International Corporation (RIC), which purchased the guitar-related parts of his father's Rickenbacker Inc and Electro String companies. In 1989 Rickenbacker moved its factory from Kilson Drive after some 27 years, consolidating factory and offices at the corner of South Main and Stevens in Santa Ana. A new idea during the late 1980s was the production of numbered limited-edition signature models. Rickenbacker's first eight artist guitars were made in editions of between 250 and 1,000: Pete Townshend (1987), Roger McGuinn (1988), John Kay (1988); Susanna Hoffs (1988), John Lennon (1989); Tom Petty (1991); and Glenn Frey

Another peculiarity from the Santa Ana workshops of Rickenbacker was this 360SF model (main guitar) from 1968, with slanted frets. The company's publicity insisted that the skewed frets matched "natural finger angle," but the rest of the world stayed resolutely parallel. The 481 (far right, from 1976) used the body shape best known on Rickenbacker's basses, with a distinctive elongated bass horn. Still at home in the 1990s, Rickenbacker continued to enchant pop players looking for a certain sound, such as Adam Devlin of The Bluetones (above).

RICKENBACKER

Two Rickenbacker catalogs are pictured here: one from 1981 (right) shows the three double-necks of the period, including six-and-12 and six-and-bass versions; the other (below) from 1990 details the V-series reissues of the 325 models.

Two more Rickenbacker guitars are pictured here: a 1987 360/12 (near right) in Tuxedo, a finish option of the time, and a 362/12 double-neck (far right) from 1975.

1992). Also, a proper Rickenbacker vintage reissue program was begun. The idea of an organized line of appropriate reissue models celebrating Rickenbacker's best-loved instruments had started in 1984 with three guitars. These were the 325V59 (renamed in this new scheme as the 325V59 Hamburg, derived from the period in which John Lennon used his original model 325 guitar), the 325V63 (renamed 325V63 Miami, because Lennon first tried out his new 325 in a Miami TV studio) and the 360/12V64. The V-type suffixes indicated the vintage of the original, so that V63 indicated 1963, V59 indicated 1959, and so on.

Meanwhile, in 1992 Rickenbacker devised a new 24-fret series, the 650 models, which shared the body style of the earlier 400 and 600 "cresting wave" models, but were redesigned with wider necks and high-output pickups in an effort to compete with more mainstream instruments of the day.

The unique sound of the electric 12-string guitar made Rickenbackers just as popular during the 1990s as they had been at any other time in pop history, and many bands continued to feature them in the recording studio as well as on stage. U2, for example, used one on 'Even Better Than The Real Thing', a single from the *Achtung Baby* album (1991) where Edge played his 330/12. Or there was The Mavericks using a 360/12 on 'What A Crying Shame' (their 1994 album's title track), and The Rembrandts chimed in with a 450/12 on 'I'll Be There For You' (a '95 hit single best known as the TV theme song for *Friends*).

Rickenbacker began talking to ex-Beach Boy Carl Wilson about a signature model in the late 1990s. The firm made a prototype, but it was nothing like the limited edition that eventually appeared in 2000. It was a black 260-shape solidbody six-string with humbuckers and vibrato and plenty of checkerboard binding. That was where everyone involved in the project was headed and it was expected that this was how the guitar would turn out. But when Wilson died in February 1998 at the age of just 52, the Rickenbacker Carl Wilson model came together through musician Billy Hinsche, whose sister was Carl's wife.

Hinsche ensured that Wilson's two sons, Jonah and Justyn, were consulted, and they wanted something different. The pair went back to a version of the guitar that Carl had used in the 60s, and the results that appeared in 2000 were the 360CW and the 360/12CW, based on 1965-era rounded-body models. Rickenbacker limited the production of the Wilson models to 500 each, and a portion of the proceeds went to the Carl Wilson Foundation, which helps to fund cancer research and assist those with the disease.

Despite competition from other electric 12-string makers, Rickenbacker has estimated in recent years that it still has something like a 98 percent share of the world market in this quite specific type of instrument. Meanwhile, Rickenbacker made a small change to the headstock of some its 12-string models during 2005. On the Rick non-replica and non-vintage models, the "slots" in the headstock were now cut all the way through, where before they were routed channels. This took out a little weight, which is usually a good thing tonally in the head of a guitar – and apparently it made the guitar easier to re-string.

Rickenbacker has introduced very few new models in recent years, and the reason most often provided by the company itself is that it has such a large backlog on its existing models that there would be no point in a business sense for it to introduce more. The 380L Laguna, launched in 1996, was a pretty pickguard-less 300-series guitar with oiled walnut body, gold hardware, and dot markers on a maple fingerboard, while the 1996 model was a reissue, available first in 2006 only, based on the old Rose-Morris-style 325.

There have been a few more renamings: the 660/12TP Tom Petty became simply the 660/12 in 1999, and a "new" matching six-string was derived from it at the same

Seen here are a 660/12TP Tom Petty signature model (far left) made in 1993; a 330W (center) with walnut body from 2015; and a 2009 six-string 330 (right) in Rickenbacker's classic fireglo finish.

Tom Petty has long been a user of Rickenbacker guitars, although as this 1982 album sleeve (above) shows, he has not been averse to other axes, including Fenders.

Two more Rickenbackers grace this page: a 2017 350V63 (main guitar, right) in the company's classic natural mapleglo finish, and a 2015 660 (far right) in black jetglo finish. The 2003 ad (above) appeared two years after the introduction of the C series of vintage re-creations, here featuring the 325C58.

time, the 660. The 650 series had some name changes and lost a few models. A striking pale blue finish harking back to some specials made back in the day for Jim Reeves's band provided the Blue Boy finish for a few models, at first only for non-US distributors in January 2002, and then later in the US as well. There was also a renaming of some of the vintage models, with a C series introduced in 2001 alongside the V models amid some name changes.

Beyond the rarely-changing model lineup, there is another unusual detail that marks the company out when compared to most other modern US guitar makers: Rickenbacker still makes all its instruments in the United States.

By 2017, alongside the specific reissues – 325C64, 350V63, 360/12C63, 381V69, 381/12V69, 1996 and 5002V58 – the Rickenbacker line offered instruments with strong roots in the best guitars of its past. There was also the 620 and 620/12 "cresting wave" models, several W for walnut versions of various models, and a sole surviving 650, the 650C or Colorado.

But the heart of the Rick line remained in its 300-series 12-strings: the 330/12 (mono, two pickups, dot fingerboard markers), the 360/12 (stereo, two pickups, triangle markers; "the world's most popular 12-string guitar" claimed Rickenbacker, without much fear of contradiction), and the 370/12 (stereo, three pickups, triangle markers), with a six-string to match the 330 and the 360.

RICK TURNER

Ex-guitar repairer and folk guitarist Rick Turner was one of three original 1970 shareholders in Alembic, the pioneering California guitar-maker, along with electronics expert Ron Wickersham and recording engineer Bob Matthews. While at Alembic, Turner moved from customizing instruments to full-scale production, making distinctive guitars (primarily electric basses) that developed the use of active electronics and exotic timbers. Turner was also involved with Geoff Gould of Modulus Graphite in the birth of the graphite neck.

Turner left Alembic in 1978 and soon formed his own operation, Turner Guitars, steering more toward guitars than basses. The new Turner 1C guitar had a small body with an almost violin-like outline and a rotating pickup to change tonal response, and is best known for its use by Lindsey Buckingham. Turner had designed it initially to use Alembic scrap parts, and also as a direct contrast to the generally unpopular Alembic through-neck six-string guitars.

After a break in production Turner returned in the 1990s and along with Turner-brand custom instruments now offers from Santa Cruz, California, a line of Renaissance-brand electric, electric-acoustic and bass designs. The retro Model T with its replica of the Rickenbacker-style horseshoe pickup of the 1930s remains a testament to this highly eclectic and respected luthier.

ROBIN

Robin is now a resolutely American brand, but its early guitars were manufactured for the company by Tokai in Japan.

First to appear in 1982 were some Stratocaster-shaped six-string models, many of which featured humbucking pickups, but all employed distinctive "reversed" headstock in the style of Gibson's Explorer guitar.

Next to be added to the Robin catalog were a number of less conventional designs including the Raider that had a "left-handed" look about it, despite being resolutely right-handed. The Ranger was styled somewhat like an early Fender Precision Bass, and this has proved to be one of Robin's most effective and enduring design ideas, with several subsequent variations. The Ranger has since attracted the attention of guitarists such as Jimmie Vaughan.

Later in the 1980s the Robin's Medley superstrat, manufactured in the United States, targeted the rock guitarist, as did the much more distinctive Machete. The Machete featured an offset body with a unique stepped construction and Robin's V-shape headstock with four tuners one side, two the other.

During the mid 1990s these continuing models were joined by the single-cutaway Avalon and Savoy series, adding Les Paul-like elements to a line which remained virtually unchanged until the company ceased trading in 2010.

This Rick Turner Model T (far left) was made in 1999, while the Robin Machete Custom (left) dates from 1989. Robin's 1985 ad (above) features an angular Wedge, a Freedom Bass, and a Raider, while the 1991 ad (right) pictures Tim Kelly of Slaughter brandishing a Robin Machete Deluxe.

A cheery if little-known Syd Delmonte plays a Roger archtop with floating pickup in this 1959 ad for the German maker's UK importer, Boosey & Hawkes.

R O G E R

This was the brand used by German luthier Wenzel Rossmeisl during the 1950s and 1960s. It was originally named for Wenzel's son, Roger, who would go on to do some significant work at Rickenbacker and at Fender.

Most Roger guitars were ornate, large-bodied acoustics available with add-on pickups and controls. They often featured deep "dished" shaping around the body edges, Wenzel's trademark that is now known as the "German carve." His son used it on his US designs, inspiring Semie Moseley of Mosrite.

The only "proper" Roger electric guitar was the model 54, which was a single-cutaway semi-solidbody dating from around 1960. It had a plain "slab" body, and its pickups and controls were mounted on a large floating assembly.

R O L A N D

Established in 1974, this Japanese company championed the guitar synthesizer, developing the combination of a specialized guitar (or "controller" in Roland-speak) and a standalone synthesizer unit that produced the sounds.

The first such duo debuted in 1977, consisting of the heavy GS-500 multi-control Les Paul-shape solidbody, and the large GR-500 synthesizer unit. Wired frets provided infinite sustain, and the sounds produced were wide-ranging and impressive. However, players seemed not to be keen on the fact that one had to use the guitar supplied by

Roland. Three years later a new two-piece outfit replaced the earlier combo. This time Roland offered guitars with simplified controls: there was a G-808 or G-303 original-design solidbody, teamed with the much more compact GR-300 floor unit. This was later joined by the Fender-like G-505 and G-202 six-strings plus an even more basic GR-100 floor box. Operation was easier, but inevitably the performance was less versatile, and many players still failed to take up Roland's guitars.

Guitarists still disliked the next guitar synthesizer from Roland, the futuristic G-707 guitar, launched in 1984 with "coat hanger" stabilizer, and the enormous GR-700 pedalboard. The hi-tech image seemed to alienate any remaining guitarists not already wary of guitar synths in general and Roland's in particular.

Roland switched shortly afterwards to providing a "hex" pickup that could be added to existing guitars and plugged into GR synth units. Roland teamed with Fender in the 1990s to create a Stratocaster with sound generation built in. The joint effort resulted briefly in the VG Strat (2007) and the similar VG Stratocaster G-5 (2012).

S A M I C K

The Korean piano manufacturer Samick began making acoustic guitars in 1965, and is today one of the world's largest guitar manufacturers, producing a dizzying array of models. Samick had an early boost when it began making the Hondo brand in 1969. Quality and quantity progressed throughout the 1970s, and since 1984 many of the

This Roger 54 (near right) was made in about 1960. The 1984 Roland G-707 guitar synthesizer "controller" (center) was the last in Roland's attempts to make guitar-plus-synth outfits. The 1993 ad featuring Eric Johnson displays Roland's solution for synth-inclined guitarists who didn't want to buy a new guitar: the GK-2 synth pickup fitted any guitar, driving the GR-1 synth unit. This Samick DCV9500 (far right) was produced in 1999.

world's most recognized guitar brands have turned to Samick for budget alternatives to their premium US-made guitars. Samick began to use its name as a guitar brand in the early 1990s, and in 1993 purchased the small Valley Arts guitar company of Los Angeles, California, effectively to serve as its custom shop. By 1998 Samick had an enormous line ranging from general "copies" to more original designs, such as set-neck offset-double-cutaway guitars. Samick lost Valley Arts to Gibson, but has acquired more brands, such as Greg Bennett, JTR (ex-Gibson man J.T. Riboloff), and Silvertone.

SCHECTER

Established in 1975, Schecter initially provided high-quality replacement parts. Later there followed complete guitars, although choice was limited to "improved" Fender-style instruments. Endorsers in the 1980s included Pete Townshend, but the brand suffered a bumpy economic ride in the US, and Japanese-made models kept it going. By the end of the decade US-built instruments were back, the California line partnering the existing offshore Schecter East series. Designs remained firmly Fender-inspired. These themes more or less remained through the early 1990s, but later there were some major changes. Schecter suddenly caught the retro bug with the Tempest and Hellcat (optionally available with ten strings), while the Avenger echoed the shape of Teisco's Spectrum 5. In 1999 the Korean-made Diamond series brought Schecter to a much wider audience, and was among the first to offer affordable seven-string guitars.

S.D. CURLEE

S.D. Curlee was the first US company to license its own designs, and thus make some money from others' copies. S.D. Curlee guitars had a unique neck-through-bridge construction, natural oil finishes, and used exotic woods such as walnut or purpleheart. Begun by Randy Curlee in Matteson, Illinois, in 1975, Curlee was originally conceived to offer interchangeable exotic-wood bodies. The licenses resulted in guitars branded Aspen and S.D. Curlee International (made in Japan by Matsumoku) as well as Global and Hondo (made in Korea). Production wound down by 1981, though a few "pointy"-style guitars were imported in 1982 before the brand ceased.

SHERGOLD

Jack Golder was responsible for a line of electrics that provided many 1970s British would-be stars with good quality instruments. Golder left Burns in 1965 after Baldwin's takeover and set up Shergold Woodcrafts in Essex with Norman Houlder. Shergold guitars appeared, but Golder mostly did timber work for British brands like Burns UK and Hayman. Hayman closed in 1975 and Golder revived Shergold for reworked Haymans, including the Meteor and Modulator, plus new models like the Masquerader. Golder stopped production in 1983, continuing custom work. He resumed commercial work in 1991 with limited-edition Masqueraders, but died the following April. Barnes & Mullins bought Shergold in 2015 and relaunched it under Patrick Eggle's guidance.

The three guitars illustrated on this page are: a retro Schecter Hellcat-10 ten-string (far left) from 1998; an Aspen AE-700 (center) made in 1976 in Japan under license from the US-based S.D. Curlee company; and a Shergold Custom Masquerader (near left) that dates from 1980.

SILVERTONE

It's likely that more American musicians began their interest in guitar-playing on a Silvertone – as sold by Chicago's Sears, Roebuck & Co – than on any other beginner guitar. Supplanting the Supertone brand when Sears divested itself of the Harmony guitar company in 1940, Silvertone was a former brand for radios, record-players and records. It was first applied to guitars in 1941. A Silvertone version of the Kay Thin Twin and Sears' first Les-Paul-style Harmony solidbody appeared in 1954. That same year the first of several Danelectro-made Silvertone solidbodies appeared, followed by masonite-and-vinyl hollowbodies in 1956 (see Danelectro).

The single-pickup amp-in-case guitars debuted in 1962 (see Danelectro). The Silvertone brand appeared throughout the 1960s on solidbodies that were made by Kay (such as the Vanguard) and Harmony (the Silhouette). By 1965 Sears was offering numerous Japanese Teisco-made Silvertones, sold through the company's stores rather than its catalog. The first Japanese Silvertones appeared in the catalog in 1969, made by Kawai. By the early 1970s the Silvertone name was dropped from guitars, but it was revived in recent years by Samick for a series of reissues.

SPECTOR

Stuart Spector started his instrument company during 1976, and this American builder's basses were the first to feature the bulbous-horned body styling designed by Ned Steinberger (and subsequently borrowed by many competitors). The early Spector six-string guitars were similarly shaped, including characteristic concave-back/convex-front carving and through-neck construction.

In 1986 the Spector name was sold to Kramer. The US-made NS-6 was the only Spector six-string produced under the new ownership, partnered by Korean-made equivalents that were better than most from this source at the time.

Kramer folded in 1990, but Stuart Spector didn't regain the rights to his name for another seven years, in the interim trading as SSD (Stuart Spector Design). This period produced the bolt-on-neck Blackhawk model, which at first was manufactured in the US and was later also available as the cheaper Czech-made CR model. This proved to be Spector's final six-string model, disappearing in 1998 when the company decided to concentrate on its more successful bass guitars.

SQUIER

Beginning in the early 1980s, Japanese-made Fender instruments exported into Europe (and later elsewhere) bore the Squier brandname. The name was borrowed from a string-making company, V.C. Squier of Michigan, that Fender had acquired in

This Silvertone guitar (near right) was part of an amp-in-case set (see top of page) made by Danelectro, this one from about 1964. The Silvertone 1437 (center) was made for Sears by Teisco in Japan, and is similar to a Teisco WG-4L. It was made around 1965. This Ned Steinberger-designed Spector NS-6A (far right) was made in Korea during 1989.

In this 1983 ad (left) Fender introduced to the US market its new Squier-brand guitars – effectively authorized copies of the Fender Strat, Tele and Precision. At the time, these new Squiers were made in Japan, but since then the brand has been produced by a number of international manufacturers.

the mid 1960s. Victor Carroll Squier had been born in 19th-century Boston, the son of an English immigrant, and became a violin-maker, moving to Battle Creek, Michigan, where he founded his string-making firm in 1890.

Fender's policy was that the new 1980s Squier guitar brandname should cater for lower price points. That way, the company reasoned, it would be able to maintain its ever-expanding market coverage but, crucially, without unnecessarily cheapening the valuable Fender brandname itself. The new Squier logo – alongside a small but all-important line that read "by Fender" – appeared on an increasing number of models as the 1980s progressed.

Fender had established its Fender Japan operation with two Japanese partners – distributors Kanda Shokai and Yamano Music – during March 1982. Fender Japan at first used as its manufacturer the Fujigen factory, based in Matsumoto, some 130 miles north-west of Tokyo. Fujigen produced Fender-brand instruments for the Japanese market, plus Fender- and Squier-brand instruments for general export. Fujigen also made Fender's Japanese Vintage series instruments during the early 1980s as well as the Squier-brand versions that were initially sold only in Europe.

However, escalating production costs meant a move to cheaper manufacturing sources for Squier-brand guitars. Korea came on line in 1985, and India made a brief contribution in the late 1980s for some early "Squier II" instruments (or Sunn

equivalents – another borrowed brandname, this time from an amplifier company that had been purchased by Fender).

Fender's factory in Ensenada, Mexico – established in 1987 – also came into the picture when it produced some Squier guitars during the early 1990s. More recently a number of guitar-making factories in China and Indonesia have become new sources for the manufacture of Squier instruments, providing low-end electric guitars that have the desirable prestige of a legitimate Fender connection.

A return to Japanese production yielded impressive results with Squier's shortlived late-1990s Vista series. Courtney Love came up with a Rickenbacker-influenced design to inspire Squier's Venus model, while the Jagmaster was prompted by Gavin Rossdale's humbucker-modified Jazzmaster. Last in the Vista series was the Super-Sonic model which apparently was inspired by a 1960s photograph of Jimi Hendrix unusually playing an upside-down Fender Jaguar. The late-1990s midrange Pro Tone line offered evidence of improving Korean quality.

More recent hits include the '51 model (2004), which became a fave budget testbed for mods, the oldie-flavor Vintage Modified (2007) and Classic Vibe (2008) series, and a number of signature models. The continuing success of Squier makes it a significant support brand for Fender, and it continues often to bear qualities well beyond its apparent status as a secondary line.

Three Squier guitars are pictured on this page: a Standard Stratocaster (far left) made in Indonesia in 1999; a Stagemaster (center) made in Korea in 1999; and a Vista Series Venus (near left) made in Japan in 1997. A craze grew for modifying and adapting the popular budget Squier '51 (packing box, above), a model first launched in 2004.

STANDEL

This 1992 ad from Starfield (right) features what looks suspiciously like a dog playing a Starfield Cabriolet SJ Limited model.

S T A N D E L

Best known for amplifiers in the 1960s, this California company started by Bob Crooks in the previous decade made some distinctive electric guitars. An early association with Semie Moseley resulted in rare Mosrite-influenced guitars, but the final Standels of the late 1960s were high-quality archtops and semis made by Harptone in New Jersey.

S T A R F I E L D

Ibanez's parent company Hoshino launched the Starfield brand in 1992. It was an attempt to combine character and convention, with Hoshino trying to achieve an elusive ideal: to be different but to stay commercial.

The retro-flavored selection included Altair and Cabriolet models, offered as part of the Japanese-made SJ series or as more expensive American Series alternatives, the latter ostensibly US-made, with better woods and higher-grade hardware.

Featuring a squat, rounded Stratocaster-derived outline, the Altair came in Classic, Trad and Custom variations, later joined by an SJ Classic-only 12-string. Cabriolets comprised the American Standard and Special versions, plus the SL Limited, and all employed an offset, mutated Telecaster-like shape.

None of these models enjoyed the success expected, and by 1994 Hoshino had introduced cheaper Korean-made Starfields in an attempt to rescue the line, but to no avail. Starfield sank soon afterwards.

S T E I N B E R G E R

Ned Steinberger proved that conventional materials are not essential to the production of a first-class instrument. Art-school graduate Steinberger moved to New York in the 1970s, and designed the NS bass for maker Stuart Spector in 1977. Steinberger produced his own bass, the L-2, in 1981. It combined plastic materials with a radical new "body-less" and headless design.

A six-string Steinberger guitar, the GL, followed in 1983. As with the bass, the usual headstock was discarded, and tuners were moved to the end of the minimal body. The one-piece hollow neck and body was made of a fiber and resin composite, sealed initially with a removable "lid" on top to which the equally innovative active EMG pickups were mounted.

For a short time in the hi-tech obsessed decade of the 1980s, the Steinberger design seemed to encapsulate the future of the electric instrument. But despite use by many top players, including Eddie Van Halen and Allan Holdsworth, it proved too uncompromising for mainstream acceptance.

Subsequently, wooden-body instruments appeared made both in the US and offshore, and in 1991 the conventionally-shaped Sceptre model appeared – with a headstock. It was the designer's last project for the now Gibson-owned Steinberger company. In retrospect it is more likely to be Steinberger's hardware – notably his

This Standel Custom Deluxe (far left) from 1966 has strong Mosrite flavors; the Starfield Altair SJ Custom (near left) was made in 1992; and this Steinberger GM4T (right) dates from 1989. Mike Rutherford of Genesis (above), who helped design the GM models, is here playing an earlier mini-body Steinberger.

Jimmy Bryant made some great "hot guitar" instrumental records with pedal steel man Speedy West in the 1950s, including this 'Midnight Ramble.' The terminology of the time on the record label calls Bryant's solo a "guitar take-off."

This rare Stratosphere Twin (main guitar) was made around 1955, the first production double-neck electric guitar. Stratosphere's 12-string electrics – made in single-neck as well as double-neck form – were another first from the innovative if shortlived company.

West-coast sessionman Jimmy Bryant (below right) plays a Stratosphere Twin in the mid 1950s at the Capitol Tower studio in Hollywood. Bryant even recorded a tune called 'Stratosphere Boogie' in honor of his unwieldy new friend.

unique Transtrem vibrato, the body-end tuning system, and the gear-less tuners – that are his lasting legacy to the modern guitar world. Although the 1990s saw some new popularity fueled by 1980s revivalists such as Warren Cuccurullo, at present Steinberger guitars do not appear to be in production.

STRATOSPHERE

This shortlived brand appeared around 1954 on the first production double-neck electric "Spanish" guitar and the first electric 12-string guitar. Based in Springfield, Missouri, the small Stratosphere company was set up in the early 1950s by brothers Russ and Claude Deaver.

The double-neck Twin was the flagship model, though Stratosphere also offered a single-neck guitar in six-string and 12-string versions. As the first to market an electric 12-string (single- or double-neck) they had to invent a tuning for it. A pedal-steel-playing friend of Russ's inspired Stratosphere's suggested 12-string tuning, with the string-pairs tuned to major and minor thirds. This made chordal playing a nightmare, but harmony lead lines were instantly available.

California guitarist Jimmy Bryant was assured enough to overcome such musical obstacles, employing his Twin to good effect on sessions and solo records, including his own 'Stratosphere Boogie' 45. Later, with Stratosphere long gone, Rickenbacker defined the now accepted 12-string tuning that mixes octaves and unisons.

SUPRO

As guitar manufacturers took their first tentative steps toward the production of electric guitars in the 1930s, Supro emerged as the primarily electric budget-price line of the Los Angeles-based National-Dobro company. National-Dobro was the recombined National and Dobro companies.

The Supro brand first appeared on a cast aluminum "frying pan" Hawaiian lap-steel, a Spanish electric archtop and a number of other instruments during 1935. It would also be the principal brandname that was used by the National-Dobro operation for its amplifiers throughout the 1960s.

Following a relocation of the parent company in 1936 to Chicago, the Supro name was used on some of the earliest lap-steel guitars to feature an amp-in-case design, such as the battery-powered Portable 70. This was an idea that would resurface, if briefly, in 1955.

Supro went on to appear on a variety of lap-steel instruments through the 1960s, and was occasionally used on resonator guitars. The Supro Capitan electric archtop and Rio electric flat-top debuted in 1941, with more electric archtops such as the El Capitan and Ranchero resuming production after World War II.

In 1942 Victor Smith, Al Frost and Louis Dopyera bought National-Dobro and changed its name to the Valco Manufacturing Company. Supro's first solidbody

Two Supro guitars are pictured on this page: a wood-body Dual Tone (far left) from 1958; and a 1960 Belmont (main guitar), the wooden body of which has been "shrink-wrapped" in red pearloid plastic. Supro was one of several guitar brands by Valco; the other main one was National. This Supro catalog cover (above) dates from 1959.

electrics debuted in 1952, the Spanish-shaped Ozark and single-cutaway Ozark Cut-Away Jet, both with small slab bodies, floating pickups attached to a large housing containing the wiring harness, and a characteristic bolt-on neck that sat very high on the body at the joint. The single-cutaway Supro Dual-Tone solidbody debuted in 1954, receiving top-mounted pickups the following year. Supro's first cutaway electric archtop also appeared in 1955. In 1957 one of the brand's most distinctive features appeared, the under-bridge Bridge-Tone transducer pickup, usually used in conjunction with magnetic pickups.

In 1962 the company modified its name to Valco Guitars Inc, and the guitar line changed from wood construction to fiberglass bodies in various colors with plastic-faced "Gumby" headstocks. (See also National.) Robert Engelhardt bought Valco in 1964, changed to a more Fender-style wood-bodied guitar design in 1965, and offered Supro's first double-cutaway thinlines in 1966.

The following year, with the guitar boom at full volume, Valco bought its competitor, the Kay Musical Instrument Company... and went bankrupt in 1968. At the end, the Supro logo was applied to a variety of Kay-made acoustic instruments. The Supro name was purchased at auction in 1969, but went unused until it reappeared briefly during the early 1980s on guitars assembled from old parts, and more recently it turned up on some revived designs.

TEISCO

The leading producer of 1960s Japanese-made beginner guitars, Teisco was unusual in using mainly its own brandname.

Atswo Kaneko and Doryu Matsuda had introduced Teisco lap-steel instruments in 1946, followed by Gibson-style guitars. By 1960 Jack Westheimer began importing Fender-like Teisco models to the United States.

The Teisco Del Rey brand debuted in 1964, including the TRG-1 model that featured an amplifier and small loudspeaker built into the guitar.

In 1965 Sid Weiss's WMI company of Illinois also brought Teisco Del Reys into America, including 1966's flared-cutaway pushbutton Spectrum 5 model – now a desirable, collectable guitar. Teisco developed financial problems, and was purchased by Kawai in Japan in 1967. New Kawai-made models for 1968 included the odd-shape May Queen. In 1969 WMI bought Kay, and by 1972 were using that brand rather than Teisco. Kawai briefly revived the Teisco brand in the early 1990s.

This fiberglass-body Supro Sahara (far left) dates from around 1964; the vinyl-faced Teisco SD-4L (center) was made in about 1963; and this Teisco Del Rey May Queen (near left) is from around 1968. The Teisco Del Rey catalog (at the top of this page) was published in the US in 1966.

TEUFFEL

Teuffel's catalog from 1998 (right) lays out the unique charms of the minimalist Birdfish model.

T E U F F E L

This high-end German maker has a unique, modern approach to design. Teuffel's Birdfish appeared in 1995 and looks like a well-engineered sculpture, with a minimalist metal frame body, removable pickups and add-on resonator tubes.

The recent Coco model is almost conventional in comparison – but only by founder Ulrich Teuffel's remarkable standards.

T O K A I

In the 1980s Tokai's blatant replicas of classic American guitars highlighted the threat posed to US makers by primarily Japanese-made "copy" guitars.

Tokai was based in Hamamatsu, Japan, and produced its first electric guitars in 1967, the Humming Bird models. Styling varied, but the "reverse-body" models were heavily influenced by Mosrite, although they had their own style of savagely pointed horns. Tokai's quality at this time was adequate – better than some of the Japanese competition, but not so good as makers like Yamaha.

As with many Japanese manufacturers, Tokai's standards improved considerably during the 1970s, and the large Hamamatsu factory became responsible for a great deal of sub-contract work for other Japanese guitar brands.

Tokai did not yet export its own-brand guitars, but this changed dramatically in the 1980s. The Tokai lines included over 100 models by that time, many of which were

This bizarre metal-frame Birdfish model (near right) was produced by Teuffel in Germany in 1999. The Mosrite-influenced Tokai Humming Bird (far right) was made in Japan in 1968. The 1983 Tokai ad (right) highlights the brand's notorious role in copying classic US models, here targeting Fender's Stratocaster.

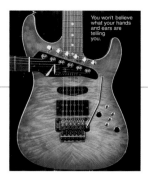

This first-year 1984 ad (left) from Tom Anderson Guitarworks features a fine example of one of the maker's beautifully figured instruments.

reproductions of popular instruments from the best American brands. Copy guitars were a well-established and commercial force in the world guitar market, but Tokai significantly increased the accuracy and quality.

Tokais began to arrive in Europe around 1981 and in the US by 1983, and were an immediate success, assisted in America by the dollar's soaring value compared to the yen, making Japanese instruments good value. The success triggered a fight from Fender, the company targeted most directly by the copying. Fender's answer was to establish its Fender Japan operation, to produce "authorized copies." This proved to be a very successful move which naturally dented the sales of Tokai and other Japanese copyists – although Japanese-made guitars continued to be popular.

Tokai catered for the Japanese market with a variety of models that ranged from the Triangle-X and Zero Fighter "reverse-body" originals to the Fender-influenced Versatile Sound selection. In the US the first line from the new Robin brand took advantage of Tokai's continuing sub-contract work. Prior to a change brought by legal challenges, Tokai itself used a very Fender-style logo. Other Tokai clones included recreations of Gibson's Les Paul, ES-series semis, Flying V and Explorer, plus various limited-production variations incorporating deluxe options.

Some Tokai originals appeared too: the 1985 Talbo had a distinctively designed aluminum body (Tokai ALuminum BOdy) while the same year's MAT series (Most Advanced Technology) was seemingly Fender-style, but with necks and bodies made from various combinations of fiberglass and carbon graphite.

By the mid 1990s Tokai had stopped exporting, and at home in Japan was limited to various synthetic-body Talbo models. In 1999 a revised Talbo in a conventional material appeared, the Talbo Woody, plus more recently a Strat and Tele copy.

TOM ANDERSON GUITARWORKS

A small-scale operation making respected high-performance electrics, this company was started during 1984 by Tom Anderson, who had previously worked for Schecter.

Tom Anderson Guitarworks is currently based in Newbury Park, California, producing some 800 guitars a year. During the 1990s the brand became synonymous with high quality. The modernized Stratocaster-style outline often employs a maple "drop top" (a method of laminating a thin maple top over the body's Strat-like contouring). Fitted to this are Anderson's own pickups and highly versatile switching, and there is an option list wider than that of many custom shops.

Models include the Pro Am Classic, the Grand Am Lam, the Drop Top T, the Hollow Drop Top and the Cobra, all in a broadly Fender- or superstrat-style. Anderson was one of the first makers to embrace the Buzz Feiten tuning system, a standard fitting since 1996. Feiten's system is a brave attempt to "correct" the compromise of equal-tempered tuning.

Three guitars are shown on this page: a 1984 Tokai Talbo A80D (far left); a Tom Anderson Guitarworks Grand Am Lam T (center) made in 1989; and a second Anderson guitar, a Hollow Drop Top (near left), made ten years later.

TRAVIS BEAN

Although not the first to feature aluminum necks, Travis Bean's guitars caused quite a stir in 1974. Based in Sun Valley, California, Bean decided he could solve stability problems and enhance sustain with light metal necks. Bean hollowed out much of the inside of his aluminum-alloy through-neck, which had a T-frame headstock and the pickups and bridge attached, the whole completed with a wooden body.

The first and most famous Travis Bean model was the equal-double-cutaway, two-humbucker TB1000, initially offered as the slab-bodied Standard but soon joined by the carved-top, block-inlaid Artist. The triangular-shaped Wedge looked and felt clumsy, but the "budget" TB500 was better. With offset cutaways and pickguard-mounted controls, this slim-bodied solid offered Fender-like flavors, as did Bean's powerful single-coil pickups.

Jerry Garcia was a famous endorser, but many players didn't like the cold feel of aluminum. Business pressures made Bean himself shut up shop in 1979. Guitarists such as Stanley Jordan and Slash have since helped raise the brand's profile, and in 1998 Travis Bean returned to the fray with a remake of the TB1000. He died in 2011.

TRUSSART

James Trussart works with steel as his primary material to make guitars that are strikingly different in appearance and tone. Born in France, he moved to the US and,

This Travis Bean TB1000 (near right) and the ad (top of page) for Bean's aluminum neck both date from 1977. The James Trussart Steelcaster Rust-O-Matic (main guitar) dates from 2016. The two ads show a pinstripe Steelcaster (top, published in 2007) and Rob Ackroyd of Florence & The Machine (below, 2008) with his Steelmaster.

eventually, located his workshop in Los Angeles in 2000. He makes custom steel-bodied guitars, basses and violins in an array of finishes, recalling the chrome look of resonator guitars and rusty discarded machinery. Billy Gibbons came up with the name for his Rust-O-Matic technique, where Trussart leaves a guitar body out in the elements for several weeks, allowing it to corrode, then treats it to stop the corrosion, sands it to add distress, and finishes it with a clear satin coat. Many of his guitars feature patterns and designs engraved or imprinted into the metal bodies or on the pickguard or headstock, including skulls, roses, and tribal art, or textures of alligator skin or plant material. Standard pickups are made for Trussart by Arcane Inc. Owners of Trussart guitars include Bob Dylan, Keith Richards, Paul Simon, Eric Clapton, Joe Walsh, Jack White, Marc Ribot and Billy Corgan.

VACCARO

Vaccaro was originally intended to revive the late-1970s aluminum-necked Kramer guitars. It was started by former Kramer principal Henry Vaccaro in 1996, using the Kramer name with revamped designs by original luthier Phil Petillo. Investment glitches led to the sale of the Kramer name to Gibson in 1997. A new Vaccaro line in 1998 had a trimmed-down, completely wood-sheathed T-bar neck (and lighter "tuning-fork" head), vintage-style pickups and sparkle finish options. The first line included an SG-style Groove Jet, flared-cutaway X-Ray, Fender-ish Generator X, and Les-Paul-Junior-like Astrolite, followed in 1999 by the less expensive V-2 X-Ray and Generator X. Vaccaro guitars stopped production in 2002.

VALLEY ARTS

Valley Arts originated from a retail operation, expanding during the 1970s to build its own high-end Custom Pro instruments. These mainly followed familiar Fender designs but with variations determined by a comprehensive list of options.

Larry Carlton was an early endorser, and the liaison resulted in a 1990s signature model. Unusually for "Mr. 335" it was a small-bodied solid. It combined Telecaster-like and Stratocaster-like styling, but hardware was more Gibson-based. The Standard version came with a pickguard; the Custom had a carved top.

The Standard Pro series introduced in the late 1980s offered less expensive US instruments, while the same period saw the addition of Japanese-made models such as the M series. This lowered prices further, as has the involvement since 1993 of the major Korean manufacturer Samick.

More recent lines have included such models as the California Pro and the IML series, which were joined during 1996 by the Studio Pro series, along with signature models such as Ray Benson's oversized-Telecaster-style Texas T.

Samick acquired part of Valley Arts in 1992, and a few years later the name was bought by Gibson.

A 1999 aluminum-neck Vaccaro Stingray (left) and a Valley Arts Custom Pro (right) from 1993. The 1990 ad (above) features Valley Arts founder Mike McGuire with endorser Steve Lukather of Toto.

V E G A

Best known for banjos, Vega nonetheless made some electric guitars including in the 1950s a novel 12-pickup stereo instrument.

Vega's roots go back to the 1880s, but the company began officially in Boston in 1903 when two Swedish brothers, Julius and Carl Nelson, renamed their company Vega (for the brightest star in the constellation of Lyra, hence the star-shape logo often used on Vegas). At first they concentrated on banjo production, and designed an unusual amplified banjo in the late 1920s.

Vega made small Martin-style "parlor" acoustics, and from the 1930s offered conventional archtop guitars, including some electrics. The Duo-Tron of 1949 had the controls and jack built into the tailpiece.

Much more unusual was the shortlived 1200 Stereo model of 1959, which followed Gretsch and Gibson's "stereo guitar" idea. Vega's instrument fed the bass notes from six individual circular pickups to one amplifier, and six treble-string pickups to another, adding electronic vibrato for good effect.

However, Vega had already begun to run out of steam, and the 1960s were a lean period. By 1970 Vega had been sold to Martin, who acquired the company for its banjo business. Around 1980 Martin sold Vega to a Korean firm, and more recently the name has been used by the Deering company for a line of banjos.

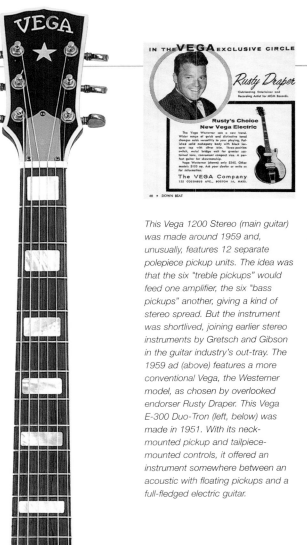

This Vega 1200 Stereo (main guitar) was made around 1959 and, unusually, features 12 separate polepiece pickup units. The idea was that the six "treble pickups" would feed one amplifier, the six "bass pickups" another, giving a kind of stereo spread. But the instrument was shortlived, joining earlier stereo instruments by Gretsch and Gibson in the guitar industry's out-tray. The 1959 ad (above) features a more conventional Vega, the Westerner model, as chosen by overlooked endorser Rusty Draper. This Vega E-300 Duo-Tron (left, below) was made in 1951. With its neck-mounted pickup and tailpiece-mounted controls, it offered an instrument somewhere between an acoustic with floating pickups and a full-fledged electric guitar.

VEILLETTE-CITRON

Joe Veillette started making acoustics in the early 1970s, soon setting up Veillette-Citron in Brooklyn which he ran with partner Harvey Citron from 1975 to 1983. Their high-end guitars were of the time, employing "organic" Alembic influences such as multi-laminated through-neck construction, exotic woods and brass hardware. The line was later rationalized to the less elaborate Standard, Classic and Limited Edition. It was at this time that Veillette's fascination began with low-tuned "baritone" guitars, using long non-standard scale-lengths. The Shark was a baritone designed in collaboration with John Sebastian, based on a Guild Thunderbird. It was later joined by a matching S series guitar. Veillette and Citron parted company not long after and each now offers an established catalog. Veillette-brand electrics and baritones began in 1993 with a revised Shark, and now emanate from Woodstock, New York.

VELENO

The shiny chrome plating on these carved-aluminum hollowbody guitars was well suited to the glam tastes of early 1970s rockers – which is why they were owned by Gregg Allman, Martin Barre, Marc Bolan, Eric Clapton, Mark Farner, Ace Frehley, Pete Haycock, Alvin Lee, Jeff Lynne, Ronnie Montrose, Dave Peverett and Lou Reed. John Veleno was a St. Petersburg, Florida, engineer and guitar teacher who began hand-making his unusual aluminum guitars around 1970, personally marketing them to

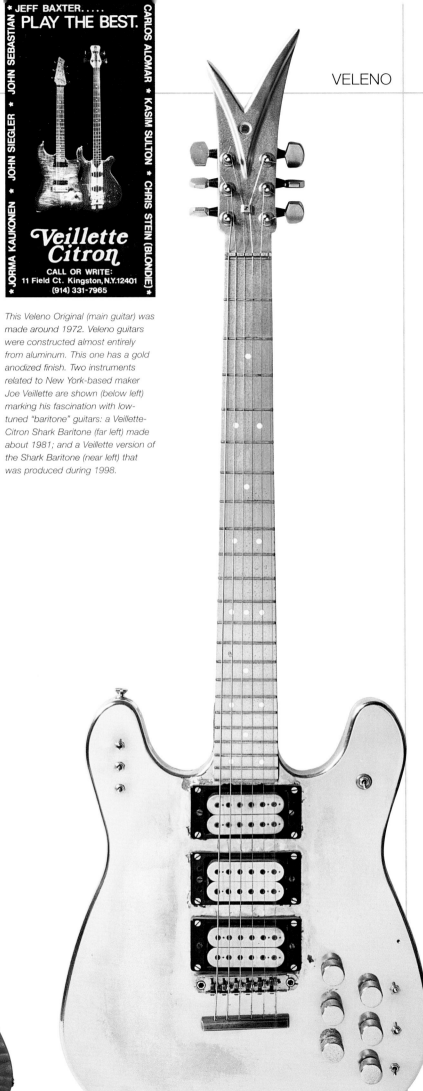

This Veleno Original (main guitar) was made around 1972. Veleno guitars were constructed almost entirely from aluminum. This one has a gold anodized finish. Two instruments related to New York-based maker Joe Veillette are shown (below left) marking his fascination with low-tuned "baritone" guitars: a Veillette-Citron Shark Baritone (far left) made about 1981; and a Veillette version of the Shark Baritone (near left) that was produced during 1998.

299

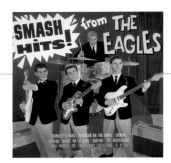

touring guitarists who passed through Florida. By 1971 Veleno's early six-tuners-in-line headstock changed to the more common three-and-three V-shape with ruby insert, for the model known as the Original.

Available in chrome, gold and other anodized colors (some with a black anodized neck), Veleno Originals primarily featured two humbuckers (by Guild, Gibson or DiMarzio) with coil-taps and phase-switching. Only between 145 and 185 Veleno Originals were made, probably until early 1977.

Inspired by a post-concert conversation with B.B. King and working with Mark Farner, Veleno also developed a mini-guitar known as the Traveller (two were made by Veleno, around ten by his son). Veleno made one bass, and built two Egyptian "ankh"-shaped guitars for Todd Rundgren in 1977 before abandoning the guitar business to become a wedding photographer.

VIGIER

The characterful instruments of French maker Patrice Vigier first appeared in 1980 with the Arpege model, a challenging design that used unusual materials. It typifies the more distinctive end of Vigier production in that it had a radical shape, was produced using non-standard construction methods, and employed "delta metal" (a type of bell brass) for the fingerboard. Another early oddity from Vigier was the Nautilus memory guitar of 1982, a multi-control instrument that enabled the recall of various player-set

tonal and other control settings. From 1984 Vigier began to offer carbon-fiber necks. Their proprietary 10/90 neck system was made using 10 per cent graphite and 90 per cent maple. In the same way as some later makers, Vigier's intention was that this dual construction would offer a useful balance in the neck's strength and feel.

Vigier also offered a more derivative Fender-influenced line, the Excalibur series, which also featured 10/90 necks, and these helped Vigier turn its relatively wild early ideas into more marketable instruments. Vigier's Excalibur Surfreter of 1997 was an unusual "fretless" guitar, as used occasionally by Gary Moore. The company had offered a fretless Arpege since 1980. Vigier celebrated the year 2000 with a lush $30,000 20th Anniversary guitar, produced in a very limited edition of two. By 2017 Vigier offered several Excalibur models.

VOX

Vox amplifiers were a great British 1960s success, but the company's stylish guitars made less impact. Vox products were originally made by Jennings in Dartford, Kent, set up by Tom Jennings in the 1950s. The factory was not equipped at first to make guitars, so most early Vox electrics – aimed at beginners on a budget – came from other UK or Italian sources.

In 1962 the first Vox original appeared from Dartford. The Phantom had an unusual body styled by Vox's own designers. Equipped with three single-coil pickups, a spear-

A Vigier Arpege V6-V (far left) from 1984, alongside two Vox guitars: an Apache (center) made around 1961; and a Mk VI (near left) that dates from about 1965. Brian Jones of The Rolling Stones (above) plays a non-standard two-pickup Mk VI.

Tony Hicks was guitarist in The Hollies and is pictured in 1965 (left) playing a Vox Phantom 12-string. He's more often seen in the 1960s with a Gibson ES-345 or a Les Paul Junior, as used on the group's 1967 album Evolution (right).

shape headstock and a "Hank B. Marvin" vibrato tailpiece, the Phantom was without curves, making it a guitar to be played only while standing.

The second Vox design landmark came with the teardrop-shape Mark series, launched in 1964: Mk VI six-string and Mk XII 12-string. Marks and Phantoms were offered from 1967 with optional active circuits, controlled by six pushbuttons on the body. Alongside these in the Vox catalog were several more low-end models, better Fender-derivatives like the Soundcaster, a line of Italian-made semi-solidbodies, and an assortment of Vox oddities such as the mini-12-string Mando-Guitar (1965) and the interesting if unreliable Guitar Organ (1966).

Vox transferred guitar production to Eko in Italy from 1966, including many models made specifically for the US market. Mounting problems led to the demise of Vox guitars in 1969. The brand was revived on a number of occasions, including three unexciting oriental Vox-brand lines in the 1980s.

Interest continued to grow in the classic Phantom and Mark originals of the 1960s, considered by many as stylish representatives of that decade, and there were several low-key reintroductions. Phantom Guitarworks in the US made a higher-profile effort, offering a number of remakes of classic Vox-style models. Then in 1998 the musical electronics company Korg launched an impressive new line of Vox reproductions, an effort that lasted to 2014.

A Vox Phantom XII Stereo (main guitar) made around 1965, with a bewildering array of controls designed to appeal to the keen 1960s soundscaper. Ian Curtis of Joy Division (above) on-stage in 1979 sings over a Vox Phantom Special made a little over ten years earlier.

The Vox Guitar Organ – this example (far right) made about 1966 – attempted to provide a guitar with the sound of a Vox Continental organ by wiring its frets to organ-tone generators. This proved unreliable, and the project was shortlived.

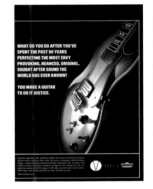

The Korg company ran a revived Vox operation from 1998 to 2014, and these two ads feature a Virage (top, 2008) and Series 33, 35 and 77 models (above, 2011).

301

Two Wandre guitars are shown here: the extraordinary Rock Oval (main guitar) was produced by the Italian maker beginning in 1958, and was used briefly if chaotically by guitarist Sal Dali in the art-rock band The Surrealists. This marginally more sedate Modele Karak (center) was produced around 1965.

Three Washburns are pictured here: a Stage A-20V (this page, far right) from 1981; a 36-fret George Washburn EC-36 (opposite page, left) made in 1988, with "monkey grip" body handle; and a Force G-40V (opposite page, right) with triple pickup, also from 1988.

W A N D R E

Among the most eccentric European guitars of any period in guitar history were those made by Antonio Wandre Pioli in Cavriago, near Reggio Emilia, Italy.

Pioli began producing primarily hollowbody electric (and some acoustic) guitars in the 1950s with a unique aluminum neck-through-tailpiece design, unusual laminated materials, wild multi-color paint jobs and often exotic shapes.

More conventional single-cutaway models included the Blue Jeans, Tri-Lam, and BB (for Brigitte Bardot), but the Bikini of 1961 was a very unusual minimalist guitar with attached amplifier and speaker (see Krundaal).

Around 1961 Wandre guitars were distributed in the UK by Vox parent company Jennings, including the blob-shaped Framez, the "deep cutaway" Rock Oval and the thin Electronica Oval-Basso.

Between 1963 and 1966 Wandre guitars were sold in the US by Chicago distributor Don E. Noble. The line featured a changed vibrato design, as well as a new solidbody, the Rock 6. In the mid 1960s some Wandres were made available in the UK with the Dallas brand, and later guitars were of more conventional design.

Around 1967 Pioli introduced the Psichedelic Sound, a take on Gibson's thinline style, as well as the Cobra variation on a Fender design and the bat-shaped Black Tulip. In 1970 Pioli sold his factory and turned to making art leather clothing.

Kiss's Ace Frehley snuggling up to his shortlived signature model in an ad (left) published in 1986.

WASHBURN

Washburn is a famous old American brandname that lives on thanks mainly to instruments of oriental origin.

George Washburn Lyon was an associate in Chicago's big Lyon & Healy company, founded in 1864. Guitar-maker Patrick J. Healy was one of the true founders of the acoustic guitar industry in the United States, but it was George Washburn Lyon's middle name that provided the brandname for the prodigious quantity of flat-top acoustic instruments produced by Lyon & Healy.

By the 1920s competition had grown and for many prominent makers in the musical instrument industry business was down. Lyon & Healy sold the Washburn name to distribution company Tonk Bros in 1928. After World War II, Tonk did not revive the Washburn name, which went unused until a small company called Beckmen used it in the early 1970s. Beckmen soon sold the name to a Chicago-based importer, Fretted Industries Inc.

Fretted Industries was owned by guitar-maker Rudy Schlacher and musician Rick Johnstone. Both were experienced in retailing and they soon realized that there was a good deal of commercial advantage to be gained from employing the Washburn brandname on a line of reasonably-priced instruments – and that Japan was the obvious source for production for the new instruments.

The new line included electric guitars, and they were the first of this type that had carried the Washburn brand. Launched in 1979, the Wing series employed high-waisted body styling with twin small-horned cutaways, through-neck construction, two humbuckers and a conventional circuit with four controls plus selector. First models were the Hawk and Falcon, soon joined by the cheaper bolt-on-neck Raven and the high-end Eagle.

The following year brought the Stage solidbodies which targeted the rock market in more overt fashion, shaped like a chopped-down Gibson Explorer and in various formats including a 12-string.

By 1983 Washburn's electric line had increased considerably. Fender-influenced Force solids partnered 335-style HB hollowbodies and the Flying V-based Tour models. Various Stages continued, while Wings had withered to the Hawk, Falcon and Eagle plus the new T Bird. The headless-neck fashion hit in 1984 and Washburn responded with Bantam mini-body guitars, including a double-neck. Washburn also followed the trend for locking vibrato systems.

As the 1980s progressed a distinctly metal theme began to dominate Washburn's lines of instruments. By 1986 the Wings had disappeared from the catalog but the Stages remained. The Force models became more superstrat than Strat-like, and the Tour V now had an offset body like a Jackson Randy Rhoads. The new Heavy Metal

Robbie Robertson of The Band (above) promotes Washburn's Chicago series in this 1989 ad.

models sported an overt, sharp-pointed body, while a series of unsubtle graphics and the newly released Wonderbar heavy-duty vibrato bridge were common features throughout the line. Artist-endorsed models were becoming increasingly common elsewhere in the industry, and included among new signature Washburns was the strange angular form of the shortlived AF40V Ace Frehley guitar.

The first Washburns to be manufactured in Korea were the Rebel series of cheap superstrats, which made their debut during 1986. Existing designs were also transferred to Korea, a source used by many brands at this time. Further models to originate from the new production base included the PRS-influenced RS8 and RS10, part of the Tour series.

By now the Washburn catalog consisted of just the Tour and Force series, between them covering a variety of instruments where common model names had little to do with consistency of features or design.

Some guitars continued to be manufactured for the company in Japan. Included among these Asian-sourced instruments were the Stephens Extended Cutaway (EC) series, which were first introduced during 1987. Also known as Spitfire models, these George Washburn-brand solidbodies catered for players who adopted the popular two-handed tapping technique of the time, the guitars' extreme carved cutaway allowing access to a 29-fret or unprecedented 36-fret fingerboard. Through-neck construction

This Nuno Bettencourt N-8 double-neck was made in 1996. One-time Extreme guitarist Nuno is featured (above) in two Washburn ads: with the N-8 and single-neck N-4 (1996, top) and with a Chicago series KC70 in 1990. Paul Stanley's signature models (1999 PS-500 far right; 1999 ad for PS-2000) were based on the Kiss man's Ibanez Iceman design.

Paul Stanley of KISS with his signature
PS-2000 CRB

and active circuitry were other features that could be found on this high-quality, US-designed super-superstrat.

The late 1980s also brought the superstrat-style Chicago series, as well as some Les Paul-style models that were marketed as the Classic series. Fretted Industries officially changed its name to Washburn International in 1987. Increased prominence for Washburn in the early 1990s came with Nuno Bettencourt's signature model. It was a popular move, and it prompted a succession of other versions made variously in the US, in Japan and in Korea.

It was during the early 1990s that the G.W. Lyon brandname was employed on a line of low-end guitars while, in a bid to plunder the more recent past, Washburn also revived a reduced Wing series.

A US custom shop was opened in 1991 to make various high-end and one-off instruments and for development and prototype work. The Mercury solid series appeared in 1992, and this comprehensive line of guitars included models made at the new US facility. The line was revamped two years later and again in 1995. Other 1990s newcomers included the Fender-style Silverado and Laredo, and the Steve Stevens signature six-string.

In 1996 the Dime series first appeared, as used by Dimebag Darrell and based on his previously favored Dean guitar. A number of variants have since been issued,

Dimebag Darrell of Pantera spurred Washburn to a number of signature models, highlighted in the 2004 ad (near left). The Dime Culprit CP2003 pictured here (main guitar) was made in 1999. A 2005 Washburn ad (far left) features Scott Ian of Anthrax with his signature model, and this X series Washburn (far left) was produced in 2007.

305

Watkins drew on its amplifier expertise for the early-1960s Circuit 4 model (catalog, right).

including the Culprit of 1999 that was like a sliced-up Explorer. Also in 1996 the US-made MG series was launched, designed by Grover Jackson, and the Peavey Wolfgang-like Billy T series appeared, evolving into 1997's Maverick series, some of which were made in Indonesia. Washburn's P series debuted in 1997, endorsed by Nuno Bettencourt, some made in the US, some in Korea.

Washburn acquired US Music Corporation in 2002 in a reverse merger, and seven years later sold US Music, including the Washburn brand, to Jam Industries. Most general production for Washburn guitars in recent years has been in China.

Nuno Bettencourt remains the brand's best known endorser, and the prime N4 model has been in production since 1990. Recent Washburn models include the "bred for shred" XM series, introduced in 2011, the Parallaxe series, introduced in 2013 and which Washburn described as its most advanced rock/metal guitars, and the budget Sonamaster series, introduced in 2016. By 2017 the catalog included several more series, such as the Hollowbody models, which included the semi-solid HB30 and HB35 as well as fully hollow electrics like the HB15 in non or single-cutaway guises, and the Jazz series of hollowbody models.

With these instruments the Washburn name remained prominent and continued to enjoy a relatively high profile around the world, which is no mean achievement in today's increasingly competitive marketplace.

WATKINS

Watkins provided cheap guitars for many fledgling British beat groups of the 1960s. The London-based company headed by Charlie Watkins originally specialized in amplification. But with Charlie's brother Sid in charge their first instrument, the Rapier Deluxe, was launched around 1959, the original of what is by far the most famous and what proved to be the longest-running Watkins model.

Styling and construction of the single-cutaway solidbody Rapier owed more to Gibson than Fender, with a 22-fret set-neck and three-tuners-a-side headstock. Body and headstock were altered around 1961 to an approximation of Fender's market-leading Stratocaster, with two (Rapier 22) or three pickups (33). The four-pickup Rapier 44 later completed the line with more comprehensive controls.

The new WEM brandname (Watkins Electric Music) first appeared on the high-end Sapphire series of 1965. The most expensive WEM instrument of the 1960s was the shortlived 5th Man, introduced in 1967, a gimmick-laden guitar with built-in effects including Sting treble-boost and Project IV sustain.

In the late 1960s Wilson, another new Watkins brand, appeared on models such as the twin-cutaway SA semi-acoustics and cheap Ranger solidbodies. By 1976 the line was much reduced, and in the 1980s the Hand Made Mercury was the flagship model with a Strat-style shape, but by 1985 instrument manufacturing had ceased.

Two Washburns from the Parallaxe series: a 2017 PX-Solar16ETC in carbon black matte (far left) and a 2015 PXM10 in quilted trans blue (center). This 2014 ad (above) features Phil Lewis and Tracii Guns of L.A. Guns. The best-known Watkins models are the various Rapiers; this Rapier 33 (right) was made in England around 1964.

WELSON

This was the brandname of the Orlando Quagliardi company. Based in Castelfidardo, Italy, and dating back to 1919, like so many accordion makers it turned to electric guitars in the early 1960s.

Some single-cutaway semi-solids appeared in the UK branded Vox. Odd-shaped Welson solidbodies adorned in garish plastics followed. The body styling was retained, without plastic, for later examples such as the Dyno II and Vedette. In contrast, late-1960s semis were straightforward Gibson-inspired equal-double-cutaway models.

A selection from the 1966 line was marketed in Germany branded for amplification company Dynacord. This badge-engineering continued with semis for the American Thomas and Wurlitzer catalogs in the early 1970s. The Welson line later included the SG-style Red Flame. The Black Pearl model was a Les Paul-alike, and one of the final Welsons was the late-1970s multi-laminated Blue Flame.

WESTONE

Starting in 1981, Westone was chosen as the in-house brandname for high quality guitars made by the Matsumoku factory of Matsumoto City, Japan, and the instruments were sold internationally.

They included the Concord, Paduak, Prestige and Thunder solidbodies, and Rainbow semi-hollows. Following its purchase of an interest in Matsumoku, St. Louis

Music of Missouri decided by 1984 to replace its Electra brand with Westone. Original designs like the minimalist Dynasty and svelte Pantera (played by Leslie West) yielded to conventional superstrats.

Around 1988 the Matsumoku factory was sold to Singer Sewing Machines and all guitar production ceased. Westone manufacturing switched to Korea, the brandname changing to Alvarez in 1991. The Westone name was revived in 1996 by original UK importer FCN, initially appearing on Korean superstrats, replaced by British-made originals the following year, but the enterprise was shortlived.

WURLITZER

Better known for its keyboards and juke boxes, Wurlitzer of Elkhart, Indiana, also distributed musical instruments – and decided to cash in on the boom of the 1960s with its own line of guitars. Wurlitzer contracted the Holman-Woodell guitar factory in Neodesha, Kansas, to manufacture the two-pickup solidbody Stereo Electric models in 1965: the Cougar, which was a relatively conventional Fender-style guitar, the Wildcat, of more exaggerated shape, and the Gemini, a pointy, asymmetrical design.

Pickups and hardware for the Wurlitzers were made by Holman. A high volume of returns, mainly due to poor painting, led Wurlitzer to cancel the contract around the end of 1966. A line of Italian Welson-made hollowbodies replaced the Holmans for another year or so, after which Wurlitzer decided to leave the guitar-making business.

The three guitars shown on this page are: a Welson Jazz Vedette (near right) made around 1967; a Westone Paduak II (center) from 1982; and a Wurlitzer Cougar 2512 (far right) produced during 1966.

YAMAHA

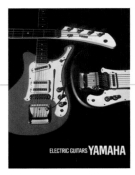

This Yamaha catalog from 1966 (right) features models from the company's distinctive early line, the SG "flying samurai" guitars.

ELECTRIC GUITARS **YAMAHA**

Y A M A H A

Although better known for a plethora of assorted products – from motorcycles to synthesizers – the Japanese Yamaha company has produced some excellent electric guitars over the years. While it's hard to pick one instrument from such a long and detailed history, perhaps the most famous of Yamaha's electric guitars is the SG-2000, once favored by Carlos Santana. For a company with such a diverse product line, the standard and quality of its electric guitars has been of a remarkably high standard throughout virtually all of its history.

Yamaha was started in the 1880s, began making acoustic guitars during 1946, and first offered solidbody electrics around 1964, although its first major line of such instruments debuted in 1966.

The 1966 solidbodies consisted of the two-pickup S-201 and three-pickup S-302 (later renamed the SG-2 and SG-3, and soon joined by a 12-string). These were bolt-on-neck models with pointed offset horns and Jazzmaster-style dual circuitry. They were soon followed by the crescent-shape SG-2C and SG-3C, and then a series of instruments that became the best-known of Yamaha's early electric instruments, the SG-2A, the SG-5A, the SG-7A and the SG-12A. These became known as the "flying samurais" for their unique asymmetrical "reverse body" shape with a dramatically extended lower horn.

The bolt-on-neck SA-15 semi-hollowbody adopted a similar outline, while several more such models, including the SA-50, employed more traditional double-cutaway styling. There were also full-size, single-pointed-cutaway archtop AE series electrics. In 1972 Yamaha's solidbody line changed to a design with a single sloping cutaway. Still called SG models, these came either with a flat body or with what's called a "German carve," a noticeable edge relief.

The following year these instruments were joined by an equal-double-cutaway series that employed a body shape which would culminate in Yamaha's most renowned SG-2000 solidbody guitar.

By 1973 the semi-hollow line had been enhanced with the fancier SA-60 and SA-90 sporting more powerful humbuckers. Two new single-rounded-cutaway hollowbody guitars were offered, the AE-12 (sunburst) and AE-18 (natural). Around 1976 the shortlived SX-800 and SX-900 solidbodies joined the line. These had two equal almost flat cutaways and sharp pointed horns.

Yamaha achieved its first big success with the SG-2000, introduced in 1976 and endorsed by Carlos Santana. It represented a big leap forward for Yamaha, and was the guitar that at last reversed the impression that Japan only produced cheap copies. It had a through-neck construction, carved top, twin humbuckers, and a bridge mounted on a brass block for added sustain.

Three proud Yamahas: an SG-5A "flying samurai" (far left) from 1967; an SA-15 (center) made about the same time; and an SG-60T (near left), with "German carve" body, dating from 1973.

Yamaha discovered that while its solidbody models had been of undisputedly high quality, they nevertheless had been too unconventional and out of the ordinary to provoke widespread take-up and popularity. However, when Yamaha tried the equally high-quality but conservatively designed SG-2000 – the instrument was in effect a double-cutaway Les Paul-style guitar – they suddenly had a successful instrument. This was an important lesson not only for Yamaha but also for a number of other Japanese electric guitar manufacturers.

Tracking the very many different Yamaha SG models that followed the 2000 model is confusing seen from today's viewpoint: in America they were called SBGs to distinguish them from Gibsons; furthermore, specifications on domestic Japanese models were quite different from those on export models with the same number. Yamaha stopped exporting the SBGs to the US in 1988, although the SBG-500 and 700 were reintroduced in 1998.

Demand for copies of American guitars picked up in Japan in 1977 just as one particular "copy era" wound down in the US. Yamaha obliged on its domestic market with high quality SR Strat-style models (SuperR'nroller) and SL Les Paul-alikes (Studio Lord). Also new in 1977 were the Strat-shape SC series, featuring blade-style single-coils, and Yamaha introduced the set-neck SF series (Super Flighter) with twin humbuckers and offset cutaways.

In 1982 Yamaha revised the SC series to reflect the old "reverse" SG body shape, now with three single-coil pickups in a Strat-style layout.

Two years later Yamaha revamped its solidbody line again, adding more SGs and a number of Tele-style SJ-series models. There were also new Strat-based six-strings called the SE series as well as variations with twin humbuckers. New Yamaha endorsers included Cornell Dupree, Barry Finnerty and Carlos Rios.

By 1984 the costs of manufacturing electric guitars in Japan had soared, and Yamaha moved most of its guitar production to a new, modern factory that was based in Kaohsiung, Taiwan. At this point Yamaha continued to make only a very few of its electric guitar models in Japan. These included the evergreen SGs as well as 1985's EX-2 and VX-2 Flying V-style models with carved-relief tops and locking vibratos.

Yamaha's new Taiwan-made line was the Strat-style SE series, introduced in 1985, with bolt-on necks, locking or traditional vibrato systems and various pickups. In 1986 Yamaha briefly offered the minimalist G-10 synth guitar controller. By 1988 top-of-the-line, through-neck models came with either passive or active electronics.

Yamaha's RGX Series debuted in 1987, sleek offset-double-cutaway superstrats with scalloped, sharp, pointed cutaways, locking vibratos and a variety of pickups, with through-neck and active models. By 1988 the RGX Custom (through-neck and ash body) and Standard (flame-maple cap) topped the line.

Yamaha's most famous instrument was the SG-2000; this 2000S (near right) was made around 1984. From its launch in 1976, the 2000 showed that Japanese-made guitars of high quality and conservative design could sell. The 1983 catalog page (below) shows the US-market SG-2000, renamed the SBG-2000, and the 1986 ad (right) features the SE series. This Gibson-style SA-1100 (center) was made in 1990, while the SC-400 (far right) from 1981 reflects Yamaha's early "reverse" body style.

Two more Yamahas are shown on this page. A luscious example from the wide-ranging and popular Pacifica series, this Pacifica 604 (main guitar) was made in 1994, while the RGX Custom (below) produced in 1989 is typical of Yamaha's superstrat period.

The ads here feature contrasting musicians who both found appeal in Yamaha's guitars. Jazzman Martin Taylor (top) is seen with a "hybrid" AEX-1500 and various AES hollowbodies in 1999, while Blues Saraceno shows off his custom plaid-finished RGX model.

A year later, in 1989, Yamaha introduced the flamed-top, set-neck Image series: Custom with LED position markers for playing in the dark; Deluxe with vibrato; and hardtail Standard. Designed at Yamaha's Kemble facility in the UK, these equal-double-cutaway solidbodies lasted only a couple years.

By 1990 Yamaha had opened a custom shop in Los Angeles, California. The SE series was history, and most RGX guitars were renamed RGZ, now joined by the new Rich Lasner-designed Pacifica line and the fancy Weddington series.

The Pacifica instruments continued Yamaha's evident enthusiasm for producing Fender-style guitars, ranging from through-neck types with carved flame-maple tops and internal sound chambers, to bolt-on-neck models that came with various pickup combinations and vibratos. Many of the Pacifica line offered excellent value and have sold very well.

The Weddington Custom (with carved quilted-maple top), Classic (carved maple top) and Special (with a flat-top mahogany body) were twin-humbucker Les-Paul-style solidbodies with an Aria PE-like sweeping curve down from the upper shoulder into the cutaway opposite.

Most of Yamaha's higher-end RGZ guitars and the Weddington instruments were gone from the line by 1995, to be replaced in 1996 by several American-made Pacifica USA models that employed bodies and necks supplied by Warmoth.

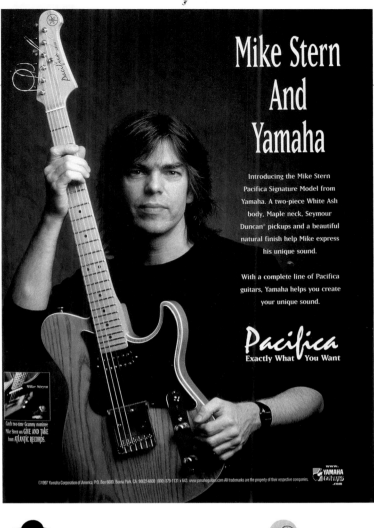

Two guitars from Yamaha's retro-style AES line are pictured: this 1998 AES-800 (near right) has hum-cancelling P-90-like pickups, while the 1999 AES-500 (center) has humbuckers. Also shown (far right) is a Yamaha Pacifica 511MS Mike Stern model, made in 1998, with an ad from that same year (top right) announcing Stern's endorsement.

By 1999 the Pacifica series included an ash-bodied Telecaster-style solidbody that gained Yamaha a valuable endorsement from guitarist Mike Stern. The AES series of solidbodies and semi-hollowbodies were also among the new models in the Yamaha catalog. These nodded to the neo-vintage revival with their exaggerated rounded single-cutaway and retro-shape pickguards, a generally 1960s image that brought Yamaha almost full circle. This continued in 2000 with the launch of a series of SGV models, which were direct revivals of the reverse-body SGs from almost 35 years earlier.

Yamaha's Silent Guitar, launched in 2001, had a simple frame-like body and nothing much more than a bridge, a pickguard, and an acoustic-like neck. Not really an electric guitar – it was designed for practice or travel with a headphone output, but could be amplified, too – and we mention it here to show Yamaha's broad view of the guitar.

The RGXA2, introduced in 2005, boasted a very lightweight body and an LED system to indicate pickup selection, and five years later the SG1820 was described as the newest incarnation of Yamaha's classic SG series, with options of humbuckers, P-90s, or active pickups. A new line of solidbody models appeared in 2015, the Revstar series, with hints of the SG but more offset, pointed horns, and with pickups provided by Asian maker G&B.

By 2017 the Yamaha electric lines were divided into four main series: the Revstar, SBG, Pacifica, and Hollow. There were eight of the new shallow-cutaway Revstars, from RS320 to RSP20CR, with traditional body sandwiches of maple and mahogany, that good selection of pickups, and what Yamaha called a stripped-down tuned-up performance. The SBGs were the modern iteration of Yamaha's classic SG models, running to a trio of relatively high-end models: the goldtop SBG1802, sunburst SBG1820 and the all-black SBG1820A.

Another classic name from the annals of Yamaha history, the Pacifica series was split into five groups: PAC100, PAC200, PAC300, PAC500 and PAC600. Each worked on and developed the Strat-derived theme, with a host of models from the budget PAC012 to the beautiful PAC611. The Hollow series was in fact just one model, the SA2200, this time recalling Yamaha's semi-solid models in a 335 style. There was also a single signature model, the long-running Tele-like PAC1611MS, for Mike Stern.

Three more Yamaha guitars are pictured here: a Pacifica from the top of that series, a 2015 PAC611HFM (far left), and a couple from the Revstar series: a 2016 RS502T (center), with P-90s, and a 2017 RS720B, with Bigsby. The ads pictured at the top of this page feature at least two genuine Yamaha endorsers: Wes Borland and Troy Van Leeuwen (top left, 2008) and "Jonny Rocker" (top right, 2007).

A leading proponent of Zemaitis guitars was The Pretenders' James Honeyman-Scott, who recorded especially dramatic guitar parts for their second album (right) of 1981.

Z E M A I T I S

Tony Zemaitis made the highest-profile British guitars of the 20th century, and is best known for the "metal front" and "pearl front" solidbodies that he built for players like Ron Wood. Zemaitis was based at Chatham, Kent, retiring in 2000 after 35 years as a professional guitar-maker. He died in 2012.

Zemaitis first came to wide attention in the early 1970s when Wood and Ronnie Lane began using his instruments, and from then his list of clients – both for acoustic and electric guitars – began to read like rock'n'roll royalty, including Hendrix, Clapton, Harrison, Richards, Gilmour, Honeyman-Scott and many others.

His electrics are flamboyant guitars for stage use, symbolizing glorious 1970s rock'n'roll decadence. They boast plenty of handwork, hand-made bridges, and engraved metal or mosaic-like pearl inlays. Some metal-front Zemaitis guitars featured work by shotgun engraver Danny O'Brien. The idea for the metal fronts started when Zemaitis shielded Strat pickups with metal foil and decided to take the idea further.

Most guitars were custom-ordered, but around 1980 with shortlived Budget student model appeared. Zemaitis instruments became desirable to later generations seeking 1970s styles, such as Gilby Clarke and Rich Robinson, and the original electrics have become highly-prized and valuable guitars. A new Japanese-based Zemaitis Guitars firm now offers instruments in collaboration with Tony's relatives.

Among the largely British clientele drawn to Tony Zemaitis's singular creations was Marc Bolan of T Rex. The metal guru is pictured (above) playing a metal-front Zemaitis. Two typical examples of the classic Zemaitis metal-fronts are shown on this page (left), along with two ads from the revived Zemaitis Guitars.

ACKNOWLEDGEMENTS

BIBLIOGRAPHY

Charles Alexander (ed) *Masters Of Jazz Guitar* (Balafon/Miller Freeman 1999)
Tony Bacon (ed) *Classic Guitars Of The Fifties* (Balafon/Miller Freeman 1996); *Classic Guitars Of The Sixties* (Balafon/Miller Freeman 1997)
Tony Bacon & Paul Day *The Fender Book* (Balafon/Miller Freeman 2nd edition 1998), *The Gibson Les Paul Book* (Balafon/Miller Freeman 1993), *The Gretsch Book* (Balafon/Miller Freeman 1996), *The Guru's Guitar Guide* (Making Music 2nd edition 1992); *The Rickenbacker Book* (Balafon/Miller Freeman 1994), *The Ultimate Guitar Book* (DK/Knopf 1991)
Tony Bacon & Barry Moorhouse *The Bass Book* (Balafon/Miller Freeman 1995)
Paul Bechtholdt & Doug Tulloch *Guitars From Neptune – Danelectro* (Backporch 1995)
Dave Burrluck *The PRS Guitar Book* (Balafon/Miller Freeman 1999)
Walter Carter *Epiphone: The Complete History* (Hal Leonard 1995); *Gibson: 100 Years Of An American Icon* (General Publishing 1994); *History Of The Ovation Guitar* (Hal Leonard 1996); *The Martin Book* (Balafon/Miller Freeman 1995).
Scott Chinery & Tony Bacon *The Chinery Collection – 150 Years Of American Guitars* (Balafon/Miller Freeman 1996)
Paul Day *The Burns Book* (PP 1979)
A.R. Duchossoir *The Fender Stratocaster* (Mediapresse 1988); *The Fender Telecaster* (Hal Leonard 1991); *Gibson Electrics – The Classic Years* (Hal Leonard 1994)

Tom & Mary Anne Evans *Guitars: Music, History, Construction And Players* (Oxford University Press 1977).
Jim Fisch & L.B. Fred *Epiphone: The House Of Stathopoulo* (Amsco 1996)
S.P. Fjestad *Blue Book Of Guitar Values* (Blue Book 1994)
Chris Gill *Guitar Legends: The Definitive Guide To The World's Greatest Guitar Players* (Studio Editions 1995).
Alan Greenwood *Vintage Guitar Magazine Price Guide* (VG Books 1998)
Hugh Gregory *1000 Great Guitarists* (Balafon/Miller Freeman 1994)
George Gruhn & Walter Carter *Electric Guitars And Basses* (GPI 1994); *Gruhn's Guide To Vintage Guitars* (Miller Freeman 2nd edition 1999)
Phil Hardy & Dave Laing *The Faber Companion To 20th-Century Popular Music* (Faber 1990)
Terry Hounsome *Rock Record 7* (Record Researcher 1997)
Steve Howe & Tony Bacon *The Steve Howe Guitar Collection* (Balafon/Miller Freeman 1994)
Adrian Ingram *The Gibson ES-175* (Music Maker 1994)
JTG *Gibson Shipping Totals 1946-1979* (JTG 1992)
Colin Larkin (ed) *The Guinness Encyclopedia Of Popular Music* (Guinness 1992)
Mark Lewisohn *The Complete Beatles Chronicle* (Pyramid 1992)
John Morrish (ed) *The Classical Guitar: A Complete History* (Balafon/Miller Freeman 1997); *The Fender Amp Book* (Balafon/Miller Freeman 1995)
Hans Moust *The Guild Guitar Book 1952-1977* (GuitArchives 1995)

ACKNOWLEDGEMENTS

Michael Naglav *Höfner Guitars – Made In Germany* (Musikkeller undated c1996)
David Petersen & Dick Denney *The Vox Story* (Bold Strummer 1993)
Norbert Schnepel & Helmuth Lemme *Elektro-Gitarren Made In Germany* English translation J P Klink (Musik-Verlag Schnepel-Lemme 1988)
Pete Prown & H.P. Newquist *Legends Of Rock Guitar* (Hal Leonard 1997)
Rittor *60s Bizarre Guitars* (Rittor 1993)
Marc Roberty *Eric Clapton – The Complete Recording Sessions 1963-1995* (St Martin's Press 1993)
Jay Scott *Gretsch: the Guitars Of the Fred Gretsch Company* (Centerstream 1992); *50s Cool: Kay Guitars* (Seventh String Press 1992)
Harry Shapiro & Caesar Glebbeek *Jimi Hendrix: Electric Gypsy* (Heinemann 1990)
Mary Alice Shaughnessy *Les Paul: An American Original* (Morrow 1993)
Robert Shaw *Great Guitars* (Hugh Lauter Levin 1997)
Richard R. Smith *Complete History Of Rickenbacker Guitars* (Centerstream 1987); *Fender: The Sound Heard 'Round The World* (Garfish 1995)
M.C. Strong *The Great Rock Discography* (Canongate 1995)
John Teagle *Washburn: Over 100 Years Of Fine Stringed Instruments* (Amsco 1996)
Paul Trynka (ed) *The Electric Guitar* (Virgin 1993); *Rock Hardware – 40 Years Of Rock Instrumentation* (Balafon/Miller Freeman 1996)
James Tyler *The Early Guitar: A History & Handbook* (Oxford University Press 1980)
Thomas A Van Hoose *The Gibson Super 400* (GPI 1991)
Tom Wheeler *American Guitars* (HarperPerennial 1990)
Michael Wright *Guitar Stories Volume 1: The Histories Of Cool Guitars* (Vintage Guitar Books 1995)
YMM Player *History Of Electric Guitars* (Player Corporation 1988)

Magazines & periodicals that we found useful during research for this book: *Beat Instrumental*; *Down Beat*; *The Guitar Magazine*; *Guitar Player*; *Guitar World*; *Guitarist*; *Melody Maker*; *The Music Trades*; *Vintage Guitar*; *20th Century Guitar*.

THANKS

I**n addition** to those named elsewhere in this section we would like to thank: Ken Achard; Julie Bowie; Julie Calland; Jamie Crompton; John Darnley; Lorenzo German; Barry Gibson; John Hall; Rick Harrison; Danny Jones; Christine Kieffer; Rich Lasner; Mike Lewis; Chris Martin; Stephen Maycock; Brian McConnell; Barry Moorhouse; Jun Nakabayashi; John Peden; Phil Richardson; Robert Roberts; Mark Snelling; Sally Stockwell; Mick Taylor; John Veleno; Patrice Vigier; Randall Whitney; Jon Wilton; Robert Witte.
SPECIAL THANKS to Dave Hunter at *The Guitar Magazine* for letting us plunder the picture files; Andrew Large for the M1 trek; Neville Marten at *Guitarist* for rummaging trannies and a CD; Staff Sgt Graham Rees, bomb disposal officer, for making the UXB stay a UXB; Robert Witte for pix, info and friendly help.

AUTHORS

This book was written by Tony Bacon (TB), Dave Burrluck (DB), Paul Day (PD) and Michael Wright (MW). The following key indicates the main writer for each entry or section, and where relevant (in brackets) a secondary writer who added material or rewrote parts of the original. Thanks also to Robert Witte for help with the Jackson entry. All text was edited for style, content and fit by Tony Bacon. The book was updated by Nigel Osborne and Tony Bacon in 2017.
History Of The Guitar TB; Acoustic MW; Airline TB; Alamo MW; Alembic TB; Alvarez PD; Ampeg TB; Aria MW (PD); Baldwin PD (TB); Bartolini PD; B.C. Rich MW; Bigsby MW; Bond DB (TB); Brian Moore DB (TB); Burns PD (TB); Carvin MW; Casio PD; Chandler PD; Charvel PD (TB); Coral TB; Cort MW; Custom Kraft MW; Danelectro MW; D'Angelico TB; D'Aquisto TB; Dean MW; De Armond PD; Domino MW; Dwight TB; Eggle DB (TB); Egmond PD (TB); Eko MW (PD); Electar TB; Electra MW; Electro TB; Epiphone MW; ESP PD; Fender TB; Fenton-Weill PD (TB); Fernandes PD (TB); Framus MW (PD); Futurama PD (TB); G&L PD (TB); Gibson TB; Gittler MW; Godin DB (TB); Godwin PD; Gordon-Smith DB (TB); Goya MW; Gretsch TB; Grimshaw PD; Guild MW (PD); Guyatone PD (TB); Hagstrom MW (PD); Hallmark PD (TB); Hamer PD (TB); Harmony MW; Harvey Thomas PD (TB); Hayman PD (TB); Heartfield PD; Heritage TB; Hofner PD (TB); Hondo MW; Hopf PD (TB); Hoyer PD; Ibanez MW; Jackson TB (PD); James Tyler DB (TB); John Birch PD: Kapa MW; Kawai PD; Kay MW; Kent MW; Klein DB (TB); Klira PD (TB); Kramer MW; Krundaal PD (MW); LaBaye MW; Magnatone MW; Martin TB; Maton PD (TB); Melobar MW; Messenger MW; Micro-Frets MW; Mighty Mite MW; Modulus DB (TB); Mosrite PD (TB); Music Man PD (TB); National TB; Ovation MW (PD); Parker DB (TB); Peavey MW; Premier MW (TB); PRS DB; Rick Turner PD (TB); Rickenbacker TB; Robin PD; Roger PD; Roland PD; Samick MW; Schecter PD (TB); S.D. Curlee MW; Shergold PD (TB); Silvertone MW; Spector PD; Squier TB; Standel PD (TB); Starfield PD; Steinberger DB (TB); Stratosphere PD (TB); Supro MW; Teisco MW; Teuffel PD; Tokai PD (TB): Tom Anderson DB (TB); Travis Bean PD; Vaccaro MW; Valley Arts PD; Vega TB; Veillette PD (TB,DB); Veleno MW; Vigier DB (TB); Vox PD (TB); Wandre MW; Washburn PD (TB); Watkins PD (TB); Welson PD; Westone MW (PD); Wurlitzer MW; Yamaha MW (PD); Zemaitis DB (TB).

TRADEMARKS

Throughout this book many trademarked names are used. Rather than put a trademark symbol next to every occurrence of a trademarked name, we state here that we are using the names only in an editorial fashion, primarily as references to standard industry designs, and that we do not intend to infringe any trademarks.

IMAGES

Most of the guitar photographs are from the Balafon Image Bank. Other guitar pictures were taken or supplied by Garth Blore; Nigel Bradley; Brian Moore Custom Guitars; Burns London; Matthew Chattle; Richard Conner; Richard D. Cummings; Fender Japan; Fender Musical Instruments; Paul Goff; Fred Gretsch Enterprises; *The Guitar Magazine*; *Guitarist*; Rittor Music Inc/Bizarre Guitars of the 60s; Rosetti Ltd; Sotheby's; Strings & Things; Keith Sutter; Robert Witte; Michael Wright.
Memorabilia illustrated in this book – catalogs, pictures, record jackets etc – came from the collections of Charles Alexander; Tony Bacon; Balafon; British Film Institute; Chinery Collection; Jennifer Cohen; Paul Day; André Duchossoir; Ross Finley; Dave Gregory; Gruhn Guitars; George Martin; National Jazz Archive; Nigel Osborne; PRS Guitars; Bill Puplett; Ian Purser; Rickenbacker International; Alan Rogan; Arthur Soothill; Robert Spencer; Steve Soest; Raymond Ursell; John Veleno; Bert Weedon; Michael Wright.
Original advertisements came from the pages of *Beat Instrumental*; *Guitar* (Japan); *Guitarist*; *The Guitar Magazine*; *Guitar Player*; *Guitar World*; *The Music Trades*.
Artist pictures were supplied principally by Redfern's. Photographers are indicated by the following key: AP Andrew Putler; AS Ann Stern; BK Bob King; CB Chuck Boyd; CM Chris Mills; CZ Charlyn Zlotnik; DE Dave Ellis; DM Dede Millar; DR David Redfern; EL Elliott Landy; ER Ebet Roberts; FC Finn Costello; GAB Glenn A Baker; HB Henrietta Butler; ID Ian Dickson; JD James Dittiger; JLK John Lynn Kirk; K&K K&K Archive; KM Keith Morris; MC Mike Cameron; MH Mick Hutson; MOA Michael Ochs Archive; NJS Nicky Simms; NMA Nigel Adams; PB Peter Brüchmann; PF Patrick Ford; RA Richie Aaron; RH Rick Hardy; RK Robert Knight; RP Roberta Parkin; SM Sue Moore; SM Susie MacDonald; SR Simon Ritter; VW Val Wilmer.
Pictures are listed in the format: page number, subject (photographer key): 21 Richards DR; 34 Coombes MH; 40 Howe DE; 43 Page MG; 56 McCartney DR; 62 Gallagher PF; 68 Phair AS; 70 Richard/Shadows RH; 74 Moore ER; 76 Harrison SM; 80 Owens DR; 82 Hendrix EL; 85 Clapton CB; 91 Edge BK; 95 Beck DR; 96 Yorke PF; 97 Coxon HB; 98 Richards EB; 104 Harrison PB; 105 Cantrell ER; 106 Christian MOA; 109 Hall DR; 110 Howe ER; 117 Fripp SM; 118 Young/ Jam ER; 120 Page RK; 122 Richards VW; 123 Clapton SM; 124 Green GAB; 128 Wheeler NJS; 135 Clapton CB; 136 Whitney FC; 137 Lifeson FC; 139 Clapton SM; 141 Manzanera SM; 164 Beatles K&K; 167 Atkins MOA; 168 Duffy ER; 169 Setzer RK; 170 Thayil JD; 185 May AP; 204 Benson DR; 206 Miller MOA; 209 Petrucci JLK; 210 Vai SR; 211 Satriani FC; 226 Van Halen CZ; 231 Young RA; 235 Ramone ID; 238 Lee DM; 260 Santana RP; 272 Beatles DR; 274 Weller ID; 275 Buck MC; 277 Devlin NMA; 284 Rutherford ER; 295 Curtis CM; 294 Jones DR; 305 Bolan KM.
Owners' credits Guitars photographed were owned at the time of photography by the following individuals and organizations, and we are most grateful for their help. Akai UK; Terry Anthony; Arbiter Group; Scot Arch; Aria UK; Chet Atkins; Tony Bacon; Robin Baird; Colin Barker; Barnes & Mullins; The Bass Centre; Jeff Beck; Steve Boyer; Dave Brewis; Brian Moore Custom Guitars; Clive Brown; Ron Brown; Burns London; Dave Burrluck; Simon Carlton; Julian Carter; Carvin Guitars; Doug Chandler; Chandler Guitars; Chinery Collection; Eric Clapton; Don Clayton; Russell Cleveland; Brian Cohen; Country Music Hall Of Fame; Neville Crozier; Paul Day; Chris DiPinto; Jerry Donahue; Mark Duncan; Dynamic Audio Industries; Duane Eddy; Edinburgh University Collection; EMD International; John Entwistle; FCN Music; Fender Japan; Fender Musical Instruments; Fred Gretsch Enterprises; Lou Gatanas; Debbie German; David Gilmour; Dave Gregory; Gruhn Guitars; Robin Guthrie; Horniman Museum; Alan Hardtke; George Harrison; Head Stock; Keith Henderson; Tony Hicks; Rick Hogue; Adrian Hornbrook; Steve Howe; Peter Ilowite; Adrian Ingram; James Tyler Guitars; Jim Jannard; Scott Jennings; Gerard Johnson; Joe Johnson; Clive Kay; Korg UK; Andrew Large; Jay Levin; Adrian Lovegrove; Adam Malone; Garry Malone; Robert Malone; Mandolin Brothers; Phil Manzanera; Martin Guitars; Bill Marsh; Graeme Matheson; Paul McCartney; Charles Measures; Paul Midgeley; Modulus Guitars; Albert Molinaro; Gary Moore; Lars Mullen; Music & Audio Distribution; Music Ground; John Nelson; Carl Nielsen; David Noble; Marc Noel-Johnson; Steve Ostromogilsky; Jimmy Page; Peavey Electronics; Nick Peraticos; PRS Guitars; Bill Puplett; Pat Quilter; Patrick Eggle Guitars; Buzz Peters; Tim Philips; Arthur Ramm; John Reynolds; Rick Turner Guitars; Rickenbacker International; Alan Rogan; Rosetti ; Todd Rundgren; Carlos Santana; Schecter Guitars; Floyd Scholz; Selectron; Sensible Music; John Sheridan; John Hornby Skewes; Nicky Skopelitis; John Smith; Samuel Reed Smith; Sarah Laine Smith; William Warren Smith; Sotheby's; Robert Spencer; Strings & Things; TE.D; Teuffel Guitars; Tom Anderson Guitarworks; Paul Unkert; Valley Arts Guitars; Veillette Guitars; Arthur Vitale; Washburn UK; Mick Watts; Bert Weedon; Bruce Welch; Paul Westlake; Lew Weston; Charlie Whitney; Gary Winterflood; Robert Witte; Michael Wright; Yamaha-Kemble Music; Bryan Zajchowski.

Jeff Beck can take a guitar that has no intonation and a bent neck, and make it sound awesome, just with his fingers. Slash.